Cervantes and the Mystery
of Lawlessness

CERVANTES

AND THE MYSTERY OF

LAWLESSNESS: A Study

of El casamiento engañoso

y El coloquio de los perros

ALBAN K. FORCIONE

Princeton University Press

Princeton, New Jersey

Library of Congress Cataloging in Publication Data will be
found on the last printed page of this book

ISBN 0-691-06588-8

Publication of this book has been aided by a grant from
The Andrew W. Mellon Foundation

This book has been composed in Linotron Garamond type

Clothbound editions of Princeton University Press books
are printed on acid-free paper, and binding materials are chosen
for strength and durability.

Printed in the United States of America by Princeton
University Press, Princeton, New Jersey

For
LUIS MURILLO
and
MICHAEL, MARK, and DOUGLAS
companions of a long night

CONTENTS

Introduction. "Desatinos de Propósito": The Ugly   3
Shapes of Satire

PART ONE. THE MYSTERY OF LAWLESSNESS

I. The Anatomy of the Monster   21

A Satirical Hybrid   21
The Patterns of Narrative Disorder: Saturation, Variegation,
Fragmentation: Dialogue as a Mode of Disarticulation   26
The Patterns of Narrative Disorder: Dismemberment of
Coherent Form through Anticlimax and Parody: The
Main Plot of the *Colloquy*   36
Two Types of Parody: The Descent to the Underworld in
the *Colloquy* and the *Quixote*   48

II. Cervantes' Apocalypse: The Descent   59
into the Grave

The World of Witches and the Mystery of Lawlessness   59
Probing the Witch: The Imaginative Center of the
Colloquy of the Dogs   72
Cañizares' Sleep and the Travesty of the Sacred   88

III. The Imaginative Unity of the *Colloquy*:   100
The Center and the Parts

The Reiterated Narrative Movement in the Episodes   102
The Recurrent Symbolic Imagery in the Episodes   108
The Fugal Structure of the *Colloquy of the Dogs*   126

PART TWO. THE AWAKENING AT THE END
OF THE NIGHT

IV. God's Infinite Mercy: *El casamiento*   131
engañoso as a Christian Miracle

v. The Survival of the Humanist Vision   146

The Conquest of *Feritas*: Teachers as Heroes   146
The Ethical Vision of the *Colloquy*: Dogs as Heroes   153
The Unassertive Satirical Voice: Dialogue as a
Liberating Force   170

vi. Language: Divine or Diabolical Gift?   187

Don Quixote and the *Colloquy of the Dogs*: Two Perspectives
on the Plurality of Languages   187
Sermo Carnis—Sermo Spiritus: The *Colloquy* and
Erasmus' *Lingua*   213
Criticism, Literature, and the Language of the Earth   226

Index   237

Cervantes and the Mystery
of Lawlessness

"Desatinos de Propósito": The Ugly Shapes of Satire

The delight that the mind conceives must arise from
the beauty and harmony it sees, or contemplates,
in things presented to it by the eyes or the
imagination; and nothing ugly or ill-proportioned
can cause us any pleasure.
—The Canon of Toledo[1]

IN THE STORIES which begin and conclude his collection of exemplary novels, *La Gitanilla* and *El casamiento engañoso y el coloquio de los
perros*, Cervantes is directly concerned with the reordering of vision,
and at the climax of each the protagonist and reader are rewarded
with a striking nocturnal revelation, in which an intense visual experience concentrates the imaginative power and the doctrinal content
of the entire work. In each case a human face comes into view. In *La
Gitanilla* the questing hero has purified his love of blinding instinctual forces, and, releasing the divine powers that have been slumbering in his soul, he gazes on the face of the beautiful Preciosa as an

---

[1] "El deleite que en el alma se concibe ha de ser de la hermosura y concordancia
que vee o contempla en las cosas que la vista o la imaginación le ponen delante; y
toda cosa que tiene en sí fealdad y descompostura no nos puede causar contento
alguno" (*El ingenioso hidalgo Don Quijote de la Mancha*, ed. L. A. Murillo, 2 vols.
[Madrid, 1978], 1:564-65. All subsequent page references to the *Quixote* are to this
edition). To provide English versions of my quotations from Cervantes' works, I have
used a number of translations, occasionally modifying them to bring out the sense of
the Spanish necessary to my argument. They are: J. Ormsby's and J. M. Cohen's
translations of *Don Quixote*, N. MacColl's and W. Starkie's translations of *The Exemplary Novels*, H. Oelsner's and A. B. Wellford's *Galatea*, E. Honig's *Interludes*, and
L. D. Stanley's *The Wanderings of Persiles and Sigismunda*. Translations of all other
works cited are my own unless otherwise indicated.

image of the starry heavens with their orderly movements and ineffable harmonies.

> Look upward, Clemente, and see the starry veil
> In which this chilly night
> Competes with the day,
> Adorning the heavens with lovely lights;
> And if your divine genius can reach so far,
> Figure in this image
> That face
> Where the highest degree of beauty is to be found.[2]

In the *Colloquy of the Dogs* the protagonist has stumbled along the entangled, involuted paths of his misadventures and found that they have led him to the center of a labyrinth, where he is rewarded with a bewildering set of enigmas and the vision of a monstrous human being. The face that looms out of the shadows is far different from that of the dancing maiden of the first story, but its hold on the contemplator is no less powerful: "her lips were blackened, her teeth rotted, her nose hooked and bony, her eyes starting from their sockets and crossed, her hair disheveled, her cheeks eaten away, her throat scrawny."[3] Overwhelmed with nausea and fear, the hapless Berganza experiences a strong desire to bite the ugly creature, but he finds himself instead riveted in contemplation of its mystery through most of the night.

One of the principal subjects of *La Gitanilla* is the value and the proper use of poetry, and its climactic hymn to Preciosa is one of its most eloquent affirmations of the power of poetry to civilize human beings and bind them in a perfect society of friendship, the very power its author would exploit as he leads his readers to share the discoveries of his characters. In the *Colloquy of the Dogs* Cervantes assumes a very different position regarding the powers of poetry, and in the alienation and fascination which his canine contemplator experiences at the sight of the repugnant monster, he may well have had in mind the intended effects of his story on its readers. The *Colloquy* is, in fact, the most literarily self-conscious of the *Exemplary Novels*, and in one of its numerous self-referential moments, it clearly

---

[2] "Mira, Clemente, el estrellado velo / Con que esta noche fría / Compite con el día, / De luces bellas adornando el cielo; / Y en esta semejanza, / Si tanto tu divino ingenio alcanza, / Aquel rostro figura / Donde asiste el extremo de hermosura" (*Novelas ejemplares*, ed. F. Rodríguez Marín [Madrid, 1962], 1:102).

[3] "Denegridos los labios, traspillados los dientes, la nariz corva y entablada, desencasados los ojos, la cabeza desgreñada, las mejillas chupadas, angosta la garganta" (*El casamiento engañoso y coloquio de Cipión y Berganza, Novelas ejemplares*, ed. F. Rodríguez Marín [Madrid, 1957], 2:305. All following page references are to this edition).

proclaims its interest in exploiting the aesthetic potential in the ugly. Cipión, speaking both as moralist and as literary theorist, reprimands his comrade Berganza, whose irrepressible garrulity has caused him once again to lose sight of the important distinction between legitimate, well-intentioned criticism and slanderous vituperation. In his ridicule of ignorant impostors and learned fools who ostentatiously display their knowledge of the classical tongues, Berganza appears to be straying toward the forbidden area of literary utterance which Cipión has designated "sátiras de sangre"—"satires of blood"—and attempted to distinguish from the legitimate criticism of "sátiras de luz"—"satires of light." While Cipión's rebuke and the dialogue which it provokes point directly to such issues in their immediate context as decorum, the potential for deception in language, and the importance of discretion in proper conversation, they offer one of Cervantes' most illuminating comments on the tone, purpose, genre, and general meaning of the novella with which he concludes his collection.

CIPIÓN: And you call slandering philosophizing? That's a nice state of affairs! Canonize, Berganza, canonize the accursed plague of backbiting, and give it whatever name you please; it will cause us to be called cynics, which is the same as calling us backbiting dogs; so for pity's sake I beg you to be silent now and to go on with your story.

BERGANZA: How am I to continue if I hold my peace?

CIPIÓN: I mean that you should follow it consecutively without making *it look like an octopus by the way you go on adding tails.*

BERGANZA: *Speak correctly; the arms of an octopus are not called tails.*

CIPIÓN: This is the mistake he made who said it was not stupid or vicious *to call things by their proper names, as if it were not better,* if it be necessary to name them, *to speak of them by circumlocutions and paraphrases that diminish the repulsion caused when we hear them called by their proper names.* Decent words give an indication of the decency of the one who utters them or writes them.[4]

The exchange is characteristic of Cervantes' entire literary production, as it dramatically presents the queries, objections, and recommendations of a highly informed literary critic, observing an author in the

---

[4] "Cipión.—¿Al murmurar llamas filosofar? ¡Así va ello! Canoniza, canoniza, Berganza, a la maldita plaga de la murmuración, y dale el nombre que quisieres; que ella dará a nosotros el de cínicos, que quiere decir perros murmuradores; y por tu vida que calles ya y sigas tu historia. Berganza.—¿Cómo la tengo de seguir si callo? Cipión.—Quiero decir que la sigas de golpe, sin que la hagas que *parezca pulpo, según la vas añadiendo colas.* Berganza.—*Habla con propiedad; que no se llaman colas las del pulpo.* Cipión—Ese es el error que tuvo el que dijo que no era torpedad ni vicio *nombrar las cosas por sus propios nombres, como si no fuese mejor,* ya que sea forzoso nombrarlas, decirlas *por circunloquios y rodeos que templen la asquerosidad que causa el oírlas por sus mismos nombres.* Las honestas palabras dan indicio de la honestidad del que las pronuncia o las escribe" (pp. 251-52; italics added).

creative act. It brings into the very work in which it appears the
process of the creation and reception of that work. The literary encounter might remind us of the composition of the prologue to *Don
Quixote* I, which takes place within its prologue, so to speak, and in
the presence of a very outspoken expert on the conventions of pro-
logues, or of the various confrontations of creating artists and critical
audiences in the *Quixote* (for example, Master Pedro's recitation of the
deliverance of Melisendra and Sancho Panza's narration of the tale of
La Torralba).[5] In the case of the *Colloquy of the Dogs*, the author at
work is a satirist, and his pronouncements are marked by the unsparing candor of the Cynic philosopher, whose association with satirical
literature is at least as old as the age of Menippus.[6] He is so intolerant
of artificiality of any type that his only reaction to the unpleasant
phrase by which his critical audience describes his narrative methods
is to insist that the hideousness of the comparison not be mitigated
by an intrusion of euphemism.[7] His uncompromising sense of propriety demands "the proper names of things," the open display of "things
that cause disgust," and apparently he is not terribly moved by the
scruples of his civilized companion. For shortly after the warning he
once again begins flaying the dunces who cite Latin in ignorance, and,
invoking the imagery of torture and mutilation for which he has a
disturbing predilection throughout his narration, he expresses the horrifying wish that they be placed in presses to have the "juice of their
knowledge" squeezed out "so that they might no longer go about
cheating the world with the glamour of their tattered Greek and their
false Latin, as the Portuguese do with the Negroes of Guinea" (p.
254).

[5] For the importance of such scenes in Cervantes' exploration of his artistic practices
and theories, see my *Cervantes, Aristotle, and the "Persiles"* (Princeton, 1970).

[6] In his other major satirical short story, *El Licenciado Vidriera*, Cervantes connects
a critique of the pride, inhumanity, and false knowledge of the Cynic philosopher
with an examination of the moral problems underlying satire (see my *Cervantes and
the Humanist Vision* [Princeton, 1982], chap. 3). For the common association of Cynic,
satirist, and dog in Renaissance letters, see the treatise on satire written by the neo-
Aristotelian literary theorist, F. Robortello. As examples of the constructive possibilities in this "venemous" form of imitation, he mentions Socrates, as well as "Menippus, & Diogenes Cynici. Nam hic ideo se Canem appellari dicebat, quod ho-
minum vitia morderet ac peruelleret" (*Explicatio eorvm, omnivm, quae ad satyram pertinent,
In librum Aristotelis de arte poetica explicationes*, facsimile reproduction of the edition of
Florence, 1548 [Munich, 1968], pp. 26-34).

[7] Cipión's euphemism—"tail" ("cola")—is prompted by the offensive connotations
of the proper word for the octopus's arms—"rabo"—which could mean "tail end" or
"backside." J. Caro Baroja points out that "poner rabos" is a popular carnivalesque
form of derision (*El Carnaval* [Madrid, 1965], p. 89).

No doubt the effects which this discussion and several others like it bring to the *Colloquy* are varied and complex. Certainly they soften the impact of the overwhelmingly negative vision emerging in Berganza's narrative by drawing attention to his unduly harsh and hence partially unreliable judgments. As I pointed out in a recent study of Cervantes' other satirical tale, *El Licenciado Vidriera*, the traditional theme of the satirist satirized generally has a redemptive implication in literature, as the excessive nature of the satirist's demands makes the evils of human beings that he denounces somehow less reprehensible, in view of the natural inadequacy and limitations of the human condition that he obviously overlooks.[8] One could in fact reasonably argue that the presence of the discussion of Berganza's narration enables Cervantes to have it both ways, to yield to the Juvenalian indignation which, as Cipión points out, is "difficult to resist," to give vent to his feelings about the evils of society, and simultaneously, by turning his criticism back on himself, to avoid violating the principle of humane, "fraternal" reprehension, which he maintains so stoutly elsewhere. In the condemnation of the destructive satirist of the *Persiles*, Clodio, Cervantes' spokesman points out that "corrective criticism among human beings must be fraternal." And in one of his most appealing speeches Don Quixote responds to a vicious tirade hurled at him by a parasitic ecclesiastic merely by reminding him that "reprehension" is justifiable only if it is "good," "holy," and "well-intentioned."[9] At the same time it is valid to conclude, in agreement with numerous analysts of Cervantes' ambivalent relations with the popular picaresque fiction of his contemporaries, that such self-critical comments stem from and reflect the author's well-known antipathy toward any pronouncement on life that suggests finality and the closed, general truth of dogma, the type of pronouncement that filled the best seller of the age, Mateo Alemán's *Guzmán de Alfarache*.

At this point I am concerned primarily with the implications of the dogs' comments in relation to Cervantes' understanding of the genre of his final novella. For they contain, despite Cipión's insistence on euphemism, circumlocution, obliquity, decorum, and high moral-

---

[8] See *Cervantes and the Humanist Vision*, chap. 3. The fundamental study of the self-examination frequently found in great satire is R. C. Elliott's *The Power of Satire* (Princeton, 1960).

[9] *Los trabajos de Persiles y Sigismunda*, ed. J. B. Avalle-Arce (Madrid, 1969), p. 119; *Don Quijote*, 2:283. Perhaps some uneasiness about the propriety of his own satirical writings is discernible in Cervantes' boast in his autobiographical *Viage del Parnaso*: "Nunca voló la pluma humilde mia / por la region satirica, baxeza / que a infames premios y desgracias guia" (ed. R. Schevill and A. Bonilla [Madrid, 1922], p. 55).

ity, their author's acknowledgment that his subject matter is ugly, that the effect for which his work strives is disgust, and that its dominant formal principle is the monstrous, the disproportionate.[10] Cervantes may have had in mind the contemporary treatise on literary theory *Cisne de Apolo*, whose author, Luis Alfonso de Carvallo, speaks of the poetry that addresses itself to man's lowest faculties, the imagination and the senses, as similar to the temptations of the devil. Carvallo compares it to the "head of the octopus," which tastes good but causes uncomfortable digestive aftereffects, disruptive passions, and terrible nightmares.[11] The peculiar association of the monster and language had, in fact, appeared in Erasmus' somber analysis of the vast potential for evil in the tongue, the *Lingua*, a work which, I suspect, influenced the conception of Cervantes' final story in a fundamental way. In its capacities for hypocritical utterance the tongue can take more shapes than the metamorphosing forms of any octopus; in its destructive venom it is the equal of the hideous squid: "the squid is a small creature, and, nevertheless, the power of its poison is so great that anything which it touches disintegrates so completely that its bones do not even remain.[12]

Whatever its derivation, Cervantes' image of the octopus with its

---

[10] Satirists have frequently introduced such monstrous emblems in order to comment on the genre, aim, form, effect, and reception of their texts. One can compare Lucian's association of his "literary novelties" with the grotesque satyrs which put to rout the Indian armies that are amused by them (*Dionysus, Lucian*, trans. A. M. Harmon [Cambridge, Mass., 1961], 1:49-59); Rabelais' recollection, as he introduces *Le Tiers Livre*, of Ptolemy's account of a black camel and a striped, black-and-white slave, "mistakes of nature," which arouse fright and indignation in their beholders; Erasmus' meditations on the Sileni Alcibiadis; and Mateo Alemán's description of the hideous monster of Ravenna, which causes wonder and conceals a message of redemption (*Guzmán de Alfarache*, ed. S. Gili y Gaya, 5 vols. [Madrid, 1964-1968], 1:70-71). Cervantes' self-deprecatory allusion to the *Quixote* as an ugly child of his fantasy, an "hijo seco, avellanado, antojadizo y lleno de pensamientos varios," engendered in a jail rather than in a *locus amoenus*, and his comparison of it to the unrecognizable cock of Orbaneja's artless improvisation belong in part to such traditional emblematic signs of satire's self-awareness.

[11] Ed. A. Porqueras Mayo (Madrid, 1958), 1:128. In its evocation of the lowest order of animal life and its suggestion of the ingestion of food, the reference focuses two of the central patterns of demonic imagery of the *Colloquy*, with all their destructive energies, directly on the reality of the work itself and on the problematic value of its blighted discourse.

[12] "Linguam subinde vertamus in plures species, quam vllus se vertat polypus . . . seps minutum animalculum est, et tamen ea veneni vis est, vt quem attigerit sic totus extabescat, vt ne ossa quidem supersint" (*Lingua*, ed. F. Schalk, *Opera Omnia*, vol. 4, pt. 1 [Amsterdam, 1974], pp. 332, 290). For the influence of the *Lingua* on the *Colloquy*, see below, my final chapter.

shapelessness and unlimited number of tentacles offers a striking inversion of the figure which nearly every literary theorist of the age invoked to describe the coherence of the perfect work of literature— the well-formed body, in which parts are perfectly proportioned to each other and to the whole so as to yield a single unified effect of beauty and harmony. Cervantes was fond both of the analogy and the aesthetic principles that it implied. His principal spokesman for literary theory, the Canon of Toledo, categorically denies that anything that has "any ugliness or disproportion about it can give us any pleasure," and he goes on to lament that the *fábulas* of the romances of chivalry do not engage the intellect of their readers, condemns their authors' failures to achieve the unity of the perfectly formed body, and remarks that "they compose them with so many limbs that it seems that they intend to form a chimaera or a monster rather than a well-proportioned figure."[13] The analogy is perhaps visible in Cervantes' odd expression of concern about the radical nature of his techniques of disposition in his *Persiles*, "a book that will venture to compete with Heliodorus, that is, if for its audacity it does not retire with its hands on its head."[14]

Throughout his writings Cervantes expresses the belief that poetry must strive for harmony and proportion, and the effect of civilized pleasure that always attends the apprehension of such qualities. Probably the most striking indication of his attachment to this view is his recurrent resurrection of another figure which contemporary literary theorists and iconographers frequently presented as an embodiment of their high ideals of literary art—Maiden Poetry, "a tender, young and extremely beautiful maiden," who is served by all the sciences and is "formed of an alchemy of such virtue that anyone who knows how to treat her will transform her into purest gold of inestimable price." He who would honor her must live up to the high ideal which she represents and be careful lest he defile her by dragging her into the commercial market or allow her to "run to vile satires or impious

[13] "Los componen con tantos miembros que más parece que llevan intención a formar una quimera o un monstruo que a hacer una figura proporcionada" (*Don Quijote*, 1:565).

[14] "Libro que se atreve a competir con Heliodoro, si ya por atrevido no sale con las manos en la cabeza" (prologue to the *Novelas ejemplares*, *Obras completas*, ed. A. Valbuena Prat [Madrid, 1956], p. 770). The body analogy, which recalls the famous monstrosity to which Horace likened poems composed haphazardly and Aristotle's description of the tragic plot as a body which can be embraced in a single view, was omnipresent in Renaissance poetics. For its implications in Cervantes' writings, see my *Cervantes' Christian Romance* (Princeton, 1972), chap. 1.

sonnets."[15] The emblem reappears at the very beginning of the *Exemplary Novels*, in *La Gitanilla*, the story which, in its contrasts in themes, actions, characters, and narrative form, provides an instructive frame of reference for an understanding of the artistic coherence of the final tale. In the radiant figure of Preciosa Cervantes displays not only the wonders of man the microcosm, but also the civilizing virtues that distinguish his poetic creations. She reminds a youthful writer that poetry is "a most precious jewel" and herself stands before him as Maiden Poetry, who is "chaste, virtuous, lively, clear-sighted, and modest" and who always "remains within the limits of the most lofty refinement."[16] Cervantes reluctance to allow the poet to work in the realm of the ugly is nowhere more forcefully expressed than in the words of the narrator of the *Persiles*: "the excellence of poetry is as clean as clear water, which improves all unclean things; like the sun it passes through all *impure things without being contaminated by any of them . . . it is a beam of light which comes forth from where it is contained, not burning but rather illuminating* all it meets with; *it is a well-tuned instrument which sweetly cheers the senses*, and brings with it, at the same time as pleasure, *virtue and profit*."[17]

When we consider these passages, their recurrence, their consistency, and their forcefulness, it becomes clear that Cipión's seemingly casual description of his comrade's narration as a monstrosity implies a good deal more than is immediately apparent. It may be the closest the author can come to the admission that in his last tale he is deliberately immersing himself everywhere in "impure things," that their foulness is truly "contaminating," and that it is impossible to speak of poetry here as the perfect form that addresses the intellect, as the retiring maiden whose virtue and knowledge edify, or as the well-tempered instrument that soothes the senses. If in fact his work illuminates, it does so only as do the consuming fires of a final judgment, and its effect is not one of harmony and joy, but rather of disgust, or, to recall Carvallo's analogy of the octopus, of the disgust akin to

[15] "Una doncella tierna y de poca edad, y en todo estremo hermosa . . . hecha de una alquimia de tal virtud, que quien la sabe tratar la volverá en oro purísimo de inestimable precio . . . correr en torpes sátiras ni en desalmados sonetos" (*Don Quijote*, 2:155).

[16] "Una joya preciosísima . . . casta, honesta, discreta, aguda, retirada, y que se contiene en los límites de la discreción más alta" (*La Gitanilla*, p. 49).

[17] "La excelencia de la poesía es tan limpia como el agua clara, que a todo lo no limpio aprovecha; es como el sol, que pasa por *todas las cosas inmundas sin que se le pegue nada . . . es un rayo que suele salir de donde está encerrado, no abrasando, sino alumbrando; es instrumento acordado* que dulcemente alegra los sentidos, y al paso del deleite, lleva consigo la *honestidad y el provecho*" (*Persiles*, p. 284; italics added).

indigestion. While the candid description, containing as it does a harsh indictment of the work, can be interpreted as the author's own withdrawal from his satirical spokesman, or as a reemergence of the theme of the satirist satirized, it must be recognized that Cervantes is in any case acknowledging the terrible logic of satirical mimesis and implicitly offering an apology for his final tale. Satire is an "evil" literary genre, in the same sense that, as very many satirists have reminded us, law and medicine are "evil" professions. All owe their existence to a great extent to man's imperfection. Before death and the knowledge of good and evil entered man's experience, there was, of course, no need for satirists and their oblique, ironic, and destructive discourse, just as there was no need for lawyers and doctors. Cervantes makes this point quite clearly in another of the literary exchanges between the dogs, where Berganza acknowledges that the impulse which stimulates his devastating pronouncements is traceable to Adam's fall and emerges as an instinct even in the most uncorrupted of creatures, the newborn infant, who, on discovering his "divine" capacity to speak, invariably chooses to exercise it by hurling the epithet "whore!" at his mother or nurse.[18]

Cervantes, the most lucid of writers, had no illusions about the nature of his medium and his artistic objectives. He knew that effective satire addresses itself to the irrational recesses of the mind, exploiting, through the imagery and actions of the monstrous, man's darkest fears and aggressive impulses, just as he knew that the genre of romance reaches into that same area to release and satisfy man's deepest irrational needs for perfection. In his understanding of such powers in literary art, Cervantes went well beyond the limits of the fashionable literary theories of his contemporaries. As I have argued in connection with *El Licenciado Vidriera*, the neo-classical aesthetic, from which he derived most of his literary principles, emphasized rationality, harmony, and decorum in literature and looked suspi-

---

[18] This vindication of satire is proclaimed by the most famous railer of the age, Mateo Alemán, whose popular picaresque novel, *Guzmán de Alfarache,* had a profound impact on Cervantes' conception of his final tale (see below). In the grotesque *captatio benevolentiae* of Part II of his confession, the protagonist describes himself as a madman hurling stones in all directions and assuming that, since everyone has "eaten the apple," all his victims deserve the wounds he inflicts on them. He offers a series of analogies describing the work and its reception in the imagery of punishment, suffering, and purgation—e.g., the blunderbuss which kills, the viper which poisons, the radish which nauseates, the executioner who displays a "fine tapestry" of corpses. All of this leads to an assault on the reader, in which he compares the reception of his work to the enjoyment of bear-baiting by a bloodthirsty mob (*Guzmán de Alfarache*, 3:69-83).

ciously on any art that gratified man's "lower" faculties, and Cervantes could not but have discerned behind its superficial prudential and cautionary pronouncements concerning satire and romance a blindness to the sources of their power and to the principles of their coherence which he intuitively understood so well.[19]

While Cervantes is unflinchingly honest about the ugliness of his creation, its destructive purposes, its questionable morality, and its debasing effects, he is certainly aware of its imaginative power, its moral justifiability, and its ultimately constructive intentions. At one point in the dialogue Cipión insists that there is a crucial difference between "bloody" satires, which presumably revel in inflicting wounds and laying bare the crimes of society, and "illuminating" satires, which would expose not primarily in order to destroy but rather to heal, just as the cauterizing fire of the surgeon burns in order to cleanse.[20] If the distinction suggests that a coherent philosophy of criticism underlies the disturbing fictions of the story, a remark in Cervantes' autobiographical mock-epic, *Viage del Parnaso*, reveals the author's view that the coherent literary form for the expression of that philosophy would in fact confront its reader with incoherence. As he proclaims his commitment to the classical ideal of harmony in literary composition, Cervantes allows that *nonsense, discord*, and *disproportion* can be the dominant features of a coherent work of art.

> Never does my narrow wit open its doors
> To *incongruity*, and *harmony* continually
> Finds them wide open.

[19] See my *Cervantes and the Humanist Vision*, chap. 3. Alvin Kernan has argued that satire is a means by which civilized man controls aggression, releasing it and channelizing it in a useful direction. He attempts to account for the persistent distaste for the most powerful satire, which is at least as ancient as Aristotle's reference to satirists as "vicious and contemptible" men, by suggesting that they exploit man's deepest fears, call forth his forbidden aggressive impulses, and produce an intense concentration of the irrational which can only be disturbing to the rational ego defenses ("Aggression and Satire: Art Considered as a Form of Biological Adaptation," in *Literary Theory and Structure: Essays in Honor of William K. Wimsatt*, ed. F. Brady, L. Palmer, and M. Price [New Haven, 1973], pp. 115-29).

[20] The distinction accords with the precepts of Renaissance literary theorists. Cervantes' designation recalls El Pinciano's dialogues, which present legitimate satire as striking at "vicios generales, y no a personas particulares," teaching virtue, and hence needing no strategy of concealment: "podrá vsar della clara y abiertamente, y, assí como el que no haze mal ama la luz, podrá el tal poeta hablar claramente delante del mundo todo, y él viuirá entre la gente más seguro" (A. López Pinciano, *Philosophía antigua poética*, ed. A. Carballo Picazo [Madrid, 1953], 3:238).

How can an *absurdity be pleasing,*
Unless it is done *with a purpose,*
Guided by *wit and grace?*[21]

Elsewhere Cervantes boasts that in his *Novelas ejemplares* he has opened a path, "on which the Castilian tongue can display an *absurdity with propriety,*"[22] and, if we are to judge by the number of self-critical and self-justificatory statements within the stories themselves, it is probably the *Coloquio de los perros* which he had in mind in these references.[23] In no other work does Cervantes so exhaustively explore the absurdities and disorderly conduct of which man is capable, and in no other work does he appear to be striving so relentlessly for an effect of riotous disorder in his narrative form.

For all its absurdities, the *Colloquy* remains for Cervantes an *exemplary* story, and its climactic position in the collection of *Exemplary Novels* is certainly not fortuitous. And yet it is undeniable that its ugliness is nearly overwhelming. It continually assaults the reader with its challenge, and the author makes no efforts to conceal from him the questions that it raises. Are we simply to avert our glance from its repugnant features, ascribe them to the crudity of taste of other ages, and open our eyes only to its "picturesque display of customs," as many of its most enthusiastic modern students have done?

---

[21] "Nunca a *disparidad* abre las puertas / mi corto ingenio, y hallalas contino / de par en par la *consonancia* abiertas. / ¿Cómo pueda *agradar vn desatino* / si no es que de *proposito* se haze / mostrandole el *donayre* su camino?" (*Viage del Parnaso,* pp. 84-85; italics added.) In *El pensamiento de Cervantes,* Americo Castro notes the importance of this passage and suggests that in it "Cervantes resume su credo intelectual y artístico al reflexionar sobre el curso de su vida literaria" ([Barcelona, 1972], pp. 25-26). See E. C. Riley's analysis of the importance of harmony, rationality, and purpose as fundamental principles of Cervantes' art and literary theory (*Cervantes's Theory of the Novel* [Oxford, 1962], pp. 19-23; "Teoría literaria," *Suma Cervantina,* ed. J. B. Avalle-Arce and E. C. Riley [London, 1973], pp. 293-322).

[22] "Yo he abierto en mis Nouelas vn camino, / por do la lengua castellana puede / mostrar con propiedad vn desatino" (*Viage del Parnaso,* p. 55).

[23] See particularly the Ensign's introductory description of his manuscript as "esos sueños o disparates" (p. 208). Riley speculates (*Cervantes's Theory of the Novel,* p. 22) that the *desatino* most likely refers to the inverisimilitude of the talking dogs and contains Cervantes' acknowledgment of the possibility of an artistic error. I agree that Cervantes' comment is attributable to the apparent improprieties of the final tale but suspect that it refers primarily to its moral dissonances and that, rather than artistic error, Cervantes is affirming the paradoxical artistic coherence of satire. The satirical elements in the tales certainly attracted the attention of Cervantes' readers, if Avellaneda's homage—the novellas are "más satíricas que ejemplares"—is an accurate indication of their contemporary reception.

Are we to follow one of the leading formalist critics of the twentieth century and retreat from the problems presented by its formal complexity by dismissing it as a banal agglomerate of episodes haphazardly thrown together?[24] On the final page of the story Cervantes reminds its reader that, however ugly its tattered manuscript and the fictions it contains may be, its pleasures are those of the intellect, for its appeal is directed at the "eyes of the understanding," the same lofty faculty to which he had presented Preciosa's vision of perfection. The admonition to activate the mind's eye to seek beauty concealed behind the complete "inversions" of an absurd exterior recalls Erasmus' influential meditations on the "Sileni Alcibiadis," the paradoxical figures which, in their combination of the profound and the ridiculous, the sublime and the humble, the inner and the outer, the reality and the appearance, and the spirit and the letter, offered Cervantes' humanist ancestors such a fascinating image of their ideals, spiritual preoccupations, and methods of teaching.

If one may attain to a closer look at this Silenus-image, that is, if he deigns to show himself to the purified eyes of the soul, what unspeakable riches you will find there.[25]

In the following study I propose to look closely at Cervantes' own "Silenus," seeking behind the alienating "desatinos" of its forbidding exterior its inner coherence, both as an individual work of narrative art and as a constituent part of a larger vision which its author had inherited from his humanist ancestors and which informs his entire collection of short stories.

The relation of Cervantes' final tale to the humanist cultural heritage is probably more complex and paradoxical than that of any other exemplary novel. In its repugnant content and deep pessimism its

---

[24] Viktor Sklovskij's unfavorable judgment of Cervantes' story is cited by O. Belic, "La estructura de 'El coloquio de los perros,' " *Análisis de textos hispanos* (Madrid, 1977), pp. 81, 107.

[25] *The "Adages" of Erasmus*, ed. and trans. M. M. Phillips (Cambridge, 1964), p. 272. See W. Kaiser's discussion of the implications of the "Silenus" in the writing of Erasmus and Rabelais and in particular its suitability as an image for the new "mixed style" of the Renaissance, in which "earnestness could be both contained and concealed within jest" (*Praisers of Folly* [Cambridge, Mass., 1963], p. 60). See also B. Könneker's observations on Erasmus' description of the "Sileni" and his exploitation of the mock encomium as an instrument for affirming the relative character of truth and exploring its complexities (*Wesen und Wandlung der Narrenidee im Zeitalter des Humanismus* [Wiesbaden, 1966], pp. 291ff.). For the popularity of Erasmus' adage in Spain, where it was translated and read as an independent essay, see M. Bataillon, *Erasmo y España*, trans. A. Alatorre (Mexico, 1966), pp. 309-11.

author would appear to be renouncing the utopian aspirations that are so prominent in certain of the preceding tales and moving toward a full rapprochement with the ascetic vision animating the contemporary literature of *desengaño*, a literature which, in its obsession with man as a creature hopelessly torn between the irreconcilable extremes of *feritas* and *divinitas*, bestiality and divinity, showed virtually no interest in that vast middle ground of *humanitas* to which the humanist program for spiritual *renovatio* was primarily addressed.[26] Readers have often been tempted to find in the *Colloquy's* relentless drive toward the unmasking of illusion an overwhelming destructive climax of the entire novella collection which refuses to spare any of the idealism of the foregoing works. Throughout my study I attempt to deal with the ambiguities in Cervantes' apparent attraction to the antihumanistic currents of his time, particularly the picaresque novel and the imposing work to which the *Colloquy* owes so much, Mateo Alemán's *Guzmán de Alfarache*. If Cervantes' final tale transcends the literature of delinquency which attained such popularity in Spain of Philip III, it does so only after thoroughly assimilating it in a critical dialogue, and the complexity of its disengagement from it can be evaluated properly only if we provisionally lay aside the facile generalizations concerning Cervantes' deep antipathy to the picaresque vision of man which are so fashionable among contemporary Cervantists.[27] The *Colloquy of the Dogs* is permeated with ascetic Christian

[26] See G. Paparelli, *Feritas, Humanitas, Divinitas: L'essenza umanistica del Rinascimento* (Naples, 1973).

[27] Américo Castro's penetrating insights into the significant differences separating Cervantes' writings from *Guzmán de Alfarache* and other picaresque works (*El pensamiento de Cervantes*, pp. 228-35; "Perspectiva de la novela picaresca," *Hacia Cervantes* [Madrid, 1967], pp. 118-42; *Cervantes y los casticismos españoles* [Madrid, 1966], esp. pp. 42-75) have been confirmed and repeated frequently by subsequent studies: e.g., C. Blanco Aguinaga, "Cervantes y la picaresca: Notas sobre dos tipos de realismo," *Nueva Revista de Filología Hispánica* 11 (1957):313-42; C. Guillen, "Genre and Countergenre: The Discovery of the Picaresque," *Literature as System* (Princeton, 1971), pp. 135-58; M. Bataillon, "Relaciones literarias," *Suma Cervantina*, pp. 215-32. A characteristic example of the way in which a fine critical insight can become a facile generalization of literary history and, as such, an obstacle to an appreciation of the complexity of the very issues which occasioned the original insight is F. Lázaro Carreter's recent disposal of the question of Cervantes' place within the development of picaresque fiction: "Es evidente que si Cervantes ha de figurar en la historia del género, habrá de ser en cuanto debelador del mismo. Trató de pícaros, pero no escribió picaresca porque se opuso a su poética punto por punto" (*"Lazarillo de Tormes" en la picaresca* [Barcelona, 1972], pp. 227-28). In two recent studies, which reached me following the completion of this manuscript, Gonzalo Sobejano has reviewed and criticized this traditional interpretation, acknowledging its significant contribution to our understanding of Cervantes' fiction but pointing out that it stands in need of

doctrines and the imaginative formulations which typify the literature of *desengaño*. Rather than dismissing them as alien or peripheral aspects of the work, we should recognize their centrality and their expressive power within its total design. By examining them closely and considering the religious and literary traditions which they bring into the tale, we can correctly respond to the paradoxical energies that enliven Cervantes' dialogue on evil, at the same time gaining a measure of insight into the tensions troubling and deepening his allegiance to the vision of his true spiritual fathers.

The humanist vision was an expansive, syncretic vision, deeply concerned with the entire field of man's multifarious activities, the broad range of his potentialities, and the varied registers of his language. Its most authentic discourse was open and expansive, reflective of man's variety and vitality and directly responsive to the freedom to criticize and create which was the distinctive feature of his humanity. The dialogue, as well as a varied assortment of narrative hybrids pulsating with the restless life of the dialogue, was the form of verbal expression that allowed this inner freedom to manifest itself most directly and to provoke the listener to exercise his own freedom in the acts of interpretation and response.

The liberating discourse of humanism is audible throughout Cervantes' writings, and I have argued elsewhere that the *Novelas ejemplares*, in their complex, experimental reconstructions of traditional narrative forms, in their disquieting manipulations of their audience's codes of literary genre, and in their imposition of the responsibility for interpretation on their individual readers, are in reality attempting through fictional means to fulfill the humanists' lofty goal of lifting man out of the realm of necessity which he shares with the beast, the condition of *feritas*, in which he can all too easily find himself hopelessly alienated from his true self. The *Colloquy of the Dogs* is a seemingly endless and unrelieved exploration of the spectacular activities of man as beast, lost in the mire of *feritas*, and its efforts to affirm the humanist faith in man's powers to escape his enslavement are not immediately visible. However, if its subject matter and doctrinal commentary suggest the kind of dogmatic stance that would deny the validity of what the preceding novellas implicitly affirmed, its formal

revision. As my consideration of the picaresque features of the *Colloquy* makes clear, I am in full agreement with Sobejano concerning the misleading simplifications of both Alemán's and Cervantes' works which it encourages. See "El *Coloquio de los perros* en la picaresca y otros apuntes," *Hispanic Review* 43 (1975):25-41, and "De Alemán a Cervantes: monólogo y diálogo," *Homenaje al Profesor Muñoz Cortés* (Murcia, 1977), 2:713-29.

affinities with them might lead us to suspect that Cervantes is carrying the methods of his enlivening discourse to the furthest extreme, that is, increasing the burden of his reader's freedom beyond anything that has gone before.

The *Colloquy of the Dogs* is certainly the exemplary novel that is most demanding and difficult to read. It is written as a dialogue which exploits all the possibilities for the destruction of linear exposition inherent in the form and thoroughly conceals its constructive energies within its dominant critical movement. At the same time it represents the most complex process of hybridization of narrative forms which we observe in Cervantes' collection of short stories. In its assimilation and refashioning of traditional genres—including the picaresque novel, the Lucianic satire, the philosophical dialogue, the miracle narrative, the devotional and consolatory treatise, the sermon, the fable, the aphorism, and the anecdote—it goes beyond any of Cervantes' other works except the *Quixote*, with the result that a kind of literary experimentalism and doctrinal instability pervade the text in a way that at first glance recalls the novelistic masterpiece more than any other of the novellas.[28]

One of the peculiar effects of the *Colloquy* which any attentive reader feels is its heavy thrust toward dogmatic assertion and its simultaneous resistance to that very thrust. A double elusiveness seems to penetrate the narrative, the one easily recognizable as having something to do with its obsessive presentation of the mysterious, insubstantial forces of evil, the other, far more difficult to account for, but clearly part of an overall narrative strategy of avoiding the rigidity and con-

[28] The affinities of the *Colloquy of the Dogs* and the *Quixote* have been repeatedly affirmed, frequently accompanying a theory of "two Cervanteses," one genuinely creative, revolutionary, and realistic, the other imitative, conservative, and romantic. The obvious similarities of the two works—their "realism," satirical methods, interest in demythologizing, antiheroic themes, portrayal of low-life characters, comedy of situation, critique of dogmatic assertiveness—have encouraged readers to adopt the view that they are of a single piece or that the *Colloquy*, in its peculiar formlessness and panoramic depiction of society, represents a kind of preliminary stage in Cervantes' development as a novelist (see, for example, J. Casalduero, *Sentido y forma de las "Novelas ejemplares"* [Madrid, 1969], p. 243; A. de Amezúa y Mayo, *Cervantes, creador de la novela corta española*, 2 vols. [Madrid, 1956-1958], 2:396-409; C. Blanco Aguinaga, "Cervantes y la picaresca"). This view can easily interfere with a proper understanding of the *Colloquy's* non-novelistic aims and methods, and it inevitably leads to an unfavorable value judgment by comparison with Cervantes' masterpiece. There are important differences separating the two works, some fundamental, some differences of degree or emphasis, and I would draw attention to them, particularly to those visible in their differing methods of parody and their different responses to their insight into the plurality of language.

venience of definitive pronouncement. The former is a compelling and perfectly intelligible manifestation of the contemporary metaphysics of evil. The latter is an effect which we attribute to the distinctive character of Cervantes' mature artistic voice. It is more resistant to interpretation, but it is what ultimately lifts the work far above the authoritarian literature of *desengaño*, tribulation, and consolation with which it has so much in common. While in his final tale Cervantes is determined to integrate evil as a meaningful element in the total vision of human experience which informs the *Exemplary Novels*, he is not content simply to fall back on the theological mysteries championed by the contemporary spokesmen of ascetic Christianity. His voice is far more tolerant, far more humane than theirs, and though it shies away from all clamor and solemnity, it too has its mysteries. Like the voice of his humanist ancestors, it is an unassertive but firm voice, gently reminding and subtly prodding its listener to remember his forgotten powers of self-transformation and make his way confidently through the night world of lawlessness. If my study proceeds from the *"desatinos"*—"swerves from the mark"—which distinguish the difficult discourse of this great work of fiction, it does so only because Cervantes would lead us into a long and nearly endless night. But light is ultimately there as our reward, and, once it is perceived, we recognize that it has been there all along, and that, like the flickering glow of Berganza's lantern, it shines all the more brightly and warmly because of the menace of the surrounding darkness.

PART ONE

The Mystery of Lawlessness

Can thus
Th' Image of God in man created once
So goodly and erect, though faulty since,
To such unsightly sufferings be debas't
Under inhuman pains? Why should not Man,
Retaining still Divine similitude
In part, from such deformities be free . . . ?
—John Milton, *Paradise Lost*

CHAPTER I

The Anatomy of the Monster

. . . vociferating in a mixed and bastard,
though intelligible, jargon.
—Berganza[1]

A SATIRICAL HYBRID

Keep quiet and listen. . . . it is easy to add
to what has already been invented.
—Berganza[2]

IN HIS OUTBURST of frustration at Berganza's narrative methods,
Cipión, Cervantes' surrogate reader, pleads with his "author" to "follow the events of his story consecutively." Quite apart from its general
aesthetic and moral implications, his image of the octopus with its
proliferating tentacles concentrates in a powerful visual focus the dy-
namic principle of design that appears to govern the narrative of the
Colloquy of the Dogs.[3] At every point we observe the dialogue striving
for an effect of uncontrolled variegation, expanding as if in a process
of continual self-generative growth. Such features are, of course, traditional in satirical plotting, and we need only glance at the terse,
unenthusiastic remarks by the contemporary neo-Aristotelian, El Pin-

---

[1] ". . . daba voces, diciendo en lenguaje adúltero y bastardo, aunque se entendía"
(p. 263).

[2] "Tenle [silencio], y escucha. . . . sea cosa fácil añadir a lo ya inventado" (p.
282).

[3] In his fine observations on the structure of the *Colloquy*, J. Casalduero notes the
appropriateness of the image of the octopus as an analogy of the narrative form of the
story. He argues that the work represents a revolutionary break with traditional
narrative structures and reveals Cervantes in the process of discovering the truly modern form, which he will perfect in the *Quixote* II, "la forma interna que surja de la
vida sentimental y psíquica" (*Sentido y forma de las "Novelas ejemplares"* [Madrid, 1969],
pp. 242-44).

ciano, to observe how the disposition of satire strikes the rationalistic theorist as excessively spontaneous, capricious, and formless: "it does not have any integral part, nor a beginning nor an end: it enters wherever it takes a fancy, and it begins from wherever it wishes, *ex abrupto*."[4]

If we inspect the anatomy of Cervantes' literary monstrosity closely, we observe that it is swollen and bursting with objects, that there is tremendous variety in its substance, narrative shapes, subject matter, character types, ideas, styles, tones, and voices. Saturation and narrative chaos would appear to be its dominant general features. Both the fictitious author of the *Colloquy*, the Ensign Campuzano, and its principal narrator, the dog Berganza, seem to be aware of its expansive tendencies. As he offers the transcription of his dream vision to his friend, Campuzano describes the "things which it treats" as "significant and different." At the beginning of his narration Berganza claims that he must take advantage of the "divine gift of speech" and hasten to tell everything he can remember, "even though it be confusedly and helter-skelter," pointing to the improvisational character of his recitation and the bewildering effects of its disconnected assortment of recollected experiences. As is often the case with Cervantes' storytellers, both the dog and the convalescent know a good deal about literary forms and principles of composition, and their statements present a fairly accurate description of the concluding tale in the *Novelas ejemplares*. Of all the short stories it is certainly the most formless, the one in which Cervantes reveals the least concern for the coherence of the total design of his plot in Aristotelian terms, that is, as a single action progressing linearly through conflict toward a climactic anagnorisis or peripeteia which resolves both the conflict and the thematic problems implicit in it. Even the *Licenciado Vidriera*, the work which most resembles the *Colloquy* in the prominence within its total design of a panoramic, apparently chaotic satirical vision, maintains by comparison a plot that is tightly and coherently developed toward a resolution in the parable of the protagonist's ill-conceived pursuit of knowledge, his fall into insanity, and his redemption. William Atkinson has gone so far as to maintain that there is no plot at all in

---

[4] "No tiene parte alguna ni principio ni fin: entra do se le antoja y comiença de adonde quiere, ex abrupto" (*Philosophía antigua poética*, 3:240). In his discussion of the conventions of Menippean satire, or anatomy, N. Frye emphasizes the normality in the genre of "violent dislocations in the customary logic of narrative" and notes that "there is hardly any fiction writer deeply influenced by it who has not been accused of disorderly conduct." However, the "appearance of carelessness that results reflects only the carelessness of the reader or his tendency to judge by a novel-centered conception of fiction" (see *Anatomy of Criticism* [Princeton, 1957], pp. 310-313).

the *Colloquy* and that consequently it is not a short story. Emphasizing its doctrinal and representational elements and its affinities with the treatise, he speculates that, although a masterpiece in its own right, it may be viewed as Cervantes' capitulation in his efforts to work in a genre that demanded compositional procedures to which his genius as a writer was not well suited.[5]

If we are to deal meaningfully with the structure of Cervantes' final tale, I would suggest that we must first put aside all vulgar assumptions concerning what constitutes effective fictional action, the neo-Aristotelian definition of plot, with its concentration on quantitative features and consequent limitation of the concept to the tightly organized action with beginning, middle, and end, and the prestigious modern theories of novella construction which conform very closely to such traditional notions.[6] A broader view of plot is called for, one perhaps truer to the original Aristotelian conception—that plot is an imitation of an action or actions which are coherently assembled according to an informing idea or vision. In his recent study of the plot of satire, Alvin Kernan admits that, according to traditional standards, satire is generally deficient in plot or altogether plotless. However, he goes on to isolate certain basic actions, variegating and confusing, magnifying, and diminishing—actions that can be viewed as translations into narrative of such effective tropes of satirical communication as catachresis, hyperbole, and anticlimactic parallelism—and he points out that satirists have exploited them with remarkable consistency from antiquity to the present. It is in such actions, in their combinations and variations, Kernan argues, that the plot of satire is to be found, and a close inspection of the "disorder" of the greatest satires generally reveals their coherent development.[7] The fol-

---

[5] "Cervantes, El Pinciano, and the *Novelas ejemplares*," *Hispanic Review* 16 (1948): 189-208.

[6] The emphasis on the tight, coherent plot as the defining characteristic of short-story writing is a legacy of nineteenth-century theorists who derived the principle from what they erroneously understood to be the practices of Boccaccio and other masters of the classical short story. Goethe's description of the "unerhörte Begebenheit" and Heyse's "Falcon theory" are classical statements of this view. The briefest glance at Cervantes' varied tales will reveal that these theories are of little value to a critic who would account for their formal principles and effects and that, insofar as they encourage the adoption of the values implicit in Atkinson's judgment, which similarly echoes Renaissance neo-Aristotelian definitions, they can hamper the critic's efforts to understand the subject.

[7] See *The Plot of Satire* (New Haven, 1965), esp. chap. 7. Kernan finds an instructive theoretical formulation of such actions, "the 'master tropes' of satire," in the classification of the rhetorical figures of "sinking" in Pope's parody of Longinus' *On the Sublime, Peri Bathous: or Martinus Scriblerus His Treatise of the Art of Sinking in Poetry*, a satirical anatomy of the bad style of contemporary poets which, when read

lowing survey of the anatomy of Cervantes' monster will make it clear that the *Colloquy of the Dogs* is no exception.

As various studies have noted, there are in fact two narrative planes in the *Colloquy*, one formed by the events narrated in recollection by Berganza, the other formed by the dialogue of the dogs, who generally comment on the happenings in Berganza's life but frequently employ them merely as points of departure for wide-ranging reflections on society and rambling discussions of various philosophical, moral, and literary themes. The two narrative planes can be viewed as derived respectively from the picaresque novel and the Lucianic dialogue, and their combination gives the work an unusual hybrid character, difficult to classify according to the theories of genres both of Cervantes' contemporaries and of nearly all historians of Spanish literature.[8] Neither the satirical colloquy nor the picaresque novel was a literary form that was restricted by the demands for economy and unity of the so-called Aristotelian plot. Quite the contrary, each in its particular way was expansive and open-ended, and, if the movement of its narrative was confined in any way, its limits were set not by laws inherent in its form, but rather by the extent of the subject it chose to portray. The picaresque novel, despite its emphasis on the hero's assimilation of his experience, his consequent moral development (downward or upward as the case may be), and the progressive movement of his confession (whether sincere or ironic), was firmly focused on the evil of the society around the picaro, and its fictionalized survey of that evil took the form of the episodic, chaotic plot, a succession of loosely related events with little apparent development linking them.[9] As

---

ironically, becomes a manual for the coherent absurdities of satire, i.e., a rhetoric of satire (see pp. 27-35).

[8] As I have pointed out above, one of the most striking characteristics of Cervantes' writings is the freedom and originality with which he manipulates and experiments with the traditional generic systems of prose fiction. The complex hybridization that occurs in the creation of *El coloquio*, in fact, goes well beyond the fusion of picaresque and Lucianic narratives. If we consider the presence of the framing tale, *El casamiento engañoso*, together with the dog's dialogue, we discover the informing presence of the Christian miracle, the confession, the novella, the *exemplum*, and the devotional and consolatory treatise, all of which, to be sure, had already been assimilated by the picaresque novel (see below). In his ability to knit together such a variety of forms in an imaginative unity, Cervantes certainly was, as he boasted in his *Viage del Parnaso*, "aquel que en la inuencion excede / a muchos" (p. 55).

[9] For the principles of structure in picaresque fiction, see Ulrich Wicks, "The Nature of Picaresque Narrative: A Modal Approach," *PMLA* 89 (1974):240-49. The sharp focus on the existential development of the picaro in *Lazarillo de Tormes*, which, since F. Courtney Tarr's influential study ("Literary and Artistic Unity in the *Lazarillo de Tormes*," *PMLA* 42 [1927]:404-21), has been repeatedly emphasized by critics

moralists and satirists have traditionally reminded us, the *proliferating* character of evil is one of its defining features, and the variety, aimlessness, and the seemingly haphazard arrangement of episodes in most picaresque plots are logical formal characteristics of a type of fiction that would explore human inadequacy in a spectacular way.[10] By the time of Cervantes the philosophical-satirical dialogue had become a very flexible literary genre, and men of letters employed it to develop and expound their ideas on a variety of subjects—customs and manners, philosophy, literature, politics, geography, and theology.[11] Unlike picaresque narrative, its approach to its subject was analytical and intellectual, and the fictionalizations which it employed were clearly subordinate to the ideas that they either exemplified or evoked. With such a clear subordination of fiction to theme, the dialogues cultivated the brief, demonstrative anecdote, often of classical derivation, and allowed, indeed encouraged, the fantastic fictionalizations that had effectively served the didactic purposes of satirists from Menippus and Lucian to such contemporaries of Cervantes as Leonardo de Argensola and Francisco de Quevedo: for example, classical myths, marvelous flights, talking animals, wise fools and shepherds, underworld journeys, and dialogues with dead people. In such works the intellect could move freely, dialectically developing a single idea, gliding eas-

---

interested in the novelistic aspects of the work, is exceptional within the early history of the genre.

[10] See Américo Castro's early interpretation of picaresque literature as informed by a pervasive preoccupation with man's theologically fallen nature and intended to display "el espectáculo de la insuficiencia humana" ("Prologue" to his edition of Quevedo's *Historia de la vida del Buscón* [Paris, 1916]). Alexander Parker has argued most forcefully for this assessment of the emergence of the genre. *Guzmán de Alfarache*, the prototype of the picaresque novel, is "an earnest attempt to investigate the nature of moral evil" (*Literature and the Delinquent: The Picaresque Novel in Spain and Europe, 1599-1753* [Edinburgh, 1967], p. 43).

[11] See, for example, T. Tasso's exploration through dialogue of the nature and importance of courtesy (*Opere*, ed. B. Maier [Milan, 1964], 4:538-48), Pedro de Luxán's Erasmian colloquies on courtship and married life (*Coloquios matrimoniales*), Antonio de Torquemada's wide-ranging survey of the customs and geography of the northern part of the world (*Jardín de flores curiosas*), Pedro de Mexía's encyclopedic presentation of facts from numerous areas of interest, for example, medicine and astronomy, in his *Coloquios o diálogos nueuamente compuestos . . . en los quales se disputan y tratan diuersas cosas de mucha erudición y doctrina*; El Pinciano's discourses on literary theory (*Philosophía antigua poética*), and Luis de León's exposition of the mysteries of his Pauline Christianity in *De los nombres de Cristo*, a work that recalls the lofty philosophical tone of the Platonic symposium. For the variety in the dialogues of sixteenth-century Spain, as well as their central didactic aims and analytical procedures, see L. A. Murillo, "Cervantes' *Coloquio de los perros*, a Novel-Dialogue," *Modern Philology* 58 (1961):174-85.

ily from one idea to another, cultivating the witty transition, pouring forth erudition, and in general allowing no requirements of form to impose constraints on its restless, digressive nature.[12]

It is easy to see that any work of literature that springs from the alliance of such genres would have enormous potential for variety and disorder. And it is clear that Cervantes was striving for such effects in the conception and creation of his final tale. He packs his narrative with the subject matter and satirical techniques appropriate to each of the two genres—the portrayal of the series of masters into whose hands the hapless picaro falls, the episodic development of comic and generally destructive actions, the moralizing commentary concerning the picaro's involvement, the hastily sketched caricatures, the brief demonstrative anecdotes, the witty disquisitions on decorum and discretion in social conduct, the discussions of literature and language, and the examples of literary styles. At the same time, he superimposes the plane of dialogized commentary onto the plane of recollected experience in an irregular pattern, so as to alter radically the rhythm of his narration, vary its tonalities, and endow its narrator with a protean capacity for shape-changing that goes well beyond the notorious powers of accommodation and disguise which one encounters in the picaresque hero.[13]

THE PATTERNS OF NARRATIVE DISORDER:
SATURATION, VARIEGATION, FRAGMENTATION:
DIALOGUE AS A MODE OF DISARTICULATION

Perhaps the most striking example of the complicating effects caused by Cervantes' uneven distribution of what we might call picaresque

[12] For the conventions of Menippean satire, see N. Frye, *Anatomy of Criticism*, pp. 308-14.

[13] See Richard Alewyn's analysis of the significance of Simplizissimus' encounter with the stone figure "Baldanders," who in his constant metamorphoses appears as the protective spirit of the picaro and the symbol of the picaresque vision, in which "das Leben ein ständiger Wechsel ohne Ordnung oder Einheit oder Sinn ist" and "in der Welt nichts beständiger ist als die Unbeständigkeit" ("Der Roman des Barock," *Pikarische Welt: Schriften zum Europäischen Schelmenroman*, ed. H. Heidenreich [Darmstadt, 1969], pp. 397-411; see pp. 407-408). As I shall point out below, the most protean feature of Cervantes' accommodating hero, Berganza, is to be found in his ironic discourse with its indirections, frequent shifts of tone, and general elusiveness. The moralizing tirades and sardonic witticisms which dominate the commentary of such famous shape-changers as Guzmán de Alfarache, known by Ben Jonson's accolade as the "Spanish Proteus," and Quevedo's Don Pablos are, by comparison, quite uniform and predictable.

narrative and Lucianesque commentary is in his development of the episodes of Berganza's sojourn in Sevilla in the service of a merchant and a local constable. The action of the episode with the merchant is saturated with digressions, and the dogs' commentary continually ranges far beyond any relevance to the events that inspire it. At times it would appear to follow a logic of intellectual free association, and it literally swallows up the narrative containing it. In this segment of the *Coloquio* we find in their most concentrated form all the techniques of narration by which Cervantes charges his final tale with the powerful centrifugal energy characteristic of great satire. A close inspection of it will in fact reveal the grammar of narrative disorder that controls the action of the entire work.

As soon as Berganza describes his departure from the shepherds and his entry into the service of a rich merchant, Cipión interrupts to comment on the lamentable absence of "good masters" in Spain. Introducing the imagery of clothing and contracts which is characteristic of the entire work (see below) and pointing to its central theme of the tyranny of illusion throughout society, he notes the difference between God, who offers, in his "book of wages," a contract for service to anyone who lives with humility, poverty, and purity (*limpieza*) of heart, and "the lords of the earth," who grant employment to servants only after thoroughly examining their lineage, cleverness, dress, and general appearance. Berganza reprimands his friend for the moralizing digression but immediately follows with one of his own, a little sermon celebrating humility as the foundation of all the virtues, ostensibly to explain the propriety of his obsequious solicitations of a master in Seville. He proceeds to describe briefly his activities in the house of a rich merchant, and then paraphrases and interprets Aesop's fable of the loving but imprudent ass whose efforts to caress his owner meet with disastrous consequences, a fable which he claims guided him in his respectful but distant relationship with his master. The exegesis of the fable leads to a sophisticated speech on decorum and the enunciation of the principle of hierarchy, a principle that no one in the disordered world of the story except the dogs and a few very marginal figures such as God, the good judge, the good prince, and the good captain would appear to respect. Despite Cipión's admonitions, Berganza cannot repress his desire to moralize, and he follows up his speech on decorum with a satirical outburst directed at gentlemen who violate the principle. He offers anecdotes describing one who "makes a buffoon of himself and prides himself on his skill in dicing and thimblerigging and his proficiency in dancing the chaconne" and another "who boasted that at the request of a sacristan, he had cut out thirty-two paper flowers to stick on the black hangings on a monument, and made such a song about those cuttings that he even took his friends to see them as if he were taking them to see the pennants and trophies captured from the enemy that were hung over the tomb of his parents and grandparents."[14] At this point Berganza returns to his narration of his life with the merchant, and he mentions his master's concern with the elegance and education of his son, whereupon Cipión immediately offers a generalizing digression on merchants, noting that their ambitions frequently drive them to use their business dealings and contracts to seek social advancement for their children by the ostentatious display of wealth and the purchase of titles. Berganza follows this satirical digression, which incorporates a pervasive preoccupation of picaresque fiction,[15] with a lengthy speech about the evils of calumny, including two anecdotes that demonstrate its universality. He swears to bite his own tongue if he lapses into its practice again, but his declaration of good intentions is qualified by another anecdote, in which he describes the model for his resolution: an inveterate swearer who, in his effort to reform, determined to pinch himself and kiss the earth every time he indulged his evil habits and who, despite such drastic methods of mortification, persisted in his swearing. He now abruptly returns to his narration with a description of his visits in the company of the merchant's son to the school of the Jesuits, praises the order and its method of teaching, offers some general comments on education, and observes, with a refined sense of humor which accords well with the light tone of this part of the *Colloquy*, that, since his games with the children interfered in their studies, he was expelled from school by "a lady whom . . . they call in these parts 'reason of state,' for when her needs have to be met, many other reasons have to fall into abeyance."[16] He describes his resumption of the duties of a chained watchdog and immediately offers a rhetorical lament about the vicissitudes of fortune, reminiscent

[14] ". . . se hace chocarrero y se precia que sabe jugar los cubiletes y las agallas, y que no hay quien como él sepa bailar la chacona! . . . se alababa que, a ruegos de un sacristán, había cortado de papel treinta y dos florones para poner en un monumento sobre paños negros, y destas cortaduras hizo tanto caudal, que así llevaba a sus amigos a verlas como si los llevara a ver las banderas y despojos de enemigos que sobre la sepultura de sus padres y abuelos estaban puestas" (pp. 237-38).

[15] Arguing that the emergence of the picaresque novel can be understood properly only if we approach it in the context of social psychology, M. Bataillon points out that it is thoroughly penetrated by "las preocupaciones por la decencia, la honra externa y las distinciones sociales" (*Pícaros y picaresca: La Pícara Justina* [Madrid, 1969], p. 214).

[16] "Una señora, que, a mi parecer, llaman por ahí razón de estado, que cuando con ella se cumple, se ha de descumplir con otras razones muchas" (p. 246).

of the conventional discourse of the picaresque commentator,[17] and requests that his companion allow him "to philosophize a little bit." Cipión assents but not without offering a digression of his own concerning the demonic temptation of knowledge and the ease with which the devil seduces a man to the practice of sinful calumny cloaked in the dignified disguises of philosophical truths. Berganza's philosophical discourse turns out to be in reality a tirade against ignorant people who pretentiously display their minute and frequently incorrect knowledge of Latin. The outburst would appear to be the product of his rapidly associating mind and his recollection of the Jesuit school and the teaching of Latin. Cipión eagerly follows the line of the argument, denouncing the assininity of the numerous people who know Latin well but are ignorant as to when it is proper and improper to use it and who pour it out like water even when speaking to shoemakers and tailors. The discussion moves on to include another condemnation of vituperation, now associated with the Cynic philosopher; a comparison of Berganza's narration to an octopus; and a consideration of the civilized use of euphemism. At this point Berganza returns to his tale briefly to mention the Negro servants' nocturnal encounters, the conflict of conscience that his acquiescence in their dishonorable activity aroused, and his determination to resist their bribes. Suddenly the narration of the "picaro's adventures," which has been swallowed up amid the exfoliating digressions, seems to be about to assert itself and to take a new rhythm, as a conflict that creates suspense and demands resolution emerges. However, as if he were tantalizing his reader, Cervantes immediately shifts back to the plane of commentary and allows his dogs to offer digressions on a subject that they have already covered more than adequately—the ostentatious display of knowledge by ignorant people and the evils of slander. In the elaboration of the theme of slander, however, the satirical dialogue glides in new directions. Cipión recalls his companion's determination to bite his tongue, and the latter narrates the classical anecdote of Carondas, the ruler whose obedience to his own law was so firm that he executed himself for violating it. Concluding rather cynically that the present is no time for such heroic acts, Ber-

---

[17] See, for example, Guzmán de Alfarache's meditations on freedom and predestination and his numerous references to the turning wheel of fortune in his account of his disastrous marriage to Gracia (Part Two, III, iv-v) or Lazarillo's repeated attributions of his misadventures to the whims of fortune (Juan de Luna, *La segunda parte de la vida de Lazarillo de Tormes*, ed. E. R. Sims [Austin, 1928]). U. Wicks has taken the theme to be a defining convention of picaresque narrative ("The Nature of Picaresque Narrative: A Modal Approach").

ganza gives voice to a theme which surfaces several times through the work and which is one of the recurrent themes of satirical literature in practically every age—when measured by the perfections of previous epochs, the present must be viewed as a dying age in need of universal purgation: "now things are not carried out with such strictness and rigor as in the days of antiquity; today a law is made, and tomorrow it is broken, and perhaps it is fitting that this should be so."[18] At the conclusion of his declaration that he is determined to abide by the tenor of times, Berganza adds that he is particularly unwilling to perform an honorable act when no one can see him, provoking a response by his companion on the evils of hypocrisy.[19] Now Cipión admonishes Berganza to return to the tale and cease with his "impertinentes digresiones." The latter appears to accede to the demands of the impatient listener, who certainly expresses the feelings of frustration that Cervantes has by now aroused in his reader; for he resumes his tale and proceeds rapidly to the point of maximum suspense—the approach of his adversary in the darkness. At this moment, when the plot looms up to offer a binding force for the aimlessly crowding commentary, Berganza once again breaks off his narration to offer a digression on bribes, which includes the gloss of an ancient adage "habet bovem in lingua" and a discussion of its applicability to the present case. Although exasperated by the fragmentation of the narrative and the display of classical erudition by his companion, who has just censured the pedants, Cipión too cannot resist the temptation to enlarge on the digression by pointing out that he could give one thousand examples of the power of bribes. Finally, after interminable delay, Berganza offers the "vanishing" climax and the denouement of his tale—his attack on the servant, her attempt to poison him, his well-intentioned but unsuccessful struggle with the adversary, whose power is too great to be withstood, and his characteristic flight from a demonic foe who remains in control of the battlefield.

Through this point Berganza's account of the events in Seville has been dominated by a tendency toward unlimited amplification, in which digressions pour forth to overwhelm a thin plot line which,

---

[18] "Ahora no van las cosas por el tenor y rigor de las antiguas: hoy se hace una ley, y mañana se rompe, y quizá conviene que así sea" (p. 255).

[19] The ironic modulations in Berganza's voice and the resulting changes in his attitude toward his subject matter and in his general identity and stance as a satirical narrator add to the complexity and apparent formlessness of the *Coloquio*. At this point I am concerned only with the structure and effects of its narrated actions. Below I will deal with the nature of the narrator's voice.

while struggling to rise to a climax, is constantly on the verge of collapsing into nothingness. What appears to be narrative disorder is in fact designed according to the traditional logic of satirical plotting, for beneath its surface chaos we observe the organizing actions of variegating and diminishing which, as Kernan points out, have been used by satirists consistently from antiquity to the present.[20] If my survey of the proliferating "desatinos"—the "swerves from the mark"—seems overly detailed and wearisome for my own reader, it is nonetheless the only way of accurately revealing the narrative mischief of Cervantes' apparently aimless dialogue and the effects that he would achieve—precisely the kind of effects that lie behind Sklovskij's reaction to the work as banal and disorderly.

As the dog turns to the next episode, his sojourn in Seville, Cervantes proceeds a step further in his assembly of disparate narrative rhythms. Following an introductory moralizing discussion of the turning wheel of fortune and the hypocrisy of people who explain away their inadequacies and failures by referring to its power, commentary nearly vanishes from the narration. Berganza recounts his experiences with the constable in a swiftly paced dramatic narrative which moves with no interference toward a climactic scene of farce. Instead of the multitudinously interspersed, quickly sketched anecdote and the unrestrained self-generating commentary, Cervantes turns at this point to the dramatic techniques which he exploits so successfully in his *entremeses* and the inn scenes of *Don Quixote* I. The episode is a masterpiece both of Cervantes' characteristic tumultuous comedy of situation—e.g., the disappearance of the Breton's trousers, the confusion and suspicion it arouses, and the scene of chaos as the society of evildoers disintegrates in mutual distrust and abusive railing—and of his scathing comedy of character—e.g., the declamation of the innkeeper's wife, a torrent of words which rises in its absurdly inflated protestations of nobility and purity of blood and sinks in the speaker's failure to conceal the nudity of her scantily attired figure, in her mutilation of correct speech, and in the travesty of a venerable official language in her hysterical invocation of the Latin phrases of the certificate of *hidalguía*.[21] While such scenes of dramatic satirical unveil-

---

[20] *The Plot of Satire*, chaps. 4, 5.

[21] The references to the respected document belong to a pattern of travesty penetrating the entire tale with its disordering effects. See my discussion of its most striking development in the aborted recognition scene of the main plot (below). For a theoretical treatment of the reductive technique which Cervantes employs in his description of the innkeeper's wife and its place in satiric fiction, particularly in the presentation of caricatures, see Kernan, *The Plot of Satire*, chap. 3, where it is des-

ing are reminiscent of picaresque fiction and contrast sharply with the proponderant Lucianesque dialogue of the preceding events, there is nothing in the episode that alters the narrative movement of the *Colloquy* more radically than the verbal style by which Cervantes pushes it toward its climax. In the proliferating preterites of verbs of action, which, following a brief sketch of necessary background information, literally pour forth in Berganza's narration, Cervantes appears to be compensating for the irregular, coiling rhythm and the disappearance of action in the lengthy preceding episode. It would be difficult to find in his writings another passage that is so bare of anything except the essential action and that offers as pure an example of his so-called *"veni-vidi-vici"* style—the rapid listings of occurrences in short phrases, each introduced by a verb of action in the preterite tense—a style which, as Hatzfeld has suggested, conveys a sense of compressed, bursting energy that goes beyond the expressive power of the specific words it employs:[22]

It happened, then, that Colindres (for this was the name of the police officer's mistress) hooked a greasy Breton; she arranged with him to dine and spend the night at his lodgings; she tipped off her friend, and scarcely had they undressed when the constable, the attorney, two policemen, and I descended on them. The lovers raised a fuss; the constable exaggerated the seriousness of the offense; he ordered them to get dressed as quickly as possible so that he could take them off to prison; the Breton lamented, the attorney, moved by charity, intervened, and, through his persuasions, the constable reduced the fine to one hundred reales only. The Breton asked for his trousers. . . .[23]

---

ignated "magnification." He notes that "Pope calls attention to the fact that the magnifying tendency is also manifested by a fondness for amplification, sheer multiplication of words and indiscriminate amassment of vast numbers of sounds" (pp. 37-38). Cervantes' *Coloquio* is, like many other satires, full of such magnifying actions and the diminishing or falling actions to which they generally lead. See, for example, the poet whose grandiose statements concerning the perfections of his neo-classical historical drama are followed by the deflationary action of his meticulous division of the bread crumbs and raisins with Berganza and the farcical anticlimax in which the bored spectators disappear during the performance of his play. See also the titanic aspirations of the final four caricatures—the alchemist who would find the philosophers' stone, the mathematician who would square the circle, the *arbitrista* who proposes a remedy for Spain's financial ruin, and the poet who has spent years struggling to produce the perfect heroic poem—and their "fall" into the ravages of syphilis and the pesthouse of Valladolid.

[22] Helmut Hatzfeld, *"Don Quijote" als Wortkunstwerk* (Leipzig, 1927), pp. 205-10.

[23] "Sucedió, pues, que la Colindres, que así se llamaba la amiga del alguacil, pescó un bretón unto y bisunto; concertó con él cena y noche en su posada; dió el cañuto a su amigo, y apenas se habían desnudado, cuando el alguacil, el escribano, dos corchetes y yo dimos con ellos. Alborotáronse los amantes; exageró el alguacil el delito; mandólos vestir a toda priesa para llevarlos a la cárcel; afligióse el bretón; terció,

As if deliberately to make his reversal of narrative procedures as complete as possible, Cervantes not only replaces his anticlimax with a theatrical, prolonged climax, which in fact totally dominates and absorbs the narrative elements preparing it, but also follows the desultory "nonmovement" of the narrative of Berganza's confrontation of the lustful servants with the exaggerated linearity of a single plot in which every narrated element contributes to a rapid progression toward its anticipated goal.

The examination of Berganza's recollection of his adventures with his third master, the commentary they provoke, and the tremendous shift in narrative tempo in the following episode suggests some obvious conclusions concerning the basic features and effects of Cervantes' final novella. The most obvious is simply that the tale is a work of tremendous variety, that it is literally packed with information, ideas, characters, actions, and styles, and that it develops nearly all its subject matter with a moralizing and generally satirical interest, embracing a variety of traditional satirical methods in the process.[24] If the first part of Cervantes' *Tale of the Captive*, with its "novelistic" survey of history, politics, geography, and customs in the Mediterranean, provides a good example of what Kenneth Burke has described as the tendency of literary form to "atrophy" in the presence of the "hypertrophy of information," the *Colloquy of the Dogs*, for all its alleged "realism" demonstrates how in satirical writing voluminous information never quite succeeds in emancipating itself and establishing its own inherent interest, for, by continuing to remind us of its violations of formal requirements, it continues to reassert its subordination to a transcendent formal design.[25] The dialogue indeed appears to be bursting with pressures from within, an effect produced not only by the sheer volume of its subjects and the interlocutors' rapidly paced, improvisational manner of presenting them, but also by the way in which it intimates that the principal narrator is overwhelmed by his material, which constantly threatens to slip from his control. While his companion continually scolds him for his irrepressible

---

movido de caridad, el escribano, y a puros ruegos redujo la pena a solos cien reales. Pidió . . ." (pp. 262-63).

[24] In its overflowing variety the *Coloquio* is a satire in the purest sense, exemplifying perfectly the fundamental meaning of the Latin term *satura—mixture* or *medley—* which was originally used to designate the type of literature created by Lucilius (see R. C. Elliott, *The Power of Satire*, pp. 101-102). Kernan observes: "Though largely forgotten, the root meaning of 'satire' remains functional, for the world of satire is always a fantastic jumble of men and objects" (*The Plot of Satire*, p. 68).

[25] "Lexicon Rhetoricae," *Counter-Statement*. (Berkeley and Los Angeles, 1968), p. 144.

digressions, Berganza insists that he is struggling to condense and frequently reminds his reader that in the fallen world of his experiences there is immeasurably more than what he is able to depict, that its material is pressing upon him and overflowing the narrative molds to which he would confine it, and implicitly that the confused jumble of his narration is only a fraction of the utter confusion which it would reflect were it to incorporate the whole truth. There are in reality "a thousand more examples" which it could easily include. Early in his tale Berganza responds to Cipión's admonitions concerning the formal requirements of coherent stories with an agreement to struggle with his material, but he suggests that there is a disorder in his subject that may defeat his efforts to avoid the shapelessness of babbling indefinitely (p. 219). Later he exclaims that words "fly to his tongue like mosquitos to wine" (p. 240), that he is not so much astounded by what he tells as frightened by what he leaves out (p. 230), that only the restraining influence of his companion is keeping his heated mouth from reciting an "entire book" (p. 229), and, in a portentous tone, that a time will come when he will tell all "with better arguments and better discourse than now" (p. 229). Recalling the night in Monipodio's den, he claims: "If I were to try to tell you all that took place in that house, the supper that was served up . . . I would entangle myself in a labyrinth from which I could never extricate myself, try as I might."[26] The analogy, labyrinth-narrative, accords well with Cipión's earlier description of the tale as a monster and with the important role at its imaginative center of the greatest monstrosity which it depicts—the figure of the hideous witch Cañizares. At another point Berganza laments: "[There are] so many things to tell that I do not know how or when I shall be able to finish them, particularly as I am fearful that when the sun rises we shall be groping in the dark, devoid of speech."[27] Cipión's rejoinder that he should not worry, for "Heaven will do it better," picks up the thread of impending apocalypse running through the story and associates the purgative effects of the tale with the consuming flames of the last days, but it fails to end Berganza's worries about the tormenting pressure to speak. As the night rushes on toward dawn and the return of silence and his narration quickens toward the swift portraiture of the four madmen

---

[26] "Quererte yo contar ahora lo que allí se trató, la cena que cenaron . . . sería meterme en un laberinto donde no me fuese posible salir quando quisiese" (pp. 272-73).

[27] "Tantas cosas por decir, que no sé cómo ni cuándo podré acabarlas, y más estando temeroso que al salir del sol nos hemos de quedar a escuras, faltándonos la habla" (pp. 255-56).

dying in the hospital, Berganza appears to be wrestling with a gigantic subject beyond his powers of coherent presentation, just as in his numerous encounters with the evil adversaries, despite his good intentions, he appears to be up against a force that he cannot quite master. "Oh, Cipión, what things I could tell you of what I saw in this and two other acting companies with which I traveled! But as it is impossible to reduce it all to a short, concise narrative, I shall have to postpone it for another day. . . . Yet all you have heard is nothing to what I could tell you of what I have noted, learned and seen of these people . . . with an infinite number of other things."[28]

[28] "¡Oh Cipión, quién te pudiera contar lo que vi en esta y en otras dos compañías de comediantes en que anduve! Mas por no ser posible reducirlo a narración sucinta y breve, lo habré de dejar para otro día. . . . todo lo que has oído es nada, comparado a lo que te pudiera contar de lo que noté . . . con otras infinitas cosas" (pp. 327-28). Cipión recommends that his companion save the experiences with the actors for a "cuento particular" (p. 318). One should compare Cide Hamete Benengeli's allusion to all that he "ha dejado de escribir" in the interest of preserving unity and the large number of "intimated tales" which Cervantes attaches with the most tenuous bonds to the narration of Don Quixote's adventures and invites the reader to "fill in," e.g., the tale of Saavedra, a story which, as the Captive puts it, "fuera parte para entreteneros y admiraros harto mejor que con el cuento de mi historia" (1:486); the romance of Pedro de Aguilar's deliverance, the renegade's narrated "[caso] más estraño que jamás sucedió en aquellas partes, donde a cada paso suceden cosas de grande espanto y de admiración" (1:493); the story of the young soldier who has left the court in disillusionment to join Spain's forces abroad; the biography of Ginés de Pasamonte, whose deeds, when fully recorded, will make the world forget *Lazarillo de Tormes*; the conclusion of the tale of Doña Clara, Don Luis, and the judge; the fortunes of the romantic daughter of Diego de la Llana; and indeed the other redactions of the *Quijote* itself ("Autores hay que dicen que la primera aventura que le avino fue . . . otros dicen que" [1:81-82]) and its future versions—the one for which Don Quijote offers the opening line (1:80) and the one which Cervantes invites his readers to contemplate at the conclusion of Part I, invoking Ariosto's untold tale of Angelica, which, in its invitation to the imagination of the reader, appealed to him so much that he could not resist returning to it in Part II: "Y cómo del Catay recibió el cetro / quizá otro cantará con mejor plectro" (2:52). Such provocative fragments are, in their effects, very different from the *Coloquio*'s allusions to "tales that might have been added" by the narrator to illustrate the contagious powers and proliferating characteristics of evil and to contribute to its satirical vision of moral disorder. As J. B. Avalle-Arce and E. C. Riley have pointed out, the peculiar tendency of the *Quixote* to intimate many more tales than it actually incorporates is a fundamental "novelistic" technique, a method of suggestion by which the writer creates for the reader the illusion that he is confronting the real, i.e., the "nontextual," world, in which, of course, "no hay vida humana sin su historia" ("Don Quijote," *Suma Cervantina*, pp. 47-79; see pp. 74ff.). The flow of unrealized possibilities is a characteristic of real experience, and, by reminding the reader of what might be there about him if only the circumstances of life would permit his engagement with it, the novelist brings to his awareness a sense of the mysterious potentiality which is concealed behind the ordering and delimiting routines and rituals of daily life.

THE PATTERNS OF NARRATIVE DISORDER:
DISMEMBERMENT OF COHERENT FORM THROUGH
ANTICLIMAX AND PARODY: THE MAIN PLOT
OF THE *COLLOQUY*

> For twenty-two years I have been hot on the trail of the
> fixed point, and here I miss it, there I'm close to it, and
> just when I think I've found it and it can not possibly escape,
> when I'm not watching, I suddenly find myself so far
> from it that I'm utterly amazed. . . . and so my
> sufferings resemble those of Tantalus, who stands
> close to the fruit yet is dying of hunger.
> —The syphilitic mathematician[29]

While Berganza's account of his service with the merchant of Seville, with its digressions and the irritation which they produce in his critical audience, clearly illustrates Cervantes' fundamental technique of disordering through accumulation, its contiguity with the description of the events involving the constable reveals his interest in manipulating narrative tempo for striking effects of variegation, irregularity, and contrast. At the same time we observe in these scenes still another narrative technique, which in its power of narrative disintegration goes beyond the insertion of proliferating and varied material and styles, the cultivation of irrelevant digressions, and the dislocations in narrative movement. The technique is fundamental in Cervantes' development of a main plot in the work, and, directed as it is at the dismemberment of coherent form, it brings us close to the sources of the destructive energy that permeates the entire *Colloquy*.

As I have pointed out above, Cervantes superimposes a satirical dialogue on a narration of picaresque adventures at irregular intervals and achieves a variety of effects in narrative rhythm and tone. Throughout most of the scene examined above, the recollected action is far from the foreground of the narration. As is often the case in the "plots" of the philosophical-satirical colloquy, it is a rather flimsy fictional scaffolding supporting a dense exposition of the ideas and is at most of incidental interest. However, in the middle of the episode Cervantes develops a suspenseful action within that fictional background: the intrigue of the Negro servants and Berganza's complicity,

---

[29] "Veinte y dos años ha que ando tras hallar el punto fijo, y aquí lo dejo, y allí lo tomo, y pareciéndome que ya lo he hallado y que no se me puede escapar en ninguna manera, cuando no me cato, me hallo tan lejos dél, que me admiro. . . . y así, es mi pena semejable a las de Tántalo, que está cerca del fruto, y muere de hambre" (pp. 332-33).

conflict of conscience, and determined opposition. Suddenly the narrative action moves toward the foreground, and the reader, experiencing suspense, seeks a coherent resolution of the imminent conflict. The unstructured temporality, which up to this point he comfortably accepts as the normal medium for the freely ranging intellectual play of dialogue, becomes unexpectedly a source of disturbance. As he copes with its disquieting effects, he is compelled to view the interruptions, repetitions, retrogressions, and qualifications, which dialectic discourse accommodates in order to nuance and deepen its exploration of its subject, as "abnormal," intrusive elements interfering with his desire to reach a fixed point.[30] Having awakened the reader's anticipations, Cervantes thwarts them twice. At the moment of maximum suspense he interposes a lengthy philosophical dialogue, and he heightens the mischievousness of his play with narrative rhythm and his reader's response both by having the exchange repeat material already covered in preceding dialogues and by representing dramatically the frustrations of the reader in Cipión's outburst of exasperation.

Perhaps nothing illustrates the deliberate cultivation of formlessness in Cervantes' satire more clearly than this procedure, which, by toying with the reader's legitimate desire for coherent plot movement, compels him to feel keenly a sense of narrative disintegration and to gaze on an artistic creation that is outrageously and *self-consciously unartistic*. The procedure is, as Northrop Frye has pointed out, endemic in the narrative methods of satire,[31] and Cervantes, who undoubtedly appre-

---

[30] For the relatively free temporal structure distinguishing dialectically composed dialogue from other forms of dialogue in literature, see G. Bauer, *Zur Poetik des Dialogs* (Darmstadt, 1969), pp. 223-28.

[31] "A deliberate rambling digressiveness, which in a *Tale of a Tub* reaches the point of including a digression in praise of digressions, is endemic in the narrative technique of satire, and so is a calculated bathos or art of sinking in its suspense, such as the quizzical mock oracular conclusions in Apuleius and Rabelais and in the refusal of Sterne for hundreds of pages even to get his hero born. An extraordinary number of great satires are fragmentary, unfinished, or anonymous" (*Anatomy of Criticism*, p. 234). If Cervantes' juxtaposition of the merchant and constable episodes reveals a narrative design analogous to the figure of catachresis as it is defined in Pope's catalogue of the rhetorical devices of confusion through variegation, the technique that he employs in developing the merchant episode itself, as well as the main plot, exemplifies the principal figure of diminishing—anticlimax: "when the gentle reader is in expectation of some great image, he either finds it surprisingly imperfect, or is presented with something low, or quite ridiculous. A surprise resembling that of a curious person in a cabinet of Antique Statues, who beholds on the pedestal the names of Homer, or Cato; but looking up, finds Homer without a head, and nothing to be seen of Cato but his privy member" (*Martinus Scriblerus, Peri Bathous: or of the Art of Sinking in Poetry*, in *Alexander Pope: Selected Poetry and Prose*, ed. W. Wimsatt [New York, 1972], pp. 396, 402).

ciated it in the works of such writers as Ariosto and Apuleius, was fascinated with its exploitation and effects. In the comic *Don Quijote* he develops the technique in a variety of ways. For example, in a well-known scene, his narrator interrupts the protagonist's battle with an adversary at the moment of climax, when his sword hangs in the air, poised for the decisive blow, and informs the reader that the manuscript which he is transcribing has come to an end. In his description of Don Quixote's angry reaction to Sancho Panza's aborted tale of La Torralba, he presents a scene in which the comic effect derives in part from the exasperation of an unfulfilled reader, and which offers an ingeniously contrived "literary parallel" to the scene "in life" that surrounds it, Don Quixote's intolerably suspenseful vigil through the night, which literally concludes in bathos with the discovery that the thunderous roar of his "demonic antagonist" was produced by the mechanical falling of the fulling mills.[32] Even in his heroic romance, the *Persiles*, Cervantes cannot resist the appeal of the technique, and on at least two occasions he fragments the development of his plot at a suspenseful moment with an authorial digression which threatens the generally dominant tone of high seriousness with reductive notes concerning the conventions and provenance of the work; moreover, in the figure of Mauricio, he subjects to comic examination the demands and frustrations of readers as they apprehend the literary plot that defiantly and self-consciously fails to exemplify the controlled "Aristotelian" movement toward climax and closure.[33]

[32] *Don Quijote*, 1:ix, xx. The narrator cannot resist reminding the reader here of his delight in frustrating him, intruding at the moment of climax with a parenthetical remark concerning the dreadful antagonist "que tan suspensos y medrosos toda la noche los había tenido": "Y eran—si no lo has, ¡oh lector!, por pesadumbre y enojo—seis mazos de batán" (1:248). In having his narrator act in his narration like the mischievous Sancho in the literary tale, which is marred by a mass of parenthetical insertions, one of which appears at the moment of climax and leads to its disintegration, Cervantes is appearing, as writer in his tale, in his characteristic pose of ironic self-deprecation; for in reality the relationship of the "parallel suspenseful texts" is one of contrast—on the one hand, meaningful, artistically designed suspenseful plotting, on the other, the unstructured, irritating flow of contingent reality. See my "Cervantes and the Freedom of the Artist," *Romantic Review* 61 (1970): 243-55.

[33] See, for example, the narrator's complex interferences with the movement toward climax in the miraculous deliverance and recognition of the pilgrims as their capsized boat drifts into the haven of King Policarpo's kingdom (2:i-ii); also, the narrator's intrusion at the moment of Periandro's seemingly fatal fall from a tower in order to consider the differences between the scene and a conventional fictional representation of it (3:xiv). For the implications of these scenes, in which the disordering of form points to constructive processes of artistic creation rather than to the moral chaos distinguishing the depicted world of the *Colloquy*, Cervantes' critical engagement

In the *Colloquy of the Dogs* the effects of this narrative procedure are much more pronounced than in Cervantes' other works, as they emerge in the author's manipulation of its central plot. Moreover, they are perfectly consistent with the other formal techniques of the work, its basic themes, and its dominant tonality. Unlike the heroic *Persiles* and the novelistic *Quixote*, the *Colloquy* offers very little to offset the powerful disintegrating impact of the technique on its fictional world. Quite the contrary, Cervantes would exploit its maximum potential for disorder, and he does so by employing it at the center of his narration and by combining with it an elaborately contrived parody of the plot of romance and a powerful religious travesty. In other words, in his strategy of alienating his readers through techniques of diminishing, of offering "too little" in the midst of "too much," Cervantes exploits their general sense of plot coherence and their natural desire for orderly movement toward closure—a desire that Berganza recognizes when wondering whether the peculiar order in his narration of "middles" before "beginnings" has irritated his companion (p. 230)—while at the same time playing upon their capacity to recognize certain archetypes of literary form and any violations of their integrity.

In the apparent disorder of the *Colloquy* it is easy to overlook the various references by which Cervantes carefully suggests that his narrative is moving toward a climactic anagnorisis which will clarify a mystery surrounding the origins of the protagonist and his acquisition of the power of speech. Following the opening discussion, in which both dogs discourse with exemplary awe, piety, and humility on the miracle by which God has offered them the "divine gift of speech," Berganza begins the tale of his life, but he immediately withholds information concerning his birth, and, by drawing attention to his selective procedures, arouses curiosity and suspense in his listener: "It seems to me that the first time I ever saw the sun was in Seville, in its slaughterhouse outside the Meat Gate, where I should imagine (were it not for what I shall afterward tell you) that my parents must have been mastiffs."[34] In the commentary that interrupts the episode of the shepherds, Cipión admonishes his comrade to curb his indignation and remember with humility his animal nature. Berganza's

---

with problems of narrative in his treatment of Mauricio, and the importance of Ariosto's artistic principles and techniques in Cervantes' fiction, see my *Cervantes, Aristotle and the "Persiles,"* chaps. 6-8.

[34] "Paréceme que la primera vez que vi el sol fué en Sevilla, y en su Matadero, que está fuera de la puerta de la Carne; por donde imaginara (si no fuera por lo que después te diré) que mis padres debieron de ser alanos" (pp. 214-15).

response is full of ambiguities, but it contains hints that the miracle of their speech may not be, as they originally thought, a gift from heaven; that the dogs may in fact some day be endowed with capacities superior to those of animals; and that there is a terrifying secret behind all these hints, a secret that he should have revealed at the beginning of his tale. Cipión manages to elicit from him the information that it has something to do with a witch, but Berganza then refuses a clarification, justifying his silence as proper to the suspenseful disposition of narrative: "That I shall not do until the proper time; do be patient and listen to my adventures in their order; *in that way they will give you more pleasure, if you don't worry yourself trying to know the middle before the beginning.*"[35] In Berganza's arbitrary dealings with his listener, Cervantes is manipulating his own audience as he arouses restlessness and curiosity by acknowledging that they are natural reactions to such tantalizing hints and by promising a pleasurable reward for the reader's patience.

As the narration continues on its meandering course, Cervantes occasionally allows the reader to glimpse briefly the thread that will presumably bind all episodes in a meaningful configuration. When Cipión observes that Berganza's methods of approaching a prospective master are remarkably like his own, Berganza suggests that the similarity is not mere coincidence and enigmatically promises to explain his remark "when the time is right." In describing the tricks that he learned while serving the drummer, he observes: "he began to teach me to dance to the beat of the drum and to perform other monkey tricks that no other dog but myself could have learned, as you will understand when I tell you about them."[36] He adds that his skill could have easily led some to believe that he was possessed by a demon (p. 281). Thus, through recurrent, fragmentary hints concerning the mysterious identity of the dogs, the presence of a horrible secret lurking behind it, and the distinct possibilities of witchcraft, metamorphosis, and demonic possession, as well as through repeated adumbrations of a climactic revelation, Cervantes has by the midpoint of his narrative created a plot and sustained its development while allowing the episodes and commentary to burgeon with no apparent confining shape or limitation. As Berganza describes the performance on

---

[35] "Eso no haré yo, por cierto, hasta su tiempo; ten paciencia, y escucha por su orden mis sucesos, que *así te darán más gusto, si ya no te fatiga querer saber los medios antes de los principios*" (p. 230; italics added).

[36] "Comenzó a enseñarme a bailar al són del atambor, y a hacer otras monerías, tan ajenas de poder aprenderlas otro perro que no fuera yo, como las oirás cuando te las diga" (p. 279).

the patio of the hospital in Montilla, he interrupts to inform the reader that the long-awaited revelation is at hand: "The first command of that day (memorable among all those of my life) was. . . ."[37] He introduces his narration of the encounter with the witch shortly thereafter by drawing attention to his suspenseful disposition of the entire recitation: "What I now wish to relate should have been told at the beginning of my story, as we would then have had no reason to wonder at finding ourselves able to speak."[38]

The figure of Cañizares and her lengthy confession—the confession within the confession within the confession in this peculiar narrative, which, in its increasing involution, seems to contract and turn inward even as the expansive energies of its crowding subject matter appear to be surging beyond its powers of control—are of fundamental importance to the entire *Colloquy*, to its most essential themes of evil, suffering, death, regeneration, and meditation, to the redemption of the dreamer, and to the formation of the mature perspective of the narrator in his role as moral apprentice and confessor. In the following section I shall consider the encounter of the dog and the witch in more static terms, as thematically the most important single episode of the work and the source of its impressive imaginative and symbolic power. For the moment, however, I would like to deal solely with Cañizares' function in the movement of the main plot. On this level she appears as the principal agent of the climactic anagnorosis and the anticipated restoration of the hero's lost identity. The witch is analogous to such figures of Cervantes' romantic tales as the Gypsy mother who presides over Preciosa's recognition, the steward of *La ilustre fregona*, who, before dying, discloses the mysterious tokens of Costanza's restoration, and Doña Estefanía, who arranges Leocadia's theatrical recognition banquet in *La fuerza de la sangre*, as well as to their remote ancestors in Cervantes' favorite romances—Heliodorus' Calasiris and Charikles and the nurse of the *Book of Apollonius*. The former serve as custodians of the orphaned heroine's magical tokens and texts, transmit prophetic dreams, interpret oracles, and connect most directly the heroes' ordeals and triumphs with the divine powers overseeing them. The latter, on the point of death, reveals to Tarsiana that she is in reality the daughter of King Apollonius, describes her mother's magical tokens, and gives her the plan for restoring her true identity by

---

[37] "El primer conjuro deste día (memorable entre todos los de mi vida) fué . . ." (p. 284).

[38] "Esto que ahora te quiero contar te lo había de haber dicho al principio de mi cuento, y así excusáramos la admiración que nos causó el vernos con habla" (p. 288).

embracing the statue of her father.[39] Addressing Berganza repeatedly as her child and expressing her relief that she will not die holding the unrevealed secret of his identity, Cañizares draws him apart to explain the mystery surrounding his origins, his metamorphosis from man to beast through the infernal offices of La Camacha, and his separation from his mother. She recites an oracular prophecy in verse, claiming that it announces his imminent return to his original state.

Following her long confession and the beginning of the next episode, the dogs study the prophecy, and Cipión, invoking the terminology and employing the traditional methods of allegorical exegesis, extracts from it both an allegorical and a literal meaning, and he claims that the events which are to precipitate its fulfillment have already occurred.[40] On the allegorical level it announces that the restoration will follow the overthrow of the proud and the exaltation of the humble by the turning of fortune's wheel. On the literal level, the restoration will occur when, in a game of bowling, the pins are cast down and set up once again. As both conditions have been met countless times in their lives and they remain in their canine state, the skeptical Cipión concludes that what "appear to be prophecies" are in reality no more substantial than the numerous other deceptive texts that his companion encounters in his wanderings. Emphasizing his repugnance through the imagery of mutilation and the monstrous with which he has earlier referred to Berganza's entire narration, he denounces the prophecy as "an old wives' tale, such as those about the headless horse."[41] In words that explode the anagnorisis toward which the narrative has been moving, the hero politely but firmly turns away from his "restoration": "And so Camacha was a false deceiver, Cañizares an artful rogue, and Montiela a wicked and malicious fool—I say this meaning no offense, *in case she may have been the mother of both of us, or rather your mother, for I won't have her as mine.*"[42] Berganza admits that Cipión's argument, "wiser than he had supposed,"

[39] My references to the *Book of Apollonius* here and in the following are based on the Spanish version in Juan Timoneda's *Patrañuelo*, which was undoubtedly one of the sources of Cervantes' knowledge of the tale.

[40] For the implications of this burlesque exercise in textual exegesis in relation to Cervantes' distaste for conventional allegorical modes of writing and interpretation and the general background of Renaissance literary theorizing on allegory, see my *Cervantes' Christian Romance* (Princeton, 1972), pp. 51-57. See also E. C. Riley's "The *Pensamientos escondidos* and *Figuras morales* of Cervantes," *Homenaje a William L. Fichter*, eds. A. Kossoff and J. Amor y Vázquez (Madrid, 1971), pp. 623-31.

[41] "Cuentos de viejas, como aquellos del caballo sin cabeza" (p. 310).

[42] "La Camacha fué burladora falsa, y la Cañizares embustera, y la Montiela tonta, maliciosa y bellaca, con perdón sea dicho, *si acaso es nuestra madre, de entrambos, o tuya; que yo no la quiero tener por madre*" (p. 311; italics added).

has convinced him and concludes: "from what you have said I'm inclined to believe that all we have hitherto experienced and are experiencing is a dream and that we are dogs."[43] The illumination offered by the carefully prefigured revelation suddenly turns into deeper obscurity. The promised point of repose in the narrative immediately becomes a source of greater instability in the reader's grasp of the work; for the characters within what is ostensibly a dream announce that they are dreaming and menace with an abrupt reversal the uneasy distinction between reality and dream by which the reader has separated the Ensign's account of the deceitful marriage from the narration of the dogs. In the ensuing confusion the reader might momentarily pause to wonder whether the Ensign, too, might be a figment of the dogs' dream. The dogs join the others who are not certain whether what they experience is dream or reality—Cañizares in describing her nocturnal flights to the witches' sabbat and the Ensign in discussing the credibility of the dogs' conversation, which he overheard in the darkness of his hospital chamber—and, as the anagnorisis fades into ambiguity, the reader has the bewildering sense of the narrative slipping out of his grasp like an elusive recollection of his own dream.

As I have suggested above in connection with Cañizares' role as an agent of recognition, the aborted anagnorisis of the *Colloquy of the Dogs* should be seen as an inversion of the traditional conclusion of romance, where plots generally develop through conflict and disorder toward some climactic struggle or revelation, which restores all usurped identities, resolves all tensions, and establishes an order that is pleasurable to the reader. Cervantes' scene is in fact based on a complicated set of romantic conventions, and their visibility heightens considerably the disintegrating effects of the vanishing climax. The most obvious is the return of the orphaned hero following a protracted separation from his family and a fall from his original high estate, a fall generally attributable to some shameful circumstances surrounding his birth or some catastrophe occurring in his childhood or youth. We need only glance once again at Cervantes' favorite romances for examples: the illegitimate Amadís is cast into the sea by his fearful mother Elisena, who encloses with him in the bitumened chest the tokens that will reveal his lofty origins later in the romance. In a more complex, "double" version of the convention, King Apollonius sets his apparently dead wife adrift in a coffin and simultaneously deposits in Tarsus his newborn daughter, the beautiful, virtuous Politania-Truhanilla, who grows up in ignorance of her illustrious iden-

---

[43] "Más discreto de lo que pensaba; y de lo que has dicho vengo a pensar y creer que todo lo que hasta aquí hemos pasado, y lo que estamos pasando, es sueño, y que somos perros" (p. 312).

tity, is menaced with death by her envious, powerful foster mother, and falls into the ugly world of the brothel, before finally being restored to her father and "resurrected" mother. Cervantes may have had in mind the specific situation as it is developed in Heliodorus' *Aethiopika*, the work which he probably esteemed above all other prose romances and which he openly imitated in the *Persiles*; for here a shameful metamorphosis of the child at birth is responsible for its removal and suffering. Chariklea's mother, the Ethiopian queen, has the misfortune of gazing at the picture of Perseus on the wall of her bedroom at the moment of the heroine's conception. The image contaminates the proceedings, and the child is born with white skin, such a scandal in a country of black-skinned people that the frightened mother secretly casts the child out into exile, supplying its custodian with a garment whose secret signs, when deciphered, will enable her subsequent recognition and restoration. Berganza and his brother are the products of a fateful metamorphosis at birth, and their exile is the result of the shameful nature of that event, which, as La Camacha insists, must "be buried in silence" (p. 293). Their metamorphosis is a fall from a high estate into bondage within a lower order, and a mysterious oracle, maintained in the memory of their protectress, can reveal the conditions necessary to their restoration if it is properly interpreted.

Up to this point, the negative energies released at the climax of Cervantes' text depend on the reader's desire for a coherent ending and his capacity to respond to the scene's elaborate ironic exploitation of the conventions of romance for grotesque effects of disarticulation and disfigurement. With the declamation of Cañizares' prophecy, Cervantes introduces another order of verbal violence, one dependent on the reader's ability to recognize an intertextual foundation of the entire scene. The oracle is by far the most important of the various parodies of romance conventions that orchestrate the *Colloquy's* central theme of the destructive powers of evil, a theme that emerges at this point in its most concentrated and direct expression as the narrative moves through the horrible world of the witches.

> They shall return to their true form
> When they with quick diligence see
> The fall of the high and the mighty
> The rise of the lowly downtrodden,
> By the power of a mighty hand.[44]

---

[44] "Volverán a su forma verdadera / Cuando vieren con presta diligencia / Derribar los soberbios levantados / Y alzar a los humildes abatidos, / Por mano poderosa para hacello" (p. 310).

The poem continues to develop the incongruous play with conventions surrounding the birth and destiny of the hero of literary romance. In it we observe ironic variations both of the mysterious tokens or ciphers that reveal the identity of the lost hero and of the apocalyptic prophecy of the advent of a mighty power who will come amid the turmoil afflicting the world and redeem the time. However, more striking is the fact that the verses of the prophecy incorporate specific citations of two of the most valued texts in Cervantes' culture and imaginatively bring to the *Colloquy* two sacred historical moments. On the one hand, we find in Cervantes' "derribar los soberbios levantados y alzar a los humildes abatidos" an echo of Virgil's "parcere subiectis et debellare superbos." This line of Anchises' prophecy (*Aeneid* VI), its moment of triumphant vision, and its promise of a fulfilled destiny enjoyed tremendous prestige, and we need only look at its appearance in a numinous moment of prophecy in Tasso's *Gerusalemme liberata* and in the concluding angelic chorus hailing Christ's victory over Satan in Milton's *Paradise Regained* to appreciate the elevating effects that it might be expected to bring to a text incorporating it.[45] On the other hand, we find in the witch's prophecy an even more distinguished text, which actually enfolds the Virgilian lines in a complex case of double citation parody. It is nothing less than the New Testament and its liturgical descendant in the Magnificat, Mary's song praising the Lord and thanking Him for choosing His lowly handmaiden in His grand design for the redemption of man: "He has shown strength with his arm / he has scattered the proud in the imagination of their hearts, / he has put down the mighty from their thrones, / and exalted those of low degree."[46]

[45] Amezúa has noted the Virgilian echo and gone on to describe the prophecy as one of the most obscure passages of the *Exemplary Novels* and to suggest that in it Cervantes' tale ("*El casamiento engañoso y El coloquio de los perros,*" *Bulletin of Hispanic* conventional prophecies of the romances of chivalry (*El casamiento engañoso y el coloquio de los perros,* ed. A. de Amezúa y Mayo [Madrid, 1912], pp. 620-21). For Tasso's exploitation of the imaginative power of Anchises' vision as a "sacred text," see *Gerusalemme liberata,* where the deeds of the hero's descendants include "premer gli alteri, e sollevar gli imbelli, / difender gli innocenti, e punir gli empi" (x, 76; ed. L. Bonfigli [Bari, 1930], p. 244); for the same procedure in Milton, see *Paradise Regained,* IV, 604-605: "And Thief of Paradise; him long of old / Thou didst debel, and down from Heav'n cast" (*Complete Poems and Major Prose,* ed. M. Y. Hughes [New York, 1957], p. 529).

[46] Luke 1:51-52. J. L. Woodward has suggested that there is a connection between the incorporation of the Biblical passage, its presence in the ceremonies of festive metamorphosis on Holy Innocents' Day, and the central theme of metamorphosis in Cervantes' tale ("*El casamiento engañoso y El coloquio de los perros,*" *Bulletin of Hispanic Studies* 36 [1959]:80-87).

The clear allusion, coupled with the foregoing discussion of the mysterious birth of Berganza, the bewilderment of his mother on discovering the fruits of her pregnancy, the suggestion of a supernatural consort ("this doggish birth comes from another source [than my man], and there is some mystery in it"),[47] associates ironically the birth of the dogs with the birth of Christ. The travesty is completed when the prophecy, resonant with Biblical and liturgical overtones and suggestive of grand and meaningful movements of history and imminent eschatological events, is interpreted as referring to the rise and fall of ten pins.[48] The game imagery, with its suggestions of aimlessness and irrational fatality, is characteristic of Cervantes' demonic lower worlds, whether its articulation is comic or serious (e.g., Durandarte's reference to playing cards, the tennis match in Altisidora's vision of hell, the gambling dens of *La Gitanilla* and the *Persiles*, Gaiferos' absorption in a game of "tablas" while his beloved languishes in the tower of the dark kingdom of Sansueña), and it provides here a strikingly incongruous analogue of the meaningful cycles of Christian history.[49] At the same time, Cervantes offers in the

[47] "Este perruno parto de otra parte viene, y algún misterio contiene" (p. 293).

[48] In his analysis of the comic, Freud speaks of a reduction of the lofty as essential to parody and its effects: "Karikatur, Parodie und Travestie, sowie deren praktisches Gegenstück: die Entlarvung, richten sich gegen Personen und·Objekte, die Autorität und Respekt beanspruchen, in irgendeinem Sinne *erhaben* sind. Es sind Verfahren zur Herabsetzung, wie der glückliche Ausdruck der deutschen Sprache besagt" (*Der Witz und seine Beziehung zum Unbewussten*, cited by W. Karrer, *Parodie, Travestie, Pastiche* [Munich, 1977], p. 172). Throughout my study I employ the term "travesty" to describe a type of parody distinguished by its employment of an exceptionally elevated model and its particularly destructive disfiguration or debasing reduction of it. As Karrer points out, travesty, whether one considers it a subspecies of parody or an independent literary mode, projects a model that possesses an "*unbedingten* Anspruch auf Erhabenheit" and hence produces comic effects that are tinged with "*Schadenfreude*, der boshaften Lust an der Erniedrigung einer Grösse" (p. 164). Whether it intends pleasant or unpleasant effects, travesty brings to the reader an experience of desecration. It can, of course, strike at the sanctity of the models which it employs, but it need not do so. As in so much medieval parody and in works such as Quevedo's *Buscón* and Cervantes' *Colloquy*, it can invoke the model behind the distortion as the standard by which a perpetrator's acts of profanation are condemned as aberrant. For the complex problems of interpretation raised by this literary procedure, see my discussion of the central imagery of the *Colloquy* below, Chapter II, n. 57.

[49] One can compare the disorienting effects of Rabelais' juxtaposition of the climactic oracle at the conclusion of Gargantua's triumphs and the establishment of his utopian community and its double exegesis, one emphasizing its allegorical coherence and concealed apocalyptic message concerning the providential design of history, the other claiming that there is no "other sense concealed in it than the description of a game of tennis wrapped up in strange language" (I, lviii; see *Gargantua and Pantagruel*, trans. J. M. Cohen [Suffolk, 1955], p. 163).

detail of his parody a "precise" image of the bathos or narrative sinking which distinguishes the entire scene, an image that we might compare to the "meaningless" movements of the fulling mills in his most interesting study of anticlimactic plotting in the *Quixote*.

With the mysterious oracle at the center of Cervantes' *Colloquy*, the text within the text within the text, we reach the supreme moment of anticlimax in the story. In contrast we might recall *La ilustre fregona*, where a text, literally torn apart, is knitted together to cast a numinous glow over the restoration and denouement. Incorporating recognizable citations from the most valued texts of his culture and showing no hesitation to tear them savagely to bits, Cervantes' system of parody at this point expands to activate religious as well as literary codes in its reader and to surround its moment of climactic collapse with the corrosive energies that are always released by the violation of the sacred. The illuminating oracle rewarding Aeneas at the moment of vision and ascent from the underworld, the epiphany of the divine order and the promise of universal redemption in Mary's humble chamber, both loom behind the scene of entrapment and failed vision at the most intense moment of divine absence in Cervantes' tale.[50] One could say that this little text at the center of the *Colloquy*, in its methods of condensing and disfiguring two venerable model texts and in its effects of bewildering, alienating, and ultimately infuriating its readers, epitomizes the linguistic violence of the entire story and its diabolical discourse.

To appreciate the full power of the elaborate parody of romance conventions with which Cervantes ends his *Novelas ejemplares*, we should recall their prominence throughout the collection. For example, in *La Gitanilla* and *La ilustre fregona* we find the exiled child, metamorphosed and fallen into a lower order, from which she is eventually

---

[50] The prophecy is an interesting case of concentrated "citation parody," in which one model text incorporates within itself a second model text compatible with it, but far more interesting is the increased corrosive energy which the double travesty—the simultaneous desecration of two sublime models through the incongruities in the surrounding context of their receptor text—brings to this crucial moment of anticlimax in the *Colloquy*. The convergence of sacred texts on the moment that fails to exemplify them includes Cañizares' comparison, which immediately follows the oracle, of the anticipated disenchantment of Montiela's children to "el que se dice de Apuleyo en *El Asno de oro*, que consistía en solo comer una rosa" (p. 294). *The Golden Ass*, with its spectacular conversion of the protagonist into an ass, its extensive satirical development of his adventures, and its concluding liberating metamorphosis and mysterious rites, was commonly interpreted as an allegorical depiction of the fall and redemption of the Christian soul, and it undoubtedly had a considerable influence on Cervantes' conception of his final tale.

delivered; the mysterious signs and tokens necessary for the climactic restoration; the benign elderly person who is custodian or interpreter of those signs; and, of course, the noble, long-suffering parents who receive their lost child with jubilation. In *La señora Cornelia, La fuerza de la sangre*, and *La española inglesa*, the comic resolution hinges to a great extent on the restoration to their parents of children who are orphaned shortly after their birth. Moreover, in *La Gitanilla* there are songs celebrating the birth of the true redeemers, Christ and Philip IV, and imaginatively identifying their restorative acts with the return of the lost maiden, and in *La ilustre fregona* the heroine is associated with the Virgin, as her birth occurs without pain and her adoration is linked poetically with the cult of Nuestra Señora del Carmen. At the same time it is worth recalling the numerous moments of apocalyptic revelation—puzzling oracles and songs—that are granted the questing catechumens of Cervantes' heroic romance, the *Persiles*, as they move through their ordeals toward triumphant restoration: for example, the underworld prophecy of Soldino, who, in tones evoking Virgil's Anchises, looks forward to the advent and victories of the heroic youth, Don Juan de Austria; Feliciana's mysterious hymn on the Immaculate Conception; and the vision of universal history that Auristela experiences among the penitentiaries at the climax of her pilgrimage in Rome.

TWO TYPES OF PARODY: THE DESCENT TO THE UNDERWORLD IN THE *COLLOQUY* AND THE *QUIXOTE*

Since *El coloquio de los perros* contains a good deal of literary satire—for example, mockery of the conventions of pastoral romance and lyric love poetry, as well as burlesque of the efforts of neo-classical poets to write perfect dramas and epics—and since Cervantes created, in his masterpiece, perhaps the greatest and most complex literary satire ever written, I should hasten to add here that the type of negation that springs from his parodistic development of the romance themes of descent and recognition at the climax of the *Colloquy of the Dogs* is fundamentally different from that surrounding his exploitation of similar formal procedures in other contexts of his work. A brief look at his most famous ironic treatment of the lower world of romance in the *Quixote* will quickly reveal the difference and illuminate through contrast the function of the same parodistic techniques in the respective works. In Don Quixote's descent into the Cave of Montesinos we note many of the conventions of the romance anagnorisis that also appear as Berganza moves into the claustrophobic cell to hear the witch's confession and prophecy. The innocent young maiden, Dulcinea del Toboso, has been separated from her beloved, cruelly metamorphosed in appearance, and cast into a state of bondage by a diabolical antagonist. The fate of the faithful Guadiana and the duena Ruidera and Durandarte's resigned request to "let the cards be dealt" indicate that Cervantes' lower world, like many of its literary antecedents, is a place where life is frozen into inferior forms of being and the inhabitants are subject to the absurd laws of an irrational necessity.[51] Along with various chivalric heroes, Dulcinea is awaiting the advent of her redeemer, whose prophesied arrival after a perilous approach bears the promise of liberation of the heroes, restoration of a heroic age, removal of a curse, and reunion of the lovers. As in the case of Berganza's quest, various venerable texts, including the *Aeneid* and several chivalric romances, loom in the background with their radiant visions of romantic descent and liberation. None of the anticipated events, of course, comes to pass in Don Quixote's "exploit." The knights and ladies remain immobilized in their enchanted realm, and much doubt is expressed as to whether the hero really did encounter them after all. Don Quixote emerges from the cave asleep, and the proximity of the unfolding events to the world of dreams envelops the entire episode in the same kind of ambiguous hallucinatory atmosphere which causes Berganza to falter in his recollection of the confrontation with the witch. In the underworld Don Quixote meets figures whose appearances and concerns are strangely inconsistent with those of his heroes. Durandarte reacts to the presence of his redeemer and the prophecy of restoration with an indifference reminiscent of the lion's yawn of contempt at Don Quixote's challenge, rolling over mechanically on his catafalque and expressing his resignation to his bondage in oratory which comically sinks in an anticlimax of colloquial phrasing: " 'And if that should not be,' replied the afflicted Durandarte in a faint whisper; 'if that should not be, cousin, I say: patience and shuffle the cards.' And turning upon his side he resumed his customary silence and said not a word more."[52] Montesinos is concerned to correct a false report in the world above that he performed the surgical act by which he removed Durandarte's heart

---

[51] For the descent themes of romance, see N. Frye, *The Secular Scripture* (Cambridge, Mass., 1976), chap. 4.

[52] "—'Y cuando así no sea, respondió el lastimado Durandarte con voz desmayada y baja, cuando así no sea, ¡oh primo!, digo, paciencia y barajar.' Y volviéndose de lado, tornó a su acostumbrado silencio, sin hablar más palabra" (*Don Quijote de la Mancha*, 2:217).

with a poniard rather than an awl. And Dulcinea receives her redeemer with the request for a loan of six reales, and, like the indifferent lion and Durandarte, she turns her back on him and races away across the gentle fields of the underworld.[53] Moreover, Don Quixote's account of his adventure is hedged about with several discussions with his companions concerning the possibility that it never really occurred, that it was perhaps a dream or a lie, and the whole episode concludes with the narrator's assertion that the reader alone must decide as to whether he should believe it or not.

These are but a few of the reductive details and techniques that Cervantes brings to this climactic scene of the *Quixote*, and I mention them merely to show how similar his methods are to those of the *Coloquio* and yet how different their effects can be. Each text telescopes recognizable literary models with deformed incarnations of them, and, as the models are, according to the prevailing hierarchy of cultural norms, "elevated" ones, the process releases in the receptor text the destructive energy that frequently characterizes parody. The irreverent metamorphosis of such models produces the effect of a dismemberment of form of the type which is traditional in satirical literature with its cultivation of all devices which bring about narrative disorientation and force the reader into a stance of detachment, ranging from repugnance to amusement, as he contemplates the objects of the fictional world. In the *Quixote* the negative energy flows primarily in the direction of the incorporated models and serves the purposes of the literary satire which Cervantes sustains throughout the work, from his "friend's" declaration in the prologue that his intention is to "destroy the ill-founded edifice of the books of chivalry," (p. 25), to the final line, when Cide Hamete's pen affirms that his single desire has been to "arouse men's contempt for all fabulous and absurd stories of knight-errantry."[54] In his anti-romance Cervantes is concerned with "demythologizing," undermining the sanctity of the golden worlds of romance by pointing up the distances separating them from the ordinary world of experience, in which even knights-errant have to eat

---

[53] Looming behind the comical scene is the pathetically sublime figure of Dido as she turns her face from Aeneas and flees into the forest of the underworld (*Aeneid* VI, 466-476). For the various evocations of Virgil's epic in the dense literary parody of the episode, see A. Marasso, *Cervantes: la invención del Quijote* (Buenos Aires, 1954), pp. 147-50. A comprehensive treatment of the literary echoes of the incident is available in H. Percas de Ponseti's *Cervantes y su concepto del arte* (Madrid, 1975), pp. 448-583.

[54] "Derribar la máquina mal fundada destos caballerescos libros. . . . poner en aborrecimiento de los hombres las fingidas y disparatadas historias de los libros de caballerías" (1:58; 2:593).

and sleep, pay for their lodgings, and make wills as they age toward death. Although in Part II Cervantes' satire expands enormously in its complexity, multiplies its directions, and abandons its primary focus on the literary concerns which dominate the first sally entirely and remain central in the second, only exceptionally do the models introduced from the chivalric world and its literary manifestations remain sacred and reflect ironically on the follies of a real world that falls absurdly short of their sublimity. But there is a far more significant function of the *Quixote*'s parody and its negations; and without it, the work would belong merely to the remote family of Renaissance burlesque narratives and certainly would not be read as the first, and perhaps the greatest of all novels. This function lies in its contribution to the characterization of the protagonist and the development of the profound philosophical themes implied by his psychological state. As H.-J. Neuschäfer has pointed out, Cervantes' major innovation as a parodist of romance was to shift the relatively predictable flow of "heroic" events from its traditional position in the foreground of the narration, a position which it continued to enjoy in the other great literary parody of the Renaissance, Ariosto's *Orlando Furioso*, to the background and to focus the interest not on the unfolding of the event but rather on its origin in the unusual psyche of an individual situated in the real "nonliterary" world.[55]

In his "heroic" descent into the Cave of Montesinos, Don Quixote, a real human being rather than a satirical mouthpiece or incarnation of folly, is glimpsing the impossibility of his lofty aspirations and encountering, if only in his subconscious mind, his most unyielding adversary and, in a sense, the real adversary of the system of chivalry and the literary form that celebrates chivalric ideals—mortality, time, decay, and history. It has nothing to do with demonic powers or divine purposes. It is all the more formidable because of its indifference to them. The incongruities that Cervantes accumulates in his description of the knight's underworld journey for the purpose of lit-

---

[55] "Hier ist also die Parodie zugleich selbst schon ein Aspekt der *locura* und damit der Personenhandlung, so dass im *Quijote* selbst dort, wo eine Vorstruktur vorliegt, diese doch immer mit einer Motivierung von innen zusammenfällt und dadurch neutralisiert wird." "Hier beginnt also jener Übergang von der *Wie-Spannung* zur *Ob-überhaupt-Spannung*, der nach C. Lugowski für den Schritt vom epischen Geschehen zur romanhaften Handlung kennzeichnend ist." Neuschäfer notes that the love madness of Orlando, unlike Don Quixote's "literature-producing" *locura*, belongs to the conventional literary world. It is in one sense simply another romance event. See *Der Sinn der Parodie im Don Quijote* (Heidelberg, 1963), pp. 39-43. Also, for these aspects of the parody of the *Quixote*, see Ortega's *Meditaciones del Quijote* and Castro's "La estructura del *Quijote*," *Hacia Cervantes* (Madrid, 1957).

erary parody are, in fact, not at all incongruous in the context of his coherent portrait of the psychic derangement of his protagonist. Manifesting the logic of dreams, they plausibly assimilate forms deriving from his real experiences—e.g., the somersault of Dulcinea's servant, the peasant features of Belerma, and various images of physical decay, as well as Durandarte's gesture of indifference, Montesinos' student dress, and Dulcinea's request for money, which recall the lion, the humanist cousin, and Basilio's financial needs respectively—and they reflect with the concentrated symbolic power of nightmare visions Don Quixote's growing self-doubt and his emerging awareness of the confinements of reality, which has surfaced occasionally from the earliest parts of the work and in Part Two impinges on his consciousness with increasing frequency until finally he renounces his identity as the knight Don Quixote and welcomes death as Alonso Quijano el Bueno.[56]

At the same time there is a coherent system of references in the numerous details disfiguring the contours of the fictional world of romance which points beyond both literary satire and characterization to the most profound philosophical implications of Cervantes' antiromance. A preoccupation with the movement of time permeates the entire episode, from the narrator's precise indications of the duration of Don Quixote's descent and the hour of the beginning of his account, to Cide Hamete's concluding speculations concerning the questionable veracity of "such a vast complication of absurdities," which could not have been invented "in so short a space of time." Such skeptical considerations are echoed by the audience within the work, the humanist cousin and Sancho Panza; and their commentary on such matters as contemporary knife merchants and the origins of playing cards humorously points up the reality of historical change, which hovers mysteriously over the whole adventure. Much more striking, however, is the intrusion of the theme of time within Don Quixote's narration. Montesinos discusses his decision to pour salt on Durandarte's heart so that it would not putrefy and stink when he delivered it to Belerma. When Don Quixote spies Belerma, he observes that her teeth are few and that the heart of her slain lover, which she is carrying in her mourning procession, is now dried and shriveled. Montesinos remarks to Don Quixote that the rings under the lady's eyes are the effects of her grief and are not to be attributed to monthly disorders, for such ills have long ago ceased to trouble her. Don Quix-

[56] For the importance of the scene in the development of Don Quixote as a novelistic character, see S. de Madariaga, *Guía del lector del "Quijote"* (Madrid, 1926), pp. 177-88, M. Durán, *La ambigüedad en el Quijote* (Xalapa, 1960), pp. 210-28, and J. B. Avalle-Arce and E. C. Riley, *"Don Quijote," Suma Cervantina*, pp. 55-59.

ote, of course, clings to the temporal rhythms of romance with its recurrent restorative cycles and its characteristic suspension in "a season of perpetual spring-like summer."[57] He views his mission to the underworld as a restoration of past centuries, and he insists, despite evidence to the contrary based on the careful measurement of time by his rationalistic friends, that he was in the cave three days. Yet the disturbing images of destructive time spring from his inner self, and his enigmatic words on awakening, "now indeed do I know that all the pleasures of this life pass away like a shadow and a dream, or fade like the flower of the field"[58] may indicate his awareness that the conception of temporality governing the fictional world of romance is no more than a beautiful illusion.

The dreaming Don Quixote, in fact, appears to be at the threshold of a revelation which, despite his own incapacity ultimately to confront it, remains absolutely clear for the reader: a vision of the hopeless estrangement of the individual consciousness from a world that, to recall the language of Lukács' *Die Theorie des Romans*, the gods have abandoned.[59] The assault on the ideal model, the fabric of romance, in the Cave of Montesinos creates a metaphysical absence, a "rooflessness," which is far more threatening than the demonic mistreatment of the divine in Berganza's underworld vision. The model is rent beyond all repair, and all that remains is a world totally disenchanted and the neutral continuum of time, implacably flowing in its destructive course, while a pathetic hero tries unsuccessfully to render his life and his relation to the world about him meaningful through a scheme of ideals which has no warrant other than his own isolated subjectivity. At this point Cervantes is not ready to soften the experience of total *desengaño* which his foolish hero is struggling to ward off with the conventional shift toward the verities of Christian doctrine which he undoubtedly accepted and which are ultimately grasped by his dying knight. Here we are at the darkest moment of the first modern novel, and perhaps the only wisdom that it implies to offset the overwhelming negativity of its revelation is what Lukács calls the irony

[57] L. A. Murillo, *The Golden Dial: Temporal Configuration in Don Quijote* (Oxford, 1975), p. 18; for the juxtaposition of divergent conceptions of time in the cave episode, see pp. 144-48. See also, Harry Sieber, "Literary Time in the 'Cueva de Montesinos,' " *Modern Language Notes* 86 (1971):268-73.

[58] "Ahora acabo de conocer que todos los contentos desta vida pasan como sombra y sueño, o marchitan como la flor del campo" (2:210).

[59] *Die Theorie des Romans* (Neuwied/Berlin, 1965), pp. 85-88. "Der Roman ist die Epopöe eines Zeitalters, für das die extensive Totalität des Lebens nicht mehr sinnfällig gegeben ist, für das die Lebensimmanenz des Sinnes zum Problem geworden ist, und das dennoch die Gesinnung zur Totalität hat" (p. 53).

of the poet, the paradoxical recognition both of the insubstantiality of a decaying world and the alienation of its inhabitants and of the value of the individual's efforts, despite the frustration that inevitably meets them, to find in the flimsy resources of his own interiority the means of investing his life with universal significance.[60]

For Lukács this irony, a "docta ignorantia" or "negative mysticism of godless ages," is the constitutive element of the modern novel. Herein the genre reveals its objectivity, its concern with empirical reality rather than with essences, and the "unzerreissbare Gebundenheit an das Dasein und das Sosein der Wirklichkeit" which links it to its great literary ancestor of "those more perfect times" before the identity of life and essence was shattered, the epic.[61] Whether or not we accept Lukács' analysis of the general historical developments in the human consciousness which account for Cervantes' creation of the "first great novel of world literature," it is clear that his depiction of the interplay of the isolated subjectivity and a neutral, demythified reality was to become the central theme of the modern novel, that his literary parody achieved the emancipation and isolation of the individual consciousness, and that the mechanics and implications of his parody are disclosed most starkly in the climactic descent into the Cave of Montesinos. There is certainly important literary satire here, and it is quite possible that Cervantes, as well as his contemporary readers, understood the scene merely as one of his most amusing bur-

---

[60] "Sie [die Ironie] bedeutet, als formelles Konstituens der Romanform, eine innere Spaltung des normativ dichterischen Subjekts in eine Subjektivität als Innerlichkeit, die fremden Machtkomplexen gegenübersteht und der fremden Welt die Inhalte ihrer Sehnsucht aufzuprägen bestrebt ist, und in eine Subjektivität, die die Abstraktheit und mithin die Beschränktheit der einander fremden Subjekts- und Objektswelten durchschaut, diese in ihren, als Notwendigkeiten und Bedingungen ihrer Existenz begriffenen, Grenzen versteht und durch dieses Durchschauen die Zweiheit der Welt zwar bestehen lässt, aber zugleich in der wechselseitigen Bedingtheit der einander wesensfremden Elemente eine einheitliche Welt erblickt und gestaltet. Diese Einheit ist jedoch eine rein formale; die Fremdheit und die Feindlichkeit der innerlichen und der äusserlichen Welten ist nicht aufgehoben, sondern nur als notwendig erkannt, und das Subjekt dieser Erkenntnis ist geradeso ein empirisches, also weltbefangenes und in der Innerlichkeit beschränktes Subjekt, wie jene, die zu seinen Objekten geworden sind" (*Die Theorie des Romans*, p. 73). Lukács notes that this conception of irony originates in romantic aesthetic theory. One recalls Solger's observations on *Don Quixote* and the link between epic "Gleichgültigkeit" and novelistic irony. "Mit der Besonderheit hängt die Ironie zusammen, die sich im Roman vorzüglich aussprechen muss, da der Charakter hier als wesentlicher, und doch zugleich als nichtig erscheint" (*Vorlesungen über Aesthetik*, cited by W. Brüggemann, *Cervantes und die Figur des Don Quijote in Kunstanschauung und Dichtung der Deutschen Romantik* [Münster, 1958], p. 99).

[61] Lukács, *Die Theorie des Romans*, pp. 42, 90.

lesques of the extravagances of literary romance, its authors, and its readers. It is also possible, as I have argued elsewhere, that in his unsettling mixture of the luminous fantasies of romance and the harshest facts of physiology, Cervantes intended to ridicule the numerous literary theorists of his time who, themselves reacting against the fantastic excesses of chivalric fiction, burdened the creative artist with an excessive demand for verisimilitude, forgot the distinction between assertive and imaginative writing, and, in effect, demanded too much "truth," representation, and information in fiction.[62] The conscious and elaborate rending of the fabric of romance in the Cave of Montesinos must be seen, however, at its deepest level of significance as a process in Don Quixote's mind, as probably the most important episode in his movement toward self-knowledge and disillusionment, and as the most concentrated expression of the work's most disturbing and exhilarating philosophical theme—man's discovery of his subjection to time and of the inadequacy of his dreams of immortality.[63]

Considered in the perspective both of literary and of cultural history, the parody of the *Quixote* should be judged truly subversive and revolutionary. Thus Lukács speaks frequently of the novel as the genre of a mature, "roofless," and liberated humanity, and *Don Quixote* stands as the preeminent example for the numerous literary theorists who

[62] *Cervantes, Aristotle, and the "Persiles,"* Chap. 2.

[63] The blindness to the contextual density and variability of the parody in the *Quixote* which one observes in Cervantes' contemporaries, most pre-romantic readers, their current descendants (see, for example, P. E. Russell, " 'Don Quixote' as a Funny Book," *Modern Language Review* 64 [1969]:312-26; Anthony Close, *The Romantic Approach to "Don Quixote"* [Cambridge, 1978], and various literal-minded critics who espouse a "hard view" of *Don Quixote* and reduce its dimensions to those of the cautionary tale on folly), and perhaps in Cervantes himself, who clearly intended and regarded his work as a funny book, does not in the slightest vitiate the "romantic" insight into the philosophical implications of Cervantes' irony. The fact is that Cervantes' humor is far from uniform and calls for discriminations of the type which its analysts have seldom attempted to make. To recognize this fact, we need only consider the one-dimensional literary parody of the two prophecies of the *Quixote* which Amezúa recalls in his attempt to "explain" Cañizares' burlesque prophecy (Malambruno's prophecy of the disenchantment of Antonomasia and Don Clavijo, who have been metamorphosed into a bronze monkey and a metal crocodile [2:337], and Maese Nicolás' prophecy of the release and ascent of the imprisoned Don Quixote [1:555-56]; see *El casamiento engañoso y el coloquio de los perros,* ed. A. de Amezúa, p. 621). Despite the parallels on the level of the mechanics of parody in these scenes, their effects are totally different not only from those of the witch's oracle, but also from those of the complex engagement with the implications of romance prophecy in the Cave of Montesinos. If we could validly lump together all these humorous treatments of romance conventions under the rubric of "literary parody," as Amezúa would appear to do, then indeed *Don Quixote* would be nothing but a funny book.

attribute to parody a dignified role of destruction and creation in the evolution of literary forms.[64] Cervantes' "novelistic" parody has no true literary antecedents. If, in its destructive moment, it recalls the epistemological context and the animating skepticism of Lucian's comical underworld journey, where the sobering vision of death and destructive temporality and the claustrophobic freedom and fearlessness of the Cynic philosopher are all that remain in the ruins of the dreams of poets and the heroes' pathetic aspirations to glory,[65] its constructive reaction to such a vision looks entirely to the future, to the anatomies of disenchanted consciousness in the literary worlds of Flaubert, Dostoevski, and Proust.

The "diabolical" parody of the *Colloquy of the Dogs* is, by comparison, much more limited in its range of implications. It is fundamentally conservative and orthodox, and its effects are radically different. It unfolds in a moral, rather than an existential context, and it stands directly in the rich tradition of moral satire descending from the middle ages and flowering in the great picaresque novels of Cervantes' contemporaries.[66] The negative energies released by its aborted ana-

---

[64] ". . . as a method which undermines and violates other literary works and traditions which is used by deviating literary works and which in itself is never a completely realized form—parody brings about many and varied generic developments and changes. In this respect parody is progressive" (T. Shlonsky, "Literary Parody: Remarks on its Method and Function," *Proceedings of the IVth Congress of the International Comparative Literature Association*, ed. F. Jost [The Hague, 1966], 2:797-801; see p. 801). For the destructive-constructive role of parody in literary evolution, see J. Tynjanov, "Dostoevskij und Gogol: Zur Theorie der Parodie," *Texte der Russischen Formalisten*, ed. J. Striedter (Munich, 1969), 1:300-371, esp. 331. See also W. Karrer's analysis of the numerous implications of parody concerning literary, cultural, and social history, his discussion of the Russian Formalists' characteristic conception of parody as a procedure which reveals in a most concentrated form the dynamics of literary evolution, and his clear exposition of the theories on the subject of J. Tynjanov, V. Sklovskij, and J. Lotman (*Parodie, Travestie, Pastiche*, pp. 100-119).

[65] *The Dialogues of the Dead, Lucian*, Vol. 7, trans. M. D. MacLeod (Cambridge, Mass., 1961). One should also distinguish Cervantes' descent from another of its most distinguished literary ancestors, Rabelais' account of Epistémon's underworld vision, where the parodistic uncrowning of the heroes, which, as in the *Quixote*, exploits for effects of shocking metamorphoses money, food, physiology, and odd professional concerns, is simultaneously both an affirmation of the unity of mankind at the elemental level of healthy bodily life and within the true regenerative time of history and a celebration of man's emancipation from his alienated condition within the illusory world of official myths and hierarchies (*Pantagruel*, xxx). See M. Bakhtin, *Rabelais and his World*, trans. H. Iswolsky (Cambridge, Mass., 1968), pp. 381-403.

[66] For the generally conservative nature of medieval parody, see P. Lehmann, *Die Parodie im Mittelalter* (Munich, 1922). J. A. Yunck's distinction between "exemplary" and "stylistic" parody illuminates these fundamental differences between the *Quixote*

gnorisis and the incongruous attire of its romantic elements and its sacred texts move in a very different direction from those penetrating the crucial descent of Don Quixote. Rather than exposing the unreality of the romance order and by implication the futility of man's existential desire to transcend the present by flight into its utopian worlds, the parodies of the *Colloquy* point with a harsh denunciation to the failures of the present, to the enormous distance that separates them from the excellences which man normally associates with the formal perfections of romance and celebrates in his sacred texts. In a sense the *Colloquy*, like the anti-romantic genre with which it has obvious affinities, the picaresque novel, actually preserves romance by assuming and utilizing the moral power of its imaginative archetypes. In other words, it accepts the vocabulary of it golden world, using it as a sign that is absolutely immune to any treatment as a hypothesis, and exploiting its travesty to bring to the climactic scene powerful effects of desecration.[67] The hideous vision of decay that rewards the

---

and the *Colloquy* very sharply: "Ages—or individuals—which respect tradition and value orthodoxy, unlike our own, tend to parody those works which they value most, rather than those which they wish to ridicule. The product is Exemplary Parody, superimposing the ancient sublime on the current ridiculous, the old ideal on the contemporary reality. It is composed by artists, and addressed to audiences, who admire old, familiar ideas. . . . The text is the parodist's weapon, not his target. His parody's concern is primarily intellectual and ethical, its essence figurative, its attitude traditional and conservative. Stylistic Parody is essentially a manifestation of the free critical spirit and a rudimentary instrument of critical analysis. . . . Its standard of judgment is not that of tradition or authority, but that of the individual educated reader. It subsists, like Exemplary Parody, on established or popular literary texts, but unlike Exemplary Parody it ignores or impugns their dignity or authority. It appeals to the iconoclastic spirit in its readers. Its text is its target, not its weapon" ("The Two Faces of Parody," *Iowa English Yearbook* 8 [1963]:29-37, esp. 36-37). For the different satirical functions of parody, see Karrer, *Parodie, Travestie, Pastiche*, pp. 42, 126-27.

[67] With his characteristic literary and linguistic self-consciousness, Cervantes incorporates in his "picaresque" saint's life, *El rufián dichoso,* a brief exposition of the travesty model which informs the idiom of disorder that he articulates throughout *El coloquio de los perros* and *Rinconete y Cortadillo.* Outraged by the ruffians' references to the "padre" and "alcalde" of an "order," which is in reality the world of the brothel, Tello, the spiritual father of the protagonist, remarks: "Bien el nombre se profana / en eso de alcaide y padre, / nombres honrados y buenos" (*Obras completas*, ed. A. Valbuena Prat [Madrid, 1956], p. 339). The abuse of the vocabulary of the sacred is visible not only in such verbal profanations but also in analogous narrative patterns such as dismemberment of coherent plot structures, anticlimax, and disfiguring metamorphoses of the reversals and recognitions of romance and comedy. In another "underworld" scene of the *Quixote* we observe Cervantes revealing his fascination with the idiom of disorder when Don Quixote, like Tello, discloses the overthrow of customary linguistic hierarchies on which it is based as he is baffled by the argot of

questing Berganza—the outstretched body of his "mother," the witch
Cañizares—is in fact radically different from Don Quixote's seemingly
comparable glimpse of the withered figure and haggard face of Belerma as she officiates in the bizarre ceremonial display of the shriv-
elled heart of the hero. Rather than a means by which Cervantes strips
off the illusions that man has projected into his romance creations,
she is a terrible reminder of the immense distance that man has fallen
in his failure to pursue his destiny of moral perfection. That is to say,
she is a frightening embodiment of sinfulness, her decrepitude is a
manifestation of her moral ugliness, and, in her preoccupation with
the destructive flow of time and the universal ending of all things,[68]
she represents temporality as the designed medium of death, damnation, and salvation, rather than, as in the case of the *Quixote*, the
meaningless continuum, which is, in reality, the most inexorable antagonist of man's strivings to impose universal significance on his life.
Unlike the helpless Don Quixote, who stands in bewilderment as the
beautiful figures of romance decompose and display the awful effects
of time, Berganza can savagely attack Cañizares, meditate on the parody "mother" of his restoration, and join his companion in exclaim-
ing, in a climactic affirmation of man's power to resist evil, "I won't
have her for my mother"—"yo no la quiero tener por madre."

---

the galley slaves: "¿Por músicos y cantores van también a galeras? . . . Antes he yo
oído decir . . . que quien canta, sus males espanta. . . . No lo entiendo." The
prisoner informs him that "acá es al revés," and the guard's clarification adds a note
of religious travesty to the startling inversion: "cantar en el ansia se dice entre esta
gente *non santa* confesar en el tormento. A este pecador dieron tormento y confesó su
delito . . ." (1:267). However, it is characteristic of the *Quixote* that the "discourse
of disorder" does not point exclusively at the ideal texts disfigured and the moral
judgment which they cast on their desecrators, but rather at the existential backgrounds which "validate" the language as an authentic instrument of expression and
communication (see my discussion of Cervantes' conception of language in Chapter
VI).

[68] See p. 303 and below, Chapter III. For this conception of time, see my "Lope's
Broken Clock: Baroque Time in the *Dorotea*," *Hispanic Review* 37 (1969):459-90.

CHAPTER II

Cervantes' Apocalypse: The Descent into the Grave

. . . the house of clay (which is the grave) is the school
of true wisdom, the place where God is wont to teach
his doctrine to his own. . . . Descend then,
oh man, with your spirit to this house,
and there you will see who you are!
—Luis de Granada[1]

THE WORLD OF WITCHES AND THE MYSTERY OF LAWLESSNESS

THE DEPICTION of the witch Cañizares at the center of the *Colloquy of the Dogs* is one of the most powerful scenes in Cervantes' entire literary production. We have reached the monster at the center of the labyrinth, and, as we move through the aborted anagnorisis and witness the two dogs groping futilely for a correct exegesis of the prophecy that holds the promise of release, the narrative grinds toward a halt, leaving us with the impression of a dreamer mesmerized by a relentlessly oppressive nightmare. The briskly paced flow of episodes and the enlivening movement of the retrospective commentary, which have swept us along rapidly if somewhat aimlessly, are suddenly suspended, and the analytical texture of the work thickens toward the density of a metaphysical treatise. The tightening involutions of the tale, its continuing thrusts inward from dream into dream and from confession into confession, appear to be approaching a climactic dead

---

[1] ". . . la casa del barro (que es la sepultura) es la escuela de la verdadera sabiduría, donde Dios suele enseñar a los suyos su doctrina. . . . Desciende pues ¡oh hombre! con el espíritu a esta casa, y ahí verás quién eres" (*De la oración y consideración, Obras del V.P.M. Fray Luis de Granada*, B.A.E. 8:35).

center of convergence, and the narrative itself seems to exert that menacing, constrictive force that we observe everywhere in the imaginary space of the novella and that becomes stifling in the tiny cell and in the spiritual abysses (the "sima de su miseria") from which the hag vainly attempts to extricate herself. At this moment of maximum narrative enclosure we find ourselves, together with the dreamer and his persona, in the depths of the grave, compelled to share with them the horror and the elation of their discoveries. As Cañizares proceeds monotonously through her interminable confession, we experience a recollection of numerous elements, which, scattered chaotically throughout the preceding narrative, here coalesce and obtrude with the intensity and concentrated symbolic power of dream visions. As she considers such philosophical and theological mysteries as the origin of suffering and the troubling complicity of the powers of evil in God's providential design and as she probes the psychology of the sinner in her unsparing self-analysis, laying bare the spiritual disease of the sick soul in the "triste noche del pecado," we plunge into the most profound strata of meaning infolded in the tale. Cañizares' confession is Cervantes' most spectacular epiphany of evil, and it forms the poetic heart of his final novella, the source of the imaginative energy that pulsates in all the details of its multiple episodes. Here we confront directly the central vision that animates the entire work, and we hear most clearly the dark tonic chord of its principal theme, which is echoed in numerous motifs playing across its surface.[2]

The encounter with Cañizares resembles many other scenes in Cervantes' works in which narrative movement decelerates and the central imagery of the work is concentrated and connected quite explicitly with the basic themes that it embodies and that inform the surrounding action. In the *Novelas ejemplares* Preciosa's songs, her speech to Juan informing him of the conditions of his courtship, the elder's description of the organization of the Gypsy world, and the poems of the *Ilustre fregona* and the *Celoso extremeño* are such highly charged, "static" moments in their respective works. However, it is the *Persiles* that offers the most instructive parallels, in the various scenes of visionary intensity that follow on a moment of liberation in Periandro's

---

[2] J. Casalduero, P. Waley, and M. Molho have emphasized the importance of this scene in Cervantes' development of the theme of sinfulness in the tale (see *Sentido y forma de las "Novelas ejemplares,"* pp. 257-61, "The Unity of the *Casamiento engañoso* and the *Coloquio de los perros,"* *Bulletin of Hispanic Studies* 34 [1957]:201-12, and "Remarques sur le *Mariage trompeur at Colloque des chiens,"* in *Le Mariage trompeur et Colloque des chiens*, ed. and trans. M. Molho [Paris, 1970], pp. 59-67, 80-82).

and Auristela's movement toward their goal of Catholic instruction in Rome and marriage. For example, the heroes' miraculous deliverance from the barbarians in the opening scene leads them through a winding labyrinthian cave to shelter, where they listen to the words of the Credo; following their escape from the fires of Policarpo's kingdom, they find refuge on a paradisiacal island, enter the chapel of a hermitage, and contemplate the images of Christ, the Virgin, and St. John the Divine. And, of course, following their arrival at Rome, they are rewarded with instruction in the mysteries of Christianity concerning the history of the world and man's destiny. In *El coloquio de los perros* the depiction of Cañizares comes as a similar type of climactic epiphany, a vision that rewards and enlightens the questing hero and clarifies the meaning of his adventures. Yet while in its structural function the vision parallels those of the *Persiles*, in its significance and effect it should be viewed as their complete inversion. It is in fact an epiphanic vision of evil, as intense and extensive in its survey of the forces of disorder as is any vision of order and harmony in the *Persiles*. There is an encounter with lawlessness in nearly every novella—for example, the demonic Gypsy society of the *Gitanilla*, the violent picaresque order of the *Ilustre fregona*, or the barbarous Turkish world in the *Amante liberal*—and the germs for the development of the figure of Cañizares are clearly present in the northern adventures of the *Persiles*, most specifically in Antonio's nocturnal encounter with the talking wolf and Rutilio's dark vigil over the metamorphosed corpse of the witch who had attempted to seduce him. However, in such works the demonic antagonists and their worlds are contained and subordinated within a narrative progression toward the celebration of order; for Cervantes is concerned less with exploring the powers of disorder than with exploiting them as agents of conflict and contrast in a celebration of the order that emerges after overcoming all obstacles to it. Only in *Rinconete y Cortadillo* does Cervantes reveal a similar fascination with the world of lawlessness and a willingness to allow his narrative to be dominated by its perverse forms. Indeed, one of the most interesting of the numerous resemblances linking the novella describing the *hampa* of Seville with the *Coloquio* lies in its organization of a series of loosely connected, fragmentary episodes and truncated plot lines around a powerful central scene presenting a monstrous embodiment of disorder, in whose grotesque, hieratic apparition and ceremonious adoration by the congregation of rogues we find imaginatively concentrated all the destructive energies animating this tale of an "anti-natural" underworld.[3] However, in *Rinconete y Corta-dillo* the depiction of villainy is stylized for humorous effects, and the rapidity of its condensed, conventional action and gesture, the exaggerated comedy of situation, and the processional caricature endow the entire work with the playful tonality and the highly contrived character of a puppet show rather than with the seriousness of a philosophical tale.[4]

In her stature, centrality, and imaginative dominance of the tale in which she appears, and as the embodiment of a profoundly disturbing vision of evil, Cañizares has no parallel in Cervantes' other works. It is as if Cervantes the writer for once could not resist the mysterious appeal of the realm of sinfulness and destruction about which he had expressed his uneasiness when referring to probably its most spectacular literary exploration in the age—Fernando de Rojas' *Celestina*: "a book, in my opinion, divine, if only it would conceal the human more than it does." To be sure, if we were to look for literary characters resembling Cañizares in her hideously insensitive conscience, in her capacity to pervert sacred knowledge, in her dedication to the pleasures of the flesh, and in her diabolical connections and activities, we

---

[3] Rinconete, a youth of "buen entendimiento" and "buen natural," observed that "casi al descubierto vivía en ella [Sevilla] gente tan perniciosa y tan contraria a la misma naturaleza, y propuso en sí de aconsejar a su compañero no durasen mucho en aquella vida tan perdida y tan mala, tan inquieta, y tan libre y disoluta" (*Novelas ejemplares*, ed. F. Rodríguez Marín [Madrid, 1962], 1:217-18). Monipodio's underworld is a demonic society in which the order of the "bien intencionada naturaleza," which Cervantes celebrates in *La Gitanilla*, is completely inverted, and as such it is analogous to the Gypsy society of thieves, with its "ancha libertad" and its perverted natural law. In addition to its exploitation of the same grammar of narrative disorder and its inclusion of the powerful epiphany of evil, *Rinconete y Cortadillo* resembles *El coloquio de los perros* in its cultivation of the imaginative power of profanation and travesty, its articulation of what I refer to below as the "language of the flesh," its satirical observation, and its focus on a relatively innocent, questing hero who must gaze on the apparition of evil, which objectifies in an exaggerated and grotesque form his own potential for evil, meditate on its significance, and reject it.

[4] One can compare Cervantes' analogous playful manipulation of romance conventions in *El amante liberal* with its highly contrived plot, its complex pursuits, its unexpected reversals, its caricatures, and its spectacular scenes. Such works lay bare the literary forms—e.g., the narrative archetypes and structures, the characteristic imagery, and the basic character types—out of which their more complex congeners, such as *El coloquio de los perros* and *La Gitanilla* are built, but which are frequently obscured by the numerous "impurities" of the rich thematic concerns informing them. In a sense they are Cervantes' "purest" or most "literary" works of literature, and, as such, they provide a kind of grammar of his favorite narrative forms. For the stylization of the picaresque in *Rinconete y Cortadillo*, see A. Castro, *El pensamiento de Cervantes*, p. 232.

would have to turn to the *Celestina*, Quevedo's *Buscón*, and perhaps *Lazarillo de Tormes* to find her congeners. However, it must be emphasized that even in his most somber work Cervantes situates his own exploration of evil within the metaphysical framework provided by orthodox Christianity and celebrated in consolatory and confessional writings from the Book of Job and Augustine's *Confessions* to innumerable contemporary devotional and ascetic treatises, as well as in such popular literary works reflecting their influence as *Guzmán de Alfarache* and *La conversión de la Magdalena*. All confirm the paradoxical notion that the miseries which afflict the human being in his life on earth—whether the result of man's sinfulness or the natural infirmities and catastrophes to which he is heir—are somehow necessary ingredients in the highest good to which he can aspire and are part of an ultimately benevolent providential design. As Pedro de Rivadeneira put it in his consolatory *Treatise on Tribulation* (1589), man's miseries, when properly understood in the light of the grand mystery of lawlessness, are in reality "the gentlest of fruits," "the richest treasures of inestimable valuables," the "sweetest honeycomb in the mouth of the dead lion," and the medicine that "perfects and refines the spirit."[5] In a conceit much more abstract but equally characteristic of the metaphysical style of contemporary religious oratory, Cervantes turned to geometry for his most concise expression of the religious paradox. Toward the end of his prose epic of tribulations, *Los trabajos de Persiles y Sigismunda*, his sententious narrator introduces the climactic resolution by invoking the venerable mystery: "good and evil are separated so slightly from one another, that they are like two concurrent lines, which, although they spring from separated and different beginnings, yet end in a single point."[6] All the unfathomable mysteries surrounding the complicity of God and the forces of darkness which are latent in the orthodox Christian vision of evil are powerfully evoked in Cervantes' monster. She reminds us that "all the misfortunes that befall men, kingdoms, cities, and villages, and sudden deaths, shipwrecks, and falls—in short, all the evils that are termed disasters, [*males de daño*]—come from the hand of the Almighty and His permissive will," insists that her murder of innocent children and all of our "disasters and evils that are termed of culpability [*males de culpa*]," while we must ultimately bear responsibility for them, are nonetheless permitted by God ("all of this God permits because of

---

[5] *Tratado de la tribulación*, B.A.E. 60:360.

[6] "El bien y el mal distan tan poco el uno del otro, que son como dos líneas concurrentes, que aunque parten de apartados y diferentes principios, acaban en un punto" (p. 464).

our sinfulness; for without His permission, I have seen by experience, the devil cannot hurt an ant"), and suggests that there is a great mystery lurking behind her pronouncement, which Berganza will be privileged "to understand when he becomes a man."[7] It is as if it were given to the monsters of the Book of Job to speak from the whirlwind in justification of the destruction that they must wreak in fulfilling God's darkest designs. As in the much less elaborate incident in the *Persiles*, in which a wolf emerges from the darkness to reveal to the wrathful Antonio the mysterious workings of Divine Grace even while reminding him of the loathsomeness of his sins, the appropriateness of the grotesque scene must be sought in the decorum of the nightmare with its concentrated symbolic language and its readiness to collapse the categories and distinctions by which we maintain our precarious hold on reality in waking life. In these cases we glimpse the nightmare of the Christian soul tormented by the unendurable contiguity of good and evil, by all the truth that is concealed beneath the paradox of fruitful evil.

Throughout Cervantes' age writers and thinkers were obsessed with the mystery of lawlessness. They continually exhorted men to consider the "logicality" and justness of evil and suffering according to God's most lofty purposes, and they ridiculed the foolishness of those who would hope to render that justice intelligible in terms of man's capacities for understanding. Thus Luis de León recalls Paul's statement that Christ was perfected and crowned with glory through sufferings (Heb. 2:9-10) and suggests that every man must make Christ's discovery that "scarcely has the light been born when evil begins to persecute it," if he is to know the glory of the blessed.[8] In his manual *Guía del Cielo* (1534), Pablo de León reminds his readers that they must not despair in sin and suffering, that God has permitted their fall "for the better," and, approaching the paradoxical truths so disturbingly embodied in Cervantes' monster, he declares that "where

---

[7] "Todas las desgracias que vienen a las gentes, a los reinos, a las ciudades y a los pueblos, las muertes repentinas, los naufragios, las caídas, en fin, todos los males que llaman de daño, vienen de la mano del Altísimo y de su voluntad permitente . . . daños y males que llaman de culpa . . . todo esto lo permite Dios por nuestros pecados: que sin su permisión yo he visto por experiencia que no puede ofender el diablo a una hormiga . . . podrás venir a entender cuando seas hombre" (p. 300).

[8] "Apenas ha nascido la luz, y ya el mal la persigue" (*De los nombres de Cristo*, ed. F. de Onís [Madrid, 1969], 2:93-94). In his commentary on Job 14:17, Fray Luis writes that "Dios no solamente castiga todo lo malo, mas aflige y da penas de castigo y penas de mejoramiento, y Dios las reparte todas conforme a su providencia, haciendo justicia en lo uno, y en lo otro manifestando su amor" (*Exposición del Libro de Job, Obras completas castellanas* [Madrid, 1957], 2:260).

crime was abundant, there grace was superabundant." He concludes with the affirmation "although He may kill me, in Him shall I place my hope," a revealing appropriation of Job that indicates his desire to emphasize the most appalling implications of faith.[9] Employing a metaphor which was commonplace in Christian discussions of the question of evil and sinfulness and which was to dominate the imaginative atmosphere of Cervantes' *Coloquio*, Luis de Granada follows a relentless exposition of all the sufferings that plague man on earth with the reminder: "all of this was punishment for sin, but it was a merciful and medicinal punishment, for that sovereign Providence arranged it all in such a way in order to remove our hearts from an excessive love of this life. Thus he placed for us so much of the bitter juice of aloes in its breasts, in order to wean us from it."[10]

Cervantes' contemporaries were intent on opening their eyes to what Erasmus, in his meditations on the Psalms, called the "other face of God," the "clouded face which human infirmity can not endure," a countenance etched with the most troubling mysteries of the divine will and universal justice.[11] The fiction of the age—with its picaros,

---

[9] "Donde abundó el delicto sobreabundó la gracia. . . . Aunque me mate, en él esperaré" (ed. V. Beltrán de Heredia [Barcelona, 1963], pp. 153-54).

[10] "Todo esto fué castigo del pecado, pero fué castigo piadoso y medicinable, porque todo esto ordenó así aquella soberana Providencia para apartar nuestros corazones del amor desordenado desta vida. Por esto nos puso tanto acíbar en sus pechos, para destetarnos della" (*De la oración y consideración, Obras del V.P.M. Fray Luis de Granada*, B.A.E. 8:32).

[11] "Facies nubila, quam infirmitas humana ferre non possit" (*In Quartum Psalmum, Opera Omnia*, ed. J. Le Clerc, 10 vols. [Leiden, 1703-1706], 5:256). Pedro de Rivadeneira interrupts his enumeration of the miseries and ordeals of life with an outburst acknowledging that a grand and frightening mystery lurks in this nightmare of the fervent believer: "Cosa es que pone espanto considerar que siendo Dios una bondad infinita, y que ama infinitamente la virtud y la galardona con gloria eterna, y aborrece infinitamente el pecado y le castiga con pena de infierno, y que dió su propia sangre y murió en un madero para matarle y destruirle, permite en el mundo tantas maldades y tan feas y tan abominables, que son más propias de bestias fieras y demonios que no de hombres" (*Tratado de la tribulación*, p. 417). A sign of the widespread fascination with this mystery was the tremendous appeal of Job in the religious and literary culture of the time. His exemplary inner heroism and his classical role in the manifestation of the paradoxes of divine justice were frequent concerns of Biblical commentary and paraphrase, devotional lessons, theological discourses, pulpit oratory, and ethical treatises synthesizing Stoic and Christian values, and it is not surprising that he should appear in the lofty literary role of epic hero in Diego Enríquez Basurto's *El triumpho de la virtud y paciencia de Job* (1649). For the popularity of Job in the literature of *desengaño*, see H. Schulte, *El Desengaño: Wort und Thema in der Spanischen Literatur des Goldenen Zeitalters* (Munich, 1969), pp. 116ff., and Raúl del Piero, "Two Notes on Quevedo's Job," *Romanic Review* 50 (1959):9-10. In view of the importance of syphilis in Cervantes' development of the themes of sinfulness

penitents, converts, sinners, saints, and tormented visionaries—bore eloquent witness to the depth and pervasiveness of this cultural preoccupation. In the enormous survey of disorder and depravity, *Guzmán de Alfarache*, in which Mateo Alemán claims that he wishes to depict the development of a perfected human being, the protagonist moves through a world of evil toward a miraculous conversion, and at the climactic moment of his inner illumination and deliverance, he introduces the profound theme with an analogy which, like Cervantes' monster, suggests that there is something unnatural at the heart of the mystery of fruitful evil and suffering. The narrator recounts an anecdote of a man who orders a picture of a horse, discovers that the artist has painted it upside down, and, on complaining, is advised by the "discreet painter" simply to invert the painting. The repentant picaro's interpretation of the analogy offers the vision of God as a supremely demanding, "baroque" artist, who provokes his public by paradoxical expression and encodes the most profound secrets of his text within startling conceits: "God's works will often appear to us like this horse which lies wallowing in the mire." However, if we invert "the painting made by the sovereign Artificer," we discover a perfect work:

As we have said just now, ordeals seem harsh to us; we fail to grasp their true significance, for we understand little of them. But when he who sends them reveals the mercy that he has stored in them and we see them right side up, then we will take them for pleasures.[12]

According to the workings of logic, the paradox, like most other paradoxes, is ridiculous, and it remained for Quevedo to exploit its ridiculousness in creating one of the most abject of the hoards of contemporary literary sinners—Pablos, the "Buscón." Of all the actions and utterances that contribute to the sense of moral revulsion which the reader feels on beholding this "stinking Lazarus," who is

---

and providential suffering in the *Colloquy*, it is perhaps worth noting that in the sixteenth century the Mass of St. Job was celebrated for the multitudes of victims of the illness (see F. Buret, *Syphilis in the Middle Ages and in Modern Times*, trans. A. H. Ohmann-Dumesnil [Philadelphia, 1895], p. 215).

[12] "Las obras de Dios, muchas veces nos parecerán el caballo que se revuelca . . . la tabla hecha por el soberano Artífice. . . . Hácensenos, como poco ha decíamos, los trabajos ásperos; desconocémoslos, porque se nos entiende poco dellos. Mas, cuando el que nos los envía enseñe la misericordia que tiene guardada en ellos y los viéremos al derecho, los tendremos por gustos" (ed. S. Gili y Gaya [Madrid, 1967], 5:157-58). Guzmán learns that God "nunca envió trabajo que no frutificase de bienes" and that "a sus amigos y a sus escogidos, con pobreza, trabajos y persecuciones los banquetea" (5:11, 154).

incapable of emerging from his grave, one of the most striking is his blasphemous perversion of the traditional consolatory paradox. On reading the humorously eloquent letter from his uncle, the hangman, describing the execution, mutilation, and cannibalism of his father and the sentencing of his mother for witchcraft, the lowly picaro, following the practices of Guzmán de Alfarache and Berganza and the recommendations of countless preachers, meditates on his sufferings and finds consolation in contemplating the significance of the catastrophe: "I can not deny that I was deeply moved by the new disgrace, but I took comfort in the consolation which it provided: parents' vices can achieve so much that they console their children for their misfortunes, however great they may be." The curious piece of nonsense makes sense only as a sardonic deformation of commonplaces of consolation which surround the depiction of sin in contemporary fiction, as a deliberate play with the convention and the readers' informed expectations concerning it, and as one of Pablos' numerous profanations of the sacred, in this case, the venerable notion of fruitful evil and the form of literature that gives it expression. [13]

The cultural obsession with the paradoxes of divine justice was intimately connected with the current hysteria concerning witchcraft, which infested the spiritual life of the whole of Europe and in Spain reached its maximum intensity precisely during the period in which the *Coloquio de los perros* was conceived. [14] Cañizares' account of her

[13] "No puedo negar que sentí mucho la nueva afrenta, pero holguéme en parte: tanto pueden los vicios en los padres, que consuelan de sus desgracias, por grandes que sean, a los hijos" (*La vida del buscón llamado don Pablos*, ed. F. Lázaro Carreter [Salamanca, 1965], p. 93). It is, of course, possible to construe Pablos' words according to the bizarre psychological coherence which we glimpse behind his actions, characteristic pronouncements, ambitions, and familial anxieties, but in such a context the *sententia* is far more elliptical than in its literary and philosophical frame of reference and requires far more speculative elaboration by the reader. The aggressive prologue of the *Buscón*, whoever its writer may have been, cynically sneers at the sanctimonious view of evil as a source of edification. The paradox of fruitful evil, which justified so many anatomies of sinfulness in literary and devotional writings of the period, is in reality a mask behind which readers and authors conceal their own taste for the sensational and their delight in witnessing depravity. Quevedo's picaresque work begins by exposing the "lie" of picaresque edification which Mateo Alemán had promoted so forcefully ". . . no poco fruto podras sacar del si tienes atencion al escarmiento; y quando no lo hagas, aprouechate de los sermones, que dudo nadie compre libro de burlas para apartarse de los incentiuos de su natural deprauado" (p. 7).

[14] H. R. Trevor-Roper notes that the 1590s were a period in which the belief in witches was most widespread and most fervently championed and in which the few advocates of skepticism and dissent were overwhelmed by the powerful voices of such encyclopedists of witchcraft as Martín del Río and Nicholas Rémy. In the years

nocturnal flights to the mountain sabbats in the Pyrenees, the orgies of feasting and sexuality, the distorted sermons of the goat-god, the murder and cannibalism of children, and the various *maleficia* that give her pleasure and do honor to Satan, matches in all details the official versions of the witches' sabbat, which haunted the popular fantasy and was attested to by innumerable confessions which inquisitors extracted, frequently through torture, from accused witches in the sixteenth and seventeenth centuries.[15] The origins of this scenario, as well as its powerful hold on the European mind for two centuries, have yet to be fully explained by historians, but it is clear that it provided the imagination of the period with a powerful mythology of evil and enabled an embattled religious authority, in an age of schism, complex spiritual turmoil, and increasing secularization, to draw together its ranks and pursue a satisfying crusade against its most ancient and easily identifiable adversary. If the enemy was engendered in large part by the anxieties of those in need of victory, his imputed powers were no less spectacular and his predictable defeat no less reassuring.

The nocturnal armies of Satan were unleashed all over Europe, and the successes which they enjoyed under his banner were readily explained by theologians according to the traditional Christian doctrine of providential evil. As I have pointed out above, Cañizares' confession is marked by a peculiar doctrinal self-consciousness, which she displays in analyzing herself as a sinner and offering a metaphysical *apologia* for the suffering she and her cohorts inflict on human beings. The doctrine that she invokes thoroughly penetrated contemporary thinking concerning witchcraft, and one of the most interesting testimonies to its importance can be found in the refreshing arguments

---

during which the *Coloquio* was written, the center of the European witch-craze was the Pyrenees. See *The European Witch-Craze of the Sixteenth and Seventeenth Centuries, and Other Essays* (New York, 1967), pp. 150-56. Various Cervantists have connected the genesis of the Cañizares episode with the famous *auto de fe* of Logroño in 1610 (see Amezúa, *El casamiento engañoso y el coloquio de los perros*, pp. 154-55).

[15] See Norman Cohn, *Europe's Inner Demons: An Enquiry Inspired by the Great Witch Hunt* (London, 1975), chaps. 6, 9, 12, and Keith Thomas, *Religion and the Decline of Magic* (New York, 1971), chap. 16. Amezúa presents numerous examples of *maleficia* described in inquisitorial records, notes that accounts of full-scale sabbats of the type which Cañizares describes were rare in Spain, and argues, misleadingly, that Cervantes' depiction of the witch owes less to them than to his personal experiences in Montilla, where, according to popular legend, a group of crones known as Las Camachas had existed and had, among other acts of evil, brought about the metamorphosis of a young noble into a horse (*El casamiento engañoso y el coloquio de los perros*, pp. 168-76).

of Pedro de Valencia against the enthusiasm, cruelty, and superstition of the Inquisition's witch hunters.[16] While acknowledging that there have always been witches, that demons exist with powers to perform "marvelous acts," and that God allows their successes in order to punish man's evil and subject his faith to trial, Valencia calls for the exercise of prudence in dealing with the cases of accused individuals, and urges skepticism concerning the popular myth of witches' sabbats. He openly expresses his doubts about the possibility of the alleged transformations of men into beasts, their invisible penetration of walls, their flights through the air, and their sexual encounters with a supernatural being known as the goat-devil. He insists that inquisitors seek explanations of the origins of the marvelous phenomena, which so many swear to have experienced, in natural causes— charlatanism, debauchery, opportunistic exploitation of fear and ignorance, hallucination rooted in physiological processes, and forced confessions—and he reminds them that there have been analogous cases of superstition and mass hysteria in pre-Christain history. However, the most eloquent part of Valencia's argument is addressed to the theological foundation of the belief in witchcraft, a matter that he considers so important that he feels obliged to include absolutely everything relevant to a "true judgement" and to ask his readers to suffer his prolixity on the subject. While he grants the existence of the devil, the rationalistic Valencia finds deeply perverse the fundamental belief in "God's permission," a belief which, as we have seen, Cañizares underscores and which the orthodox portrayals of witches' activities, such as the influential encyclopedia of demonology of the Jesuit Martín del Río (1599-1600), repeatedly invoked to account for the spread of witchcraft and the spectacular successes of Satan. With a possible trace of irony Valencia notes that del Río and others "presuppose the harshest permissions which have ever been heard about the divine goodness" and proceeds to argue that "in regard to God's permission mountains of difficulties present themselves."[17] The con-

---

[16] *Discurso de Pedro de Valencia, acerca de los quentos de las brujas y cosas tocantes á magia, dirigido al Ill.mo S.r D. Bernardo de Sandoval y Roxas, Cardenal Arzobispo de Toledo, Inquisidor General de España*, ed. M. Serrano y Sanz, *Revista de Extremadura* 2 (1900):289-301, 337-47. For the traditional religious attitudes and theological doctrines which nourished the belief in witchcraft, see K. Thomas, *Religion and the Decline of Magic*, chaps. 4, 15. Thomas notes that "the witch may sometimes have seen herself as an instrument of God" (p. 512). In Cervantes' fictional witch this kind of awareness is highly developed, and it is informed by the refined theological considerations essential to the most basic themes of the *Colloquy*.

[17] ". . . Presuponen las mas duras permisiones que jamás se an oido de la divina bondad . . . en quanto á la permision de Dios se representan montes de dificultades" (*Discurso*, p. 339).

ception that God would tolerate such triumphs by the devil and visit
such afflictions on helpless women and children would appear to be
at odds with the belief in His omnipotence and goodness, and Valencia recoils from a bewildering paradox with indignation:

I fail to understand how those people who affirm this view of God's permissive will and defend it by referring to it as a great piety while denouncing
as a victim of an impious fancy anyone who refuses to believe it can themselves maintain with proper piety and reverence the doctrine of divine goodness and abominate with proper hatred and contempt the devil. I at least do
not wish to believe the words of those who have offered to him the submis-
sion that they confess. . . . Did ever God grant to the devil so that he might
use it against Indians, devourers of human flesh, or Egyptians, worshippers
of garlic and onions, such an infamous power as that which is given to him
by these tales of evil old crones for his use against Catholic Christians? And
can it be said that one honors God by believing this?

Without having to endorse the uncompromising skepticism of the
"political thinkers, the Epicureans, and the Lucianists, who believe
in no more than nature and the physical things which they experience
in the course of life," one can legitimately refuse to lend credence to
"all the old wives' tales," "all the pagan fables," "all the metamorphoses in Ovid," and of course, all the extravagant marvels detailed
in the infamous confessions.[18]

Valencia's penetrating critique of the superstitions of his contemporaries is animated by the powerful skeptical spirit of a man who is
repelled by the irrationality and inhumanity about him, who is not
prepared to account for such suffering by praising the mysteries of a
darkened divine countenance, and who perhaps senses the sinister potential for ideological tyranny lurking in the traditional consolatory
doctrines of Christianity such as sanctified affliction and fruitful evil.
In Cervantes' *Colloquy of the Dogs* we observe a similar skeptical spirit
informing the dogs' discussion of the fantastic metamorphoses of the
witches' world and the enigmatic oracle, which Cipión describes as

---

[18] ". . . no se donde tienen la dotrina i la piedad i la reverencia de la divina
bondad, i el odio, desprecio i abominacion del demonio los que esto afirman i defien-
den i con nombre de grande piedad i vituperando con nombre de impío afecto á los
que no se lo quieren creer; yo á lo menos no quiero creer á los que le an hecho el
reconocimiento que confiessan. . . . ¿Concedió jamás Dios al demonio contra indios
que comían hombres, ni contra Egypcios que adoravan ajos i cebollas, tal infamia i
superioridad como la que le dan estos cuentos de malas viejas, contra christianos
cathólicos?; i que se diga que es honra de Dios creer esto? . . . políticos, epícureos i
lucianistas que no dan crédito mas de á las cosas corpóreas i naturaleza que esperi-
mentan en el uso de la vida . . . todas las consejas de viejas . . . todas las fábulas
gentilicas . . . todas las transformaciones de Ovidio" (*Discurso*, pp. 341-43).

"fairy stories or old wives' tales, like those about the headless horse and the magic wand, with which people while away the long winter nights beside the hearth."[19] But Cervantes does not focus his skepticism on the theological mysteries that emerge in Cañizares' confession and Berganza's anguished meditation over the lifeless husk of the hag, from which the spirit has evidently departed on its travels to the orgiastic sabbat. Whether or not Cervantes actually believed in witches—and the dogs' sarcastic rejection of the oracle, its promise of metamorphosis, and any kinship with the crone would indicate that he was certainly skeptical about the miraculous events commonly said to transpire at the demonic sabbats—it is nevertheless clear that he was well aware of the imaginative power of the myth of witchcraft, that he effectively introduced its vision of annihilating energy and its vocabulary of horrible inversion at the moment of climactic disintegration in his narrative, and that he exploited its theological implications to pursue to its most profound depths his major theme of the nature of evil.[20] When Berganza meditates on the loathsome cadaver of the witch in the darkness of the night, the series of troubling questions that he poses—"Who made this wicked old woman so wise and so evil? From where does she know which are evils of calamity and which are evils of culpability? How does she come to know so much about God and speak of Him so often, while her works are those of the devil? Why does she sin so much out of pure malice, not being able to offer the excuse of ignorance?"—far from exposing the contradictions in a perverse theology, intimates rather the mystery of a paradox which conceals a dread but liberating secret.[21]

[19] "Consejas o cuentos de viejas, como aquellos del caballo sin cabeza, y de la varilla de virtudes, con que se entretienen al fuego las dilatadaas noches del invierno" (p. 310).

[20] To appreciate the power of the myth of witchcraft in the imagination of the period, we need only look at Valencia's description of the diabolical pact: "Pero que á descubierto i por pacto determinado se quiera un hombre apartar de Dios i declararse por su enemigo i pasarse al reino i campo contrario del Príncipe de las tinieblas para seguir sus vanderas, i esto no trasformándose Satanás en angel de luz ni representando dulcura y divinidad sino mostrándose en figura feísima y torpísima con hediondeces i profesión de maldad i opposición á todo bien, suavidad i luz, esto excede en perversion á todas las abominaciones de los idólatras, bárbaros, i tiranos, i atheistas, i merece qualesquiera castigos, i que se corten tales miembros podridos i hediondos, del cuerpo sano destos reinos, i se ataje el cancer á fuego i sangre sin delacion" (*Discurso*, p. 292).

[21] "¿Quién hizo a esta mala vieja tan discreta y tan mala? ¿De dónde sabe ella cuáles son males de daño y cuáles de culpa? ¿Cómo entiende y habla tanto de Dios, y obra tanto del diablo? ¿Cómo peca tan de malicia, no excusándose con ignorancia?" (pp. 305-306).

PROBING THE WITCH: THE IMAGINATIVE CENTER
OF THE *COLLOQUY OF THE DOGS*

At this point, rather than directly pursuing the theological implications of Cañizares' presence and confession, I turn to the imagery
and motifs that are concentrated about the witch, for the scene provides the imaginative center of the work, the source of life that ra-
diates to all points of its circumference. Once we have possessed it,
we can see much more clearly the relationships among its apparently
disorderly parts and between its parts and the unified whole that they
compose. If Cervantes' plot construction reveals a mastery of what I
have called a grammar of narrative disorder, which is intelligible to
all readers, but which depends to some extent for its most powerful
effects on their recognition of the specific principles of plot structure
manifest in certain narrative forms that were popular in his age, his
principal imagery is drawn from the archetypal imagery of the literature of disorder, but a full, correct response to it depends on the
readers' awareness of a distinctive body of associations and themes that
surround it in the contemporary Christian literature of sinfulness and
divine retribution. In what follows I would like to examine the central
images of the tomb, confinement, night, sleep, physical infirmity,
animality, mutilation, torture, cannibalism, and disorientation, with
some reference to the other works of literature of the age which exploit
their imaginative power and which are comparable in some ways in
meaning, purpose, or effect to the *Coloquio de los perros*.

I would stress at the outset that the imagery and the themes with
which it is charged are in themselves commonplaces, as they derive
for the most part from the Bible and are always close to the surface
of any anatomy of sin, whether in didactic or imaginative writing,
within the Christian tradition. It is precisely because they are commonplaces, orchestrated with particular frequency and intensity in
Cervantes' own religious culture, with a tremendous impact on the
literary production of the age—an age that we remember for the beast-
man and the fortunate thieves of Calderón, the sleep of Segismundo
and Tirso's "Desconfiado," the repentant and nonrepentant picaresque
heroes, the theological trickster, Don Juan, the contrite Magdalena,
the martyr, and the saint—that they resonate with such power
throughout his tale and organize its total design. For these very reasons I would also emphasize that when I call attention to the presence
of such traditional imagery and to its associative values in the religious
writings of Cervantes' age, I am not at all arguing for the causal
connections which have interested traditional source studies. There is

only one true source of the *Coloquio de los perros*, and that is Cervantes' own vision of evil and its forms, powers, consequences, origins, and necessity in the redemptive process, as well as whatever personal and existential factors were responsible for shaping that vision. I am concerned only with meaning, expressive power, and imaginative impact and resonance in the vocabulary that gives literary shape to Cervantes' vision, and, although his vocabulary remains our vocabulary, its range of associations is much less precisely defined in our culture, its imaginative power much more diffuse, and its metaphysical resonance much more muted. If we are to respond intensely to the rich imagistic texture of Cervantes' literary world or if our response to it is to be directed at what is central to his text rather than at peripheral details which are more immediately striking and more readily intelligible according to the priorities of our "modern" imagination and critical interests, our own philosophical orientation and moral values, or our own conceptions of Cervantes and Cervantes' Spain, then we must recognize how its overwhelming vocabulary of disorder draws power and meaning from the Christian culture of the age, and we can do this effectively only by glancing at works representative of that culture.

At the center of the Cañizares episode we watch as the witch moves from a "room that was dark, narrow, and low-ceilinged, illuminated only by the feeble glow of a clay lamp," into a "tiny room even narrower than the other," where she anoints herself, "stretches out on the floor like a dead woman," and falls into a trance. Berganza can detect no breathing in her motionless form, and, as he stares at the "skeleton of bones," he is seized with an uncontrollable fit of terror. Before entering the room, Cañizares describes the diseased condition of her soul, a state in which she can recognize with a keen intelligence her sinfulness and yet summon no energies from a totally flaccid will that would free her from her bondage in sensuality. She describes herself as a typical sinner, her soul wallowing and "sunken in the profound abyss of its own misery,"[22] incapable of lifting a hand upward toward the hand that God is extending in her direction. The images of moving into the grave and sinking into the abyss, with their strong associations of constricted space and bottomlessness, certainly add powerful visual support to the effects of the narrative movement of the work, which at this climactic point plunges deeper and

---

[22] "Aposento, que era escuro, estrecho y bajo, y solamente claro con la débil luz de un candil de barro . . . otro aposentillo más estrecho . . . se tendió en el suelo como muerta . . . toda era notomía de huesos . . . sumida en la profunda sima de su miseria" (pp. 288, 301, 304, 305).

deeper into central recesses that appear to hold the promise of clarification and release from suspense only to become sources of greater
confinement and mystery. As I have pointed out above, both the
confessions within the confession and the dreams within the dream
lead us to a central void.

However, the images of the grave and the abyss, as well as the
cadaverous body whose foul-smelling mouth has repelled Berganza,
are primarily meaningful as traditional symbols of the condition of
sin as a state of death in life. This fundamental Christian view, expressed so forcefully in Paul's epistles, is omnipresent in the devotional and ascetic writings of the sixteenth century. For example, at
the beginning of his widely read manual for the true Christian warrior, the *Enchiridion*, Erasmus surveys the powerful enemies he must
confront and repeatedly describes sinfulness as a "death of the soul."
He invokes the fifth psalm—"their throat is an open sepulcher"—
exploits the similarity in the Greek words for body and grave to suggest a link based on etymological reasoning, and alludes to the four-
day death and stink of the entombed Lazarus, a Christian archetype
of spiritual regeneration which was to enjoy a spectacular resurrection
in the devotional and literary writings of the following one hundred
years:

. . . your soul is dead! *If the body does not feel a small pin prick*, we say that it
is not alive. And shall we say that the soul is living which is insensible to
the wounds that sin inflicts upon it? . . . Within the sepulcher of the sinner's
breast lies stretched out a dead and stinking thing, which is his soul, *giving
off those foul odors that infect all who stand close by.* . . . The bodies of the good
and the just are temples of the Holy Spirit; those of the wicked and unjust
are tombs of dead things. So that the declaration of the grammarians fits
them very neatly: that the word *Soma*, which is Greek and signifies *body*, is
very close to the word *Sima*, which signifies *pit* or *grave*; because the breast,
wherein lie the heart and the thoughts, is a grave, and *the mouth and throat
are its cracks and openings, through which the evil odor rises. You can be certain
that no body bereft of its soul remains as lifeless as the soul of one whom, in his
sinfulness God has abandoned*; and no corpse in its physical putrefaction so
offends the human nostrils as the stench of the soul that has been dead for
four days, that is to say, a soul completely corrupted by the habit of vice
and buried in sin, offends the nostrils of God and all the saints.[23]

[23] ". . . tu ánima está muerta. *Si el cuerpo no siente una punçada pequeña de un alfilel,*
dezimos que no está bivo. ¿Y diremos que está biva el alma que a tales heridas está
sin sentido? . . . Dentro del sepulchro de su pecho está tendida una cosa muerta y
hedionda, que es su ánima, *de donde proceden aquellos malos olores que inficionan a los que
están a par dél.* . . . Los cuerpos de los buenos y justos, templos son del Espíritu
Santo; los de los malos y injustos son sepulchros de cosas muertas. De manera que

In an Easter sermon based on the resurrection of Lazarus, Juan de Avila rebukes his listeners for remaining in the "sepulcher of their sins" and refusing to throw open the tombstone which confines them in the darkness of evil and which is an emblem of their stony hearts. In another sermon he turns to Job for a similar image and set of associations: "God is most powerful, and with great pleasure He uses His power to deliver souls from sins. And it is written in Job: 'He will deliver you from the narrow mouth and the bottomless pit.' "[24]

If the grave and death are frequently appearing symbols of sinfulness, they are also sources of enlightenment concerning man's mortality and his inclination toward sin. In his lonely vigil through the night, Berganza finds himself both terrified and fascinated by the sight of the living corpse, and, as he gazes at it attentively, "squatting beside her, watchful, staring into her hideously ugly countenance," he ponders its significance, "meditating on the terrible vision of her body and the worse occupation of her soul. . . . In such meditations as these the night passed and the day came."[25] The continuing "descubrimientos" of evil which punctuate the entire tale reach their climax in the fixed stare of the protagonist, riveted, as in the tormenting obsession of a nightmare, on a horror that refuses to vanish. Astonishingly, the dread fixation almost immediately becomes the initial phase of a spiritual exercise. At the very center of the *Coloquio de los*

---

encaxa en ellos muy bien aquella declaración que hazen los grammáticos, diziendo que este vocablo o palabra Soma, que es griego, y quiere decir cuerpo, está muy cercano de Sima, que quiere dezir hoya o sepultura, porque el pecho donde está el coraçón y donde están los pensamientos es un sepulchro, y *la boca y garganta son los resquicios y aberturas por donde sale el mal olor dél. Ten assimesmo por cierto que ningún cuerpo queda tan muerto* quando se ha apartado el ánima de las carnes, quanto queda el ánima a quien Dios desampara por el pecado; y ningún cuerpo assí muerto y podrido huele acá tan mal a las narizes de los ombres como hyede en el acatamiento de Dios y de todos los santos el ánima que está ya de quatro días muerta, quiero dezir, por luenga costumbre toda corrompida y sepultada en los vicios." (*El Enquiridion o manual del caballero cristiano*, ed. D. Alonso [Madrid, 1932], pp. 122-23, italics added). It is likely that Cervantes was acquainted with Erasmus' influential treatise in the popular sixteenth-century Spanish translation by Alonso Fernández de Madrid. See also the discussion of the death of sin in *De Immensa Misericordia Dei, The Essential Erasmus*, trans. J. P. Dolan (New York, 1964), pp. 253-54.

[24] "Poderosísimo es Dios, y de buena gana emplea su poder en sacar ánimas de pecados. Y escrito está en Job: El te librará de la boca angosta y del pozo que no tiene suelo" (see *Obras completas*, ed. L. Sala Balust [Madrid, 1953], 2:258, 947).

[25] ". . . en cuclillas, atento, mirando su espantosa y fea catadura. . . . considerando la mala visión de su cuerpo y la peor ocupación de su alma. . . . me preguntaba yo a mí mismo: '¿Quién hizo a esta mala vieja tan discreta y tan mala?' . . . En estas consideraciones se pasó la noche y se vino el día" (pp. 305-306).

perros, we observe in fact the type of meditation that was celebrated and presumably widely practiced in the age.

In his manual for the proper reflection of the devout, *De la oración y consideración*, Fray Luis de Granada repeatedly urges the Christian to open the "eyes of his spirit" and marvel at the darkest truths of existence: "the whole of life is subject to so many miseries and ordeals, both of the spirit and of the flesh, that it would be more fittingly called death than life." For all its deceptive appearances it is in reality "narrow and brief; only in ordeals and afflictions is it rich and long." Man lives in "blindness" in the state of the "frenético"; like the spider he consumes himself in spinning out his creations which then are as fragile as the web that vanishes in the wind. He is the helpless victim of sicknesses, wars, earthquakes, and floods. In his sinfulness he has perversely used all the goods that the Creator has placed at his disposition and persecutes his fellows with a cruelty unmatched in the realm of the beasts. He is sick in his evil and resembles the victim of a nagging malady who is constantly tormented by a raging fever. Man is always lapsing into the state of forgetfulness which Cañizares describes, failing to remember that his true destiny is to live, not "here with the beasts," but rather "in heaven with the angels," and that the destiny of his flesh is to fall into "a pit seven feet in length in the company of other dead bodies." The devil's mission is aimed at making man forget: "For this reason one should believe with all certainty that the devil works as hard as he can to make man lose this memory." Luis de Granada's outline of the methods and directions of disciplined meditation reveals a sequence that we observe in the Cañizares episode of Cervantes' exemplary tale; for, following the catalogue of the afflictions of the traditional *miseria hominis*, he moves to the consideration of "death, which is one of the most profitable meditations which a Christian can have," and exhorts his reader to descend into the grave and there listen to the most frightening and profound words of God:

God told the prophet Jeremiah to go down into the house where the potter was fashioning clay, because he wished to speak with him there. God could well have spoken with His prophet in any other place, but He wanted to speak to him in this one, *in order to make it understood that the house of clay (which is the grave) is the school of true wisdom*, where God is wont to teach his doctrine to His own. There He teaches them how great is the vanity of the world, the misery of the flesh, the brevity of life; *and above all he teaches them to know themselves*, which is one of the highest truths of philosophy which one can know. Descend, oh man, with your spirit into this house and there you will see who you are, what you are made of, in what you will finish, and what end awaits the beauty and the glory of the world! And so you will learn to despise everything the world adores, *as it does not know how to look upon it correctly*.[26]

Granada emphasizes that in the grave man is forced to behold the nakedness of his elemental self, and that, when he discovers that just as he is born naked, so will he die, he will at that instant realize that in pursuing the pomp with which he clothes himself in life on earth he is in reality building towers of wind on foundations of sand. He will stare at the decaying flesh and find himself compelled to ask: "How could the man who there sees how he is the food for worms worship his belly as his God?"[27]

[26] "Eso que hay de vida (tanto cuanto) está subjecto a tantas miserias y trabajos, así de espíritu como de cuerpo, que mas se puede llamar muerte que vida . . . estrecha y breve, en solos trabajos y miserias es rica y larga . . . acá con las bestias . . . en el cielo con los ángeles . . . un hoyo de siete pies de largo en compañía de los otros muertos. . . . Por esto es de creer cierto que el demonio trabaja cuanto puede por hacernos perder esta memoria . . . paso de la muerte que es una de las mas provechosas consideraciones que un cristiano puede tener. . . . Al profeta Hieremías dijo Dios que descendiese a la casa donde se labraba el barro, porque quería hablar allí con él. Bien pudiera Dios hablar en otro cualquier lugar con su Profeta, mas quísole hablar en este, *para dar á entender que la casa del barro (que es la sepultura) es la escuela de la verdadera sabiduría*, donde Dios suele enseñar á los suyos su doctrina. Allí les enseña cuán grande sea la vanidad del mundo, la miseria de la carne, la brevedad de la vida; y sobre todo *allí les enseña á conoscer á sí mismos*, que es una de las mas altas filosofías que se puede saber. Desciende pues ¡oh hombre! con el espíritu a esta casa, y *ahí verás quién eres, y de qué eres, y en qué has de parar, y en qué para la hermosura de la carne*, y la gloria del mundo. Y así aprenderás á desprecir todo lo que el mundo adora, *por no saber mirarlo*" (*Obras*, B.A.E., 8:31-35; italics added). Compare Rivadeneira's words: "cuando muere y duerme el cuerpo en la sepultura, entonces se abren los ojos del alma, para ver y conocer que todas las cosas deste mundo son una representacion y vana figura" (*Tratado de tribulación*, p. 389). For the emphasis on correct vision in the spiritual writings of the time and their strategies of shocking the reader into an "opening of his eyes," so that he can "penetrar con los ojos del entendimiento la verdad que está encubierta," as Fray Diego de Estella puts it in *De la vanidad del mundo*, see S. Gilman, "An Introduction to the Ideology of the Baroque in Spain," *Symposium* 1 (1946):82-107, and H. Schulte, *El Desengaño: Wort und Thema in der spanischen Literatur des Goldenen Zeitalters*, pp. 151ff. Campuzano's concluding observations on the value of the *Coloquio de los perros* as a work which has refreshed the "ojos del entendimiento," as well as the numerous allusions to meditation in Berganza's actions and words (see below), are clear indications of the affinities of Cervantes' final tale and contemporary devotional literature. Throughout his writings Erasmus stresses the necessity of seeing with the spiritual eye, and he chooses, as the monstrous embodiment of disorder in his colloquy which most resembles Cervantes' dialogue in its fundamental themes, the one-eyed Cyclops, who outrageously perverts all Christian values and teachings (see *The Colloquies of Erasmus*, ed. and trans. C. R. Thompson [Chicago, 1965], pp. 415-22).

[27] "¿Cómo tendria por Dios á su vientre quien allí mirase como es manjar de gusanos?" (*De la oración y consideración*, p. 35).

Berganza's description of the naked body of the moribund Cañizares is certainly the most shocking of the numerous passages of a work that cultivates the ugly at all levels, and its most ugly detail is the description of her gigantic belly.

. . . it frightened me terribly to find myself shut up in that narrow room with that figure before me, which I shall describe to you as best I can. She was over seven feet in length; she was completely a skeleton of bones, covered with dark, hairy, and wrinkled skin. *With her belly, which was like a sheepskin, she covered her shameful parts, and it even hung halfway down her thighs*; her nipples resembled two dry and wrinkled cow udders; her lips were blackened, her teeth rotted, her nose hooked and bony, her eyes starting from their sockets and crossed, her hair disheveled, her cheeks eaten away, her throat scrawny, and her breasts flabby.[28]

The belly, of course, has been a prominent symbol in the Christian iconography of sin since St. Paul, and it is certainly that doctrinal context which Cervantes had in mind in creating this scene, whether or not there may have been, as Amezúa insists, real witches in Montilla whose life, physical appearance, and customs he wished to depict.[29] Here in the grave, Berganza, the dreaming Ensign, and the reader must gaze at the power, the contagion, the bestiality, and the ugliness of sin. For Luis de Granada, wonder and shock are the proper reactions to such a spectacle, but it is the wonder that stirs the mind to ask pointed questions and make its way through their frightening answers toward profound spiritual illumination: "if you consider at-

[28] ". . . me dió gran temor verme encerrado en aquel estrecho aposento con aquella figura delante, la cual te la pintaré como mejor supiere. Ella era larga de más de siete pies; toda era notomía de huesos, cubiertos con una piel negra, vellosa y curtida; *con la barriga, que era de badana, se cubría las partes deshonestas, y aun le colgaba hasta la mitad de los muslos*: las tetas semejaban dos vejigas de vaca secas y arrugadas, denegridos los labios, traspillados los dientes, la nariz corva y entablada, desencasados los ojos, la cabeza desgreñada, las mejillas chupadas, angosta la garganta y los pechos sumidos" (pp. 304-305; italics added).

[29] Erasmus' archsinner, Polyphemus, notes: "My kind have four gospels. Four things above all we gospelers seek: full bellies; plenty of work for the organs below the belly; a livelihood from somewhere or other; finally, freedom to do as we like." Several details of Erasmus' anatomy of the world of lawlessness in his dialogue suggest that Cervantes may have had it in mind as he conceived the climactic scene of his own colloquy: its central doctrinal concern with sinfulness and redemption and the relations between free will and Divine Grace, its concentration of a vision of universal disorder in a monstrous being, its description of the demonic metamorphoses of men into beasts, its allusion to the hand of Christ and the responsibilities of man to receive that hand correctly, the unregenerate sinner's knowledge and perversion of theological doctrine, his abject reliance on divine mercy, his satirical catalogue of disasters and his apocalyptic intimations of an approaching end of the world, his decision to react

tentively all the miseries which I have enumerated, then your eyes will suddenly open, and you will be amazed at the blindness of men; and you will begin to say: 'How is it that this miserable race of Adam feels such pride? Where does so much puffing up of spirit come from? From where so much haughtiness in their hearts? From where such great disdain for others, such esteem for themselves, and so much forgetfulness of God?"[30] The exposition of a theological, Biblical, or moral issue followed by a series of questions concerning its implications for the meditator or an injunction that the meditator raise such questions is a basic rhetorical method of Granada's treatise and of religious oratory in general, and we see how close Cervantes' scene is to such "kinetic" writing as Berganza's ponderings in terror lead him to raise a series of questions concerning the mysterioius union of in-

---

to his awareness of such matters by returning to his orgies, his ironic inclusion of Erasmus' own colloquy among the disasters (see my observations on the self-indictments of Cervantes' colloquy below), and, most interestingly, the concluding exchange between him and his innocent adversary, which plays on the fact that the latter's name, Cannius, implies "dog." See *Cyclops or The Gospel Bearer, The Colloquies of Erasmus*, pp. 415-22.

Perhaps nothing reveals the fundamental differences in the respective visions animating the *Coloquio* and *Don Quixote* more effectively than a comparison of the prominent stomachs of Cañizares and Sancho Panza. The latter is the literary descendant of a type of folkloric character (e.g., St. Pançart) who represented the elemental, creative power of bodily life and enjoyed considerable prestige in traditional carnivalesque culture and the literature reflecting its influence. In such figures the insatiable belly is conceived of as the "saintly" belly, the focus of man's development toward wholeness of being, the locus of his most intimate contact with the natural world, and the center of bodily creation, linking past and future, death and birth, and endowing life with its indestructible continuity (see M. Bakhtin, *Rabelais and His World*, trans. H. Iswolsky [Cambridge, Mass., 1968], chaps. 4-5). In Cañizares' gigantic, dried-up belly we find inverted all the creative, nourishing powers of the saintly stomach. It epitomizes her voracious appetite for the debilitating stimulants of sin, her self-nourishment from the detritus of the moribund, the "fertilization" of her womb by the sulphurous effluvia of her demonic paramour, and her cannibalism of children. In his heroic attack on the monster, Berganza seizes her by the heel, associated both in Christian tradition (Gen., 3:15) and in the *Coloquio* ("Yo, que tenía entonces el juicio, no en la cabeza, sino en los carcañares" [p. 184]) with the power of Satan, and he sinks his teeth into the "luengas faldas de su vientre." The ascetic moralization and abuse of the creature of the stomach was, of course, common in the literature of *desengaño*. One can compare Berganza's savage rending of the belly with Pedro el Justiciero's threatened mutilation of the fool in Calderón's *El médico de su honra*.

[30] "Si consideras atentamente todas estas miserias susodichas, luego se te abrirán los ojos, y maravillarte has de la ceguedad de los hombres; y comenzarás á decir: ¿pues de qué se ensoberbesce este miserable linaje de Adam? ¿De dónde tanta hinchazon de ánimo? tanta altivez de corazones? tan gran menosprecio de los otros? tanta estima de sí mismo, y tanto olvido de Dios?" (*De la oración y consideración*, p. 33).

telligence and evil, divine wisdom and diabolical practice, in the object of his considerations (see above).

As she probes the depths of her spiritual malaise, Cañizares employs an image that appears frequently in contemporary theological discussions centering on the mystery of divine mercy and the problem of free will and man's responsibility to earn salvation. After repeating the commonplace, "the habit of sinning becomes a second nature," and describing the state of forgetfulness which sensual indulgence has induced in her, she adds that her will is "manacled" in its sinful delights and that her soul "is unable to lift its powers of proper consideration sufficiently even to harbor any good thought; and thus, letting itself become engulfed in the deep abyss of its own misery, *it does not care even to lift its hand to grasp the hand that God in His mercy continually holds out to it so that it might arise.*"[31] Throughout the sixteenth century the Catholic world responded to the Protestants' denial of free will by proclaiming that man must cooperate with God and that, even though his resources are wretchedly small in comparison with the colossal powers of the divine will, he must use them in order to merit grace through works. And following the composition, in 1524, of Erasmus' *De libero arbitrio*, a polemical work that bases a good deal of its argumentation on Ecclesiasticus' injunction: "to act faithfully is a matter / of your own choice. / He has placed before you fire and water: / stretch out your hand for / whichever you wish" (15:15-16), the image of man extending his hand toward a merciful God in an exercise of his freedom was a familiar figure in theological treatises, sermons, and works of imaginative literature which wished to render the doctrine in a powerful and readily apprehensible visual shape.[32] A sermon on the Nativity of the Virgin by Juan de Avila reveals similarities to Cervantes' passage in theological conception and imagery which are so striking that they suggest that we are dealing with a topic of religious oratory. After exhorting his listener to "awaken from the sleep of sinfulness," to emerge from the "sad night" in which he lives, and to walk by the "light of the Virgin," he urges him: "Brother, do not be more imprudent than children, animals and infidels, who, if they fall into a well or a filthy swamp, not only raise their hands to whoever helps them out, but even call out loudly that somebody

---

[31] "La costumbre del vicio se vuelve en naturaleza . . . no puede levantar la consideración siquiera a tener algún buen pensamiento; y así dejándose estar sumida en la profunda sima de su miseria, *no quiere alzar la mano a la de Dios, que se la está dando, por sola su misericordia, para que se levante*" (pp. 301-302; italics added).

[32] *Discourse on Free Will*, ed. and trans. E. F. Winter (New York, 1967), pp. 21-36.

might assist them . . . and if God gives you light and ever removes you from among the sleeping and the dead, you will also weep because you sinned and because, in sinning, you failed to raise yourself with the aid which God was promising you, stretching forth his hand to save you."[33] At the opening of *Guzmán de Alfarache* the disillusioned and repentant picaro reminds his reader that God's helping hand is present to assist him as he struggles with his recalcitrant human nature, and over and over again he insists that man must also do his part in the redemptive process. Like Cervantes' archsinner, Alemán's picaro is given to tormented meditation on his spiritual disease. He frequently marvels at the mysterious obstinacy of human nature when enslaved by evil. In recalling his climactic descent into the realm of the beggars, a demonic order which, in its bizarre inversions, its blasphemous "sacred text," and its presiding monster of the flesh, corresponds to Cervantes' world of witches as an epiphany of lawless-

---

[33] "Despertar del sueño del pecado . . . triste noche . . . lumbre de la Virgen. . . . Hermano, no seas más imprudente que los niños, y que los infieles, y que los animales, que, si en un pozo caen o en cieno hediondo, no solo alzan la mano luego a quien les ayuda para salir, más aun con voces llaman a quien les socorra . . . y si Dios te da lumbre y algún tiempo te saca de entre los dormidos y muertos, también llorarás tú porque pecaste y porque en pecando no te levantaste con el socorro que Dios te prometía, extendiendo su mano para tu remedio" (*Obras completas*, 2:945). In a sermon written in the year of his *Discourse on Free Will* (1524), Erasmus celebrates the gift of divine mercy and at its climax exhorts man to show himself worthy of receiving this immense treasure. In his depiction of the habitual sinner who "despairing of himself, prefers to grow old in evil," we find the familiar imagery and doctrine: "The Lord is always with us, calling us to Himself. Why do you unhappy men not go to Him? Why continue in the garments of your misfortune? The altar of mercy is ready to receive you, and you turn to the chains of madness. The asylum of the divine compassion is open, and you fly to the pit of miserable despair. The Savior holds His hand out to you, and you turn away. Heaven is reserved for you, and you plunge into the abyss. The bosom of the divine goodness is open to you, and you flee to the noose" (*De Immensa Misericordia Dei, The Essential Erasmus*, p. 265). The imagery and the doctrine behind it appear frequently in Felipe de Meneses' *Luz del alma cristiana* (1554), a popular catechistic work which Don Quixote praises as a perfect example of a genre which his sinful countrymen are in sore need of: "—Estos tales libros, aunque hay muchos deste género, son los que se deben imprimir, porque son muchos los pecadores que se usan, y son menester infinitas luces para tantos desalumbrados" (*Don Quijote*, 2:520). Explaining the mystery of redemption, Meneses writes that "queriendo el hombre nunca le faltará Dios por la Ley y asiento que él por su misericordia quiso hacer con él de no le faltar en semejante caso y así los sanctos doctores encaresciendo este tan señalado beneficio suelen decir que está Dios tan presto y aparejado para dar la mano al que está caido en el pecado, que en el mesmo punto que él la pidiese se la da, y no ha él dicho, señor ayúdame, cuando ya está con él" (ed. I. V. Pensado [Madrid, 1978], p. 427; see also pp. 486, 519, 537, 543).

ness, he deplores his rejection of the "benefits of God" offered to him through the hands of a saintly cardinal who would lift him from his wretched state. He proceeds to contrast God, a true Father in His faithfulness, patience, and mercy, with his own father, who "would have hated him and let go of his hand." Subsequently Guzmán recognizes that, if he is to emerge from the "swamp of his vices" ("cenegal de los vicios"), he must toil by day in the vineyard, with the good intentions of his hands guiding the good works of his hoe. As he recalls his alienation amid the deepest abysses of his depravity, he rebukes himself and his listener because "we do nothing to help ourselves" and utters a discourse on sin in which he likens God to a gentle father taking His child by the hand and supporting and directing his first steps. When the father releases the hand to allow him to venture on alone, the child must walk in His direction; He remains ever near, so that, if he stumbles, "he falls into His arms; God receives him into them and does not allow him to fall to the ground." And at the moment in which the wayward picaro finally does turn toward the merciful father and tastes the fruitfulness of all his own sufferings, Guzmán decides to "lift his arm" and "purchase Grace," and he prays that God "might take him by the hand," employing the same phrase that Cervantes' Ensign uses as he recounts the strange events that prevented him from suicide and murder when he discovered the treachery of his wife ("Once again God held me with His hand!"—"¡Aquí me tuvo de nuevo Dios de su mano!").[34]

But in the world of the *Coloquio de los perros* human beings are for the most part like Cañizares, incapable of reaching out for divine mercy, and it is the vengeful, rather than the forgiving hand of God that looms in its shadows, the "powerful hand" poised to "overthrow the proud who have been exalted." At two important points in the narrative we witness characters extending their hands, but they are hands of deception and depredation—the bejeweled fingers of Doña Estefanía which obsess the Ensign ("She excited me still further by revealing a white hand with very handsome rings"; "I was all on fire because of the white hands I had seen")[35] and "those clean and white hands" whose beauty is unforgettably etched on Berganza's memory despite the rapacity that guides them in the theft of the meat (p. 220). The theological implications in Cañizares' speech resonate in these incidents and surround them with the type of imaginative power

[34] *Guzmán de Alfarache*, 1: 71; 2:286, 288; 3:253; 5:11-12, 153.

[35] "Sacó la señora una muy blanca mano, con muy buenas sortijas. . . . Yo quedé abrasado con las manos de nieve que había visto" (pp. 180-81).

which we experience in Tirso de Molina's development of the hand symbolism in the age's most famous desecrator of orthodox doctrine concerning the efficacy of good works—Don Juan Tenorio.

The Cañizares episode brings to a climax the development of another body of imagery that is instrumental in establishing the dominant tonality of the work and conveying its essential themes. As the title suggests, the world of the *Coloquio* is a world of beasts. Its inhabitants and their activities are continually associated with animals, and it is generally the rapaciousness and violence of the animal world that are evoked by the comparisons. As the sensible dogs remind the reader, in the hierarchical scale of the creation beasts belong to an order which is inferior to that of man and his civilization. However, in the disoriented world envisioned in Cervantes' *novella*, we observe human beings everywhere descending to the level of the beast, and we quickly realize that the only heroism visible in its murky atmosphere is ironically to be found in the pathetic figure of a dog, whose principal defense against the swarm of evil adversaries is an ability to flee. The elaborate animal symbolism of the work contributes significantly to its overwhelming vision of people living by instinct, gratifying primitive impulses, allowing themselves to be dominated by the elemental needs of food and sex, showing no charity, preying on one another, living in fear of one another's rapacity, and drawing together only in the form of the pack or mob, the community of the ravenous beast united in the hunt and in the slaughter of the outsider. Such are the implications of the animal imagery which runs through the work and appears in its most concentrated form in Cañizares' confession, and like most of the central imagery which emerges here, we feel that it draws its power from a deep Christian tradition.

The association of man's inhumanity with bestiality in Christian writings is, of course, as ancient as the Bible. In emphasizing the power of Divine Grace to bring man's reason and will into harmonious cooperation so that he can love and pursue what he understands to be right, Luis de León recalls the darkness and animal imagery of the Psalms to describe the transformation of the justified Christian:

And just as happens in nature and in the changes of night and day, wherein, as David tells in his Psalm: 'With the coming of night the beasts come forth from their lairs and, strengthened and guided by the shadows, roam about the fields and wreak destruction at will, but, as soon as the day dawns and light begins to appear, these very beasts withdraw and hide in their caves'; such are the bestial licentiousness of the body and the disruptive rebelliousness of its movements; for when our fallen will found itself in the night of its misery, they roamed about freely and brought fire and bloodshed in their universal devastation, but, as soon as the rays of good love began to shine and the day of goodness, to reveal itself, then immediately they turn their foot backward and hide in their cave and allow what is truly the human being in us to come forth into the light and to engage in his proper occupation from sunrise to sunset.[36]

The sun finally does rise on the world of the *Coloquio de los perros*, and the dawn brings a breath of relief to its inhabitants, as they stumble about in its suffocating atmosphere, but the light seems dim, and we might wonder whether the nightmare which we share with the sleeping audience within the book is really over. It is certainly the spectacular movements of the creatures of darkness that Cervantes is interested in displaying in the work, and at the center of the nightmare we enter a world of bestiality where we behold the devil, the source of all evil, appearing in the form of a goat to reward his flock with sexual favors; where we hear of mysterious metamorphoses, in which his worshippers turn themselves into cocks, owls, and crows, transform men into asses, and give birth to dogs; and where we must contemplate the hideous body of the moribund witch with its breasts resembling "two dry and wrinkled cow udders" and its gigantic "belly of sheepskin." The world of the beast is a world of savagery, depredation, and mutilation, and in the Cañizares episode there is a striking concentration of the imagery of dismemberment and violence which

---

[36] "Y como acontece en la naturaleza y en las mudanças de la noche y del día, que, como dize David en el psalmo 'En viniendo la noche salen de sus moradas las fieras, y esforçadas y guiadas por las tinieblas, discurren por los campos y dan estrago a su voluntad en ellos, mas luego que amanece el día y que apunta la luz, essas mismas se recogen y encuevan; assí el desenfrenamiento fiero del cuerpo y la rebeldía alborotadora de sus movimientos, que cuando estava en la noche de su miseria la voluntad nuestra cayda, discurrían con libertad y lo metían todo a sangre y a fuego, en començando a luzir el rayo del buen amor y en mostrándose el día del bien, buelve luego el pie atrás y se asconde en su cueva, y dexa que lo que es hombre en nosotros salga a luz y haga su officio sossegada y pacíficamente y de sol a sol" (*De los nombres de Cristo*, 2:184-85). The demeaning comparison of man and animals, as well as the connection of sin and the beast, is common in the picaresque novel. See, for example, Guzmán de Alfarache's "Terrible animal son veinte años . . . Es bestia por domar. Trae consigo furor y poco sufrimiento" (3:251-52). And following a scathing critique of the dominance of illusion in society and a satirical review of numerous professions, each engaged in the predatory struggle which pulsates beneath the seemingly smooth surface of society, Guzmán concludes: "Todo anda revuelto, todo apriesa, todo marañado. No hallarás hombre con hombre; todos vivimos en asechanza los unos de los otros, como el gato para el ratón, o la araña para la culebra, que hallándola descuidada, se deja colgar de un hilo y, asiéndola de la cerviz, la aprieta fuertemente, no apartándose della hasta que con su ponzoña la mata" (2:54). For the dehumanizing effects of animal imagery in *Lazarillo de Tormes*, see A. Deyermond, *"Lazarillo de Tormes": A Critical Guide* (London, 1975), pp. 68-70.

runs through the entire work, from the initial descriptions of the ravages of syphilis and the carnage of the slaughterhouse to Berganza's concluding confession of his desire to rip to pieces the lap dog which epitomizes parasitic favorites. In the central scene we are told of the slaughter of children and the use of their blood for ointments. We learn of the branding of Cañizares by the harsh judge, and witness the probing of her body with sharp pins, pushed in "from the point all the way to the head,"[37] Berganza's savage tearing of the stomach of the screaming witch, and the drubbing of the well-intentioned dog by the mob which swiftly forms amid the lightening shadows of dawn and characteristically lends its support to the evil antagonist to drive . away the hapless hero.

From the opening paragraph, in which we observe a young man, his face ravaged nearly beyond recognition, stumbling forth from a hospital, to the final pages, which describe Berganza's frustrated attempt to talk with the *corregidor* concerning the rampancy of syphilis and the need for social reforms, imagery of physical infirmity, disease, decrepitude, filthiness, and death dominates the imaginative world of the *Coloquio de los perros*. In the Cañizares episode it moves into the foreground of the narrative most powerfully in the gruesome details of the naked body which Berganza must contemplate through the night—the decayed teeth, the crossed eyes, the emaciated cheeks, the disheveled hair, the scrawny throat, the flabby breasts, and the foul-smelling mouth—all of which fill him with so much disgust that he cannot bear to bite her. Cañizares is literally a mountain of decrepitude, moving about in her hospital among the dying, drawing her life from the remains of the dead, whose clothing she delouses, rationalizing her failure to do good works by enumerating all the ailments of old age that afflict her, clinging desperately to the pleasures that her withering flesh is still capable of enjoying, and in moments of despondency suffering in the awareness that her life is ebbing away.

The imagery of physical infirmity and disease is, of course, prominent in Christian depictions of sin, its contagious power, and its consequences, from the Bible on down to the sermons, manuals of piety, guides for sinners, and religious fictions of Cervantes' time. For example, Erasmus describes the "sickness of the soul" as analogous to the state of bodily infirmity in which "the knees and legs are buckling, unsteady, and bent, and the other limbs are so weak, feeble,

---

[37] "desde la punta hasta la cabeza . . . se sintió acribada de los alfileres, y mordida de los carcañares, y magullada del arrastramiento" (pp. 306-307).

and heavy that you can scarcely drag them along or even move them,"[38] a state very similar to that of the Ensign as the story begins. Employing an image which might remind us of Berganza's recoiling from the mouth of Cañizares as she seeks a kiss, he emphasizes the contagious powers of evil by likening it to the foul odor that emerges from the breast of a person sick with sin. In discussing the miraculous power of grace to enter the sinner and to dispose his rebellious will to pursue the good in freedom from all compulsion and fear, Fray Luis de León refers to "this efficacious medicine of grace" which cures the "person who is sick and in poor health" and heals the "malicia del mal" of the justified.[39] Fray Luis de Granada follows a powerful denunciation of the sinfulness which besets the various ages of man— the child, who is "a brute animal in the shape of a human being," the youth, who is "a wild and unbridled horse," and the old man, "a sack of ailments and pains"—with the conclusion: "And so men wander around like the sick patient, who does nothing but toss about from one part of his bed to another, believing that with these changes of place he will find more peace than before, but he fails to find any; for the cause of his restlessness lies within himself, and it is his illness."[40] Cervantes' presentation of the ailing old woman as suffering from the spiritual disease described in Christian anatomies of the soul brings the power of a deep tradition not only to the central incident but also to the numerous other scenes of the work that introduce disease motifs (see below).

Finally, I would point to the concentration of imagery of disorientation surrounding the figure of Cañizares. At the opening of each part of the story we abruptly discover that we are in a world in which things seem to have been violently wrenched out of their normal functions, contexts, and relationships: the sword of a warrior has been transformed into the staff of a convalescent; a man has been perspiring profusely although the weather is not hot; a standard-bearer of the Spanish army in Flanders is mysteriously seen stumbling along the streets of Valladolid; and two dogs have suddenly received the power

---

[38] *El Enquiridion*, p. 121. "The first step is to put away evil. The physician first bleeds the body so that wholesome fluids can be let in. Then the sinner should discharge the evil desires that God despises: lust, arrogance, avarice" (*De Immensa Misericordia Dei, The Essential Erasmus*, p. 268).

[39] *De los nombres de Cristo*, 2:175-76.

[40] "Y así andan los hombres como el enfermo, que no hace sino dar vuelcos en la cama a una parte y a otra, creyendo que con estas mudanzas hallará mas descanso del que tenía, y no lo halla; porque dentro de sí tiene la causa de su desasosiego, que es la dolencia" (*De la oración y consideración*, p. 32).

to reason and speak. Moreover, as if Cervantes wished to draw our attention to the dislocation of ordinary experience in such events and their implications, he follows them immediately with the reaction of a character expressing wonder and emphasizing that an inversion of the natural order of things has occurred. The licenciate greets his comrade with disbelief, claiming that he should be in Flanders "trailing a pike there instead of dragging a sword here," and the dogs agree that a miracle has occurred because their ability to speak rationally violates the laws of nature and overturns the universal hierarchy, in which "the difference between the brute beast and man is that man is a rational animal and the beast irrational."[41] These scenes introduce a relentless vision of derangement, in which we continually confront situations that conflict with our expectations and assumptions concerning the customary design in nature, society, and the universe. Heavenly bodies desert their orderly courses to become meteors; ministers of justice reward the guilty and condemn the innocent; constables assist criminals in their rapacious acts; marriage brings two people together to prey on each other; soldiers act as if their kings were the enemy; society adores the deceitful and persecutes the honest. In the blasted world of the witches we reach an order of total inversion and the source of the anarchy detailed throughout the rest of the work. Here we encounter forces capable of darkening the sun in the middle of the day and of unleashing at will the most destructive powers of nature. Here human beings procreate and beget animals, roses bloom in December, and wheat is harvested normally in January. The workers in a hospital draw sustenance from the death of the people they are to cure, and language serves as an instrument of concealment rather than communication. The bier of a corpse is viewed as a bridal bed bedecked with flowers, good works are defined as the destruction of a vineyard and the murder of innocent children, and the eulogy of a deceased mother is perceived by her surviving son as "knife thrusts into his heart." Cervantes embodies all this chaos in the monstrous denizen of this world, Cañizares, who worships the devil and pursues destructiveness as if it were a virtue. Like her master, who speaks "with distorted phrases" ("con razones torcidas"), and her literary ancestors of the world of La Celestina, she is capable of generating striking effects of derangement in her peculiar way of

[41] "Le hacía en Flandes, antes terciando allá la pica que arrastrando aquí la espada . . . que la diferencia que hay del animal bruto al hombre es ser el hombre animal racional, y el bruto, irracional" (pp. 176-77, 210).

wrenching proverbial utterances out of their normal contexts.[42] But
the central dislocation of this topsy-turvy world is revealed within the
spirit of Cañizares, and, although the shape by which Cervantes manifests it is extravagant and grotesque, it is nonetheless the inversion
that Christians traditionally find in every sinner. The body has enslaved the will, the will pursues as natural what habit has sanctioned,
and memory and understanding have been displaced from their positions of authority in the soul. Cañizares' knowledge of theology and
the pathology of her spiritual condition, coupled with her incapacity
to act on the counsel of her understanding, renders her inner derangement all the more unnatural and provokes the climactic outburst of
questions in Berganza's meditation, which in their antithetical formulations recall the queries of the licentiate and the dogs at the beginnings of the two parts and their amazement on beholding such
consequences of the powers of lawlessness (e.g., "How does she know
so much about God and speak of him so often while her works are
those of the devil?"). His questions, which we as readers share, are
the most important of a series of unanswered questions hovering enigmatically in the thickening atmosphere of the tale and intensifying
the mystery that is only partially resolved at its conclusion. Just as
the plot unravels about its central void, the probing queries of the
meditator are suspended and lead to silence.

CAÑIZARES' SLEEP AND THE TRAVESTY
OF THE SACRED

If the description of the naked Cañizares in the dark, narrow chamber is the most important elaboration of the central imagery of the
tomb and death and reveals quite explicitly the themes embodied in
it, the scene is at the same time the climax in the development of
another closely related body of imagery—that of sleep, night, and
awakening. This is undoubtedly the most complex image pattern in
the work, and the particular effects of derangement which Cervantes
achieves in its articulation require special consideration. Again it is
necessary to emphasize the archetypal character of these elements within
Christian tradition.

I would point to two fundamental symbolic associations of sleep,

---

[42] See, for example, her application of "el deleite mucho mejor es imaginado que
gozado" to the question as to whether the pleasures of her encounter with the devil
are imaginary or real (pp. 303-304).

both of which Cervantes exploits at the climactic moments of the *Colloquy of the Dogs*. On the one hand sleep is imaginatively equated with death and sinfulness. The notion appears repeatedly in the New Testament, where the awakening to the light of day is invoked to express most vividly the process of the redemption and rebirth of the new man through Christ's grace: "Awake, O sleeper, and arise from the dead, / and Christ shall give you light" (Eph. 5:14); "Besides this you know what hour it is, how it is full time now for you to wake from sleep. For salvation is nearer to us now than when we first believed; the night is far gone, the day is at hand. Let us then cast off the works of darkness and put on the armor of light" (Rom. 13:11-14); "For since we believe that Jesus died and rose again, even so, through Jesus, God will bring with him those who have fallen asleep" (1 Thess. 4:14).[43] Now, precisely because sleep is the prelude to awakening to new life, it is also viewed traditionally as a restorative force which renders the soul open to the infusion of divine grace and capable of undergoing the mysterious healing metamorphosis of redemption and conversion. It is a darkness that nourishes the "eyes of the soul" with a light that clarifies the deepest mysteries of existence, even as it blinds the "eyes of the body," riveted as they are on the things of this world.[44] And it is, of course, the time when God can reward the sleeper with the higher vision, even if his dream, like that of Cervantes' Ensign, is a torment of purgation. As Elihu tells Job, "For God speaks in one way, / and in two, though man does not perceive it. / In a dream, in a vision of the night, / when deep sleep falls upon men, / while they slumber on their beds, / then he opens the ears of men, / and terrifies them with warnings" (Job 33:14-16). Thus Augustine interprets Adam's sleep as the sleep of illumination,[45] and in the *Confessions*, a work that had a significant impact on the religious culture of Cervantes' age and the major literary modes by which it gave expression to the Christian mysteries of sin and redemption—the picaresque novel and religious drama—he describes his own difficulties in arising from the sleep of death and sinfulness.

[43] Compare Mateo Alemán's *Libro de San Antonio de Padua* (Tortosa, 1622), p. 341: "Hombres que vivis muriendo en quanto durmieredes aqueste sueño temporal . . . [Paul said] levantate hombre dormido, levantate de con los muertos, y darate Christo su luz, con que camines a el antes que anochezca."

[44] As Augustine describes the experience of conversion in Calderón's *El sacro Parnaso*, "me ilumina / hoy un rayo bello, / que hace vea más / cuando estoy más ciego" (ed. A. Valbuena Prat, *Obras completas* [Madrid, 1967], 3:787.

[45] *De Genesi ad Litteram* 9, 36; *Patrologia Latina* 34, 408; for the importance of sleep in the visionary experience in Christian tradition, see M. A. Lücker, *Meister Eckhart und die Devotio Moderna* (Leiden, 1950), pp. 26-27.

The passage resembles Cañizares' analysis of her own *acedia*, the spiritual sickness that poisons her soul, and, as it is important to see that Cervantes' witch, for all the sensationalism and grotesque effects that she brings to the work, is a vehicle for the introduction of profound and venerable theological concerns, it is worth looking at Augustine's words.

Thus by the burdens of this world I was sweetly weighed down, *just as man often is in sleep*. Thoughts wherein I meditated upon you were like the efforts of *those who want to arouse themselves but, still overcome by deep drowsiness, sink back again*. . . . I had no answer to give to you when you said to me, "Rise, you who sleep, and arise from the dead, and Christ will enlighten you." . . . In vain was I delighted with your law according to the inward man, when *another law in my members fought against the law of my mind, and led me captive in the law of sin which was in my members*. *For the law of sin is force of habit, whereby the mind is dragged along and held fast, even against its will but still deservedly so*, since it was by its will that it had slipped into the habit. *Unhappy man that I was!* Who would deliver me from the body of this death, unless your grace through Jesus Christ our Lord?[46]

As she prepares for her sleep, Cañizares confesses to Berganza how habit has made sin second nature to her, how the pleasures of the flesh have so dulled her soul that it has lost its faith and forgotten its Christian identity and God's laws, and how she strangely can understand what has happened to her but nevertheless do nothing to remedy her plight, since her will, hopelessly enslaved by her appetite, refuses to respond to her understanding.[47] She too is tormented by the tra-

---

[46] *The Confessions of St. Augustine*, trans. J. K. Ryan (Garden City, New York, 1960), pp. 189-90. Italics added.

[47] ". . . la costumbre del vicio se vuelve en naturaleza, y éste de ser brujas se convierte en sangre y carne, y en medio de su ardor, que es mucho, trae un frío que pone en el alma, tal, que la resfría y entorpece aun en la Fe, de donde nace un olvido de sí misma, y ni se acuerda de los temores con que Dios la amenaza, ni de la gloria con que la convida . . . y así, quedando el alma inútil, floja y desmazalada, no puede levantar la consideración siquiera a tener algún buen pensamiento" (p. 301). The seriousness and the unequivocal character of the doctrinal pronouncements of Cervantes' witch stand out sharply when we compare her to her greatest literary ancestor, La Celestina. The latter's invocation of theology is uniformly perverse and iconoclastic. For example, she introduces the doctrine of providential evil to endow with dignity Claudina's public exposure as a criminal; she finds the traditional conception of habit nourishing sin ("pero del pecado lo peor es la perseverancia") defined and exemplified by Claudina's admirable determination to win honor for her professional excellence as a witch; and she invokes the pious commonplace of Christian theodicy, "cuando el alto Dios da la llaga tras ella envía el remedio," to describe the "remedy" which she proposes for Melibea's uncontrollable passion (Fernando de Rojas, *La Celestina*, ed. D. S. Severin [Madrid, 1969], pp. 124, 159). La Celestina, whose recur-

ditional *tristitia vitae*, the unhappiness of the sinner who despairs in his ineffectual efforts to extricate himself from the "manacles on his will" and to rise from the "profound abyss of misery" into which he has sunk and who fails completely to understand the mysteries of God's mercy and the hope that it provides. "Let death come and take me from this weary life . . . thus my thoughts are bound always to be evil, and yet I know that God is good and merciful and that He knows what is in store for me; so that is enough, and let us drop this conversation, for it truly saddens me."[48]

It makes little difference for our purposes whether or not Cervantes read St. Augustine's *Confessions*; for these essential Christian ideas and symbolic images and motifs were undoubtedly mediated to him through sermons, devotional works, and popular fiction, notably the picaresque novel and the best seller of the age, *Guzmán de Alfarache*.[49] From the very origins of the genre, the death and resurrection, the sleep and awakening of Lazarus can frequently be glimpsed in the backgrounds of the picaresque narratives. The myth was a favorite of religious writers of the time, as it had been since the earliest eras of Christianity, for the symbolic representation of the mystery of sinfulness and

---

rent motto is, "¡O buena fortuna, cómo ayudas a los osados!' (p. 102) is anything but a victim of *acedia* or "debilitating sinfulness," and the parody of religious motifs which pervades her discourse is intimately connected with her celebration of an abundant nature, instinctual vitality, and the creative aspect of the elemental bodily life of humanity in its energies for renewal and growth (see pp. 65, 101, 150). Like Sancho Panza (see above) she belongs in part to the traditional family of carnivalesque figures, to which Renaissance literature, in its response to the increasing orientation of society toward the claims of the secular world, was particularly hospitable. Despite her demonism and depravity, Celestina remains a powerfully ambivalent figure, and the metamorphosis which she undergoes in *El coloquio* was for Cervantes undoubtedly a "rewriting" which "encubre más lo humano," even as it was a reinterpretation of the witch that was perfectly compatible with the most ascetic tendencies of the theological climate of his time. For all the imaginative power of the moralized witch and her epiphany of evil, Cervantes' Cañizares is a figure of reduced dimensions when considered beside her illustrious predecessor, and Cervantes' deletion of "lo humano" of the witch is just as devastating as Calderón's rigid moralization of the other great ambivalent spokesman for the body in sixteenth-century European literature—the fool (see above).

[48] "Venga la muerte y lléveme desta cansada vida . . . así, que siempre mis pensamientos han de ser malos, con todo esto, sé que Dios es bueno y misericordioso, y que El sabe lo que ha de ser de mí, y basta; y quédese aquí esta plática, que verdaderamente me entristece" (pp. 289, 303).

[49] F. Rico has recently emphasized the general impact of St. Augustine's doctrines and writings on Alemán's picaresque novel and suggested that a close study of texts might reveal that the nature of the former's influence was far more concrete than is commonly supposed (*La novela picaresca y el punto de vista* [Barcelona, 1970], p. 77).

redemption and the powers of grace and God's mercy. There were few contemporary discussions of sinfulness that failed to introduce the tomb, the sleep, the sickness, the stink, the voice of Christ, the cure, and the awakening. "Lazarus, however, was already rotting in the tomb. . . . It was not difficult for the Lord to raise up one who had been dead for four days. It is a more difficult matter to raise up someone who has lived in sin all his life and has become rotten as well. . . . Every day He calls, 'Maiden arise!' 'Young man, arise!' 'Lazarus, come forth!' But there are many who are more than dead, who do not hear Him when he calls them back to life."[50] Fray Luis de Granada writes that the call of grace has the power to awaken the most hardened sinner, to transform him into a new Lazarus, and to summon him forth from the "tomb of his wickedness."[51] The concluding scene of Juan de Luna's somber picaresque novel, *La segunda parte de la vida de Lazarillo de Tormes*, depicts the protagonist in a state of utter misery but presumably on his way toward conversion, huddled in a church and covered by a mantle which the priest has taken from a sepulcher.[52] In the sprawling panorama of disorder and vice of Alemán's novel, the confessor refers to the necessity of opening the "eyes of the understanding" and awakening from the sleep of sinfulness ("if with all of this I would not awaken from the sleep of my sins"), and at the moment of his conversion, in the darkness and stillness of the night aboard the galley, he ponders his sinfulness and God's grace, exhorts himself to "wake up from his sleep," sheds tears of contrition, falls asleep, and awakens to a new identity and a new life: "I fell asleep, and, when I awakened I found myself another man, no longer I and no longer the person with that old heart of before."[53]

[50] Erasmus, *De Immensa Misericordia Dei, The Essential Erasmus*, p. 254; see also *Enquiridion*, pp. 122-23.

[51] "Otro beneficio fué . . . llamarte con tan poderosa voz, que con ella resuscitases de muerte a vida, y salieses como otro Lázaro del sepulcro tenebroso de tus maldades, no ya atado de pies y manos, sino suelto y libre de las prisiones del enemigo" (*De la oración y consideración*, p. 62). See also *Guía de pecadores*, where Granada recalls Augustine's interpretation of the four-day sleep of Lazarus as four stages through which the sinner passes as he becomes habituated in vice (ed. M. Martínez Burgos [Madrid, 1966], p. 78). An interesting summary of the doctrinal concerns connected with the Lazarus myth and the associations which it possessed in the culture of the sixteenth century can be found in a sermon by Juan de Avila which is based entirely on it— "Llora Jesucristo tu Alma, llora también tú" (*Obras completas*, ed. L. Sala Balust [Madrid, 1953], 2:246ff.).

[52] Ed. E. R. Sims (Austin, 1928), p. 91.

[53] "si con esto no recordare del sueño de los vicios . . . recordar de aquese sueño . . . me quedé dormido y, cuando recordé, halléme otro, no yo ni con aquel corazón viejo que antes" (*Guzmán de Alfarache*, 4:79, 5:153). The importance of sleep and

If St. Augustine's struggles with the sleep of sinfulness lead him to an awakening to the new life and if his spiritual descendants in the picaresque novel are occasionally rewarded with the same experience, it must be noted that there are also unregenerate sleepers who discover no way out of the nightmare. Writers fascinated with their spiritual malaise did not shrink from evoking the promise of Augustine's and Lazarus' destinies in order to underscore their failures. Following her confession, Cañizares sinks into her sleep, a sleep of orgiastic communion with the devil in which we witness a hideous climax to all the scenes of carnal indulgence and bestiality, banqueting and sexuality, running through the *Colloquy* ("there he gives us dull, saltless food, and there certain things take place which . . . are filthy and indecent").[54] For her there is no release from the manacles of sin, and her awakening in rage and violence is a demonic parody of the awakening to new life which traditionally rewards the redeemed Christian and which in the tale rewards the Ensign following his night of expiation and, by implication, his double, the reader, who imaginatively shares his slumbers. Similarly her "ointments" ("unturas"), which enable her to sink into that sleep and make rapturous contact with her devil-goat, represent a grotesque inversion of the divine grace which inspires the visionary sleeper and enables the redeemed Christian to "turn the wheel of good works."[55]

---

awakening in the iconography of conversion can be readily seen in the *Quixote*, both in the final chapter, in which "Don Quijote durmió de un tirón, como dicen, más de seis horas" and awoke a new man ("ya yo no soy don Quijote") and in Sancho Panza's acquisition of self-knowledge and his determination to return to his "antigua libertad." He is "resuscitated" from his "muerte presente" and seeks his "antigua libertad." In the latter case Cervantes employs the venerable motifs with their aura of religious solemnity to dignify what is an entirely secular experience.

[54] "Allí nos da de comer desabridamente, y pasan otras cosas . . . sucias y asquerosas" (pp. 295-96).

[55] Describing the redemptive power of grace, Fray Luis de Granada observes: "cura nuestros males, sana nuestras heridas, alumbra nuestro entendimiento, inflama nuestra voluntad . . . de tal manera que las que antes estaban como atadas e inhábiles para bien obrar, con esto se hacen hábiles y lijeras para todo bien. Por donde con mucha razon comparan los teólogos estas virtudes y hábitos celestiales a la uncion con que se untan los ejes donde van las ruedas de un carro, porque así como estas se mueven muy lijeramente cuando el eje va untado y bañado en aceite, así las potencias de nuestra ánima se mueven muy suavemente a todas las obras virtuosas, cuando están desta manera ungidas con la unción y olio del Espíritu Sancto" (*Memorial de la vida cristiana, Obras*, B.A.E., 8:289). See M. Molho's fine observations on the satanic inversions marking Cañizares' world: the "Hospital of God" is metamorphosed into the "Hospital of the Devil," and the "theological virtues" proclaimed are "Froidure, Désespérance et Mépris du prochain" ("Remarques sur le *Mariage trompeur et Colloque des chiens*," pp. 66-67).

In the description of Cañizares' sleep Cervantes is, then, releasing in his text the powerful negative energies of a travesty of the sacred. He is employing a basic technique for the full orchestration of horror which had emerged as a convention in Spain's literature of disorder of the previous century and which his contemporary, Francisco de Quevedo, was developing for unprecedented effects in narrative. We have briefly noted Cervantes' mastery of this technique in his elaborate parody of the plot of romance, in the unraveling of the clearly anticipated climactic anagnorisis of the *Colloquy* and the sounding of the Magnificat as a grotesque accompaniment of the supreme moment of disintegration. To amplify on some of my observations in Chapter I, the basis of this method of travesty is the association of the act or speech of a character which arouses disgust and moral outrage with something that is sacred or valued. The valued model may, of course, be anything which the writer's audience esteems—sacred myths, legends, rituals and texts, historical and religious figures, venerated actions and gestures, moral doctrines, lofty institutions, or literary conventions. Through the process of association the action described becomes an incongruous incarnation of what is sacred, and its impact is all the more disturbing as it defiles its model and activates about itself in the text the destructive energy always generated by the violation of taboos.[56] The procedure is undoubtedly as old as literature itself, and the medieval Christian literature of sinfulness certainly developed a rich tradition of disorderly imaginary worlds which exploit the vocabulary and the power of profanation. For example, in a dramatic work which Paul Lehmann discusses as illustrative of the typical methods, effects, and didactic purposes of the medieval parody that utilizes profanation of religious motifs, a "gamblers' mass," written and pre-

---

[56] In the wide-ranging panorama of violated sacred models in *La Celestina*, the work that set the tone for the literature of disorder which flourished in Spain during the following two centuries, we observe how an author can find in the valences of words and images which are less exclusively determined by the sanctions of cultural and literary codes the potential for such destructive energy. Suspecting that Melibea's invitation to Calisto is in reality a trap, Pármeno describes the maiden in a simile that violently wrenches language out of its customary experiential, as well as literary and cultural, context: "Así como corderica mansa que mama su madre y la ajena, ella con su segurar tomará la venganza de Calisto" (p. 166). A text may, in fact, incorporate a key to its grammar of profanation, as in Tello's discussion of the perverted idiom of the criminal world of *El rufián dichoso* (see above) or Rinconete's scorn for the language of Monipodio's "bendita comunidad" (*Rinconete y Cortadillo*, p. 216). Pármeno's ejaculation in the face of Calisto's religious associations of his idolatrous love is similar: "¡Desvariar, Calisto, desvariar! Por fe tengo, hermano, que no es cristiano. Lo que la vieja traidora con sus pestíferos hechizos ha rodeado y hecho, dice que los santos de Dios se lo han concedido e impetrado" (*La Celestina*, p. 175).

sumably produced by the monk, Gottschalk Hollen, the church in which the "holy rite" is enacted is an inn, the attending cardinals are devils dealing at the gaming tables, the priest is the innkeeper, and the chalice and the paten are goblets brimming with wine and the wagered coins. The mass begins with the Introit—the solemn entry of the "priest," accompanied by an anthem exhorting the faithful to gamble. The responsories and the Kyrie which follow are arguments over who has the first play, and the doxology and "Dominus vobiscum" are blasphemies and curses. The Epistle begins with the address to the congregation by the devil Titivillis, "apostolus princeps tenebrarum," who urges his flock: "Brothers, now be drunk!" and the Gospel is a lament over gaming losses. The response which it receives ("proficiat tibi") might remind us of the burlesque of traditional consolatory doctrines which we discover in such descendants of these devils as Celestina, in her reminiscences of Claudina's suffering, and don Pablos, in his reaction to the news of the mutilation and scattering of his father's corpse (see above).[57]

The technique which we observe in this simple work was developed effectively in Spain's most complex and powerful poetic vision of disorder, La Celestina. Its diabolical protagonist, always a master of the devil's art of perverting sacred scripture, cites the Beatitudes to assure a young man that his grandmother, although a witch, is in heaven, counts maidenheads in need of restoration on the beads of her rosary, receives the homage of the holy pilgrimage, and, in her processional apparition in church, displaces onto herself the divine adoration of the congregation and, when looking back on the scene, describes her infernal purposes in language that evokes the beautiful maiden of popular ballads, "la dama de Aragón," whose wonder-working chastity recalls the quasi-divine heroines of Greek romance.[58] In Lazarillo de Tormes the procedure becomes central to the entire work. The impact of its irreverent reconstruction of the religious confession, where all converges on the significant moment of illumination which endows the modern Lazarus' life with meaning, springs in part from its elaborately developed imagery of the tomb and death in life and its ironic resonances of the true Lazarus' awakening from the grave.[59] In fact, a

[57] Lehmann, Die Parodie im Mittelalter, pp. 14-15.

[58] For the effects and implications of Celestina's Biblical parody, see S. Gilman, "Matthew V:10 in Castilian Jest and Earnest," Studia Hispanica in Honorem R. Lapesa (Madrid, 1972), 1:257-65. For the irreverent treatment of traditional elevating literary models in the work, see A. Castro, "La Celestina" como contienda literaria (Madrid, 1965), esp. pp. 66, 95.

[59] See H. R. Jauss, "Ursprung und Bedeutung der Ich-Form im Lazarillo de Tormes,"

seemingly unlimited variety of valued models emerges in the background of the antihero's confession and adventures—the Beatitudes and the Biblical myth of the beggar Lazarus' heavenly reward, the Augustinian confession and the *via illuminativa*, so prominent in spiritual writings of sixteenth-century Spain, the sacraments, the birth and education of the hero of romance and folk tale, the humanist epistle, the ancient "case of fortune," the *Homo Novus*, the self-made man celebrated in numerous humanist writings, and the heroes and grand events of recent Spanish history. Through comic contrast they emphasize his spiritual depravity, and, as he constantly violates their sanctity through inadequate representation, they endow his "ascent" with the aura of triumphant negation which is traditionally associated with the most absolute form of evil.[60] *Lazarillo de Tormes* bequeathed

---

Romanistisches Jahrbuch 8 (1957):290-311. The basic thesis of this controversial genre study—the intimate connection between traditional confessional literature and the origins of the picaresque novel—has not been addressed by its various critics. Its validity is in fact strengthened by the recognition of the ironic evocations of the Lazarus myth in the text of the *Lazarillo*. The perverted confession records and celebrates a perverted resurrection. For critics' recent consideration of the importance of Lazarus of Bethany in the structure and imaginative atmosphere of the work, see Deyermond, *"Lazarillo de Tormes": A Critical Guide*, pp. 29-32.

[60] For the presence of these various valued models in the imaginative world of the *Lazarillo*, see the following: S. Gilman, "Mathew V:10 in Castilian Jest and Earnest" and "The Death of *Lazarillo de Tormes*," *PMLA* 81 (1966):149-66; B. W. Wardropper, "El trastorno de la moral en el *Lazarillo*," *Nueva Revista de Filología Hispánica* 15 (1961):441-47 and "The Strange Case of Lázaro Gonzales Pérez," *Modern Language Notes* 92 (1977):202-12; A. Deyermond, *"Lazarillo de Tormes": A Critical Guide*; M. J. Asensio, "La intención religiosa del *Lazarillo de Tormes* y Juan de Valdés," *Hispanic Review* 27 (1959):78-102; F. Lázaro Carreter, *"Lazarillo de Tormes en la picaresca"*; F. Rico, *La novela picaresca y el punto de vista*, pp. 15-55; R. W. Truman, "Lázaro de Tormes and the 'Homo Novus' Tradition," *Modern Language Review* 64 (1969):62-67; C. Guillen, "Introduction" to his edition of *Lazarillo de Tormes* (New York, 1966). Quite apart from the difficulties involved in determining what specific forms of disorder in his society a writer wishes to connect with his consistent debasement of his protagonist (e.g., for Asensio, the utterances of Lazarillo's "disfigured religious consciousness" point to the external, ceremonial character of traditional religious experience which contemporary Erasmists and *alumbrados* found so offensive; for Gilman, they point to the flood of pious commonplaces facilely invoked by contemporary Spaniards to rationalize and conceal its flight from a confrontation with some very disturbing social realities), the general implications of the willingness of a particular author or a particular audience to introduce a sacred or official sign in a context of profanation, frequently comic in tone, can certainly be very complex, and they can be of great interest to social and cultural historians, particularly if they are seeking undercurrents of crisis, skepticism, and dissatisfaction hidden behind the canonized forms of cultural expression (see W. Karrer's discussion of Hegel's and Marx's views of parody in relation to historical change and periods of transition, *Parodie, Travestie, Pastiche*, pp. 102-105). A. Castro and S. Gilman have recently examined contexts of

this narrative technique to the picaresque novel, and we observe Mateo Alemán employing it effectively in his description of the beggar society in Rome, whose elaborate ordinances and activities institutionalizing the exploitation of Christian charity travesty the organization of religious orders and inspire in the narrator one of the most startling

---

this type in *La Celestina* and *Lazarillo de Tormes* and argued that such combinations, while reducing the stature of the evil character responsible for the profanation, strike out at the conventional hierarchy of values dominating an illusion-ridden society and implicitly present in the valued models with which the characters are so incongruously associated. As Gilman has suggested, Celestina's ironical reference to Claudina's salvation might imply the "sarcasm of a skeptical 'converso'" concerning the existence of an afterlife, and Lazarillo's frequent allusions to the role of God in his ascent might suggest that "if God is to blame for such wretchedness and for such a 'buen puerto,' He Himself is the real 'pícaro' of the story." Castro goes even further in his interpretation of the destructive energies released in *La Celestina*'s parodistic engagement with valued literary models. The work is an "enorme axiomachía," a spectacular conflagration, in which traditional values and their literary manifestations function as "llama consuntiva." It is the reflection of a society in crisis, afflicted with social tensions, suspicions, cynicism, and moral chaos, and nothing is spared amid its grandiose ruins except a purged literary order from which the modern novel, with its problematic stance toward values and individual experience, can spring up (see *"La Celestina" como contienda literaria*). The hypothetical character of such conclusions brings us face to face with the enormous difficulties of interpretation raised by this technique, which is fundamentally irreverent and ironic and which, to recall Freud's observations on parody and travesty, is based on the "Herabsetzung des Erhabenen" (for Freud's views, as well as a consideration of the problems standing in the way of a reliable critical method of dealing with the phenomenon of parody reception, see W. Karrer, *Parodie, Travestie, Pastiche*, pp. 165ff.). It can in fact rarely be asserted that the destructive energy released by such a combination moves in a single direction. Thus a ridiculous incarnation of something sacred might render itself all the more ridiculous by contrast, but the sacred object will generally remain tarnished, if ever so faintly, by the association. P. Lehmann is probably right in his fundamental thesis that medieval parody generally points unequivocally toward the object deforming the ideal rather than toward the questionable value of the ideal and in his admonition that we must recognize that the "medieval man" could enjoy the humor of profanation without experiencing a threat to his beliefs. Moreover, if we are to avoid allowing our own values and anxieties to dominate our interpretations of iconoclastic elements in texts of other ages, it is well to bear in mind Yunck's distinction between conservative, "exemplary" parody and critical, "stylistic" parody (see above) and Freud's psychological theories concerning the way in which parody can provide a civilizing release from necessary restraints and inhibitions. An interesting observation by Bartholomé de Villalba y Estaña suggests that there were Spaniards who saw nothing sinister or seriously troubling in the irreverences of *Lazarillo de Tormes* and in fact found in them a source of immense amusement even as they distanced themselves morally from the deranged sensibility which produced them: "Tanbien dizen que queda muy azeda /la vida del que tanto hacia reir, / que es del muy sacro Tormes Lazarico, / que le han dejado necio, corto y chico" (*El pelegrino curioso y grandezas de España* [1577], ed. La Sociedad de Bibliófilos Españoles [Madrid, 1889], pp. 56-57).

of the various utterances of his unregenerate persona—his mock encomium celebrating the freedoms of the begging life.[61] In Quevedo's
Buscón and Juan de Luna's *La segunda parte de la vida de Lazarillo de
Tormes*, the grotesque mixture of the profane and the sacred pervades
the entire narrative and infuses it with a tone of savage negation. The
former associates the cannibalism of the remains of the picaro's father
with the ingestion of the divine body in the Holy Sacrament, and the
latter reaches a climax in a demonic marriage rite, in which the Mass,

---

However, probably in every society and every reading public, including those of the
Middle Ages, there have been, on the one hand, a share of zealots who react with
anxiety and defensiveness to any irreverent manipulation of their sacred vocabulary,
even though the total context of the pronouncement that they confront makes it clear
that the manipulation presupposes the inviolability of that vocabulary, and, on the
other hand, a share of iconoclastics and skeptics who seize any element of a text which
can be construed as irreverent and willfully read the whole utterance as irreverent,
failing to concern themselves with other elements in the context that may condition
the "subversive" passage. The inquisitors who censored Lazarillo's repetition of a
commonplace joke with irreverent implications concerning the Inquisition and the
Bible and the "critics" of the *Tribunal de la justa venganza*, which denounced Quevedo
as a minister of Satan for presenting in the *Buscón* a protagonist who, violating the
sacred rules of the Council of Trent prohibiting jests with Holy Scripture, compares
himself to the Holy Sacrament and *Ecce Homo* (see *Obras en verso*, ed. Astrana Marín
[Madrid, 1943], p. 1106) represent such readers, and, while they are responding to
an ambiguity and a power which are really in the text, we must recognize that their
response is highly selective, and in its failure to account for the total effect of the
text, fundamentally uncritical. In writings employing such profanations it is always
useful to ask to what extent the incarnation of the sacred is blackened morally by
other elements within the work. When Quevedo's Pablos and his partners conclude
a feast blasphemously associated with Holy Communion by committing mass murder,
there seems little validity in the interpretation of the profanation as striking out at
the belief in the sanctity of Holy Communion; the same would apply to Lazarillo's
hungry adoration of the offertory bread, the "cara de Dios" (see R. M. Price, "On
Religious Parody in the *Buscón*," *Modern Language Notes* 86 [1971]:273-79).

[61] *Guzmán de Alfarache*, 2:203-13. One can see in Guzmán's declamation, even
more clearly than in Lazarillo de Tormes' self-exaltation, the debt of the picaresque
novel to the rhetorical paradox, which the humanists of the early sixteenth century
developed as one of their most effective forms of philosophical and satirical inquiry.
However, what is striking in its incorporation in picaresque literature is the way it
chooses the demonic as the object of its festive eulogy of the unpraiseworthy and, in
so doing, directs its ironic assaults at the most sacred doctrines of its culture. While
it appears to surpass the irreverences of its humanist antecedents, it is far less subversive and far less ambivalent, for the framework of theological and moral values
with which it plays is fundamentally unshakeable. It represents in fact a suppression
of the enlivening instability of the humanist mock encomium, and its transformation
is analogous to that wrought in contemporary literature on two of the great paradoxical spokesmen of the earlier period—the fool and the witch. For Alemán's awareness
of the conventions of the mock encomium, see his *Libro de San Antonio de Padua*, p.
33.

with its Gospel and Epistle, provides an organizing model for its "ceremonies" of sexual humiliation, castration, and blanketing.[62] Both the *Buscón* and *Guzmán de Alfarache* introduce, in scenes that are crucial in the picaro's development, a failed sleep of regeneration which has effects of profanation that are similar to those we observe in Cañizares' demonic sleep and awakening. In one of the most striking of the travesties of sacred models by which Quevedo heightens the abjectness of his protagonist, Pablos is described as a stinking Lazarus in the grave, falling asleep and awakening to a new existence, reborn not to a life of virtue but rather to a life of total depravity.[63] At the beginning of his adventures, Guzmán falls asleep outside the Church of St. Lazarus, awakens to a forgetfulness of death and a condition of continuing sleep, and, the proper hierarchy of reason and appetite overturned in his soul, allows himself to be guided into a life of aimless wandering by his "feet," which have "assumed the function of his head." Guzmán, of course, combines in himself Cañizares, the obstinate sinner, and the Ensign, who, recalling his fall and the mysterious sleep in the Church of San Llorente, laments that he then "had his wits in his heels rather than in his head."[64] Alemán's notorious picaro is both the unregenerate and the regenerate sleeper, and, as I have pointed out above, he eventually does fall into the authentic sleep of Lazarus and awakens a new man.

[62] Cervantes' consciousness of the prominence of this technique in the contemporary literature of disorder is most evident in his humorous concentration of picaresque conventions in *Rinconete y Cortadillo*. We witness a miracle of the Virgin when a cattle thief avoids informing on his associates by collapsing under torture; the narrator details the "monastic" organization of the criminal society and the "buenas obras" of its inhabitants; he promises to write "la vida y milagros" of Rinconete and Monipodio for the "grande consideración" of the reader; and, describing the demonic banquet, he notes: "Los viejos bebieron *sine fine*; los mozos, adunia; las señoras, los quiries" (pp. 191-92). As I have pointed out above, *Rinconete y Cortadillo* incorporates very explicitly a key for the proper interpretation of the corruption of "el buen lenguaje" that distinguishes its criminal underworld (see pp. 159, 216).

[63] See T. E. May, "El sueño de don Pablos," *Atlante* 3 (1955):192-204, and "A Narrative Conceit in 'La Vida del Buscón,' " *Modern Language Review* 64 (1969):327-33; also, A. A. Parker, *Literature and the Delinquent: The Picaresque Novel in Spain and Europe* (Edinburgh, 1967), p. 71.

[64] See *Guzmán de Alfarache*, 1:103-107. The Ensign's particular formulation of the traditional conception of sin's overthrow of the hierarchy within man recalls a description of Rojas' Calisto: "si agora le diesen una lanzada en el calcañar, que saliesen más sesos que de la cabeza" (*La Celestina*, p. 78).

CHAPTER III

The Imaginative Unity
of the *Colloquy*: The Center
and the Parts

AS I POINTED out in my examination of the main plot of the *Coloquio de los perros*, Cervantes, in conceiving his final tale, found his principal generic models in the Menippean satire, which had been widely cultivated and popularized by the humanists of the sixteenth century, and in the picaresque narrative, which in Mateo Alemán's *Guzmán de Alfarache* had recently achieved a success rivaling that of his own *Quixote*. By combining the intellectualizing, analytical methods of the former with the fictionalizing methods of the latter, Cervantes created a work of tremendous variety in subject matter, style, rhythm, and tonality, a work whose aesthetic coherence is impossible to account for in terms of the traditional Aristotelian conception of literary unity which has marked most critical approaches to the short story. To recall the curiously revealing analogy by which Cervantes described his work, there are innumerable tentacles to the octopus, and some are indeed very slimly attached to the venomous central body from which they appear to proliferate. Seizing the traditional prerogative of the satirist, Cervantes wrote his final tale from his own watchtower (*atalaya*), surveying swiftly a vast landscape of disorder beneath him, compelling his reader to follow his darting gaze and ever to see with sharpened vision, with the "eyes of the mind" ("ojos del entendimiento"), as he puts it, as the objects of his anatomy momentarily tumble into the foreground of his narration and almost immediately vanish to make room for what is to follow. There is truly a multitudinous formlessness in the work, and, like the formlessness of much great satire, it points up the insubstantiality of its inhabitants' worlds, the inexhaustible powers of proliferation and reiteration in man's follies and inadequacies, and the raw destructive energy released by the *saeva indignatio*, even as, in its monotony, it hints at the myopia that generally accompanies the satirist's rage and facile destructiveness, however justified his indignation might be. And any attempt to make sense of its tumultuous catalogue of behavior, foibles, manners, professional activities, social classes, political views, and literary judgments according to some overarching, carefully wrought design will find the material intractable to such treatment and might risk overlooking the fact that to a great extent the coherence of the work lies in its pervasive amplification of its central discontinuities, in its very incoherence.[1] There is, however, more order in its incoherence than

---

[1] See, for example, O. Belic's argument, supported by quantitative measurements, that the story is an "edificio acabado," that, in fact, the extension and disposition of its episodes, "casi matemáticamente exacta," are proof of "la perfección del trabajo arquitectónico de Cervantes" (*Análisis de textos hispanos* [Madrid, 1977], pp. 79-107). The most interesting attempt to find this kind of structure in the *Colloquy* is M. Molho's analysis of the numerous dualities the work presents. Attributing the critical disagreement on the subject to an "habile trompe-l'oeil" by which Cervantes conceals an elaborate symmetrical structure, Molho adopts the view that any discontinuity in the narrative is illusory and proceeds to show how a complex system of oppositions and analogies organizes the entire *Colloquy*. He argues that "la binarité, sous une forme ou sous une autre, s'y retrouve partout" and goes so far as to conclude: "La morphologie de l'édifice résulte, au vrai, d'un ensemble de rapports dont l'opérateur est le nombre 2, habile à informer le jeu dialectique des antithèses" ("Remarques sur le *Mariage trompeur et Colloque des chiens*," pp. 20-21). The division of the whole into systems and subsystems of two's is pursued relentlessly and frequently offers startling illuminations concerning seemingly insignificant details and unsuspected relationships. At times, however, the search for binarism leads to a juxtaposition that is more geometrical than substantial (e.g., the Gypsy as rural predator / the dupe of the Gypsy as good farmer), and the fundamental, overarching binary system subsuming all secondary systems (i.e., a system of four introductory and four concluding episodes, interrelated through formal balance and a neat conceptual opposition ["social" / "extra-social"] flanking a central, pivotal episode, itself observing the binary pattern by dividing neatly into two units [drummer / witch]) has the peculiar effect of conferring the dignity of integrity and centrality on the episode of the drummer and establishing its equivalence with the encounter with Cañizares, of which it is in reality only an introduction. At the same time both the identity which the validity of the system presupposes among the individual members of its second set (i.e., Moriscos—actors—maniacs as outsiders) and the balance which it assumes linking this set and the first set of members are less striking than the overall asymmetry which the latter creates within the tale in its drastically reduced length and the markedly different rhythms and perspectives in the narrative in which it takes shape. The attachment to the system ultimately leads to a rigidified conception of the text which fails to do justice to the dynamics of its movement, its powerful effects which depend on its apprehension by its reader in time, its spectacular discontinuities, its asymmetries, and its indeterminacy. The recurring analogies evoked by Molho's interpretation—"une architecture formelle d'un rigueur sans faille," "la rigoureuse géo-

is readily visible, and in what follows I would like to pursue its design by analyzing the way in which it assimilates the seemingly limitless set of objects of its satirical field. As I turn to its episodes, its "tentacles," I would follow the procedure I have employed in inspecting the shape of the central body, first, seeking the principles that its narrative movement observes and, second, examining how the central imagery with its symbolic implications concerning evil in its metaphysical and existential aspects penetrates the entire texture of the work, creating both a unifying atmosphere and connecting in an imaginative way the various specific forms of disorder displayed at the surface of the narrative with the sulphurous recesses of the richly thematic Cañizares episode.

THE REITERATED NARRATIVE MOVEMENT
IN THE EPISODES

In my discussion of the complex ways in which Cervantes superimposes retrospective commentary on the narrations of actions in the past, I emphasized that the narrative surface of the *Colloquy* is extremely disorderly, that it is crowded with disconnected events, uneven in the varying temporal rhythms of its action, and ragged in its irregular combinations of intrusive commentary and recounted action. However, an attentive reader quickly discovers that there is in fact a dominant narrative rhythm which organizes the story up to and beyond the Cañizares episode, even if, like most integrated forms in the murky atmosphere of Cervantes' final tale, it is at times scarcely discernible. It is visible in the main plot of the work and in numerous of the smaller units of narrative, which, in structural terms, repeat through analogy Berganza's movement toward a spectacular vision of disorder. The pattern can be described as a movement from an initial precarious state of order to a state of total disorder, at which point we frequently observe a type of climactic discovery, a sudden opening

---

métrie de l'édifice," "un tout étroitement entretissé," "le modèle binaire"—strongly suggest the tendency toward abstraction and stasis dominating his conception of the work. Cervantes' organic analogue, the self-generating monster with proliferating tentacles, is a more accurate depiction of its structure. R. El Saffar's recent "critical guide" to the work continues to emphasize its "static patterning" and mathematical design ("we note a recurrence of the numbers four and two in the underlying organization") and asserts that the initial and concluding clusters of four episodes offer "a picture of the whole society" (*Cervantes: 'El casamiento engañoso' and 'El coloquio de los perros'* [London, 1976], pp. 38-41).

of the eyes of the character and the reader to an unexpected revelation of evil. This kind of movement represents, of course, a complete inversion of the dominant narrative direction of the *Persiles* and of Cervantes' various short romances, where a movement from catastrophe to order is generally crowned by an epiphanic vision revealing a mythic or supernatural realm which imaginatively illuminates the narrative and celebrates the restoration of order and certain fundamental values implied by the action. The *Coloquio de los perros* is, in fact, just as obsessive as the *Persiles* in its repetitions, and its reiterated movement toward disintegration invests its central vision of disorder with the type of cumulative imaginative energy that surrounds the triumphant visions of order toward the end of the Christian romance.[2]

The seemingly aimless sequence of unraveling narrative units begins with the frame tale. Pursuing a "happy and comfortable life," the Ensign woos Doña Estefanía, encounters no difficulties in arranging a marriage, and enjoys a honeymoon of luxurious living and delicious sensual indulgence. When Estefanía is forced to move from the spacious home in which she has deceitfully entertained her husband, quarrels begin to trouble their relationship, and soon the Ensign discovers that he has been the victim of an ingenious deception. Following his mysterious sleep in church, he finds himself in a state of intense spiritual agitation, and, when he contemplates his empty trunk-coffin, he is in reality making the discovery of his own evil. As he ponders the significance of his wife's acts, he is, like various sinners of the *Persiles*—for example, Antonio in his encounter with the wolf, Rutilio beside the cadaver of the witch, and Ortel in pursuit of his wrathful victim—confronting a double who represents his own fallen nature. The double will mysteriously vanish but will reappear at the center of his dream in a much more frightening incarnation as the figure of Cañizares. Following this initial moment of unraveling, the narrative of the frame tale continues its downward plunge to a moment of even greater disintegration in the literal decomposition of the protagonist's body, as his hair, eyebrows, and teeth fall out, and in the great illumination of his nightmare vision of universal chaos.

This type of movement echoed in several of the major episodes of the dog's narration. For example, Berganza's recollection of his experiences in the slaughterhouse begins with an account of his birth, infancy, education, and service among the butchers. It offers a de-

---

[2] The *Persiles* can arrest its narrative movement with a discovery of evil similar to those in the *Coloquio de los perros*, and its does so effectively in the northern adventures, which, in their themes and imaginative atmosphere, resemble the *Coloquio* more closely than anything else in Cervantes' works (see above, Chapter II).

scription of their practices and customs and concludes with the narration of the event that terminated his work as a basket-carrier ("perro de la espuerta"). The robbery of the meat by the beautiful maiden is reminiscent of the traumatic first experience of disillusionment that almost immediately rewards the picaro as he begins his wanderings—for example, Lazarillo's painful encounter with the stone bull or Guzmanillo's discovery that he has eaten incubated eggs. Within the design of the novella it forms the first of the series of discoveries which Berganza makes in the darkness of his world ("One day, in the gray dawn, I was diligently on my way to bring her the portion . . . I lifted my eyes and saw a very pretty girl . . . I said to myself: 'Flesh has gone to flesh' ")[3] and which culminates in his nocturnal vigil over the moribund witch and his contemplation of the pervasive power of evil in the universe. The following scene of violence, in which Berganza narrowly escapes death at the hands of his vengeful master, is quickly succeeded by the reestablishment of order, as the picaresque dog flees to a new master, a shepherd in whose employ he thinks he has found "the haven of his repose" ("el centro de su reposo"). He proceeds to give an account of the life and customs of the shepherds, his duties as a custodian of the flock, and his discovery of the falsity of the vision of sheep and shepherds projected by pastoral fiction, and he then turns to the experiences that forced his departure. Once again in the darkness Berganza makes a frightful discovery—the shepherds are in reality the wolves, slaughtering their own flock, mutilating the carcasses, attributing the carnage to rapacious animals, and violently punishing the dogs for failing to protect their charges. To escape the beatings which become a regular part of his life, he finally flees and finds employment in the household of a merchant in Sevilla, where he is rewarded generously with food and freedom for his diligent service as a watchdog. Here he experiences his moments of greatest happiness, in the innocent world of schoolchildren, who feed him, play with him, and offer him "the life of a king." However, all of this comes to a violent end. In the darkness of the night he discovers the bestial activities of his master's Negro servants, and, in a vain effort to prevent their lewd encounters, he is beaten and starved. Barely escaping their attempts to poison him, he flees once again to seek a new master.

In Berganza's tenure as police dog in the service of a constable, we

---

[3] "Y un día que, entre dos luces, iba yo diligente a llevarle la porción . . . alcé los ojos, y vi una moza hermosa en extremo . . . dije entre mí: 'La carne se ha ido a la carne' " (p. 220).

observe the action three times following the pattern of movement toward a climactic nocturnal scene of unmasking, in which a revelation occurs that is important both in the protagonist's development and in the presentation of the satirical themes of the work. The most significant is the lengthy farcical scene in which Berganza observes the constable and his accomplices, the whore and the notary, at work fleecing an ignorant foreigner, their nude, filthy victim stumbling about and screaming in a "lenguaje adúltero y bastardo," and the half-naked innkeeper's wife contributing to the bedlam with a torrent of protestations concerning her purity of blood (*limpieza*). When the confusion finally subsides, Berganza discovers that the machinery of justice, in keeping with the inverted order which prevails in the world about him, has punished the parties involved in inverse proportion to their degree of guilt. A second night of illumination brings Berganza to the lawless world of Monipodio, where he beholds the embrace and the banquet of evildoers, a travesty of the rituals of healthy social and religious communion which appears frequently in Spain's great literature of disorder, from the *Celestina* to Quevedo's *Buscón* and Calderón's *La cena del rey Baltasar*, and which is present in a more essential frame of reference in Cañizares' banquets with the devil. Here he observes a deranged world of violence and treachery, in which the esteem that its inhabitants enjoy varies in proportion to the enormity of their criminal acts, and he discovers in the arrangement by which the underworld enables his constable to maintain the respect of the society of Sevilla, another of the perverted pacts organizing social units everywhere in the world of the *Coloquio de los perros*. On the following night, Berganza makes a discovery of how effectively the pact works, as he accompanies his master to the room where he arrests an unsuspecting brigand, "naked in his bed," and increases his stature in Sevilla through a deception that is ridiculously self-destructive in terms of its material costs to him ("the fame of my poltroon of a master increased . . . he kept up his reputation for courage, and everything he gained by his office and his talents was drained away in the support of his false valor").[4] Following his description of the way in which two horse thieves deceived his master, a brief anecdote that follows the basic narrative rhythm of the story in moving toward a climactic scene of disorder in which the evil are revealed preying on the evil, Berganza recounts the experience that ended his employment

---

[4] "Creció la fama de mi cobarde . . . sustentaba la fama de ser valiente, y todo cuanto con su oficio y con sus inteligencias granjeaba se le iba y desaguaba por la canal de la valentía" (p. 274).

as police dog. Again we observe a nocturnal scene of disorder, as the police chief discerns a man vanishing in the shadows and exhorts the dog: "Go get the thief!" Perhaps fed up with the evil of his master and the complicity forced upon him as an employee, Berganza obeys the command and attacks the constable. While the other policemen attempt to beat him and the chief acknowledges the appropriateness of his interpretation of the command, he decides to flee.

Berganza's tenure as entertainer in the service of the drummer ends in a similar scene of confusion when Cañizares interrupts his show in the midst of its own climactic satirical revelations with an outburst of vituperation and the angry public departs cursing the witch for destroying the entertainment. As in the case of the elusive prophecy of the Cañizares episode, we observe in the dog's performance a "text" that suddenly unravels and produces intense frustration in those who confront it. Such aborted texts and their disorienting effects on their "audiences" image the containing text of the *Colloquy* in its troubled relations with its internal and external readers. Together with the classical poet's play, which breaks down entirely in performance, the sick poet's unborn epic on the "holy skirt," and Berganza's interrupted *entremés* (see below), they form a series of "disintegrating" literary works inscribed in a larger "disintegrating" text—the *Colloquy* itself. In his characteristic game of incorporating into his fiction miniature analogues of the particular literary work containing them, Cervantes succeeds in creating one of the most effective of the various motifs of disorder of his final exemplary novel—the recurrent vanishing climax.

Following Berganza's service with the drummer we reach the culminating nocturnal revelation and the climax of disorder crowning the development of the main plot. As I have pointed out above, here Berganza, the dreaming Ensign, and the reader glimpse a realm of universal disorder and an apparition of Satan, the supernatural spirit who presides over it and the supreme worker of destruction. The episode ends with a violent scene of disorder. We witness the mutilation of the crone's carcass by Berganza and a group of bystanders, the hateful imprecations of the awakening witch, the formation of a mob which attempts to kill Berganza, and the disappearance of the dog into the shadows.

The episodes of Berganza's service with the constable and the encounter with the witch are those in which the *Colloquy* develops most extensively narrated action in the past, and with the contemplation of Cañizares there is a painful immediacy in the unfolding action. At the conclusion of the scene Cervantes sharply alters his narrative perspective and rhythm by presenting Berganza's experiences with the Moriscos and the Gypsies almost entirely in retrospective, generalizing commentary, in which the dog pronounces a satirical denunciation of the viperous societies which he claims are poisoning the Spanish nation. The removal of the biography of the picaresque dog from the foreground of the narrative and its replacement by a static picture which is the fruit of his observation are paralleled by the withdrawal of the satirical glance from the abyss into which it has peered in the witch's confession and its redirection toward an area of social and political issues. The abrupt change signals a new phase in the novella as a whole.[5] From this moment on, the satirical tone lightens considerably, as the narrative races toward the dawn, and the satirical vision becomes "shorter," less concerned with such essential problems as the flaw in man's nature and the source of all evil and more exclusively engaged with such topical issues as current economic and political problems, the enemies of the state, remedies for prostitution, literary controversies, and the habits of poets and intellectuals. However, here too, whenever the narrative turns to Berganza's experiences as they unfold in the past, we witness the same principle of structure as before. His pleasant association with the poet leads to the farcical scene in which the audience, thoroughly bored with the ambitious neoclassical drama, walks out during its performance and the angry actors attack its author. His successful career as an actor concludes with a nearly fatal drubbing which he receives in a riotous scene of an *entremés*. In his work with the alms collector, the good Mahudes, he approaches a *corregidor* one night to offer him some edifying ideas on prostitution and the necessity of social reform, and he is rewarded for his good intentions with a beating. During a nocturnal visit to a rich noblewoman's house, he is attacked violently by a tiny lap dog, and he finds himself compelled to suppress his indignation and endure the humiliation. As is generally the case, each defeat yields an illumina-

---

[5] The sudden change in narrative perspective resembles the unexpected displacement of Lazarillo de Tormes from the center to the periphery of his autobiography immediately following its central episode, in which he descends into the sepulchral, insubstantial world of the master of illusion, the wraithlike *hidalgo*. In each case the event has a crucial and pivotal function in the education of the hero, and it presents an unfolding biographical experience in its closest focus and its most reduced narrative tempo. At its completion the picaros are metamorphosed from participants into observers, and the succeeding events of their confessional accounts recede from the foreground not only through their temporal distancing, effected in the retrospective, generalizing, and summarizing tendency of the speakers, but also through the mediating focus of the "mature" consciousness providing the perspective of wisdom from which the events are judged.

tion concerning the ways of the world and the disheartening ascendency of the forces of disorder. For example, in the final misadventure he learns that society has no interest in wisdom when it is offered by someone who is poor and that unprincipled flatterers and favorites can tyrannize the weak with powers usurped from the strong.

In conclusion, the pressure toward disintegration, which we feel most intensely as we are drawn by the development of the main plot toward its collapsing climax, pulsates everywhere in the smaller units of the *Colloquy*, and up to the very end of the tale a narrative rhythm, which we can describe as a movement from order to disorder, is reiterated to create a powerful cumulative effect of destructiveness. The narrative rhythm of the *Colloquy* is perfectly suited to the vision of depredation, savagery, and bestiality that informs its fictional world. Cervantes continually reveals his mastery of techniques of plot construction which have always distinguished great narrative satire, and we need only recall the climactic negative visions of Lucian's colloquies, the sequence of unraveling scenes of *Le Tiers Livre*, the aborted anagnorises in Voltaire's *Candide*, and the recurrent rhythm of bondage-escape-bondage of picaresque fiction to appreciate the place of the *Coloquio de los perros* within the total structure of literature and to recognize the traditionality of the literary methods which Cervantes so effectively exploits to give coherent artistic form to his own particular vision of evil.

THE RECURRENT SYMBOLIC IMAGERY
IN THE EPISODES

If we turn to the central imagery of the *Coloquio de los perros*, we find a more significant unifying force. The motifs which I have isolated as they emerge with the intensity and concentration of a nightmare vision in the Cañizares episode are in reality omnipresent in the work. They penetrate the entire surface of its fictional world, and, while they are rarely connected so directly with the theological issues raised by the witch's confession, they imaginatively surround all the forms of disorder which Cervantes puts on display with the murky atmosphere of absolute evil. That is, even as the *Colloquy* addresses itself to current social and political problems, to man's petty foibles, to the vices that beset certain occupations, to popular literary forms, or to the pathological excesses of man's intellectual habits and aspirations, and even when the work cultivates a humorous tonality, as is frequently the case in the witty exchanges of the dogs' discussions, there is usually a suggestion that the powers symbolized so vividly in the sinister witch are never far removed. One constantly senses that there is some concrete connection between the most superficial concerns of the topical satire and that fundamental crack in the universe and the sulphurous depths from which those powers emerge. The imaginative impact of the *Coloquio de los perros* and its ability to appeal to audiences across the ages as a work of art rather than merely as a revealing document of social history lie in its insistence on going beyond the short view of the angry satirist, in its attempt to fathom a mystery of universal interest, and in its success in marshaling the aesthetic forms that speak to all men at all times concerning that mystery. It is this imaginative reach that makes Cervantes' final tale truly a philosophical vision, a "universal" *novela ejemplar*, rather than a curious but dated survey of customs. To appreciate its breadth and timelessness, we need only compare it to the other dog colloquy of the late Renaissance, Des Périers' *Cymbalum Mundi*, with its far more limited and remote satirical concerns.

The most important and pervasive body of imagery in the work is introduced by its title and exemplified in the ugly figure of the octopus which Cervantes employs as an analogous representation of his plot—the imagery of the animal world, primarily the animal world of savagery, depredation, and mutilation. In the marvelous inversions of traditional hierarchies of being and value in the Cañizares episode, people actually metamorphose into beasts—the sacristan becomes an ass, the witch, a nocturnal bird, and the devil consorts with his followers in the form of a goat. In the rest of the work people are shown everywhere through metaphor and simile to resemble animals. The two most powerful concentrations of this imagery appear in the incidents beginning Berganza's narration, which, together with the episode of the frame tale, bring us closest to the mysterious supernatural order of the witch and the themes connected with it. Berganza opens his story with a gruesome description of the world of the slaughterhouse of Seville, where he was born and educated. It is a lawless order in which we observe people rending the carcasses of animals during the night, stealing pieces of flesh, described in the work's characteristic language of profanation as their "tithes and first fruits," and cursing and stabbing each other at the slightest provocation, while a greedy throng of accomplices and mistresses gathers at dawn to fill their bags with the torn "testicles and loins."[6] In this thoroughly

---

[6] Rodríguez Marín's exclamation concerning Cervantes' wordplay, "criadas con criadillas" (p. 216): "¡Singular donaire el de Cervantes para jugar del vocablo!" has little informative value as textual commentary. However, it illustrates very well how

deranged society there is no distinction made between man and beast or indeed between beast and lower forms of life. The predators "lop and prune" the carcasses as if they were "willows or vines"; they are described as "birds of prey"; and, as Berganza watches the violent tearing of animal flesh turn into the slashing of human bodies, he makes the appalling discovery that the "butchers think no more of killing a man than a cow. For the merest trifle, and without more ado, they plunge their knife with the yellow handle into the belly of a man as readily as they would into the neck of a bull."[7] The accumulation of images of dismemberment and the reiterated associations of man and beast reach a disturbing climax in a scene in which the implications of cannibalism which hover about the entire episode become quite explicit. While Berganza is delivering a piece of meat to his employer's mistress, a beautiful young lady at a window summons him in a friendly manner and proceeds to steal his meat. She admonishes the dog to teach his master "not to trust animals," and, as if understanding the irony of her words, Berganza responds with one of the darkest pronouncements of the work: "Flesh has gone to flesh." In the climactic moment of satirical unveiling the deceptive mask of man's corporeal beauty is suddenly torn off, and we witness him imaginatively transfigured not only into the violent animal which he is in reality, but into the raw flesh that he voraciously ingests as well.[8]

---

a reader bent on approaching the *Coloquio* as a mimetic assemblage of scenes depicting the customs and conditions of Spanish life by a master observer will find such details incomprehensible, as he fails to see that Cervantes is writing as a satirist rather than as a novelist and hence is presenting a particularly ugly, deformed, and selective picture in order to produce the shocked reaction of the very type that may lurk behind the editor's exclamation.

[7] "Que las escamonden y podan como si fuesen sauces o parras. Pero ninguna cosa me admiraba más ni me parecía peor que el ver que estos jiferos con la misma facilidad matan a un hombre que a una vaca: por quítame allá esa paja, a dos por tres, meten un cuchillo de cachas amarillas por la barriga de una persona, como si acocotasen un toro" (p. 217).

[8] The symbolic impact of this scene derives to a great extent from the violent opposition and subsequent identification of the maiden's corporeal beauty and the raw flesh which her unforgettably lovely hands seize from the basket, as well as from her mysterious knowledge of Berganza's name and the ephemeral character of her intervention, which links her with other shadowy figures who momentarily loom up in the world of the novella (her imaginative connection with Doña Estefanía is most obvious). While the concentration of the elliptical episode into a few striking details indicates that Cervantes conceived the scene as starkly symbolical, the allusive nature of the specific details that compose it—the beautiful woman at the window, beckoning treacherously to the passerby who raises his eyes to 'her while she conceals rapacious hands, the confrontation with the dog, the prominence of the surrounding imagery of mutilation—suggest that he wished to enrich its imaginative atmosphere

In its presentation of a demonic elemental society and its exploitation of the powerful effects of motifs of cannibalism, the *matadero* episode of the *Colloquy* recalls the depiction of the barbarian society in the opening scenes of Cervantes' arctic romance, *Los trabajos de Persiles y Sigismunda*. Both works begin with a horrifying vision of man as an animal and a cannibal and human society as a violent community precariously held together by the common interest in satisfying its elemental needs through depredation, a community that is constantly on the verge of disintegration, as its members are always quick to turn on one another while tearing at their fallen prey. The scenes of the allegorical romance are, of course, much more abstract in character than the localized descriptions of the satirical colloquy, and, in order to lift his dialogue beyond the range of its absorbing topical themes and occupational satire, Cervantes introduces Cipión's editorializing commentary, which explicitly connects the Sevillian scene with the most essential theological and moral issues of the work. He finds in Berganza's aptitude for learning quickly to rip the ears of the bulls ("I easily became an 'eagle' [i.e., an expert] at this") an illustration—an *exemplum*—of traditional doctrine concerning the fall, man's inherited inclination to sin, and the contagious nature of evil: "since evildoing comes from a natural predisposition, it is an easy thing to learn."[9]

While such essential areas of significance are clearly visible in the foreground of the description of the *matadero*, it is also clear that the episode has a more immediate frame of reference and can be read as a satirical commentary on the real slaughterhouse of Seville, the brutality of its employees, and the corruption of the city administrators who protect the "jiferos," while the king of Spain, who is characteristically impotent in his appearances in the world of the *Coloquio*, vainly attempts to institute reform. Moreover, it is quite possible that readers

---

with the story of Jezebel, which was very familiar in the religious culture of the time. See, for example, Luis de Granada's exhortation that man descend to the grave to discover "en que para la hermosura de la carne": "así aprenderás a despreciar todo lo que el mundo adora, por no saber mirarlo; pues no mira mas que a la cara de Jezabel, que asoma por la ventana muy compuesta, y no a los extremos miserables della" (*De la oración y consideración*, p. 35). Berganza and Cipión are compelled to gaze on the "extremos miserables," but in a revealing moment in Cervantes' critical dialogue with the literature of *desengaño*, they reach a conclusion in their interpretation of the maiden's actions that is radically different from the ascetic's traditional reading of the Biblical tale (see below, Chapter V).

[9] "Con mucha facilidad salí un águila en esto . . . Cipión.—No me maravillo, Berganza; que como el hacer mal viene de natural cosecha, fácilmente se aprende el hacerle" (p. 215).

of Cervantes' time would be inclined to read it for what it reveals about Seville rather than for its grim reminder concerning the destructive potential in man's nature and its dark sources, just as they might well have preferred to read the opening scenes of the *Persiles* primarily for their anthropological value or for the exciting marvels revealed in the descriptions of the customs of contemporary primitive societies.

As we move to the second scene of the dog's narration, we find present the same two referential levels—the general and the concrete, the universal and the local. However, the episode of the shepherds is far more complex in its articulation of animal imagery, and the problems of interpretation that it presents are far less easily resolved. From its opening discussion of the shepherds' songs which find their way into contemporary books to its concluding vision of a shepherds' banquet, the episode is constructed out of the archetypes of pastoral literature, and the spare action of its surface is enriched with a broad range of implied meaning based on the expressive function of pastoral in a variety of contemporary cultural contexts. Once again we find Cervantes availing himself of the most sacred vocabulary of his culture in order to achieve the kind of shocking effects of travesty which we have observed in his construction of the main plot and in his development of the symbolic imagery of sleep and awakening.

While the first half of the episode addresses itself to contemporary fiction and reading habits and ridicules the popular pastoral romances for their conventionalized, illusory depiction of nature and shepherds, in the second half the narrative paradoxically assumes and exploits the expressive power of archetypal pastoral imagery in order to develop the satire toward those essential and timeless areas of meaning that are so disturbing in the Cañizares episode.[10] Here we observe a concentrated elaboration of the imagery of bestiality, mutilation, and cannibalism, and the corrosive imaginative energies that it releases are certainly not confined to the professional abuses in seventeenth-century Spanish society at which they are ostensibly directed. In Berganza's pastoral world men appear as a pack of wolves betraying their trust to those both above and below them in the social and natural hierarchies. On discovering the shepherds mutilating the sheep "in a very dark night," lying to their employers about the nature of the

[10] In its peculiar resurrection of pastoral to make a profound comment on the nature of man and society, immediately after dismantling the pastoral myth by juxtaposing it to the reality to which it allegedly corresponds, the episode is comparable to the interlude of Marcela, Grisóstomo, and the goatherds in the *Quixote*. The views of man that are the occasions for the abrupt turnabouts in the exploitation of pastoral could not be more distinct.

predator, and feasting on the remains of the flock, Berganza reacts with amazement at the unfolding spectacle of lawlessness and derangement: "I was horror-struck and bewildered when I saw that the shepherds were the wolves, and that the sheep were torn to pieces by the very men whose duty it was to protect them. . . . 'God help me!' I said to myself; 'who can ever put down this villainy? Who will be able to bring it home to the people that the defense is guilty, the sentinels sleep, the trustees rob, and he who protects you kills you?' " Once again a rhetoric of frightful interrogation, characteristic of contemporary religious oratory and meditative practices, punctuates the *descubrimiento* of evil. As in the case of the Cañizares episode, the series of troubling analytical queries leaves the act of response to the reader. However, Cipión picks up the movement of thought from the concrete to the abstract that informs their climactic paradoxes and, while ironically acknowledging the affinities of the whole interchange with contemporary religious rhetoric and "lightening" its didactic burden through self-criticism, he offers an interpretation of the particular events in relation to the most fundamental principle of social order— trust: "there is no greater or slyer thief than the domestic one, and accordingly many more who are trusting die than those who are wary. But the misfortune is that it is impossible for human beings to live together in the world if there is no trust and mutual tolerance. However, let us drop the discussion, for I don't want to be forever preaching."[11]

If we are tempted to reduce the whole episode to a criticism of contemporary shepherds and a generalizing commentary on domestic customs and abuses, we are not only overlooking the clear implication that the flock, as well as the employer, is the victim of man's betrayal of trust and that the moral issues raised by the slaughter include man's inhumanity as well as his treachery, but, more importantly, we are also failing to respond to the suggestive power of its symbolic imagery. Amezúa, with his characteristic respect for the literal level of meaning in Cervantes' texts, may be right in arguing that the author

---

[11] "Pasméme, quedé suspenso cuando vi que los pastores eran los lobos, y que despedazaban el ganado los mismos que le habían de guardar. . . . '¡Válame Dios!— decía entre mí—. ¿Quién podrá remediar esta maldad? ¿Quién será poderoso a dar a entender que la defensa ofende, que las centinelas duermen, que la confianza roba y el que os guarda os mata?' . . . no hay mayor ni más sotil ladrón que el doméstico, y así, mueren muchos más de los confiados que de los recatados; pero el daño está en que es imposible que puedan pasar bien las gentes en el mundo si no se fía y se confía. Mas quédese aquí esto, que no quiero que parezcamos predicadores" (pp. 232-33).

was primarily concerned with exposing the numerous abuses of power and trust which he witnessed while serving in the bureaucracy of southern Spain, but, as Casalduero has emphasized, the satire of the scene is not focused on any specific object, and, because of its abstract character and the indeterminate allusiveness of its concentrated imagery, its referential reach is far wider than the areas of topical satire that it incorporates.[12] As in the previous episode, the shocking vision of man as a cannibal and a rapacious animal consuming his fellows emerges, but here the ugliness of the spectacle is reinforced by the powerful imaginative resonances of the archetypal figure of the shepherd within the central literary, political, and religious traditions of Cervantes' age. As he traces a program for the education of the ideal prince, Erasmus points out that there is a tremendous difference between a shepherd and a thief, and he reminds us that, when Homer wishes to distinguish a king for his excellence, he refers to him as "populi pastorem" and that Plato likens the good ruler to the shepherd exercising his authority in the best interest of those who are committed to his care.[13] In traditional discussions of the social and religious community the shepherd has always enjoyed considerable prestige, and it is primarily his activity in nourishing his flock, in holding it together, and in protecting it from predators that has given him his imaginative appeal. The most important shepherd in the culture of Cervantes' Spain was, of course, Christ, the Good Shepherd, who held together, nourished, and protected the spiritual society of Christians. In Fray Luis de León's *Nombres de Cristo* we find a celebration of Christ the shepherd and a lyrical commentary on the pastoral symbolism of the Bible, and it is well to bear some of his utterances in mind as we reflect on the expressive power of Cervantes' depiction of the shepherds in the *Coloquio de los perros*. As a good shepherd Christ governs by "pasturing"; he nourishes his flock "with health and pleasure and with honor and peace"; he continually offers it his grace as a clear stream flowing from a fountain, although it frequently strays toward the muddy "cisterns" of death; he is a shepherd who enters the entrails of his sheep and infuses them with life; he watches over and protects his flock; and in order to save his sheep from "the teeth of the wolf, he consented to allow wolves to make him their prey."

[12] A. de Amezúa y Mayo, *Cervantes, creador de la novela corta española*, 2:405. J. Casalduero, *Sentido y forma de las "Novelas ejemplares,"* p. 252.

[13] "Plato Principes Reipublicae custodes appellat, ut hoc sint patriae, quod canes gregi: quod si canes vertantur in lupos, quid praeterea sperandum est gregi?" (*Institutio Principis Christiani, Ausgewählte Schriften*, ed. W. Welzig [Darmstadt, 1968], 5:172; see also p. 180).

There is no greater unity binding men than the single body in which Christ, whose "entire ministry is to unify," joins them, and he achieves and preserves this unity by offering himself as food to his flock.

thus he is a shepherd [pastor], since he is pasturage also, and his way of pasturing is to give himself to his sheep. Because Christ's manner of ruling his devoted followers and leading them to pasture is none other than having his own life hurled into them and imbibed and incorporated by them, and having his sheep, faithfully inflamed with charity, transport him into their entrails, where, thoroughly transported, he changes his sheep into himself. For in nourishing themselves from him, they strip themselves naked of themselves and dress themselves in the qualities of Christ. And as the flock increases, nourished by this happy pasturage, it quickly becomes a single thing with its shepherd.[14]

If his professional activity suited the shepherd perfectly to his symbolic role and Christian and classical writings conferred enormous dignity on him, for these very reasons the negligent shepherd and his traditional adversary, the wolf, have always been effective figures in ecclesiastical and political satire. For example, in the *Praise of Folly* Erasmus denounces contemporary bishops for leaving the care of sheep to subordinates, and in the *Sileni Alcibiadis* he claims that, if we look at contemporary magistrates with the penetrating vision demanded by the satirist, we shall discover ravenous wolves concealed beneath the disguises of royalty.[15] The Erasmian reformist program nourished the *Coloquios satíricos* of Antonio de Torquemada, a Spanish humanist whose works were known to Cervantes, and they offer an elaborate example of such pastoral satire. In a discourse on the beauty and purity of

[14] "Es assí Pastor que es pasto también, y que su apascentar es darse a sí a sus ovejas. Porque el regir Cristo a los suyos y el llevarlos al pasto, no es otra cosa sino hazer que se lance en ellos y que se embeva y que se incorpore su vida, y hazer que con encendimientos fieles de caridad le traspassen sus ovejas a sus entrañas, en las cuales traspassado, muda él sus ovejas en sí. Porque cevándose ellas dél se desnudan a sí de sí mismas y se visten de sus cualidades de Cristo; y cresciendo con este dichoso pasto el ganado, viene por sus passos contados a ser con su Pastor una cosa" (*De los nombres de Cristo*, 1:155). J. Casalduero offers an illuminating reading of the episode based on the cultural code which Luis de León's "Pastor" manifests so powerfully (*Sentido y forma de las "Novelas ejemplares,"* pp. 248-53). See also Gracián's meditation on the lost sheep which is restored to its shepherd and which gratefully nourishes itself from the open wound in his side: "¿Oh amado Pastor mío . . . Otros pastores se comen sus ovejas, y yo me como a mi Pastor" (*El comulgatorio, Obras completas,* ed. A. del Hoyo [Madrid, 1960], p. 1055).

[15] *The Essential Erasmus,* p. 156. *The "Adages" of Erasmus,* ed. and trans. M. M. Phillips (Cambridge, 1964), p. 277. The most celebrated example in Spain of a political satire depicting the disintegration and moral decay of a flock tended by a negligent shepherd was the *Coplas de Mingo Revulgo.*

nature and the spiritual riches, joy, and tranquility of the contemplative life, the shepherd Aminta recalls the illustrious shepherds of the
Old Testament and the good pagan rulers who abandoned their fields
to lead their countrymen, and he proceeds to denounce the shepherds
of the present—kings, emperors, princes, popes, cardinals, and bishops—who, driven by self-interest, ambition, and avarice, neglect their
defenseless flocks.[16] If the negligent shepherd proceeds to slaughter
and eat his flock, as is the case in Cervantes' *Colloquy*, the satirist is
presenting an even more powerful image of disorder, as it brings to
his text the disordering effects of a violent travesty. The perversion of
his function as nourisher could not be more complete and horrifying
and might even strike the mind as a desecration of the sacred meal
by which the most important shepherd, Christ, offers himself to his
flock as food in order to unite all the members to himself and each to
each other in the spiritual society of Christians.[17] It seems safe to
speculate that in the religious culture of Cervantes' time, penetrated
as it was by biblical and ecclesiastical history, teachings, and symbolism and vivified by spectacular public celebrations of the sacraments and the fundamental Christian doctrines, the myth of the Good
Shepherd of the Gospels and the sacrificial act by which he binds his
society were alive in the collective imagination, and that the vision of
a shepherd devouring his flock, insofar as it is explicitly connected
with questions of social organization and the responsibilities of governing and protecting the defenseless, should be all the more repugnant because of the manner in which it travesties Christ's nourishing
sacrifice of Himself for the unity and salvation of his flock.[18]

---

[16] *Colloquio entre dos caballeros llamados Leandro y Florián y un pastor Aminta sobre las
excellencias de la vida pastoril*, N.B.A.E. 7:514-15.

[17] For such effects, see the description of the priest of Maqueda and his weekly
banquets of sheeps' heads in *Lazarillo de Tormes* (ed. F. Rico [Barcelona, 1976], p.
29).

[18] An attempt to determine the precise extent of the religious resonances and their
effects in Cervantes' scene would undoubtedly lead us into insoluble problems concerning the way in which cultural values converge on a text and establish themselves
as actually "present" within it and the difficulties in knowing in exact terms the
degree to which an entire cultural system of meaning, historically remote from us, is
encoded in its smallest symbolic units. In the case of a spare and allusive text such
as the sheep episode of the *Colloquy*, where the cultural values which seem to loom
up are not delineated in explicit terms within it, it is perhaps safest to say that they
are "present" only insofar as they are activated in the imagination to which the text
communicates and that, as the makeup of that imagination and its codes of communication are impossible to establish with a high measure of accuracy, their "presence" must remain speculative. However, confining our view more exclusively to the
determinate forms within Cervantes' text, we can with certainty conclude that the

In conclusion, Cervantes' particular way of using the pastoral archetypes on which the second episode is based accords perfectly with the technique of profanation of the sacred that pervades the entire work. Its climactic shepherds' feast is one of a series of demonic feasts which punctuate the events of the *Colloquy of the Dogs* and which in Cañizares' orgiastic banquet at the witches' sabbat take the shape of a communion of demons and a desecration of the Lord's Supper. Looking at the total design of the *Colloquy*, we observe in these repeated meals the rituals of the damned, as the numerous evil societies which the work depicts seal and celebrate the pacts that unite them and which in fact desecrate all the communal bonds that we revere. All are violent perversions of the banquet of charity, friendship, conviviality, and health which celebrates the reintegration of the cured, redeemed Ensign into society.

The imagery of bestiality and mutilation is most concentrated and most expressive in the opening scenes of Berganza's narration. However, it is omnipresent in the work, and few episodes can be found in which Cervantes does not exploit its connotations of lawless instinct, egotism, filth, and savagery to degrade the inhabitants of his fictional world. It might be remarked at this point that the animal narrator represents a protagonist of considerably reduced dimensions, that his antiheroic figure has clear implications concerning the general absence of heroism in the fallen world of the novella, and that his mediating presence itself casts a shadow of corrosive irony over the entire narra-

---

incident, as it does personify the flock, raises the ugly spectacle of treachery, murder, and cannibalism, ethical symbols that speak clearly in the vocabulary of any sane human being, that its introduction of the shepherd in a context of theorizing concerning social order exploits a powerful symbol in our culture, and that its distinctive way of employing that symbol is consistent with a technique of desecration visible at various points in the work. While appearing to be "truer" to the literal sense of the text, such speculation as Amezúa's concerning the allusiveness of the scene to contemporary historical conditions encounters difficulties of interpretation which are just as great as those confronting an approach to its meaning through archetypal analysis, unless we are prepared to limit those "represented" conditions according to what the text literally says—simply that shepherds were killing sheep and robbing their employers. Curiously, the indeterminacy of this text lies in the expressive inadequacy of its absolutely determinate content, and the pressures which it exerts on us to go further than this banal literalist interpretation are proof of the existence and power of literary archetypes. Whatever its local, narrowly historical frame of reference might be, the context for its proper and fullest construction lies beyond the bureaucratic corruption of contemporary Spain, the existence of which is no doubt attested by voluminous documentary evidence, and is to be found rather in the general moral, social, political, and religious issues actualized in innumerable literary manifestations of the shepherd archetype in Spain's cultural traditions.

tion, assaulting our customary perceptions through the type of negative "defamiliarization" which is a common feature of satire based on
the perspective "from below."[19] Moreover, it should be recalled that
Cervantes employs the repellent image of the octopus to describe the
work itself, and that the dogs' numerous self-critical references to
their utterances in the imagery of bloodletting, wounding, biting,
and cursing relegate the dialogue as destructive satire to a subhuman
sphere of strife and savagery.

The episode of Berganza's service with the merchant of Seville cen-
ters on the dogs' mildly satirical observations concerning the customs
and attitudes of the new rich, their harsh criticisms of society's obsession with lineage and *limpieza*, and the exposure of domestic servants' disloyalty. It unfolds in a civilized urban setting, and in its
prominent social and economic concerns it initially appears to mark
an abrupt change in the course of the tale. However, beneath the
surface of middle-class respectability, maintained ostentatiously by the
merchant's family, Cervantes unveils the nocturnal order that it conceals, and it turns out to be the same elemental world of uncontrollable instinct and animal savagery that has dominated the preceding
scenes. Berganza describes his confinement, his struggles for survival
with the cats who would steal his bones, and his ferocious silent
battles in the darkness with the black slave, whom he describes as a
"bitch" descending to "disport herself" with her mate: "one very dark
night when she came down for her usual pastime, I attacked her
without barking . . . and in one instant I tore her shift to shreds and
bit a piece out of her thigh; this little prank was enough to keep her
in bed more than a week, but she made up a story for her master,
pretending that she was ill. When she got well, she came down another night, and I once again did battle with my bitch, and, without
barking or biting, scratched her all over as if I had been carding
wool."[20]

While working for the constable, Berganza must participate in the
criminal schemes of the villainous society of policemen, prostitutes,

[19] For a survey of the manner in which satirical fiction has exploited the manipulation of narrative perspective, see Dmitry Cizevsky, "Comenius' *Labyrinth of the
World*: Its Themes and Their Sources," *Harvard Slavic Studies* 1 (1953):83-135.

[20] ". . . a la cual, bajando una noche muy escura a su acostumbrado pasatiempo,
arremetí sin ladrar . . . en un instante le hice pedazos toda la camisa y le arranqué
un pedazo de muslo; burla que fué bastante a tenerla de veras más de ocho días en la
cama, fingiendo para con sus amos no sé qué enfermedad. Sanó, volvió otra noche, y
yo volví a la pelea con mi perra, y, sin morderla, la arañé todo el cuerpo como si la
hubiera cardado como manta" (p. 258).

and notaries, who exploit the power of sexual instinct "as a net and hook for fishing on dry land" and "go hunting for foreigners." They easily "hook" a "filthy" Fleming, who roars like a beast when his pursuers spring their trap, and in the ensuing scenes of chaos we find the characters occasionally associated with animals—the constable with the hare and the innkeeper's wife with the lynx. At the same time we witness Berganza in one of his few acts of depredation and demonic feasting, as he momentarily joins the rapacious group to strip the prey. Sniffing the pleasant aroma of a piece of ham which is stuffed into the pocket of the Fleming's trousers, he drags them out to the street to gorge himself on the meat ("I fell upon the ham with a right good will").[21]

Berganza compares pedants with asses, and his observation of the vast store of empty baubles hawked by puppeteers and charlatans leads him to the conclusion that "they are all good-for-nothings, useless vagabonds, wine sponges and bread weevils."[22] In his severe judgment of the Morisco's habits of hoarding money, which he describes in the characteristic imagery of confinement and darkness of the *Coloquio* as a condemnation of the *real* "to life imprisonment and eternal darkness," he again introduces degrading animal comparisons: "They are its money box, its moths, its magpies, and its weasels. They grab everything, they hide everything, they swallow everything."[23] They are "vipers" nourishing themselves secretly in the bosom of Spain, and Cipión adds that the only hope for their extirpation lies in the "most prudent guardians of the republic." In the final scene of Berganza's biography, he likens the favorites and sycophants of the court society to lap dogs who snap at the legs of the virtuous, and his

[21] ". . . les servían de red y de anzuelo para pescar en seco . . . andaban siempre a caza de extranjeros . . . me entregué en el jamón a toda mi voluntad" (pp. 261-63). One of the principal targets of the satire in this episode is the vulgar attitude toward the value of pure (i.e., non-Jewish) blood which apparently infested all levels of Spanish society of the time and was maintained most aggressively by the ignorant lower classes, here represented by the half-naked innkeeper's wife in her ridiculous obsession with her husband's *ejecutoria*, the certificate of purity. The incident is shot through with motifs of *limpieza*, disguise, and concealment, and, as Castro has pointed out, the curious detail of Berganza's discovery of ham in a foreigner's pocket, perhaps suggesting a belief among contemporary non-Spaniards that ham is a certification of purity which will impress Spanish hosts and ensure respectful treatment, might belong to this group of motifs. See Castro, *Cervantes y los casticismos españoles* (Madrid, 1966), p. 14.

[22] "Toda esta gente es vagamunda, inútil y sin provecho; esponjas del vino y gorgojos del pan" (p. 282).

[23] "A cárcel perpetua y a escuridad eterna. . . . Ellos son su hucha, su polilla, sus picazas y sus comadrejas: todo lo llegan, todo lo esconden y todo lo tragan" (p. 317).

recitation closes with his terrible wish to tear them to pieces with his teeth, effectively bringing the narration back to its point of departure, the description of the rending of animal and human flesh in the slaughterhouse.

While the field of imagery which I have described thus far is explicitly connected with the degraded practices of the figures that populate the Ensign's nightmare and with the satirical themes of the work, references to animals and mutilation occasionally emerge that do not have such pronounced thematic implications but that nevertheless contribute to the formation of a unifying atmosphere which imaginatively spreads the contagion of Cañizares' evil order to all areas of the *Coloquio's* fictional world. Some of these can appear in moments of levity and humor, as in the two anecdotes about stealing horses and mules,[24] in the ridiculous poet's contemptuous dismissal of the audience's hostile reception of his play with the proverb "pearls to swine" (p. 326), in the recollection of Aesop's fable of the fawning ass and his master, and in Berganza's playful resolution to bite off his tongue if he yields to the temptation to slander. Others appear in more somber contexts, and contribute effects that are more disturbing. For example, the dogs acknowledge that men delight in drawing blood in their vicious pronouncements, and Berganza describes the way in which slanderous words fly to his lips "like mosquitoes to wine."

A similar unifying network of imaginative correspondences that is developed throughout the work and concentrated about the figure of Cañizares is based on imagery of disease, physical infirmity, decrepitude, and filth. It is most striking in the frame tale, in which on the opening page we observe the stumbling figure and emaciated face of a convalescent syphilitic as he comes forth from a hospital and later listen to his account of the effects of the disease: "I changed my lodgings and I changed my hair in a few days, for I began to shed my eyebrows and eyelashes, and little by little my hair too began to fall out, and before my time I became bald because of a disease that is called *la pelarela.*"[25] The dogs' narration is filled with characters who are marked by physical decay and deformity. There are the other inhabitants of the Hospital of the Resurrection, the four intellectuals whose titanic aspirations to write the perfect heroic poem, cure the

---

[24] See in particular: "Fuésele a pagar a la posada, donde halló menos la bestia a la bestia" (p. 315).

[25] "Mudé posada, y mudé el pelo dentro de pocos días, porque comenzaron a pelárseme las cejas y las pestañas, y poco a poco me dejaron los cabellos, y antes de edad me hice calvo, dándome una enfermedad que llaman *lupicia*" (p. 199).

economic ills of Spain, square the circle, and find the philosophers' stone are comically reduced by the babble of their feverish minds as they sweat out the poisons of syphilis. In Cañizares' hospital we view the dying patients whose clothing is infested with lice. We see a lustful Fleming, his body covered with filth and grease, seeking the embraces of a prostitute, shepherds who pluck lice out of their hair while grunting, a ruffian who is named for his deformed face Nicolás el Romo, and a dog starved until the knots of his spine emerge from his fur. Berganza describes the Moriscos as a "slow calenture" ("calentura lenta") which is gnawing away at the life of Spain as effectively as a "burning fever" ("tabardillo") (p. 317), and he compares the prostitutes of Valladolid to a plague. When the Ensign explains to his comrade that his golden chain was a counterfeit, he employs a proverb that is consistent with this body of imagery and the tonality that it creates: " 'Don Simueque thought he could palm off on me his squint-eyed daughter, but zounds! I'm a cripple on one side, so she met her match."[26] And Berganza's joke concerning the portentous character of an overheard remark that two thousand students are studying medicine in Spain (p. 212), whatever its short-range satirical implications may be, reveals once again how Cervantes can develop the central imagery of his work in a wide range of tonalities, and with a good deal of variation in its thematic implications.

It is hardly necessary to enumerate the motifs of darkness in *El coloquio de los perros*. As I have indicated in my analysis of the structure of its narrative movement, they abound in the work and envelop its entire fictional world in a murk that becomes unbearable in the dog's vigil over the moribund witch. I would here point out the recurrent references to death and the closely related imagery of destructive time, tombs, and dark, confining space. In the central episodes of Cañizares' confession and the Ensign's discovery of his wife's treachery, the imagery is, of course, part of a powerful symbolic articulation of the Christian vision of sin as death in life. However, tombs and graves also appear in less conspicuous places in the narrative: for example, in Cipión's discussion of the traditional association of the dog with friendship and the animal's frequent appearance at the feet of dead heroes in funerary sculpture (p. 211); in Berganza's account of dogs starving to death on the graves of their masters; in his disdainful reference to contemporary nobles who spend their time making paper flowers which they then proudly display as if they were "the pennants

---

[26] "Pensóse don Simueque que me engañaba con su hija la tuerta, y por el Dío, contrahecho soy de un lado" (p. 196).

and trophies captured from the enemy that were hung over the tomb of their parents and grandparents";[27] and in the insane political adviser's (*arbitrista*'s) reference to the probable destruction of his petition: "this one too is going to end up in the charnel house."[28] Indeed, it could be said that images and motifs of death are as prominent and characteristic in the *Coloquio de los perros* as are images and motifs of birth in the novella that opens Cervantes' collection, *La Gitanilla*. While the monstrous Canizares' mentions with a horrifying matter-of-factness her occupational interest in the slaughter of children, in the *Gitanilla*, Saturn, the prototypal devourer of infants and the traditional figure of time the destroyer, appears, forgetting his melancholy and gout to dance in celebration of the birth of the prince. And just as time characteristically appears in the romantic novella in its restorative, renewing aspect, the repeated references to its passage in the *Coloquio* present it in the other traditional perspective—the time that destroys everything, shrouds men's lives in oblivion, and reveals the darkest of truths. The prophecy of the birth of the redeemer which holds so much promise in Preciosa's world here proves to be a frustrating hoax. Cañizares recalls her experience of taking Berganza's mother to her tomb, obsessively alludes to her own approaching death, and voices the melancholy generalization: "but that has already passed, and all things pass, memories fade, lives do not return, tongues grow weary, new events drive old ones into oblivion" and "I have seen and see now that life, which flies upon the light wings of time, is ending."[29] Her enervating preoccupation with the destructiveness in the general course of things is shared by others in the world of the novella. The Ensign pauses in his recollection of the joys of his honeymoon to reflect on the disintegrating powers of the time: "These days passed by flying, just as the years pass by, which are under time's jurisdiction,"[30] and the dogs are convinced that their miraculous acquisition of speech is a portent of an approaching holocaust (p. 212). After listening to the insane boasts of the four diseased intellectuals,

[27] "Las banderas y despojos de enemigos que sobre la sepultura de sus padres y abuelos estaban puestas" (p. 238).

[28] "Que éste también ha de parar en el carnero" (p. 334).

[29] "Pero esto ya pasó, y todas las cosas se pasan: las memorias se acaban, las vidas no vuelven, las lenguas se cansan, los sucesos nuevos hacen olvidar los pasados. . . . yo he visto y veo que la vida, que corre sobre las ligeras alas del tiempo, se acaba" (pp. 303, 292).

[30] "Pasáronse estos días volando, como se pasan los años, que están debajo de la jurisdición del tiempo" (p. 187).

Berganza remarks: "I was full of amazement at having heard them and in reflecting that, in most cases, people with such bizarre ideas were ending their days in the hospitals."[31] The systems of death and animal motifs intersect in Berganza's account of the constable's ill-fated purchase of the stolen horse, for he humorously evokes the steed of Sejanus, which according to legend brought suicide and other forms of violent death to all its owners.

If people are literally dying in the world of the *Colloquy* and its living inhabitants are plagued by a fearful apprehension of impending death and destruction, there is a pervasive constricted quality in the spatial settings in which they appear, and it suggests at many points, most notably in the witch's entrance into her narrow cell, the tomb and the suffocating confines of evil. Like Cañizares, whom we observe moving from the open patio to the cramped chamber and the small chest, and finally to the tiny cell of her ecstasy, the Ensign moves toward ever greater confinement, from the luxurious, spacious house of Estefanía's acquaintance, to the narrow room which is almost entirely filled by the bed, and to his imaginative entrance into his trunk, which is metaphorically transformed into the "sepulcher" for his dead body. The movement into the grave, which, as I have pointed out in Chapter II, recalls the fundamental Christian symbolism of sinfulness, the popular Christian myth of Lazarus, and the contemporary ascetics' injunction to descend into the grave and contemplate mortality and evil, reappears stripped of such profound implications in Cipión's anecdote about the attempts of faithful dogs to hurl themselves "into the same grave with the bodies of their deceased masters."[32]

At the same time the motif is echoed in numerous permutations which are less literal but figuratively far more expressive. Throughout the *Colloquy* we observe its shadowy characters inhabiting or moving into narrow spaces where the powers of darkness are energetically at work. We find Berganza chained behind the door of the merchant's house, attempting to prevent the Negro slave from entering in the darkness to enjoy his bestial encounters with his paramour. We follow him at night as he bursts into the rooms of the inns where the constable and the prostitutes have lured their victims and as, accompanying his masked master, he slips into the house of Monipodio to partake of the banquet of criminals. Everywhere in this world people are

---

[31] "Quedé admirado de haberlos oído y de ver que, por la mayor parte, los de semejantes humores venían a morir en los hospitales" (p. 336).

[32] "Con los cuerpos difuntos de sus amos en la misma sepultura" (p. 211).

enslaved, almost literally it seems, by powers of lawlessness. Both the Ensign and Cañizares, the shadow self whom he dreams into existence, refer to their chains, and, in doing so, appropriate a metaphor that was omnipresent in the traditional religious literature of sinfulness ("carnal pleasure holds my will enchained"; "carnal pleasure, which held my understanding enchained . . .").[33] However, the bondage in which the throng of manacled sinners is suffering is most forcefully manifested in the claustrophobic spatial settings in which they appear—the rooms where the whores trap their prey, the concealed courtyard in the city where thieves and murderers congregate, the bed in which the constable corners the naked ruffian, the small mat on which Berganza is chained and tormented by the marauding cats, the entrance hall ("zaguán") of the lustful Negro, the cave in which the Gypsies confine Berganza, and the vaporous hospital cubicles where feverish patients are tossed about by purgatorial nightmares, lunatics babble about their grandiose follies, witches despoil the dying and consort with devils, and dogs conceal themselves "among the mats" to discuss their lives in solitude. Even the outdoor settings that occasionally appear in the work seldom offer relief from the menacing confinement. In the dim light of the slaughterhouse, we view people stumbling about over carcasses and constantly interfering with one another's movements, and in the natural landscape of the shepherds' society we witness Berganza running about aimlessly in the murky atmosphere of the "darkest night," continually circling back to his point of departure and finally peering out from behind a bush where he has concealed himself to discover the elusive wolf. The pervasive theme of spatial entrapment reaches its most appalling expression in the satirical *contrappasso* contained in Berganza's casual observation that false intellectuals should be placed in punishment "in a press," where, "by dint of turning the screws, they might squeeze all the juice of their knowledge out of them."[34] As I have pointed out above, the

[33] "El deleite me tiene echados grillos a la voluntad" (p. 302); "el gusto, que me tenía echados grillos al entendimiento" (p. 184).

[34] Compare the Book of Job, in its imagery of death, confinement, and liberation and its world of manacles, collars, prisons, graves, chains, caves, claustrophobic cells, and murky landscapes, and its connection of all of this with the themes of sinfulness, righteousness, divine justice, and fruitful evil: "And if they are bound in fetters and caught in the cords of affliction, / then he declares to them their work and their transgressions" (36:8-9). "The godless in heart cherish anger; they do not cry for help when he binds them. / They die in youth and their life ends in shame. / He delivers the afflicted by their affliction, and opens their ear by adversity. / He also allured you out of distress into a broad place where there was no cramping, and what was set on your table was full of fatness" (36:13-16).

narrative itself, in its continuing involutions, appears to reflect the obsessive, futile movement and the suffocating confines of its inhabitants and to impose them on its readers, and it is fitting that, in a moment of artistic self-consciousness, Berganza likens his tale to a labyrinth (p. 273).

While the constricted spatial world of the novella draws its suggestive powers in large part from the images of the tomb in the two most important episodes and points primarily to the themes of sinfulness and death, at the same time it evokes the tortured inner world of the mind which brings it into existence and the tormented meditation of the sinner as he gropes about in the darkest recesses of his racked consciousness. And it is the enormous imaginative power accumulating through the reiterated variations of the tomb motif that causes us to experience as moments of intense relief those few occasions when the claustrophobic atmosphere is unexpectedly lifted and when space suddenly seems to open up and yield to the free movements of the characters—when the terrified Berganza drags the witch out into the patio ("There, by dint of gazing at the sky and finding myself in an open space, my fears left me")[35] and when, at the very beginning and concluding moments of the novella, an exiting movement (from the hospital to the street and from the licentiate's room to the garden of el Espolón) and the framing statements ("There came forth from the Hospital of the Resurrection a soldier" and "away they went") resonate with implications of a liberation from the enslaving power of sin and a restoration of hope for spiritual regeneration.[36]

---

[35] "Allí, con mirar al cielo y verme en parte ancha, se me quitó el temor" (p. 305).

[36] It should be noted that the motif of cramped space in this case belongs simultaneously to another system of motifs—those of retribution and public castigation—a system which has an important function in supporting the purgatorial effects of this tale of universal lawlessness. As in all the principal motif systems, it finds its imaginative and doctrinal center in the Cañizares episode, which, besides the "metaphysical" chains of the sinner, presents the vision of God's punishing hand, describes a judge who brands and an executioner who scourges, evokes the mythical punishment of Lucius of the *Golden Ass*, and concludes with the painful probing of the witch's body and the drubbing and attempted exorcism of Berganza. In reality the system of motifs of retribution permeates the entire work, frequently intersects with the other systems (particularly that of mutilation), and is articulated in a broad range of tonalities and thematic densities. We glimpse the infernal punishments of Sisyphus, Tantalus, and Midas looming up behind the tormented visionaries of the hospital and are reminded of the suicide of the heroic defender of law, Charondas of Thurii; we observe people being thrown into jail and condemned by judges; we hear of dreadful tortures; we witness an infant cursing its mother for having given birth to him with the burden of original sin; but at the same time we learn of the castigation of Aesop's

THE FUGAL STRUCTURE OF THE
COLLOQUY OF THE DOGS

With his characteristically fine sense of literary form, Joaquín Casalduero has suggested that the unity of the *Coloquio de los perros* should
be sought in its fugal arrangement of episodes presenting variations
on a central theme.[37] My analysis of the single narrative rhythm which
organizes the action of the main plot, the numerous episodes, and
even the smaller units of narrative contained within the episodes, and
my attempt to isolate the principal symbolic images or motifs as they
recur through all the individual narrative units, would confirm the
appropriateness of a musical analogy to describe the form and effects
of Cervantes' final tale. In terms of structure the *Colloquy* is, in fact,
closer to the seemingly antithetical *Persiles* than to any of the so-called
realistic works with which it is commonly grouped. As I have shown
elsewhere, the prose epic of heroic endurance is organized according
to principles of design that are comparable to those of fugal composition. It enunciates a dominant theme and restates it continually in
innumerable episodic variations, all of which are held together by a
recurrent narrative rhythm and a carefully patterned repetition of symbolic imagery.[38] In both the Christian romance and the Christian satire the principal effects of such a structure are the accumulation of
power through the ceaseless reiteration of the central theme, and, as
each unit of the work imaginatively contains and concentrates the
whole, the severe attenuation of any impression of chronological progression. This effect endows the narratives, for all their confusing
fragmentations, with a kind of temporal monumentality. In their repetition of decisive acts and symbols and their presentation of a sequence of similar moments of heightened intensity, both works acquire the hieratic powers that we associate with ritual, where crucial
moments reactualize sacred primal actions and events and concentrate
within themselves all subsequent repetitions of those actions and events
through history, past and future.[39] The rituals endlessly celebrated in
the *Coloquio de los perros* are, of course, demonic, and their monotonous

---

foolish ass, Berganza's banishment by the Jesuits, and Berganza's mischievous determination to punish his tongue.

[37] *Sentido y forma de las "Novelas ejemplares,"* p. 242.

[38] *Cervantes' Christian Romance*, pp. 143-48.

[39] See M. Eliade's discussion of the effect of timelessness which normally attends
ritualistic activity, the "abolition of time through the imitation of archetypes and
the repetition of paradigmatic gestures" (*The Myth of the Eternal Return: or, Cosmos
and History*, trans. W. Trask, [Princeton, 1971], p. 35).

repetitions and triumphant epiphanies of nothingness are coherent manifestations in literary form of its metaphysical conception of evil as repetitious, contagious, and fundamentally insubstantial. Moreover, the *Colloquy* is a dream vision, with all the existential immediacy of any intense subjective experience, and one clearly notes in the obsessive character of its repetitiousness a psychological dimension and a particular kind of shocking effect which are lacking in the more distanced, and hence more abstract, celebrative moments of the *Persiles*.

In its inversions of the "fugal" *Persiles*, we would expect the *Colloquy of the Dogs* to reach its appropriate climax in its most spectacular and universal ritual of evil. That is, if the prose epic moves toward Rome, the image of the Heavenly City, and the sacred space where its heroic catechumens are granted a culminating revelation, the *Colloquy* would logically move toward the witch's cell, its blasphemous declamation, and the apparition of Satan and his underworld armies. One might, in fact, expect a climactic descent into chaos of the type that Cervantes' contemporary Francisco de Quevedo depicted in tracing the fortunes of the most satanic of Spain's picaros, which ends in a blasphemous feast of the damned, a profanation of Holy Communion, and a mass murder. However, Cervantes places his "Rome of the damned" not at the conclusion of his "anti-*Persiles*," but rather at its midpoint. Once the moment of Cañizares' confession has been passed, the narrative seems to reverse direction abruptly, as if retreating from the point of maximum enclosure in its coiling involutions. As the night hastens toward dawn, it becomes increasingly clear that Cervantes would allow his questing hero the possibility of an ascent from the abyss into which he has tumbled. And with the leap outward into the frame tale, it is evident that the tormented Ensign will discover a way out of the nightmare and a hope of definitively detaching himself from the dark figment of his hallucination which images his condition of despair and obstinate sinfulness. The shadows of the long night of the *Colloquy of the Dogs* never vanish entirely, but the work does end with an awakening and the promise of a new life.

PART TWO

The Awakening at the End
of the Night

I now consider all my misfortunes were for the best,
because it was due to them that I entered the hospital,
where I saw what I shall now relate.
—The Ensign Campuzano

CHAPTER IV

God's Infinite Mercy: *El casamiento engañoso* as a Christian Miracle

"Behold, God does all these things, twice,
three times, with a man, to bring back
his soul from the Pit, that he
may see the light of life.
—Job 33:29-30

UP TO THIS point I have focused my analysis on the spectacle of lawlessness that *El coloquio de los perros* presents and the principal literary techniques that Cervantes employs to give coherent shape to his vision of universal disorder. In his fictional world the forces of evil appear to be in complete control, and, if we observe how effectively they derange the forms of order celebrated in his most ambitious utopian novella, *La Gitanilla*, we can appreciate the full force of negation emerging in the final tale.[1] The "well-founded nature" ("bien concertada naturaleza") manifest in the orderly movement of the starry heavens, in man the microcosm, and in the perfect societies of family and state, appears here irreparably damaged in consequence of man's fall. It is a nature racked by portents of impending disaster, and its laws are twisted about to gratify the impulses of evildoers. While a benign providence seems to watch over the world of *La Gitanilla*, where redeemers are born and echoes of the music of the spheres are audible to the virtuous, the *Coloquio* reminds us of all the darkness in the designs of an inscrutable and punishing God, enumerating the evils that he "permits" and emphasizing through its humble narrator the sobering lesson that "what Heaven has ordained to happen, no human effort or wisdom can prevent."[2] It reveals gigantic powers of

[1] See my *Cervantes and the Humanist Vision*, chap. 2.

[2] "Lo que el cielo tiene ordenado que suceda, no hay diligencia ni sabiduría humana que lo pueda prevenir" (p. 213).

darkness stalking the land, uttering false prophecies, darkening the sun at will, and reversing the cycles of nature. In the La Gitanilla, Preciosa's song brings peace to her society and the promise of the advent of a prince who will end all corruption at court. In the Coloquio the king is powerless to control his enemies at home while foreign wars menace the country, and his army, despite the best efforts of a good but ineffectual captain, despoils the very kingdom it would protect. Courts and the executors of justice reward criminals in direct proportion to their guilt, and society characteristically takes shape in the form of the mob, the band of predators, mockers, and cannibals. Instead of binding individuals into a genuine society of Christian marriage and producing its marvelous fruits, the erotic impulse isolates human beings, drives them into pacts that enable them to prey on each other, and rewards them with disfiguring diseases and monstrous offspring. If La Gitanilla vindicates man's ability to follow his natural reason, to civilize the "wild horse" of lawless appetite, and to exemplify in his life the lofty image projected by the doctrine of the microcosm, the Coloquio displays man everywhere enslaved by his bestial nature and in some cases literally metamorphosed into a beast. And while the opening tale affirms the power of poetry and language to celebrate man's highest aspirations and achievements and to guide him as he pursues them, the Coloquio ruthlessly and cynically exposes the rhetoric of lies and deceit common to the various idealizing genres and allegorical fictions—the heroic epic, the pastoral romance, the love lyric, and the historical drama—and seems to say that the only language which bears truth within itself is the "uncolored," "antirhetorical" language of satire, the bestial genre that, while perhaps unique among literary forms in refusing to adopt the devil's illusory discourse, the "distorted phrases" of Cañizares' master, nevertheless can at its best do no more than man in his deepest misery, as he "bites and wounds" his fellows.

The Coloquio de los perros can in fact be read as a desecration of all that is sacred in the world of La Gitanilla, which it echoes directly in its Gypsy episode, and its destructive expressive power is heightened by its position as the concluding novella in a collection initiated by La Gitanilla.[3] It is as if Cervantes determined to reverse the order

---

[3] The Gypsy society is characteristically viewed entirely in its demonic aspect. Gypsy maidens appear, for example, but we learn only of their deceitfulness, their hypocrisy, and their failure to take Holy Communion. Walter Starkie has considered the concrete connections between the episode and La Gitanilla in the context of certain facts of Cervantes' biography which they may reflect ("Cervantes and the Gypsies," Huntington Library Quarterly 26 [1963]:337-49).

of his *Persiles*, where the culminating celebration of Divine Providence, Christian values, and man's capacities to live and build a society according to those values draws a good deal of its force from its sequential connection with the opposing world of darkness, natural disorder, lustful witches, raging tyrants, and barbaric cannibals of the first half of the romance. Whatever Cervantes may have thought about the total design of his collection *Las novelas ejemplares*, it remains a fact that his concluding tale is deeply pessimistic in tone, that it conveys an overwhelming vision of disorder, and that it presents nature, man, the family, society, the state, and literature as helplessly caught in the grip of evil and wrenched into shapes that violently disfigure their proper forms as they appear in *La Gitanilla*.[4]

It has been remarked frequently that satirical literature is far more interested in displaying the ugly anatomy of its victims and ironically recording their successes than in presenting a power that rises up either to oppose them effectively or merely to enunciate a set of values by which they are to be condemned.[5] The less attention the writer

---

[4] The various efforts by Cervantists to account for the positions of the individual tales relative to one another in terms of a structural design governing the entire collection—efforts for which they have sought justification in Cervantes' words in the prologue: "y si no fuera por no alargar este sujeto, quizá te mostrara el sabroso y honesto fruto que se podría sacar, así de todas juntas como de cada una de por sí" (*Obras completas*, ed. A. Valbuena Prat [Madrid, 1956], p. 770)—have thus far failed to offer a convincing argument for the existence of such a design. Nevertheless, Casalduero is certainly right in noting the violent contrast between the beginning and concluding tales of the collection and assuming that their situation was not adventitious. See *Sentido y forma de las "Novelas ejemplares,"* pp. 24-28, 52-54. It is perhaps worth pointing out that the frame created by *La Gitanilla* and *El coloquio* establishes a movement which reverses that linking the powerful opening and closing tales of the novella collection of Cervantes' most celebrated predecessor—Boccaccio. An interesting attempt to interpret *El coloquio* as forming an interior frame for the entire collection and compelling the reader suddenly to view all the foregoing tales in the perspective of *desengaño* can be found in W. Pabst's *Novellentheorie und Novellendichtung: Zur Geschichte ihrer Antinomie in den romanischen Literaturen* (Heidelberg, 1967), pp. 131ff.

[5] See A. Kernan's observations on the traditional "scene" of satire: "Somewhere in his dense knots of ugly flesh the satiric author or painter usually inserts a hint of an ideal which is either threatened with imminent destruction or is already dead. Humanity, what man is capable of achieving, is reflected in the lovely human faces of Bosch's tortured Christ and his St. Anthony, both about to be destroyed by the monstrosities which surround and press inward on them. Far above and in the distance behind *Gin Lane* rises a church steeple, but the three balls of the pawnbroker, in the form of a cross, dominate the immediate scene of squalor and filth. . . . Although there is always at least a suggestion of some kind of humane ideal in satire—it may in the blackest type of satire exist only as the unnamed opposite of the idiocy and villainy portrayed—this ideal is never heavily stressed, for in the

gives to positive forces which might counter the evil that infests his world, the more pessimistic and disturbing his satirical vision becomes, and the more vulnerable his work is to such criticism as "sensationalist" and "nihilistic" or to some such charge as "a distasteful glorification of evildoers." Cervantes' contemporary Francisco de Quevedo produced in *El Buscón* a satire that is almost totally ironic in its treatment of its targets, and it makes moral judgment of its inhabitants so exclusively the responsibility of its audience that the critics of the *Tribunal de la justa venganza*, who denounced it as a sermon by Satan, undoubtedly spoke for many readers of the time who were troubled by its unrelieved spectacle of depravity.

In the literary techniques that I have studied in detail in the *Coloquio de los perros*—the continuous unraveling in the narrative movement, the retreat from a climactic revelation with its promise of redemption, the omnipresent demonic imagery, and the frequent cultivation of the vocabulary of profanation—Cervantes employs an ethical discourse that is intelligible to all sane men of any age, and it releases powerful energies of negation which coil around the numerous figures who move about, often triumphantly, in the crowded spaces of his fictional world. It is the same discourse that Quevedo employs, and it arouses repugnance in the reader and compels him to reject unequivocally the forms of lawlessness that he beholds. However, the *Coloquio de los perros* is a much more optimistic work than the *Buscón*, which, in the concentration that marks its discourse of negation, resembles more closely than any other picaresque novel; for its goes beyond its destructive techniques to suggest the presence of forces that would counter the triumphant procession of evildoers. In the concluding part of this study I would like to examine the positive counterweights which the *Coloquio* does develop and which indicate that even in this his darkest work Cervantes does not abandon the faith that his epic heroine Auristela affirms amid the ordeals of her journey through the dim landscapes and waters of the north: "just as light shines most brightly in darkness, so is hope most firm in time of trouble."[6] The "light" that shines feebly but firmly in the nearly overwhelming darkness of Cervantes' "sátira de luz" comes from three sources—the frame

---

satirist's vision of the world decency is forever in a precarious position near the edge of extinction, and the world is about to pass into eternal darkness. Consequently, every effort is made to emphasize the destroying ugliness and power of vice. The author of satire always portrays the grotesque and distorted, and concentrates to an obsessive degree on the flesh" (*The Cankered Muse* [New Haven, 1959], pp. 10-11).

[6] "Así como la luz resplandece más en las tinieblas, así la esperanza ha de estar más firme en los trabajos" (*Los trabajos de Persiles y Sigismunda*, p. 97).

tale and its drama of fall and redemption, the brief interlude describing the college of the Jesuits and their society of children, and the mediating voice of the dogs with its distinct style and implicit well-defined values.

I have pointed out above that the frame tale presents an incident that is closely connected with Cañizares' confession. I have suggested that its prominence in the *Colloquy* derives not only from its position at the beginning and its formal independence as a confession framing and containing a subordinate confession, but also from the elaborate set of imaginative correspondences linking it with the central, dominating episode of the work. If we examine the correspondences closely, we discover that Cervantes has insinuated various parallels linking the two confessing figures. Their similarities and differences as doubles are crucial in the development of his fundamental theme.[7] The description of the Ensign that opens the work places him immediately in the realm of sickness, debility, inversion, insubstantiality, and immorality which will take shape later in the world of the witches. As he emerges from the hospital and stumbles along the streets of Valladolid using his sword for a staff and displaying the wasted yellow face of a convalescent syphilitic, his comrade crosses himself at the sight of the "evil apparition" and admits his astonishment at discovering him "dragging a sword here" rather than "trailing a pike there" in Flanders. Like the witches, he is associated with a derangement of natural processes: although it is not hot, he has sweated for twenty days, and his subsequent claim to have heard animals speak of things that are "more suitable to be discussed by learned men than to be uttered by the mouths of dogs" provokes the licentiate's incredulous exclamation: "By Heaven! If we are not back again in the time of

---

[7] See P. Waley, "The Unity of the *Casamiento engañoso* and the *Coloquio de los perros*." While the thematic, symbolical, and literary coherence of such doubling is what is most interesting, it is at the same time perfectly plausible in psychological terms. As in the case of the numerous details which Don Quixote's subconscious mind assimilates from the realm of his experience to the dream world of his fantasy in the Cave of Montesinos, the Ensign's hallucinatory incorporation in the witch of certain elements of his self and his encounter with Doña Estefanía—e.g., the deadly female, the hand, the narrowing rooms, the chest—reveals Cervantes' extraordinary powers of observation and understanding concerning the workings of the mind and particularly of the imagination. Needless to say, the psychology of the sinner was much more conventional and much more accessible to Cervantes through his readings than the psychology of Don Quixote, and for that very reason it is much less fruitful to view the Ensign's fantasy in purely psychological terms, although, to be sure, Cervantes may have conceived Don Quixote's vision in relation to general themes to be illustrated rather than as the individualized expression of a singular personality to be explored and observed for its own inherent interest.

Maricastaña, when pumpkins spoke!"[8] The Ensign quickly informs his astonished friend that he has just sweated out "fourteen buboes," and his subsequent description of the decomposition of his ravaged body is, like Berganza's recollection of Cañizares' naked figure, one of the ugliest passages in the novella. In the ensuing conversation he makes the connection between physical and spiritual illness which is so pronounced in the Cañizares episode and in the traditional Christian vocabulary of sinfulness, and, anticipating the anatomy of spiritual disorder that Cervantes traces in his witch, whose will is "manacled by lust," he recalls: "As I then had my wits in my heels rather than in my head . . . without making any other comments than those inspired by my desire for pleasure, which held my understanding enchained, I told her. . . ."[9]

It is, however, in the soldier's confession, his account of his court-

---

[8] "Más para ser tratadas por varones sabios que para ser dichas por bocas de perros. . . .— ¡Cuerpo de mi!—replicó el Licenciado—. ¡Si se nos ha vuelto el tiempo de Maricastaña, cuando hablaban las calabazas . . . !" (pp. 204-205).

[9] "Yo, que tenía entonces el juicio, no en la cabeza, sino en las carcañares . . . sin hacer otros discursos de aquellos a que daba lugar el gusto, que me tenía echados grillos al entendimiento, le dije . . ." (p. 184). See also: ". . . saqué tantos [dolores] en el cuerpo y en el alma, que los del cuerpo, para entretenerlos, me cuestan cuarenta sudores, y los del alma no hallo remedio para aliviarlos siquiera" (p. 177). Once again it is useful to look to Erasmus' *Enchiridion* for the religious tradition animating Cervantes' central themes and imagery. Defining the Christian warrior's battle with sinfulness as more lofty than that of the traditional epic hero, pointing to the higher stakes involved in his mission, and repeatedly reminding his reader that he must freely choose to use the power which God is constantly handing him, Erasmus glosses St. Paul, "fiel alférez de la cavallería christiana," Rom. 6:23: "For the wages of sin is death," by comparing the death of the soul, which can be recognized only by the exercise of the "eyes of the spirit," to various states of physical decay, which the inferior "ojos corporales" can easily perceive. In one of his "exemplos," he describes the stumbling movements of a body enfeebled by illness, reminds his reader that he would instantaneously recognize the morbidity in such a physical condition, and asks: "¿Y no conoces la dolencia que tiene tu alma, quando para hazer qualquier obra buena o de piedad está desmayada . . . ?" As another example of the fact that "dentro del sepulchro de su [the sinner's] pecho está tendida una cosa muerta y hedionda, que es su ánima," Erasmus offers a case which looks forward to the condition both of Cervantes' Ensign and of the latter's nightmare self. "Heziste un engaño a tu amigo, o a quien quiera que sea, o cometiste un adulterio: cierto es que tu ánima ha recebido en esto una llaga mortal. Pero con todo esso no solamente estás tú sin dolor dello, mas aún te huelgas de lo que ganaste, y te alabas o tienes contentamiento del mal que heziste. Si assí es, ten por cierto que tu ánima está muerta. Si el cuerpo no siente una punçada pequeña de un alfilel, dezimos que no está bivo. ¿Y diremos que está biva el alma que a tales heridas está sin sentido?" (*Enquiridion*, pp. 121-22). The entire *Colloquy* is, as the Licentiate implies at its conclusion, an exercise in opening the eyes of the spirit, and it does so by accumulating images which are perceptible and offensive to the "eyes of the flesh."

ship and marriage, that the links between the frame tale and the Cañizares episode are clearest and most significant. Both the Ensign and his bride, Doña Estefanía, resemble Cañizares in that they cultivate hypocrisy, masterfully manipulate appearances for personal gain, and speak in the "twisted" and ambiguous language of the devil. Their goals in marriage, money and a life of sensual indulgence and idleness, violate all the purposes of the institution according to traditional Christian doctrine, and their isolation from one another as they plot their treachery is certainly a perversion of the sacrament that binds two human beings into one flesh. Their marriage is, as the Ensign puts it (echoing a common joke which found its way into Pedro de Luxan's Erasmian *Coloquios matrimoniales*), "un casamiento *por amores*" ("a marriage of passion"), which turns out to be "un casamiento *por dolores*," ("a marriage of pain"). It recalls through inversion the ideals concerning the proper goals of marriage and the emphatic repudiation of the marriage of passion that Cervantes presents in the opening novella, *La Gitanilla*[10] If the marriage of the Ensign and Doña Estefanía, when stripped of the institutional sanctions that disguise its reality, is not unlike, both in its purpose and in the fruits of its erotic energies, the only other reasonably stable erotic society that is depicted in the world of the *Colloquy*, that of witches and their lovers, their honeymoon, described as a paradisiacal world of sensual indulgence and lassitude, actually prefigures the vision of Cañizares wallowing in the abyss of her sensual delight. The allusion to Aranjuez and the orderly enumeration of the phenomena that regale the different senses of this "covetous son-in-law in the house of the rich father of the bride" ("I rumpled fine linen sheets, I lighted my way with silver candlesticks . . . Doña Estefanía and the maidservant danced attendance on me. . . . My shirts, collars, and handkerchiefs smelled like another Aranjuez of flowers, for they were drenched in scented essence of orange blossom")[11] recall traditional false paradises of the type that Cervantes created in the *Persiles* as well as the moral issues generally connected with them—e.g., the enslaving power of appetite and illusion—but the most important element to note in this description is its distinctive emphasis on eating and its imagery of food ("For six days I enjoyed my honeymoon [literally—"feasted on the bread of the marriage"] . . . I breakfasted in bed; I got up at eleven; I dined

---

[10] See my *Cervantes and the Humanist Vision*, chap. 2.

[11] "Yerno ruin en la [casa] del suegro rico . . . ahajé sábanas de holanda, alumbréme con candeleros de plata . . . bailábanme doña Estefanía y la moza el agua delante. . . . Mis camisas, cuellos y pañuelos eran un nuevo Aranjuez de flores, segun olían" (pp. 186-87).

at twelve. . . . Whenever Doña Estefanía was not by my side, she was to be found in the kitchen, wholly absorbed in the task of preparing dishes that would tickle my palate and stimulate my appetite.")[12] As I have pointed out above, the imagery of demonic and animal feasting penetrates the entire fictional world of the *Coloquio de los perros*, and it connects the honeymoon of the frame tale not only with Cañizares' banquet of devils but also with various other evil societies in which feasting is viewed as an act of rapacity and selfish appetite rather than as the restorative and binding act of a genuinely integrated individual or community.

The structure of the frame tale resembles the total design of the *Colloquy*, as well as that of the episodic units which repeat it in a seemingly endless sequence. It moves downward toward a climactic experience of disorder at its center, a moment in which supernatural powers are discernible behind the events of the narrative and a sudden illumination rewards the hero and compels him to reflect on events of profound significance. As is generally the case with the *Colloquy*'s recurrent epiphanies of evil, the dominant imagery emerges, concentrated and charged with strong symbolic power, and the most essential theological and moral themes of the tale move into its foreground. On discovering Doña Estefanía's treachery, the Ensign experiences the temptation to despair and considers momentarily the possibility of suicide. Instead he decides to pursue his wife with the intention of "inflicting upon her an exemplary punishment." He enters a church, commends himself to the Virgin, and immediately falls into a deep sleep ("Owing to my affliction, I fell into so deep a sleep that I would not have awakened for a long time if they had not roused me"). Following his awakening he is racked by spiritual torment ("Full of troubling thoughts and misgivings, I went . . ."), and he makes the discovery that, while he was asleep, Doña Estefanía chose to flee. In describing retrospectively his return to his empty room and his inspection of the empty trunk, the Ensign employs a simile that makes the symbolic significance of these strange events quite clear: "I went to see my trunk and found it open, *like a grave waiting for a dead body, and speaking rationally, it should have been mine, if I had possessed enough sense to know how to feel and to meditate on so great a misfortune.*"[13] To

---

[12] "Gocé del pan de la boda . . . almorzaba en la cama . . . levantábame a las once, comía a las doce. . . . El rato que doña Estefanía faltaba de mi lado, la habían de hallar en la cocina, toda solícita en ordenar guisados que me despertasen el gusto y me avivasen el apetito" (pp. 186-87).

[13] "Hacer en ella un ejemplar castigo . . . con la pesadumbre me tomó un sueño tan pesado, que no despertara tan presto si no me despertaran. Fuí lleno de pensa-

interpret the simile for its mimetic aptness makes as little sense as to view the Ensign's daytime sleep in the church in naturalistic terms.[14] Like Cañizares, "dead" in her tiny cell as she sleeps, the Ensign is spiritually dead, and, as he gazes upon the coffin that awaits his corpse, he is forced to ponder the implications of his sinfulness and his mortality. Like Berganza, as he follows the witch into spaces that are increasingly claustrophobic and must contemplate her cadaverous body, the Ensign must "descend into the house of clay" and return to renewed life with the self-knowledge that it provides.

While the sequence of events at the center of the frame tale emphatically reveals the spiritual death that punishes the sinner, at the same time it makes it very clear that a drama of redemption is unfolding before us. Indeed, at this point we note that the action narrated in the Ensign's confession begins to resemble the kind of Christian romance which was popularized in the numerous miracle books of the time and which had a much more profound impact on Cervantes' writings than has been commonly recognized.[15] As in various episodes of the *Persiles* and *La fuerza de la sangre*, the other novella

---

mientos y congojas. . . . Fuí a ver mi baúl, y halléle abierto, y *como sepultura que esperaba cuerpo difunto, y a buena razón había de ser el mío, si yo tuviera entendimiento para saber sentir y ponderar tamaña desgracia*" (pp. 194-96; italics added).

[14] In its inverisimilitude the event is comparable to Pablos' daytime sleep in Quevedo's *Buscón*, which, as T. E. May has convincingly argued, is intelligible only if one disregards its representational illogic and notes its symbolic significance in connection with the Lazarus archetype and the central theme of sinfulness. See above, Chapter II.

[15] Throughout the Catholic world well-organized efforts were made to collect, authenticate, and commit to official written record miracles confirming the holiness of the various shrines. Printed collections of miracles poured forth to celebrate the colossal powers of the Divine Will, the infinite mercy of God, and the intercessory powers of the Virgin and the saints. Their message was everywhere the same: only through pious devotion, exemplary humility, and total reliance on the gift of Divine Grace can man find relief as he staggers along helplessly beneath the burden of his inherited predisposition to sin. Their impact on the art of the period was enormous, and we find their characteristic themes, situations, agents, and plots infiltrating all traditional forms of literature, ranging from the refashioned "classical" epics, such as Virués' *Monserrate* and Lope's *Peregrino en su patria*, to picaresque novels (e.g., Alemán), short stories (e.g., Zayas), and drama (e.g., Calderón). The spokesmen for *desengaño* were naturally drawn to the popular form, and an interesting testimony to its appeal to them can be found in Avellaneda's "rewritten" *Quixote*, which incorporates the conventional miracle, the *Cuento de los felices amantes*, as if to replace Cervantes' ambiguous religious tale, the *Historia del cautivo*, with a doctrinaire celebration of the cult of the Holy Rosary. Avellaneda's spokesman alludes to the fact that "an infinite number of such miracles exist in print" for the edification of the faithful. For a more extensive treatment of the subject, as well as relevant bibliography, see my *Cervantes and the Humanist Vision*, chap. 4.

designed according to the structural principles of the popular religious form, we observe an abrupt plunge into disorder and a spectacle of human beings overwhelmed by the powers of sinfulness and helplessly appealing for the aid of Divine Grace. Familiar themes and motifs of the miracle books appear—an offering to the Virgin, a threat of a terrible crime, a mysterious sleep that prevents its occurrence, a renunciation of revenge, a horrible illness and its cure, a purgatorial nightmare with its recurrent suggestions of miraculous events, a debate concerning problems of authentication and transcription of those events, and a concern with providential evil and the mysteries of divine justice and mercy.

Various celebrants of Cervantes' "verismo" have dwelled on the fact that there is documentary evidence proving that Berganza's final master, the saintly Mahudes, actually existed. Intrigued by a scene which Cervantes may have enjoyed as he sat at his window every evening in Valladolid—the approach of an alms collector and two dogs with lanterns hanging from their collars, pawing at coins thrown to them— they have found in such evidence proof once again of the novelist's authenticity and originality as a "representational" writer but for the most part have failed to open their eyes to the real insight that Mahudes' existence provides into Cervantes' conception of his final exemplary novel. What the tale owes to the historical figure more than likely has less to do with his unproven ownership of dogs than with his "miraculous" recovery from sickness in the Hospital of the Resurrection and the dedication of his life to its service. Mahudes' testament indicates that he, and perhaps those acquainted with his work on behalf of the poor, perceived his fate in terms of a pattern celebrated repeatedly in the rich miracle literature of the age. He accepted his illness, probably the fruits of "sin," as a providential affliction ("the sickness which our Lord Jesus Christ had given to me for the best"), and, preparing to die, he selected the Virgin as his "lawyer."[16] Undoubtedly he regarded his cure as a miracle and his subsequent life as expiation and spiritual regeneration. The existence of Mahudes, then, while telling us next to nothing about the origin of Cervantes' dogs, tells us quite a bit about the genesis, the genre, the theme, and the spirit of this tale of the mysteries of sinfulness and redemption.

---

[16] "De enfermedad que nuestro señor ihuxpo tubo por vien de me dar" (see N. Alonso Cortés, "Los perros de Mahudes," *Revista de Filología Española* 26 [1942]:298-302, and Amezúa, *Cervantes, creador de la novela corta española*, 2:411-13; *El casamiento engañoso y el coloquio de los perros*, pp. 75-80; and L. Astrana Marín, *Vida ejemplar y heroica de Miguel de Cervantes Saavedra*, 7 vols. [Madrid, 1948-1957], 5:569).

The fact is that Cervantes' narrative "monstrosity" enfolds its picaresque novel and its Lucianic satire within the containing frame of a
Christian miracle and presents a fictional hybrid which, in its activa-
tion of traditional generic codes and its exploitation of their interplay,
is in its purely literary qualities perhaps the richest and most original
of the *Exemplary Novels*. *El casamiento engañoso y el coloquio de los perros*
is certainly a striking case of the imaginative adaptation of conventional narrative forms and the innovative experimentalism that characterize Cervantes' fiction in general, and the complexity resulting
from its literary "hybridization" goes beyond that of any of his other
works, with the exception of the *Quixote*.

Precisely because the parallels linking the central scene of disorder
in the frame tale and Berganza's encounter with the witch are so
obvious, the contrasts that Cervantes carefully develops between the
sinner and his dark double are all the more important. Unlike Cañizares, who is totally helpless to resist *acedia* and the desolation which
paralyzes her will, the Ensign finds his impulse to despair immediately countered by an inner voice, speaking in his heart and reminding
him that despair is the greatest of sins, "for it is the sin of demons."
He refers to the voice as a "good inspiration" and a "consideration"
and attributes it to his benevolent guardian angel. In his meditation
on the call of grace, Fray Luis de Granada writes that one of its
benefits is "to send you so many good inspirations and intentions,
even in the midst of your crimes, and to call you with such a powerful
voice, that through it you are resurrected from death to life, and you
come forth as another Lazarus from the dark tomb of your wickedness,
your hands and feet no longer manacled, but rather loosed and free
from the chains of the enemy."[17] Divine Grace evidently has come to
the aid of the Cervantes' "enchained" Lazarus, and its workings continue as he commends himself to the Virgin and falls asleep in the
Church of San Llorente. As in the case of Cañizares' demonic ecstasy,
Cervantes' scene plays upon the ambivalences of the symbol of sleep
in Christian tradition, pointing toward both the spiritual death of the
sinner and the mysterious suspended condition, beyond the reach of
the material and temporal order, which renders the individual most
receptive to the infusion of numinous powers. Unlike the sleep of

---

[17] "Enviarte tantas buenas inspiraciones y propósitos, aun en medio de tus mesmos
delictos" and "llamarte con tan poderosa voz, que con ella resuscitases de muerte a
vida, y salieses como otro Lázaro del sepulcro tenebroso de tus maldades, no ya atado
de pies y manos, sino suelto y libre de las prisiones del enemigo" (*De la oración y
consideración*, p. 62).

Cañizares with its traditional negative resonances, the Ensign's strange sleep is clearly restorative and connected with redemption, the germinating process in which Divine Grace fructifies in the transformed soul of the sinner.[18] The event in the church anticipates the protagonist's subsequent experiences of sleep, in which purgatorial and redemptive processes are even more directly suggested, and it is significant that, as he recalls his first sleep and his wife's escape, he exclaims: "Once again God held me with his hand!" While indicating the speaker's awareness as a reformed sinner that God's grace has saved him at the lowest moment of his fortunes, the phrase sharply contrasts the Ensign's regeneration with the damnation of Cañizares, who, as we have seen, is incapable of reaching out to grasp the hand that God is ever offering. The Ensign has responded to the call of grace in his heart, and he has appealed in prayer to the intercessory powers of the Virgin. These are the first steps of his regeneration, but like the redeemed

---

[18] Unlike the picaresque heroes, Lazarillo de Tormes, the youthful Guzmanillo, and Quevedo's Buscón, who sink deeper and deeper into sin, the Ensign is a "true Lazarus," who like the mythic prototype of all these figures is capable of awakening from the sleep of the tomb. It is instructive to contrast the Ensign's sleep and vision of his tomb with the scene in the *Buscón* in which Pablos is called a stinking Lazarus, falls asleep in the daytime, and awakens to a new life, ("otra vida"), only to proceed to pursue evil with greater enthusiasm than ever before. Cervantes' scene is closer in its imaginative conception to Alemán's account of Guzmanillo's mysterious sleep outside the Church of St. Lazarus as he sets out on his wanderings through a life of criminality. (One can compare the anecdotally presented analogue of the sleeping peasant, who would flee from the dead body and funeral of his wife into a tavern, with the Ensign's discovery of his "coffin" and the necessity of contemplating mortality; similarly the picaro's reference to his feet displacing his head as his guide and his description of his life as a state of continuing sleep suggest that Cervantes may well have been intentionally echoing the crucial scene of Guzmanillo's failed sleep.) Both Quevedo's and Alemán's scenes are, as I have pointed out above, demonic parodies of the "conversion experience" celebrated in devotional writings, in miracle books, and in such literary works as the *Coloquio de los perros* and, insofar as it ultimately moves toward conversion, *Guzmán de Alfarache* itself, and they owe their powerful impact in the portrayal of evil to their vocabulary of profanation. However, one of their most interesting implications is the familiarity and conventionality of such a scene as the Ensign's sleep in Cervantes' tale. What has proven to be a source of mystery and critical contentions for twentieth-century readers primarily concerned with finding the coherence of a literary context in its references to the real world which it allegedly "represents" was no doubt absolutely clear to Cervantes' contemporaries. See, for example, M. Bataillon's explanation of Quevedo's "conversion" scene as a witty exploitation and reflection of contemporary socio-psychological preoccupations and his general cautionary remarks concerning the kind of interpretation that would privilege the literary and archetypal allusions which it might contain (*"Défense et illustration du sens littéral*, The Presidential Address of the Modern Humanities Research Association [Leeds, 1967], pp. 26-27).

sinners whom Cervantes describes in the northern world of the *Persiles*, he must expiate his sins, and the forty sweatings and the purgatorial nightmares[19] in the suffocating cubicle of the hospital are the dreadful penance that his new self must endure as it struggles to be born.[20]

[19] Berganza's terrifying contemplation of Cañizares can be viewed as an amplified version of Rutilio's vigil over the cadaver of the witch-wolf in the endless night of Norway. One should also note that this victim of lust endures a storm lasting forty days and experiences a symbolic death and a metamorphosis into an animal state, when he dons the skins which he finds on the hanging corpse and, reduced to muteness, spends three years amusing the barbarians "saltando y haciendo cabriolas en el aire." In each case the number forty, regardless of its mimetic appropriateness or inappropriateness (a cure by forty sweatings is perhaps a more plausible reflection of reality than a storm of forty days [Amezúa's documentation indicates that the treatment through sweating lasted thirty days (*El casamiento engañoso y el coloquio de los perros*, p. 414) and F. Buret notes that the normal period of treatment of patients in the sweating-vats of the early sixteenth century was from twenty to twenty-five days (*Syphilis in the Middle Ages and in Modern Times*, p. 331)]), would appear to be part of an imaginative pattern exploiting its significance in Christian tradition and developing the theme of expiation. The Ensign's purgatorial nightmare of witches and talking animals, i.e., the entire *Colloquy*, can similarly be considered a spectacular expansion of the nightmare of "mil géneros de muertes espantosas" which torments the wrathful Antonio as he lies in his tiny boat in the darkness of the northern waters. His expiatory quest leads him to an encounter with talking animals, who remind him of the loathsome nature of his sins and hint at the mystery of God's mercy. The presence of God in such nightmares of revelation and purgation which force the sinner to the edge of the grave before releasing him to return to the light recalls the Book of Job: "For God speaks in one way, and in two, though man does not perceive it. / In a dream, in a vision of the night, when deep sleep falls upon men, while they slumber on their beds, / then he opens the ears of men, and terrifies them with warnings, / that he may turn man aside from his deed, and cut off pride from man; / he keeps back his soul from the Pit, his life from perishing by the sword. / Man is also chastened with pain upon his bed, and with continual strife in his bones; / so that his life loathes bread, and his appetite dainty food. / His flesh is so wasted away that it cannot be seen; and his bones which were not seen stick out. / /His soul draws near the Pit, and his life to those who bring death. / . . . Behold, Gods does all these things twice, three times, with a man, to bring back his soul from the Pit, that he may see the light of life" (33:14-30).

[20] As I have suggested above, it is likely that Cervantes had Alemán's *Guzmán de Alfarache* in mind as he planned and wrote the *Coloquio de los perros*. There are, of course, many general similarities—e.g., the confessional mode, the combination of picaresque and theological subject matter, the centrality of the theme of fruitful evil, the atmosphere of tormented meditation, the exploration of the inner world of the confessor, the emergence of a dark double of the sinner at the moment of his self-confrontation and self-conquest, and the presentation of a wide-ranging satire contained within a story of redemption. However, if we look at the climactic scene of Guzmán's conversion and compare it with the two central scenes of Cervantes' tale, we find similarities of a more specific type. Meditating aboard his galley during the night, Guzmán considers the importance of "alzando el brazo," of meriting grace,

Like other important works of fiction that cast a panoramic satirical vision within the framework of the drama of a sinner's inner torment and regeneration, notably Alemán's *Guzmán de Alfarache* and Tolstoy's *Resurrection,* Cervantes' *Coloquio de los perros* devotes little attention to the exemplary life of its reformed protagonist. Yet the story does end with the promise of a new life. I have remarked that the *Colloquy* presents numerous scenes of demonic feasting and that they are generally expressive of man's predatory, destructive capacities, everything in his nature that likens him to the beast in its asocial, isolated condition. It is significant that the work begins with an encounter of friends, and that almost immediately we witness them attending Mass and eating together. Offering hospitality to his suffering comrade, the licentiate emphasizes the restorative powers of food ("the stew is just the thing for an invalid"), his desire to eat together with his friend ("there we shall take potluck together"), and the "good will" with which he makes the offer. Thus the work begins and ends, since it can be said that the occurrences of the frame tale are in reality the concluding events in the story of the Ensign's regeneration, with a true banquet, in which men reveal their high aspirations toward unity and pure communication and give expression to their distinctively human impulses of friendship, charity, conviviality, and good will.[21]

---

and exhorts himself to "recordar de aquese sueño," and "comprar la gracia." He then experiences the sleep of conversion and feels the hand of God: "quedé dormido y, cuando recordé, halléme otro, no yo ni con aquel corazón viejo que antes. Di gracias al Señor y supliquéle que me tuviese de su mano." But like Cervantes' soldier he must come to understand fully the mystery of fruitful evil and suffering, the "tesoro escondido," the "trabajos y persecuciones" with which God "banquetea" his chosen— the mystery symbolized by the gold buttons uncovered by "God's divine hand" in the rats' nest on the day of the picaro's final deliverance. Just as the Ensign recalls his initial incapacity to understand the implications of his "empty coffin," Guzmán laments: "A Dios plugiera que como debía lo considerara" (5:153-55). In each case the moment of self-awareness and the beginning of spiritual regeneration are followed by expiation. Guzmán endures humiliating filth, treachery, and torture, and he acquires both the Stoic wisdom that fortune can not threaten the riches of the spirit and the Christian sense that the miseries suffered by those who are guided by God's hand are in reality pleasures. It is significant that, recalling his conversion, he immediately discourses on the inverted horse in the painting—the paradoxical mystery of lawlessness (see above).

[21] See P. N. Dunn's comments on the restorative elements in the encounter of Campuzano and Peralta ("Las 'Novelas ejemplares,' " *Suma Cervantina*, p. 115). In his phenomenological study of the important role of festive activity in man's ordering of his existence as an individual and as a member of a community, O. F. Bollnow notes that throughout history the banquet has had a particularly important function as a creative and binding act. It belongs "zu den tiefsten gemeinschaftsbildenden Funktionen. Es hebt jede Feindschaft auf. . . . Die Einzelpersönlichkeit geht dabei

Above the chaos of the animal world, an authentic society has come into being, its health restored and its taste for the pleasures of life renewed, and its prominent position at the beginning and the end of the nightmare gives us the feeling that the apparently boundless spectacle of evil may indeed be somehow less substantial, less oppressive than it seemed as we peered about in its shadows. Following the meal the Ensign sleeps for the third time, and the reader is imaginatively invited to share his sleep, as Cervantes describes him slumbering beside the licentiate while the latter reads the tattered manuscript and waking up at the very moment of its conclusion ("The completing of the reading of the *Colloquy* by the licentiate and the awakening of the Ensign occurred exactly at the same instant").[22] Here the act of reading and sleeping are closely associated in their purgatorial and restorative powers. The book itself, a miraculous gift recalling the divine communications which it records, becomes in fact the final and most complete vision bestowed upon its group of dreamers, which suddenly has expanded to include the reader. In one of his characteristic acts of narrative illusionism, Cervantes has placed us beside his characters, and at the awakening we find ourselves invited to cast down the book and the works of darkness that it encloses. In the final words of the work: "Let us go. . . . And with this away they went" ("—Vamos. . . . Y con esto se fueron"), we join the friends, who have just "shut" their own book, and share in a profound experience of release. As we accompany them out of its numerous imprisoning spaces and direct our steps toward the garden of the Espolón and its joys of life, we discern momentarily at the dim horizon of Cervantes' final tale the paradisiacal landscape of Preciosa's world of dance and song.[23]

immer mehr in einem grösseren Ganzen auf. Der Mensch fühlt sich nicht nur im Einklang mit dem andern Menschen, sondern darüber hinaus mit dem Sein überhaupt. . . . Im Fest ist keine Trennung, kein Hass, überhaupt keine Abgeschlossenheit möglich" (*Neue Geborgenheit: Das Problem einer Überwindung des Existentialismus* [Stuttgart, 1955], pp. 224-26). The most holy of banquets in Cervantes' culture was, of course, the Lord's Supper, which the interlocutors of the *Colloquy* witness before returning to their meal at the licentiate's apartment.

[22] "El acabar el *Coloquio* el Licenciado y el despertar el Alférez fué todo a un tiempo" (p. 339).

[23] The note of celebration which unmistakably sounds at the conclusion is attributable in large part to the exiting movement and the sudden expansion of space. Bollnow defines festive space as a locus which opens up and enables man to feel free and light, unburdened of the sense of confinement which reduces his movement in ordinary life. It is the space of the dance. ". . . je mehr der Mensch sich froh und heiter fühlt, um so mehr *weitet sich* für ihn der Raum" (*Neue Geborgenheit: Das Problem einer Überwindung des Existentialismus*, p. 239).

CHAPTER V

The Survival of the Humanist Vision

THE CONQUEST OF *FERITAS*:
TEACHERS AS HEROES

THE ENSIGN'S tale of redemption represents a powerful counterforce
to the dominant narrative movement of the *Colloquy of the Dogs*, but
its implications concerning man's capacities for victorious resistance
in his battle with evil are not very reassuring, and its depiction of
people living according to their fundamental responsibilities as human
beings is ephemeral. Whatever the Ensign's statement—"Well, I still
have my sword; as for the rest, I put my trust in God"—might mean
as an affirmation of spiritual growth and exemplary humility is not
made very clear by Cervantes,[1] and, as we watch the stumbling convalescent enter the garden at the end to regale his "physical eyes"
("ojos corporales"), we might be tempted to recall Guzmán de Alfarache's words immediately following his account of his sleep and conversion: "then I resolved to confess my sins frequently, reforming my
life and cleansing my conscience, in which good deliberation I continued several days. But I was flesh and blood. At each step I continued to stumble, and many times I would fall."[2] The fact is that the
frame tale, while affirming the power of Divine Grace and the infinite
mercy of God, resembles *Guzmán de Alfarache* and numerous other
contemporary works animated by the spirit of *desengaño* with its ascetic
vision of man's depravity, his near total reliance on divine mercy for
salvation, and the tremendous distance separating this world from the
order of grace. *El casamiento engañoso* is far closer in spirit to the miracle books than is Cervantes' secularized miracle, *La fuerza de la san-*

---

[1] "Espada tengo; lo demás Dios lo remedie" (p. 201). F. Rodríguez Marín interprets the Ensign's words as ironical.

[2] "Luego traté de confesarme a menudo, reformando mi vida, limpiando mi conciencia, con que corrí algunos días. Mas era de carne. A cada paso trompicaba y
muchas veces caía" (*Guzmán de Alfarache*, 5:153).

gre.[3] Its characters are for the most part human beings of considerably reduced dimensions, and the only heroism which it recognizes in the treacherous world that it displays would appear to belong to the Divine Will. However, if we turn to the *Colloquy of the Dogs*, we find two other important counterforces, and their nature reveals that Cervantes, even in his most somber work, refuses to repudiate the image of man and his capacities for perfection in this world which shines brightly in the opening novella of his collection and which recalls the utopian aspirations of Erasmian Christianity.

In the brief depiction of Berganza's experiences in the Jesuit school in Seville we witness, if only for a moment, the emergence of a powerfully drawn ideal family and society which is antithetical in every way to the numerous evil societies that fill the work. While elsewhere children characteristically appear insulting their mothers, forming mobs to persecute a scapegoat, and readily following the counselors who cultivate the "inclination to evil" that they inherit from Adam and who punish their failures violently, in this natural community they unite in friendship, play, and charity, welcome the outsider into their group with joy and communal feasting, and yield to the benevolent guidance of the "blessed fathers and teachers" who "prop up the tender shoots of their youth" by gently revealing to them the path of virtue. It is a society of innocence, spontaneity, harmony, and simplicity, and, as the children offer the dog the "life of a king" and sell their grammars to buy food for their carnivalesque banquets, we witness the dark world of Cervantes' satire suddenly illuminated by a momentary glimpse of the pastoral ideal that had been shattered so violently in the episode of the shepherds.

I grew so tame that they put their hands in my mouth, and the tiniest of the children would ride on my back; they would fling their caps or hats away for me to fetch, and *I used to return them to their hands neatly* and with signs of great delight. *They took to giving me as much to eat as they could,* and they enjoyed watching, when they gave me nuts or filberts, how I cracked them like a monkey, shedding the shells and eating the meat. One boy, to test my cleverness, brought me a great quantity of salad in a handkerchief, and *I ate it as if I were a human being.* . . . *many an "Antonio" was pawned or sold to provide my breakfast.*[4]

---

[3] See my *Cervantes and the Humanist Vision*, chap. 4.

[4] "*Domestiquéme con ellos de tal manera, que me metían la mano en la boca,* y los más chiquillos subían sobre mí; arrojaban los bonetes o sombreros, y *yo se los volvía a la mano limpiamente* y con muestras de grande regocijo. *Dieron en darme de comer cuanto ellos podían,* y gustaban de ver que cuando me daban nueces o avellanas, las partía como mona, dejando las cáscaras y comiendo lo tierno. Tal hubo que, por hacer

The passage gathers and rearticulates the central imagery of the novella, and, like the frame tale, it directly counters its normal destructive implications. In this striking carnivalesque vision man appears as
naturally good; his hand, guided by his impulses to communicate and
to share; his feasts, animated by his most civilized inclinations. Nature and human beings serve each other in harmony and joy, and, for
once, man's embrace of the beast is not treacherous, and fangs and
hands are not moved by the instinct to grasp and rend whatever they
encounter.[5] The shepherds of this community are the Jesuit teachers,
and of the various good human beings fleetingly visible in the work—
the beleaguered king, the good captain, the police chief of Seville,
the dead heroes, and the "hombre principal" who insists on decorum
(p. 237)—they are the only ones who receive any attention and whose
efforts seem at all effectual. The celebration of the Jesuits is all the
more conspicuous for the nearly total absence of heroism in the rest
of the novella. Cipión emphasizes their effectiveness as political and
spiritual leaders ("blessed men who, as statesmen for the republics of
this world, there are none so prudent as they, and as guides and
leaders on the road to heaven, few can equal them") and praises the
loftiness of the example that they set. They are "mirrors, in which are
reflected integrity, Catholic doctrine, rare wisdom, and last but not
least, profound humility, the foundation on which is erected the whole
edifice of human felicity."[6]

If Cervantes' picture of the innocent society confirms the natural
goodness of human beings and tempers somewhat the most somber
implications of the novella concerning the irreparable consequences of

---

prueba de mi habilidad, me trujo en un pañuelo gran cantidad de ensalada, *la cual
comí, como si fuera persona. . . . más de dos "Antonios" se empeñaron o vendieron para que
yo almorzase"* (pp. 244-45; italics added). In the concluding chapter, I shall discuss
the carnivalesque aspects of this scene and its implications concerning the central
theme of the nature of language.

[5] The passage inverts not only the various descriptions of predatory hands (see
above), but also the recurrent demonic embraces which mark the relations among
evildoers and their victims. It recalls specifically the treacherous kiss which the Ensign
plants on the rapacious hand of Doña Estefanía as they plot their mutual seduction
and the adoption of Berganza by the treacherous shepherd: ". . . me llegué a él,
bajando la cabeza y meneando la cola. Trújome la mano por el lomo, abrióme la boca,
escupióme en ella, miróme las presas, conoció mi edad, y dijo a otros pastores que
yo tenía todas las señales de ser perro de casta" (pp.221-22).

[6] "Bendita gente que para repúblicos del mundo, no los hay tan prudentes en todo
él, y para guiadores y adalides del camino del cielo, pocos les llegan. Son espejos
donde se mira la honestidad, la católica dotrina, la singular prudencia, y, finalmente,
la humildad profunda, basa sobre quien se levanta todo el edificio de la bienaventu-
ranza" (p. 244).

original sin, his spokesman suggests that man must be educated to cultivate his good impulses and fulfill his destiny as a Christian ("the end for which they were created"), and he describes with unconcealed approbation the educational methods of the college in Seville. In its emphasis on the moral development of the individual through the study of good letters, the rejection of coercion and punishment as instruments of guidance ("they reproved them with gentleness, punished them with mercy"), the determination to make education pleasant ("the days of youth are spent in learning and in diversion"; "they incited them with prizes and were prudently indulgent with their shortcomings"), and the advocacy of a practical approach to education which would exploit the child's imitative faculty, ("they inspired them with examples"; "they painted for them the ugliness and horror of vice and the beauty of virtue"),[7] Cervantes' description of the college reflects the fundamental theories on teaching which Erasmus had formulated one hundred years earlier and which, developed, disseminated, and applied by his followers, had provided the foundation for a widespread reorganization of European education throughout the sixteenth century.[8] Among the leaders in such reforms were the Jesuits, and it was through their celebrated colleges, which sprang up all over Europe in the second half of the century, that various of the essential doctrines of the Erasmists actually achieved their most influential realization.[9] As J.-C. Margolin has recently pointed out,

[7] "Los reñían con suavidad, los castigaban con misericordia . . . se pasa la mocedad aprendiendo y holgándose . . . los incitaban con premios y los sobrellevaban con cordura . . . los animaban con ejemplos . . . les pintaban la fealdad y horror de los vicios, y les dibujaban la hermosura de las virtudes" (pp. 242-45).

[8] In *De Pueris Instituendis* Erasmus stresses the importance of educating the child to be morally independent ("vt sua sponte recte faciat potius quam alieno metu" [ed. J.-C. Margolin, *Opera Omnia*, Vol. I, pt. 2 (Amsterdam, 1971), p. 58]), and repeatedly criticizes teachers and parents who found their relationship with their children on terror. He writes that "libenter autem ab his discimus quos diligimus. . . . Prima cura est amari, paulatim succedit non terror, sed liberalis quaedam reuerentia, quae plus habet ponderis quam metus" (p. 54). The instructor must exercise "lenitas," "mansuetudo," "charitas," and "comitas," all qualities exemplified by the perfect teacher, Jesus Christ, to arouse the love of the student and to make him view learning as a pleasant game rather than as an arduous task. The teacher must recognize and take advantage of the imitative faculty of children and work with practical examples. "Primum discant amare mirarique probitatem ac literas, horrere turpitudinem et inscitiam" (p. 62). For the influence of Erasmus' ideas and treatises on education, see J.-C. Margolin's introduction to his edition of *De Ratione Studii, Opera Omnia*, Vol. I, pt. 2 (Amsterdam, 1971), and E. Garin, *L'éducation de l'homme moderne: La pédagogie de la Renaissance (1400-1600)*, trans. J. Humbert (Paris, 1968), pp. 145-51.

[9] The Jesuits established themselves in Seville in 1554 and founded a college in the diocese of San Miguel in 1579 (W. Krauss, "Cervantes und die Jesuiten in

P. Aquaviva's celebrated *Ratio Studiorum*, which, following its definitive formulation in 1599, was to provide the model for the Jesuit educational program, is, in several of its principles concerning goals and methods and in its emphases on good letters and the attainment of eloquence in a proper course of study, a continuation of Erasmus' fundamental doctrines as set forth in his *De Pueris Instituendis* and *De Ratione Studii*.[10] For our purposes, the most important implications of

---

Sevilla," *Gesammelte Aufsätze zur Literatur- und Sprachwissenschaft* [Frankfurt, 1949], pp. 177-84). For the enormous influence of the Jesuit colleges, both in the Catholic and non-Catholic world, see A. G. Dickens, *The Counter Reformation* (Norwich, 1969), pp. 83-87; 172-74; 185-86.

[10] Introduction to *De Ratione Studii*, p. 107. Cervantes' description closely connects moral instruction and good letters ("el camino de la virtud, que juntamente con las letras les mostraban"). For the importance of the Jesuits' *Ratio Studiorum* in "safeguarding the heritage of humanism" by maintaining humanistic studies as the basis for the child's development in the face of mounting pressures for a more utilitarian approach to education, see F. de Dainville, *La Naissance de l'humanisme moderne* (Paris, 1940), esp. pp. 65-69. The *Colloquy*'s allusion to the value of the program in the creation of a "foundation" for subsequent development, its recurrent stress on the benefits of language (see below), and its formulation of the metaphor of cultivation which was so popular in Renaissance educational treatises ("enderezando las tiernas varas de su juventud"), recall the *Ratio*: "et meminisse Nostros oporteret, arborum radices ac fibras non esse spernendas: quippe sine illis nullus esset vergultorum, foliorum, florum, fructuum decor et ac venustas" (*Ratio Atqve Insitutio Studiorum* [Rome, 1586], ed. G. M. Pachtler, *Monumenta Germaniae Paedagogica* 5 [1887]:145). R. García-Villoslada has noted the general accuracy with which Cervantes' scene reflects the Jesuit methods of instruction and their success in contemporary Spanish society (*Manual de historia de la Compañía de Jesus* [Madrid, 1954], p. 279). In a subsequent study, *Loyola y Erasmo* (Madrid, 1965), he demonstrates that Erasmus' influential pedagogical works, such as *De Copia, De Conscribendis Epistolis*, and the *Adagia*, despite the various official statements of disapproval which climaxed in Paul IV's *Index* of 1559, were widely used as textbooks in the Jesuit colleges, that the Jesuits, in their private readings, were familiar with the humanist's more controversial works, and that, even after the order's first decree of an absolute prohibition, issued by P. Mercurian in 1575, Erasmus' writings continued to be used in the colleges. García-Villoslada concludes that "en lo pedagógico la Compañía debe no poco a Erasmo" (see pp. 233-70, 76). For the impact of the Erasmists' attitudes toward the value of classical studies on the Jesuits and the possibility of a link between Loyola's meditative practices and Erasmus' prefatory appendix to his *Paraphrasis in Evangelium Matthaei*, see A.H.T. Levi, "Erasmus, the Early Jesuits, and the Classics" in *Classical Influences on European Culture*, ed. R. R. Bolgar (Cambridge, 1976), pp. 223-38. For the shifts of emphasis and differences in goals distinguishing the Jesuit program from the humanists' theories of education, see E. Garin, *L'éducation de l'homme moderne*, pp. 183-89, and M. Bataillon, *Erasmo y España*, pp. 771-72. Bataillon, more recently, has noted certain affinities linking the Erasmists and the Jesuits in their attitudes toward the limited value of traditional monasticism in the great contemporary enterprise of reforming and perfecting Christendom ("De Erasmo a la Compañía de Jesús: protesta e integración en la Reforma católica del siglo XVI," *Erasmo y el erasmismo*, [Barcelona, 1977], pp. 203-44).

Cervantes' celebration of the Jesuit college of Seville, regardless of what informative value, if any, it might have concerning his personal experiences or of how accurate it might be as a descriptive document,[11] lie in its forceful affirmation of man's innate goodness and his capacities to realize his highest calling, its attribution to education of a vital function in man's most important undertaking, and its eloquent portrayal of an example of effective leadership and heroism in a world that otherwise is absolutely devoid of such qualities. At the same time, by affirming the practical value of example and pointing out to the reader the effectiveness of the Jesuit's admonition to visualize "the ugliness and horror of vice," it offers an implicit justification of the *Colloquy* and a precise reminder to its reader of the way in which he is to meditate on its panorama of evils.[12]

[11] See F. Rodríguez Marín, *Cervantes estudió en Sevilla (1564-1565)* (Sevilla, 1905), and L. Astrana Marín, *Vida ejemplar y heroica de Miguel de Cervantes Saavedra*, I (Madrid, 1948), pp. 349ff. In *El pensamiento de Cervantes*, A. Castro accounts for the favorable description of the college as a personal reminiscence but allows for the possibility that it may be offered hypocritically ("puede tratarse de una de tantas fórmulas de obsecuencia a las ideas oficiales" [p. 280]). In his most recent studies he implicitly dismisses this possibility and attributes the glowing praise to Cervantes' sensitivity to the social tensions of his caste-conscious society and his genuine respect for a religious order which refused to practice discrimination based on the statutes of "limpieza de sangre" (see "El 'Quijote,' taller de existencialidad," *Revista de Occidente* 5 [1967]:23-29, and "Sobre el no querer entender nuestra historia," *Insula* 22, no. 247 [1967]:12).

[12] J. Casalduero correctly notes that Cervantes' description of the Jesuits' program of teaching provides a revealing insight into his own moral vision and his literary practices manifesting it (*Sentido y forma de las "Novelas ejemplares,"* pp. 54-55). The various efforts which critics have made to interpret Berganza's praise as ironic are unconvincing. W. Krauss suggests that the dog's subsequent sarcastic reference to people who speak Latin at all times ("que hablando con un zapatero o con un sastre arrojan Latines como agua" [p. 249]) undercuts the eulogy of the Jesuits, as it strikes at the "anerkannten Grundsätze ihrer humanistischen Pädagogik," but he offers little evidence either from the text or from external information which he brings to bear on the problem to support the validity of his interpretation. See "Cervantes und die Jesuiten in Sevilla." In his " 'Conscience,' the Jesuits and the *Quijote*," *The Jesuits in the "Quijote" and Other Essays* (Barcelona, 1974), pp. 7-31, E. A. Siciliano presents a much more elaborate interpretation, based to a great extent on fragmentary bits of biographical information concerning Cervantes' possible unrewarding experience of Jesuits and some scattered, allegedly sarcastic allusions in his writings to the intricacies of contemporary scholastic argumentation concerning ethics. He maintains that in Berganza's account one is "struck by the dull pounding of catechismal platitudes," that the "*benditos* padres" lecturing on religion are imaginatively discredited by their subtle association with "la *buena* Camacha" and Cañizares discoursing on religion, and that the "darkness that shrouds the other types must, of necessity, cast some shadows over the Jesuits." R. El Saffar has similarly asserted that the praise of the Jesuits in the *Colloquy* is ironic, but the textual evidence to which she points is inadequate to offset the arbitrariness of her claim (e.g., the Jesuits are subtly shown

In conclusion, if the redemption of the Ensign in the frame tale points toward Divine Grace as holding out the only hope for man in his struggle with his bestial nature, the brief scene in the Jesuit school looks well beyond the narrow confines of the Christian miracle and strongly implies the possibility that man through his own efforts can escape the tyranny of instinct and live a life of virtue and rationality. In view of the sharp contrast between the civilized society of the college and the savage worlds that are omnipresent in the rest of the novella, and the echoes of the humanist principles on education clearly audible in the episode, it is worth recalling Erasmus' essential belief in the possibility and necessity of civilizing man through education. Unlike trees and beasts human beings "are not born, but rather created" ("non nascuntur, sed finguntur"). If not trained to obey reason through good letters and the precepts of philosophy, they will yield themselves over to their most destructive instincts and descend to a level of life which is in fact inferior to that of the beasts. "It is certainly true that the man who is not instructed in philosophy or any of the disciplines is an animal significantly below the beasts. While the beasts merely follow their natural inclinations, a man, unless he is formed through letters and the precepts of philosophy, is driven by the most savage instincts." In words which aptly describe the condition of the people of Cervantes' *Colloquy*, enslaved as they are by

---

to be in collusion with the *converso* merchants in their efforts to "buy" clean genealogies; they "have really abdicated their intellectual and spiritual role to take up their place in society as a clearinghouse through which the rich acquire their titles of nobility and they strengthen their financial grip on the major national industries"; "it could be that the merchant's banishment of the dog reflects his fear that the animal's lack of nobility may expose his own questionable background" [*Cervantes: "El casamiento engañoso" and "El coloquio de los perros,"* pp. 46-50].) This argument follows M. Molho's interpretation, which burdens Cervantes' slender text not only with the implication of collusion between Jesuits and a class of usurous upstarts, but also with a disclosure, in the merchant's materialism and ambitiousness, of a glimpse of the "scandaleuse silhouette de Rodrigo Calderón." Proceeding on a convenient assumption that "rien n'interdit de penser qu'il peut et doit être lu et entendu à double sens," he suggests that Berganza's praise of the Jesuits as "bendita gente para repúblicas del mundo" evokes the specter of the infernal triad of "Devil, Flesh, and World" in the background of the scene, argues that the dog's acclaim of their humility is undercut by the portrayal of his own opportunistic, false humility in the previous scene, and, citing Mariana's criticisms of abuses in the order's secular involvements, economic policies, and teaching program, suggests that similar hostile judgments must be ironically inscribed in Cervantes' illusionistic scene (see "Remarques sur le *Mariage trompeur et Colloque des chiens,*" pp. 30-39). The interpretation is extremely hypothetical, relies to a great extent on extrinsic evidence, i.e., on what is not in Cervantes' text, and places quite an exegetical strain on the few textual elements which it does seize for support.

appetite, Erasmus writes: "There is no animal more savage and harmful than the man who is driven by ambition, cupidity, wrath, envy, gluttony, and lust."[13] Cervantes, a genuine heir to the central traditions of Christian humanism, is deeply concerned with education, and, whenever he deals with it in his writings, whether it emerges as a central theme (e.g., in the *Licenciado Vidriera*, in Don Quixote's colloquy with Diego de Miranda, and in his instruction of the Christian prince, Sancho) or appears peripherally and clearly subordinate to other issues (e.g., in Antonio's Christian instruction of the naturally good human being, the barbarian Ricla, in the *Persiles*, and in the initiations of Rinconete and Cortadillo, Juan-Andrés, Leonora, and Berganza in the demonic societies of Monipodio, the Gypsies, the duenna, and the slaughterhouse), he remains committed to the Erasmists' fundamental optimistic assumptions concerning man's social and ethical nature and the value of education in molding the crowd of beasts into the civilized community of humanity.

THE ETHICAL VISION OF THE *COLLOQUY*:
DOGS AS HEROES

The portrayal of the Jesuits in the *Colloquy* implies a type of heroism that contrasts, not only with the villainy which prevails everywhere else in the work, but also, in its distinctive emphases on humility, prudence, humanitarianism, and discipline tempered by charity, with the traditional type of heroism which Cervantes celebrates elsewhere in his writings.[14] If we turn to the true heroes of the tale, the

[13] "Profecto verissimum est, hominem nec philosophia nec vllis disciplinis instructum animal esse brutis aliquanto deterius. Siquidem pecudes naturae duntaxat affectibus obsequuntur, homo nisi literis ac philosophiae praeceptis formetur, in affectus plusquam ferinos rapitur. . . . Nullum est animal efferatius aut nocentius homine quem agit ambitio, cupiditas, ira, inuidia, luxus et libido" (*De Pueris Instituendis*, p. 32). See also *Antibarbari*:"Quid enim refert bene natum esse, nisi ad *naturam accedat honesta educatio?*" (ed. K. Kumaniecki, *Opera Omnia*, Vol, I, pt. 1 [Amsterdam, 1969], p. 53; italics added).

[14] Cervantes' description of the decision to ban the dog and his disrupting influence as an act of "una señora que . . . llaman por ahí razón de estado" is a joke exploiting the topicality of the Jesuits' controversial political theories and activities. There are no suggestions of excessive severity in their insistence on discipline here. Applying the celebrated doctrine to a policy decision concerning the "subversive dog," the Jesuits appear, rather, as participants in the carnivalesque uncrowning of official hierarchies and values which pervades the entire episode. What might appear to be a reassertion of official seriousness becomes in reality another of its various festive elements. One can contrast Cervantes' treatment of the political doctrine, in its play-

dogs Cipión and Berganza, we find that these ideals are brought out forcefully throughout their dialogue, both in the recounted actions of Berganza which exemplify them and in the value judgments which mark their retrospective commentary on his experiences.

As I have mentioned above, Cervantes' choice of dogs as protagonists has ironic implications concerning the existence and possibility of heroism in the world of his tale. There is definitely a "reduced dimension" in such heroes, and, if Berganza's courageous opposition to the horde of enemies almost invariably ends in flight, Cervantes frequently reminds us of the ways in which his quest differs from that of traditional heroes. We glimpse the graves of heroes of the past and observe their statues on tombs where dogs respectfully and logically occupy their conventional position at heroes' feet. We witness contemporary behavior ridiculed by measurement against the inspiring examples recorded by Valerius Maximus; we hear a modern poet rave ridiculously about his version of the epic of the Holy Grail; we watch the descendents of heroes honoring fastidiously crafted paper flowers, which they make to decorate monuments, more highly than the spoils of combat that adorn their ancestors' graves; we listen to a fleeting prophecy of the birth of mighty redeemers, and we are tantalized with the hopes that surround mysterious births and heroic metamorphoses. Perhaps no scene in the work concentrates the antiheroic character of its heroes and their world more effectively than Berganza's description of himself disguised as a horse and bearing a pasteboard figure of a knight-errant on his back ("he made me some coverings of gilt leather and a little saddle, which he fitted on my shoulders; on it he placed a light figure of a man with a tiny lance to tilt at the ring").[15]

While all these reductive details surrounding the dogs support the general satirical tone of the work and contribute to its pervasive destructive energies, Cervantes carefully reconstitutes his protagonists as embodiments of a distinctive type of heroism even as he undoes them

---

fulness, with B. Leonardo de Argensola's denunciation of "razón de estado" as the "más horrendo de los monstruos," a tyrant who is more destructive than the Hydra, the centaurs, and the Furies, in the contemporary Lucianic colloquy, *Dédalo* (see *Obras sueltas* [Madrid, 1889], 2:161ff.).

[15] "Hízome unas cubiertas de guadamecí y una silla pequeña, que me acomodó en las espaldas, y sobre ella puso una figura liviana de un hombre, con una lancilla de correr sortija" (p. 283). Cervantes exploits the same reductive method in one of the most memorable scenes of the *Quixote* pointing up the absence of the heroic, "El retablo de maese Pedro." The introduction of statues of heroes of the past as an ironic contrast with an unheroic present is the central satirical device in the anonymous anti-Semitic *Diálogo entre Laín Calvo y Nuño Rasura*, written in the second half of the sixteenth century (see *Revue Hispanique* 10 [1903]:160-83).

by sustained ironic references to the traditional mythology of heroes. Indeed, the heroism of the dogs is in essence a "heroism of reduced dimensions," and it recalls the fundamentally paradoxical conception of heroism that Erasmus had celebrated and found authorized both in the true Christocentric philosophy of the Gospels and in the most lofty ethical doctrines of classical antiquity. As they are introduced, the dogs are immediately associated with powerful symbols pointing to the two historical traditions converging in the Christian humanists' synthesis and to two of their privileged myths—Diogenes and Christ: "two dogs with two lanterns who rove about at night with the brethren of the Order of St. John, lighting the way for them when they beg for alms . . . if by chance alms are thrown from the windows and fall on the ground, they race over at once, shine the light, and search for what falls, and they stop before the windows where they know that the people habitually give them alms. And while they prowl about there, they are so tame that they look like lambs rather than dogs, though in the hospital they are like lions and guard it with great care and vigilance."[16] On the one hand, the lion and the lamb, the two fundamental aspects of Christ—power and gentleness, justice and love, the judge and the sacrifice;[17] on the other, the lamp of

[16] "Dos perros que con dos lanternas andan de noche con los hermanos de la Capacha, alumbrándoles cuando piden limosna . . . si acaso echan limosna de las ventanas y se cae en el suelo, ellos acuden luego a alumbrar y a buscar lo que se cae, y se paran delante de las ventanas donde saben que tienen costumbre de darles limosna; y con ir allí con tanta mansedumbre, que más parecen corderos que perros, en el hospital son unos leones, guardando la casa con grande cuidado y vigilancia" (p. 202).

[17] "La flaca humanidad mostró en la muerte, / Y en el resucitarse glorioso / Soberana deidad con ella unida. / Ayer manso cordero temeroso, / Hoy llama con bramido el leon fuerte, / Para mostrar que es Dios en darse vida" (Ramírez Pagan, "A la resurrección del Señor," B.A.E. 35:55). See Luis de León's discussion of the apparent paradox of Christ as lion and lamb in the Bible (*De los nombres de Cristo*, 3:215ff.). He writes: "avéys de entender que, como Cristo lo [el león] es, no contradize, antes se compadece bien con él ser para con nosotros cordero. . . . Ansí que ser Cristo león le viene de ser para nosotros amoroso y manso Cordero, y porque nos ama y nos suffre con amor y mansedumbre infinita, por esso se muestra fiero con los que le dañan y los desama y maltrata" (pp. 220-21). Given the censorious nature of the dogs' colloquy and the subsequent allusions to Cynic philosophy, the lantern clearly evokes the figure of Diogenes, but it is possible that Cervantes, in his creation of a canine hero carrying a means of illumination in his mouth, intended an association with the great Spanish saint and defender of the Church whose biography he had purchased in Seville in 1590, St. Dominic. Before giving birth to the saint, Doña Juana, according to legend, experienced a dream vision of herself, bearing in her womb a dog holding a flaming torch in his mouth and illuminating and burning the whole world ("que'elle auoit vn chien dans son ventre, qui portoit en sa gueule vn flambeau ardent, dont il eclairoit & embrazoit tout le monde"). Through this sign God wished to reveal the mission of his saint to "bark and defend the Church against

Diogenes—the uncompromising pursuit of truth, the penetrating, discriminating power of reason, the demand for moral integrity, the intolerance of illusion. Erasmus had written eloquently of both Diogenes and Christ in his *Sileni Alcibiadis*, a work which, like nearly all satires, devotes most of its energies to a depiction of a world upside down and a harsh exposure of the numerous "anti-Sileni" of society, whose beautiful surfaces conceal inner rot, and he had stressed the paradoxical character of these true Sileni, their humble appearance and origin contrasted to the beauty and power of their ideals and exemplary lives. For Erasmus true heroism lies in endurance rather than conquest. Paul is an immeasurably finer warrior than Alexander. By the same token true vision lies in the capacity to see beyond the surface and the letter to the "unseen things" of the spirit, to look with the "purified eyes of the soul," the "ojos del entendimiento" which Cervantes would refresh in his final tale.[18]

Berganza's confession, like that of the dreamer which contains it, follows the general pattern of literary confessions, moving toward a moment of decisive change in his life, a conversion or a renewal of self, which is the intelligible result of all the experience that preceded it. There is certainly a parallel which one can observe between the Ensign's fall, expiation, and redemption and Berganza's decision to "take refuge in the church" ("acogerse a lo sagrado") after his experience of the evil of the world, which includes his own terrifying night of meditation and his own encounter with a malevolent female. However, there are important differences between the confessions, and they distinguish Cervantes' dog heroes not only from the Ensign but also in a very important way from the picaresque confessor with whom

---

the entry of the devil and to illuminate it and inflame it with his holy life and doctrine" (P. de Rivadeneira, *Les Flevrs des vies des saints* [Paris, 1667], 2:99). At the same time, in view of Cervantes' interlocutors' breed—the mastiff—and their profession as watchdogs of the Hospital of the Resurrection, one should bear in mind the common metaphor by which contemporary Spaniards referred to the members of the Holy Inquisition. In the *Persiles*, the *morisca* witch Cenotia speaks of her persecutors as follows: "Salí de mi patria, habrá cuatro años, huyendo de la vigilancia que tienen los mastines veladores, que en aquel reino tienen del católico rebaño" (p. 201).

[18] "Another Silenus was Diogenes, whom the mob considered a dog. But it was about this 'dog' that a divine observation was made by Alexander the Great, the fine flower of princes, it seems, when in his admiration for so great a soul he said 'If I were not Alexander, I would wish to be Diogenes; though he ought all the more to have wished for the soul of Diogenes, for the very reason that he was Alexander. . . . But is not Christ the most extraordinary Silenus of all?" (ed. and trans. M. M. Phillips, *The Adages of Erasmus*, p. 271). For an interpretation of the *Colloquy* as a "consecuencia y reflejo del pensamiento de los filósofos cínicos," see A. Oliver, "La filosofía cínica y el 'Coloquio de los perros,' " *Anales Cervantinos* 3 (1953):291-307.

they have so many superficial affinities, and they decisively separate the novella of lawlessness from the fundamental vision of the picaresque novel.[19] The picaresque protagonist, whether speaking as a repentant or a confirmed villain, whether he arouses revulsion at his roguery or admiration for his resourcefulness, always presents himself as belonging to or, in the convert's case, as having belonged to the world of deceit and treachery that the work anatomizes. If we look carefully at Berganza's adventures, we find that the developed moral character which is continually manifest in the retrospective judgments that he shares with his comrade Cipión is visible even in the earliest "picaresque experiences." Although in his childhood he quickly learns to tear the flesh of the carcasses in the slaughterhouse and, in his eagerness to learn, provides a lesson concerning the power of man's inherited inclination to sinfulness, Berganza is capable of reacting with moral revulsion to the activities of his masters: "nothing shocked me more or made a worse impression on me than seeing that these butchers would kill a man as easily as they would a cow,"[20] of appreciating an overheard comment by a man of "discretion" concerning the lawlessness of the slaughterhouse, of condemning the rapacity of the deceitful beautiful woman, and of overcoming the impulse to punish her violently, an act of self-conquest that distinguishes him sharply from his master and foreshadows his renunciation of vengeance preceding his withdrawal from the world at the conclusion. As he passes from one master to another, Berganza's intentions and actions frequently give evidence of his "buen natural." He welcomes the opportunity to guard the flock of sheep as a "proper and natural duty of dogs" because it is "work involving the great virtue of protecting and defending the humble and feeble against the proud and mighty." He finds self-fulfillment and happiness in his work ("I believed that I had found in the flock a haven of rest"; "I found myself well-suited to the job for guarding sheep, because I felt that now I ate the bread of my sweat and toil") and rejoices that "sloth, the root and mother of all vices," is unknown to his life.[21] The true shepherd of his flock, he

---

[19] In his recent critical discussion of the prevailing misconceptions about the relation of Cervantes' tale to picaresque literature, G. Sobejano emphasizes that "la diferencia esencial entre el *Coloquio* y el *Guzmán* reside en la bondad del protagonista del *Coloquio*" ("El *Coloquio de los perros* en la picaresca y otros apuntes," p. 40). See also J. Rodríguez-Luis, *Novedad y Ejemplo de las "Novelas" de Cervantes* (Madrid, 1980), pp. 238ff.

[20] "Ninguna cosa me admiraba más ni me parecía peor que el ver que estos jiferos con la misma facilidad matan a un hombre que a una vaca" (p. 217).

[21] "Me deparó la suerte un hato o rebaño de ovejas y carneros. Así como le vi creí que había hallado en él el centro de mi reposo, pareciéndome ser propio y natural

displays his resourcefulness in discovering the teachery of his masters, and his good impulse to expose their slaughter of sheep is frustrated only by his inability to speak.

Unlike the picaresque hero, Berganza continues to manifest an inherent goodness as he copes with his series of ordeals. He speaks of his "buen natural," and, although he is not entirely immune to the contaminating power of evil, his moral lapses are minor or temporary, and he generally yields to the promptings of his good instincts when he realizes the extent of his complicity with the perpetrators of evil. In the social world of the city, he is capable of adopting its seamy conventions for his personal advantage, playing the sycophant at the doors of various prospective employers (p. 234) and cultivating the picaro's well-known strategies of accommodation. Although he takes pride in his loyalty to the merchant and in his position, which he describes as "universal sentinel of my own and the neighboring houses," he is tempted by the gifts by which the fornicating servants would purchase his silence ("For some days the Negro woman's presents played havoc with my conscience"), and he is capable of serving the constable in his corrupt activities and even of joining in the depredation of one of his victims. However, in each case he is ultimately guided by his conscience and his "good intentions" to turn on the evildoers despite the advantages they offer him. He recalls his obligations to his master and struggles to prevent the encounters of the Negro servants ("moved by my good disposition, I desired to respond to my duty toward my master, since I drew his wages and ate his bread; and this is proper not only in honorable dogs, who thereby earn the renown of the grateful, but indeed in all who have masters to serve")[22] and, when he can no longer control his indignation at the constable's thievery, he attacks his master. In each case he must flee before the superior power of his antagonist, but there is clearly something heroic in his determination to resist the evildoers.

In the episode of the shepherds we see Berganza in the first of the numerous meditations and introspective monologues that introduce

oficio de los perros guardar ganado, que es obra donde se encierra una virtud grande, como es amparar y defender de los poderosos y soberbios los humildes y los que poco pueden. . . . yo me hallaba bien con el oficio de guardar ganado, por parecerme que comía el pan de mi sudor y trabajo, y que la ociosidad, raíz y madre de todos los vicios, no tenía que ver conmigo" (pp. 221-30).

[22] "Algunos días me estragaron la conciencia las dádivas de la negra . . . llevado de mi buen natural, quise responder a lo que a mi amo debía, pues tiraba sus gajes y comía su pan, como lo deben hacer no sólo los perros honrados, a quien se les da renombre de agradecidos, sino todos aquellos que sirven" (p. 253).

his spiritual growth as a subject of the work, mark his development toward self-knowledge, and culminate in his terrifying vigil over the carcass of the witch and in the night of his confession through the miraculously acquired "divine gift of speech." As if following the injunction familiar in the devotional literature of the age, he takes advantage of his moments of idleness to exercise his memory, recalling the evils he has experienced and pondering their significance: "And these hours of rest I did not spend in idleness, because I put my memory to work during them, remembering many things."[23] He contemplates the horrors of the slaughterhouse and the customs of its inhabitants, considers the terrible implications concerning the impossibility of social order in the shepherds' treachery, and notes the discrepancy between the community of real shepherds and the pastoral worlds described in the romances read by Nicolás el Romo's mistress.

[23] "Y estas horas de mi sosiego no las pasaba ociosas, porque en ellas ocupaba la memoria en acordarme de muchas cosas" (p. 223). Compare his words following his experiences in the Jesuit school, which again recall, in their Augustinian emphasis on the correct use of the distinctively human faculty of memory for the purpose of spiritual growth, the central traditions of Christian meditational literature: "como me estaba todo el día ocioso, y la ociosidad sea madre de los pensamientos, di en repasar por la memoria algunos latines" (p. 248). Ironically, in the *Colloquy* only the dog can remember. In Cañizares, the archetypal sinner, forgetfulness is stressed: "éste de ser brujas . . . trae un frío . . . que la [el alma] resfría y entorpece aun en la Fe, de donde nace un olvido de sí misma, y ni se acuerda de los temores con que Dios la amenaza, ni de la gloria con que la convida" (p. 301). In his directives concerning the importance of "continually remembering" in the spiritual life of the Christian, Francisco de Osuna notes that God's memory is perfect and holds registered as in a perfect book, to be read by the angels, the eternal truths of all things. He finds in forgetfulness a perversion of this divine attribute and ascribes to it the power to produce the kind of disorder that marks the entire fictional world of the *Colloquy*: "No seas, pues, tú, ¡oh hombre que eres imagen de Dios! tan olvidadizo que parezcas imagen contrahecha y muy al revés de aquello que representa; porque si en Dios todas las cosas viven y en ti todas las cosas mueren, seréis muy contrarios" (*Tercer Abecedario espiritual*, ed. M. Andrés [Madrid, 1972], pp. 356-57). It is consistent with Cervantes' development of the theme of memory and forgetfulness that Peralta should "offer to the memory" of the sinner a moral lesson contained in two verses of Petrarch's *Trionfi*, that Berganza should welcome the acquisition of speech, "para decir cosas que depositaba en la memoria, y allí de antiguas y muchas" (p. 213), that he justifies his narrative of so many things "para hacer memoria dellas, y para desengaño de muchos" (p. 328), that on the night of his purgative vision the Ensign should be lying awake in the darkness "thinking about his past adventures," and that he should, through the eating of raisins and almonds, have his memory "delicada, sotil, y desocupada." Francisco de Osuna's recommendation of "dry things," specifically "raisins and almonds," in order to clear the memory would indicate that such dietary methods of activating this faculty were common practices in current mystical circles (*Sexta parte del Abecedario espiritual*, cited by F. Rodríguez Marín, in a note, *Coloquio*, p. 206).

In such philosophical inquiry and refined literary satire, Cervantes develops through Berganza's meditations the most serious themes of his work.[24] In the city we observe Berganza revealing his appreciation of the qualities of the Jesuits and meditating on their educational methods: "I remained sitting on my haunches at the door of the hall, staring fixedly at the teacher who was lecturing at the desk . . . I took delight in seeing the loving care and the anxiety and diligence with which those blessed fathers and teachers taught those boys. . . . I reflected on how they rebuked their pupils with gentleness."[25] The encounter with Cañizares is the climax of Berganza's development as a heroic character. Here we see him emphatically rejecting the embrace offered by the witch,[26] piously resisting the temptation to tear her to pieces "so that death might not carry her off in such an evil state," raising profound questions as he meditates over her body, and finally courageously defending himself when she and the mob which she has deluded attack him.

A true descendant of the Socratic school of philosophers, Berganza is motivated by a healthy desire to observe and understand the ways of the world, to become an "hombre discreto," and he is aware that travel is indispensable to the fulfillment of his ambition.[27] The generalizing commentary which dominates his recollections of his adventures with the Moriscos and the Gypsies suggests that he has wan-

[24] In the important function of the meditation in the protagonist's development and in the enunciation of themes we observe one of the most obvious links between Cervantes' tale and both the picaresque novel and the confessional and devotional literature which nourished it. One can compare Lazarillo's striking consideration and solitary interrogation of God following the departure of the suffering *hidalgo* (*Lazarillo de Tormes*, ed. cit., p. 49), as well as the numerous monologues through which Guzmán de Alfarache meditates on the significance of his misadventures.

[25] "Quedéme sentado en cuclillas a la puerta del aula, mirando de hito en hito al maestro que en la cátedra leía . . . recibí gusto de ver el amor, el término, la solicitud y la industria con que aquellos benditos padres y maestros enseñaban a aquellos niños . . . consideraba cómo los reñían con suavidad" (pp. 242-243).

[26] To appreciate Berganza's defiant reaction to the proffered kiss, one should bear in mind the recurrent acts or gestures of demonic bonding: Monipodio's embrace of the constable, the witches' encounters with the devil, the reception of Berganza by the treacherous shepherd, who spits in his mouth and puts the collar of the dead Leoncillo on him, the deceitful marriage, and the union of the Flemish sailor and Colindres, as well as the positive counterweight to all these rituals or pacts of false societies—the gesture of the children who joyfully place their hands in the protagonist's mouth.

[27] ". . . el andar tierras y comunicar con diversas gentes hace a los hombres discretos" (p. 278). For the importance of travel in Renaissance educational theories and in Cervantes' general views on the development of the individual, see my *Cervantes and the Humanist Vision*, chap. 3.

dered through these "foreign" communities as an ideal observer, taking note of their aberrant customs, considering the problems that are raised by their existence in Spain, and developing the concerned judgments which he offers his companion. In his adventures as an actor he once again reveals his Christian heroism as he suffers a cruel wound and conquers an urge to take revenge on his tormentor ("for calculated revenge is the sign of cruelty and an evil spirit").[28] It is perhaps this moral triumph that distinguishes him most decisively from the picaresque hero. The notorious Guzmán de Alfarache can recognize at one point that vengeance is the act of a "cowardly and bestial spirit" and even affirm that "self-conquest" through the overcoming of impulses to punish one's offender is the greatest victory an individual can achieve. Yet by his own admission he is an "animal" hopelessly driven by such impulses, which "prick him like the spurs in a beast's flanks," and he relishes his ingeniously calculated acts of revenge as his most satisfying accomplishments.[29]

When Berganza can no longer endure the evils of the acting profession and prudently realizes that he has no power to correct them, he resolves to "take sanctuary" in the Hospital of the Resurrection. It is important to note that Berganza's conversion and withdrawal as a servant in the religious order of St. John of God are not motivated by an ascetic impulse to abandon the world. Throughout his life he is

---

[28] "Que la venganza pensada arguye crueldad y mal ánimo" (p. 328). A. Castro has emphasized the importance of the heroic act of renouncing vengeance in Cervantes' works (e.g., *El curioso impertinente, El celoso extremeño, El Persiles*), an act all the more striking in view of the contemporaneous celebrations of blood revenge in the public performances of the *comedia de honor*, and he has convincingly argued that the theme reveals the impact on his development of the Erasmian moral ideal and the type of heroism expounded in the *Enchiridion*. See *El pensamiento de Cervantes*, pp. 355ff., and above, Chapter I. Berganza's renunciation is another of the various elements in the text establishing parallels and distinctions simultaneously between the dog and the dreamer whose imagination he inhabits. The Ensign similarly confronts the moral problem posed by "justifiable revenge" and overcomes the impulse to perform an "exemplary punishment," but, unlike Berganza, he needs divine help, the miraculous intercession of the Virgin, to achieve his triumph.

[29] *Guzmán de Alfarache* 1:133-35; 4:115 ("tanto fué lo que siempre me aguijoneaba la venganza, que como con espuelas parecía picarme los ijares como a bestia. ¡Bien bestia!, que no lo es menos el que conoce aqueste disparate"). Both parts of Guzmán's "confession" end with spectacular acts of retribution, and throughout the work God is envisioned primarily as an avenging deity. While the benign figure of John of God looms up at the faintly hopeful conclusion of the *Colloquy of the Dogs*, in the background of *Guzmán de Alfarache*'s final scene of dismemberment, hanging, whipping, and mutilation, we glimpse the awesome figure of John the Baptist and recall his grim prophecy of universal purgation: "the chaff he will burn with unquenchable fire."

committed to activity and service for others, and he is always extremely curious concerning mankind's doings.[30] What attracts him to
the service of the "good Christian Mahudes," a redeemed sinner who
devoted himself to the order after his own cure in the hospital, is the
sight of Cipión carrying the lantern, so "content" and so "justly and
righteously occupied." And as he works with the alms collector, he
continues to reveal his interest in the secular world.[31] He meditates
on the significance of four intellectuals' diseased products, as well as
on the implications of the privileges of lap dogs. And in the concluding incidents of his autobiography, he vainly attempts to offer the
corregidor of Valladolid a program of reform that might end the pes-
tilence of prostitution, and he reveals his worldly wisdom and practicality in his decision not to attack the tiny lap dog who arrogantly
bites him in the foot.

In summary, unlike the picaresque hero and the helpless protagonist of the miracle, Berganza represents throughout his life, both before and after his decision to take sanctuary, a well-defined and appealing set of values and virtues: piety, humility, prudence, endurance,
charity, loyalty, practicality, a dedication to melioration and reform
through active service for humanity, faith in the effectiveness of rea-

[30] P. Laín Entralgo has stressed Berganza's role in the tale as an objective spectator
who indefatigably observes and records as he wanders through the world. He argues,
somewhat misleadingly, that the dog's perspective is that of the ingénu, that his
approach to reality is thoroughly empirical, that his function is that of a "mirror,"
and that he leaves all theory and analytical reflection on his experiences to his comrade, Cipión ("Miguel de Cervantes: *Coloquio de los perros*, Soliloquio de Cervantes,"
Mis páginas preferidas [Madrid, 1958], pp. 47-72).

[31] Berganza deplores the success of the charlatans, "gente inútil y sin provecho,"
who wish to "ganar de comer holgando" (p. 282), and he condemns the Gypsies for
their general idleness. The men "ocúpanse, por dar color a su ociosidad, en labrar
cosas de hierro," and the women, "a título que no hay quien se fíe dellas, no sirven,
y dan en ser holgazanas" (pp. 313-14). Berganza's affirmative attitude toward the
value of work, as well as his interest in the economic health of his country, is another
of the numerous elements which link Cervantes' light-bearing mastiffs, who address
one another as "brother," practice the examination of conscience and intention, engage in charitable work, and defend the ecclesiastical institution, with the active
religious forces of the period—e.g., the Jesuits, the Holy Inquisition, the Order of
St. John of God. H. R. Trevor-Roper has pointed out that the "sanctity of secular
work" was a central message not only of the Calvinists, but also of the Jesuits, who
were "determined to recapture from heresy the *élite* of the laity." He mentions, as a
characteristic manifestation of their attitudes toward work, the book by the Spanish
Jesuit, Pedro de Guzmán, which appeared one year after the *Novelas ejemplares*, *Los
bienes de honesto trabajo y daños de la ociosidad*. See "Religion, the Reformation, and
Social Change," *The European Witch-Craze of the Sixteenth and Seventeenth Centuries and
Other Essays*, p. 35.

soning and criticism, and a determination to combat evil. Although pathetically overmatched in his encounters with his adversaries and constantly forced to take refuge in flight or silence, the embattled protagonist clearly presents a norm by which the reader can measure and judge the flaws of the host of monsters, and despite his defeats he offers a firm vindication of the natural goodness of human beings and their capacities to cultivate their good inclination through education and to lead a virtuous life.

If we turn from the tale of Berganza's life to the multilayered satirical dialogue which folds about it, we discover that it is animated by the same set of values that is implied by Berganza's experiences. The dogs are exemplary in their expressions of piety and humility. Cipión reminds Berganza that it is folly to assume that the workings of divine providence can be fathomed by human intelligence ("what heaven has ordained to happen, no human knowledge or effort can prevent").[32] Berganza receives his "divine gift of speech" in words that recall the teachings of contemporary Christian Stoics and their putative spiritual ancestor, Job, concerning the proper attitude toward the possessions of this world, things "lent" to their holders: "I don't know when they may ask me to return this blessing, which I look upon as a loan."[33] Admitting his weakness, he trusts in God to see him through his difficulties: "To Jesus I commend myself in every event. . . . At least I shall do my best, and may Heaven make up my deficiencies."[34] Cipión insists that in God's eyes the poorest are the richest and the most humble are those of "best lineage," for, unlike numerous contemporary Spaniards in their obsession with "purity of blood," God is concerned only with "purity of heart." Berganza offers

[32] "Que lo que el cielo tiene ordenado que suceda, no hay diligencia ni sabiduría humana que lo pueda prevenir" (p. 213).

[33] "No sé cuándo me volverán a pedir este bien, que por prestado tengo" (p. 213). See, for example, the doctrine as expressed in the Greek poem of pseudo-Phocylides, a philosophical work widely read in contemporary schools and popularized by the neo-Stoics. "Nunca te aflijas / por desdichas que pases, ni te alegres / con los contentos: todos son prestados, / y como viene el mal se van los bienes" (trans. F. de Quevedo, *Obras completas verso*, ed. L. Astrana Marín [Madrid, 1943], p. 645). A. Rothe speculates that Quevedo may have become acquainted with the work in his Jesuit college and welcomed it as proof of the reconcilability of classical and Hebraic traditions (*Quevedo und Seneca* [Cologne, 1965], p. 42). H. Ettinghausen notes that the idea that "goods are given to man on loan" is frequent in Quevedo's Stoic writings and that in his demonstration that Epictetus was influenced by Job, he adds the line in his translation of the *Manual*, "pues da la vida cuanto da prestado" (*Francisco de Quevedo and the Neostoic Movement* [Oxford, 1972], p. 69).

[34] "A Él [Jesús] me encomiendo en todo acontecimiento. . . . A lo menos, yo haré de mi parte mis diligencias, y supla las faltas el Cielo" (pp. 241-42).

an eloquent speech on humility as the foundation of all virtue (p. 234), and, although there is a good deal of banter in its introduction, it makes its point forcefully and supports numerous other elements in the work that stress the importance of humility (see below).

While such references firmly found the point of view of the satirical commentators in Christian doctrine, it should be emphasized that the dogs devote little attention to the metaphysical speculations that emerge in the Cañizares episode. Their discussions are dominated by a wide-ranging interest in man's social, political, occupational, economic, and cultural activities, and their pronouncements concerning such activities are marked by a forcefulness that contrasts sharply with the bewilderment and inconclusiveness of their remarks on miracles, providence, and the witches' mysteries. There is a pronounced worldly character to the code of ethics that they advocate most definitively. Thus they can describe and unequivocally denounce the corrupt dealings of scribes, the hoarding of wealth by Moriscos and its effects on the Spanish economy, the parasitic customs of charlatans, Spaniards' obsessions with purity of blood and lineage, the ridiculous pastimes of idle nobles, the pretentious posturing in Latin of pedants, and the intellectual vices of philosophers. They can critically discuss the acquisition of power by flatterers and the ostentatious display of wealth by the new merchant class in its efforts to ascend socially. And in a speech recalling the Erasmians' pacifism and their eloquent criticism of the debasing effects of war, Berganza describes soldiers' depredations of their own country, an evil for which there appears to be no remedy, "for all or most things having to do with war bring with them harshness, severity, and inconvenience."[35]

The dogs' discussion concludes with a powerful expression of Stoic philosophy. Cipión, whose very name has been traditionally synonymous with the ideal of moral heroism propounded by the philosophers of antiquity and exemplified by its greatest heroes, reminds his friend that man is subject to the vicissitudes of fortune ("If by chance death or some other accident or fortune fells the tree on which they lean for support . . .") and that truth has little power against the tyranny of appearances within society. As he advises Berganza to curb his zeal as a reformer and implies that an honest man's only practical course of action lies in prudence, endurance, resignation, and silence, his words of disenchantment rearticulate the imagery of darkness that is perva-

---

[35] "Porque todas o las más cosas de la guerra traen consigo aspereza, riguridad y desconveniencia" (p. 280). The theme was reiterated throughout Erasmus' writings and received its most influential formulation in the oration, *Querela Pacis*, the adage, *Dulce Bellum Inexpertis* and the *Institutio Principis Christiani*.

sive in the novella: "Wisdom in a poor man is beshadowed, for need and poverty are shadows and clouds which obscure it, and if by chance it does shine through, men take it for folly and treat it with contempt." However, at this moment Cipión notices that the dim light of dawn is entering through the chinks of their vaporous cell, and he turns to the more positive aspects of his philosophy. "Virtue and good sense remain always the same, whether naked or clothed, alone or accompanied. To be sure, they may suffer in the opinion of the world, but not in the true reality of what they are worth and deserve. And with this, let us make an end to our conversation."[36] In one of its few predications that is not attenuated by the vertiginous ironies of the surrounding discourse, the *Colloquy* ends with an affirmation of the fundamental Stoic doctrines concerning the value of virtue as its own reward, man's responsibility to pursue virtue and truth and to cultivate intelligence and good sense, and the crucial distinction between the essential realm of reality and virtue and the insubstantial world of opinion and appearances, with all its enslaving allurements. Moreover, in his association of Berganza's emphatic pronouncement with dawn and light, with the awakening of the redeemed sinner, and with the conclusion of the licentiate's reading experience, we see that Cervantes has carefully integrated the declaration of these doctrines with the other elements which at the end of his tale hold out hope for regeneration, spiritual growth, and escape from the enveloping shadows of illusion and the contaminating powers of evil.

While such Stoic values are prominent throughout the *Colloquy* and are privileged through their incorporation in the climactic moments in its plot development and in its sustained elaboration of symbolic imagery, I would emphasize that the ethical vision of the tale is not entirely reducible to them and that, in its assimilation of Stoic philosophy, Cervantes' dialogue, in fact, effects a modification that decisively separates his work from the rigorous neo-Stoic ethical ideal which flourished in contemporary ascetic and imaginative writings. When one considers the nature of the *Colloquy*'s Stoic philosophy, one immediately notes the presence of powerful moderating tendencies—the simplicity, tolerance, evasiveness, and indulgence of its heroes

---

[36] "Si acaso la muerte o otro accidente de fortuna derriba el árbol donde se arriman. . . . La sabiduría en el pobre está asombrada; que la necesidad y miseria son las sombras y nubes que la escurecen, y si acaso se descubre, la juzgan por tontedad y la tratan con menosprecio. . . . La virtud y el buen entendimiento siempre es una y siempre es uno: desnudo o vestido, solo o acompañado. Bien es verdad que puede padecer acerca de la estimación de las gentes; mas no en la realidad verdadera de lo que merece y vale. Y con esto, pongamos fin a esta plática" (pp. 338-39).

and, of course, the forcefulness of their evangelical pronouncements concerning such "non-Stoic" virtues as humility and charity. In its specific content, its derivation, and its eclectic character, the moral stance of Cervantes' dogs represents a Christian-Stoic synthesis of a type that is far closer to the moral philosophy of Erasmus' *Philosophia Christi* than to that of the seventeenth-century neo-Stoics with their emphases on virtue, *sapientia*, constancy, endurance, the readiness for death, and the freedom from the slavery of worldly vanities and their interest in the Old-Testament "sources" of Stoic philosophy. It is worth recalling Erasmus' discussion of "vulgar and false opinions and judgments" in the Sixth Rule of the *Enchiridion*. His survey of the illusions and uncontrollable passions which blind men and cause them, like the dwellers of Plato's cave, to stumble about amid the shadows leads him to extol the Stoics as examples of those who insist on truth and courageously defend it despite the mockery of the benighted majority. At the same time he reminds the Christian to treat his brothers with compassion, and he proceeds in the following section of the rule to celebrate as the essential values of the spiritual man charity, love, kindness, gentleness, good will, humility, and brotherhood, and to enjoin his readers to educate the "hombres carnales" with the humanity of St. Paul rather than the asperity of the Cynic philosopher.[37]

Cervantes' critics display a similar combination of the Stoic passion for truth and the Christian commitment to charity, benevolence, and humility. Berganza admires the saintly occupation of the "buen cristiano Mahudes," is prompted by "good envy"[38] to aid him in the

[37] See, for example: "Primeramente que ningún christiano piense que nació para sí solo ni quiera bivir para sí solo . . . que todos sus bienes tenga por comunes a todos. Pues la charidad christiana no sabe tener cosa propia. Ame los buenos porque son miembros de Jesu Christo y a los malos porque lo manda Jesu Christo" (*Enquiridion*, pp. 322-23). "El próximo . . . es tu hermano en el Señor . . . y es también miembro de un mesmo cuerpo donde lo eres tú . . . ¿Quién te puede ser estrangero . . . ? ¿No vees que el bien que se haze a un miembro redunda y se comunica a todo el cuerpo . . . ? (pp. 324-25) ". . . que los unos condecendamos a los otros, y cada uno procure de aliviar y aun llevar la carga de su próximo con toda diligencia y humildad" (p. 330). "Assí que la ley determinada del christiano ha de ser querer sobrepujar a todos y ganar honrra con ellos en amor y mansedumbre y en buenas obras . . . pero en contiendas, en odio, en murmuración, en injurias y en daños, en esto tal dexarse vencer de muy buena gana y aun de los más flacos" (p. 334). Erasmus' moderated Stoicism is implicit in his words on the beauty of a "sabia innocencia, con limpieza y integridad de vida, con una severidad modesta" (p. 340).

[38] Berganza's allusion to "buena envidia" is a revealing commonplace as it reflects a favorable view of the proper, creative function of the passions and situates his ethical attitudes in the Christian-Aristotelian tradition of moral philosophy while separating them decisively from Stoic morality with its essentially negative view of the passions.

collection of alms, and ultimately finds the "buen puerto" which he has been seeking all along in a life dedicated to charitable action. He recalls his companionship with the poet, the generosity with which he shared with him the few crumbs of bread that made up his meal, and the pleasure of the drink which they enjoyed together ("we would

---

Contrasting the Peripatetics and the Stoics, Erasmus writes that the former "piensan aver en ellas [las aficiones] algún provecho, porque éstas nos fueron dadas naturalmente por espuelas y incitamientos para la virtud. Como veemos que la yra, aunque es passión, pero no siendo desmedida, es despertadora de la virtud de la fortaleza; y la embidia, siendo liviana, despierta a la industria y diligencia; y otras por el semejante" (*Enquiridion*, pp. 165-66). A fundamentally positive valuation of the affects underlies Erasmus' entire ethical philosophy and his teachings concerning the individual, the family, society, and the state. See, for example, his discussion of the dignity which Christ conferred on the natural passions by willingly experiencing, in his vigil in Gethsemane, the fear of death and implicitly rejecting the readiness and fortitude which the "inhumane" Stoics demand of their sage (*Disputatiuncula de Taedio, Pavore, Tristitia Jesu, Instante Supplicio Crucis, Opera Omnia*, ed. J. Le Clerc, 10 vols. [Leiden, 1703-1706], 5:1265-92, esp. 1276-77), Stultitia's tirade against the rigors of the Stoic wise men in the *Praise of Folly* (see *Laus Stultitiae, Ausgewählte Schriften*, ed. W. Welzig, 8 vols. [Darmstadt, 1967-1980], 2:64-72), and the eloquent advocacy of the constructive cultivation of the passions that precedes her notorious panoramic diatribe. Similarly in the *Colloquy*'s forceful affirmations of the goodness and beauty of the human body, we observe a definitive repudiation of the traditional dualistic attitudes concerning body and soul which are characteristic of such spiritualistic doctrines as Platonism and Manicheanism and which were resurrected and widely celebrated in the neo-Stoic philosophy and ascetic Christianity of Cervantes' contemporaries. In a striking scene in which Berganza appears to recoil from his initial triumph as a penetrating Stoic observer of depths, he refuses to bite the hands of the beautiful maiden whose inner corruption he has perceptively discovered, and both dogs agree that it is the "prerrogativa de la hermosura que siempre se le tenga respecto" (p. 220). To appreciate their rejection of the kind of *desengaño* championed everywhere in seventeenth-century moral philosophy, we need only look at the uncompromising demands for lucidity made by F. de Miranda y Paz in his guide for the man who would escape the universal tyranny of illusion: "La mayor hermosura es un vaso de corrupcion. La exterior apariencia en el color, bella, y apacible en perfecciones: en el interior es abominable, hedionda y corruptible. Acaso has visto belleza grande, que no sea un pedaço de estiercol oculto con una tela sútil? Ea, haz reflexion, no te niegues al conocimiento. Confesarás, que la mayor gentileza, y hermosura de hombre, o mujer, es podre" (*El Desengañado. Philosophia Moral*; cited by H. Schulte, *El Desengaño: Wort und Thema in der Spanischen Literatur des Goldenen Zeitalters* [Munich, 1969], p. 96). The tensions and ambiguities of the scene of Berganza's encounter with the beautiful woman are perhaps the clearest indications in the work of the eclectic character of its ethical vision and Cervantes' concern to disengage from the darkest implications of the Stoic morality. The reference to the body at the conclusion of the Ensign's confession, as he awakens and decides to accompany his friend to the park to refresh the "ojos corporales," is another moment in which we see Cervantes emphatically adhering to the more optimistic vision of his humanist predecessors. It is worth contrasting the conclusion of St. Theresa's confes-

repair to the waterwheel, where I, putting my head down, lapped away, and he drank out of one of the buckets; and thus both of us quenched our thirst like monarchs"). Once again for a brief moment the oppressive atmosphere of the *Colloquy* is lightened by the carnivalesque spirit of equality and authentic communication, uniting, as it were, dog, man, and monarch, and we glimpse a true banquet marked by the same spirit of friendship and good will which we observe in the restorative feast of the frame tale and in the schoolchildren's lunches. The recollection of the experience inspires Berganza to speak eloquently on the beauty of charity: "There is no better or ampler purse than charity, whose liberal hands are never poor, and so I disagree with the proverb that says, 'He who is naked gives you less than he who is hard,' as though a hard and avaricious man would ever give anything as a generous and naked man gives it, for at least

sion, where she claims that she has awakened from spiritual blindness, that, having seen with the "eyes of the soul," she understands that everything which she "sees with the eyes of the body is a mockery," and that she is dead to feelings of grieving or glorying in things which occur in the dreamworld of the earthly life (see *Libro de la vida, Obras*, ed. T. de la Cruz [Burgos, 1971], pp. 447, 494-95). The leading proponent of Christian Stoicism in Cervantes' Spain, Francisco de Quevedo, referred to the body as a "jail" and an "enemy" and reminded his reader: "tu no eres sino el alma" (see A. Rothe, *Quevedo und Seneca*, p. 75). Characteristically Quevedo interprets Christ's experience of fears in Gethsemane as an example revealing the heroism of divine love and of the soul; for such fears, the product of "human nature" and the "weakness of the body," offer Christ and his martyred descendants the occasion for spiritual victory in their ultimately joyous acceptance of death (*Declamación de Jesucristo, Hijo de Dios, a su Eterno Padre, en el huerto, Obras*, B.A.E. 48:359-63). In considering such striking moments in Cervantes' dialogue, we should recall Erasmus' words on the dignity of man and his reverence for the sanctity of the human body, the temple consecrated by Jesus Christ (see *Enquiridion*, pp. 372, 380; for Erasmus' rejection of a radical spiritualism, see A. Auer, *Die Vollkommene Frömmigkeit des Christen nach dem Enchiridion militis Christiani des Erasmus von Rotterdam* [Düsseldorf, 1954], p. 92). Perhaps most apposite to the conclusion of Cervantes' *Colloquy* is the following exchange in Erasmus' colloquy, *The Godly Feast*: "Eusebio: But while we feast our minds plenteously, let us not neglect their partners. Theo: Who are they? Eusebio: Our bodies: aren't they partners of our minds? For I prefer 'partners' to 'instruments' or 'dwellings' or 'tombs.' Tim: When the whole man is refreshed, this is abundant refreshment indeed" (*The Colloquies of Erasmus*, trans. C. R. Thompson [Chicago, 1965], p. 62). For the importance of certain fundamental Stoic doctrines in the eclectic ethic of Erasmus' *Philosophia Christiana*, see E. Troeltsch, *The Social Teaching of the Christian Churches*, trans. O. Wyon (New York, 1931), 2:764, and "Verhältnis von 'via antiqua' und 'via moderna' zu Humanismus und Reformation.—Religiöstheologische Bedeutung des Erasmus," *Aufsätze zur Geistesgeschichte und Religionssoziologie, Gesammelte Schriften*, Vol. 4 (Tübingen, 1925), pp. 762-74. "Die Theologie des Erasmus . . . geht in ihrem Kerne auf eine kritische Herausschälung der mit der Stoa identifizierten Moral des Evangeliums hinaus" (p. 773).

the latter gives good will when he has nothing else."[39] Rearticulating the recurrent imagery of clothing and nudity, Berganza's words recall the spirit of the *Sileni Alcibiadis*, emphasizing the gap between external and internal and paradoxically finding true riches in a condition of absolute poverty. The definition of the "liberal desnudo" looks back to perhaps the most Erasmian moment of the *Colloquy*, the dogs' dialogue on humility, an exchange that exploits the elaboration of a central paradox, the conventional style of religious oratory, and ironic self-deflation to support its unconventional elevation of this fundamentally "antiheroic" Christian virtue. Following Cipión's condemnation of the "lords of the earth" who judge their servants by their dress and lineage and his reminder that "the Lord of Heaven" finds the "most humble to be of the best lineage," and the righteous to be the most "limpios" ("of untainted blood"), Berganza is inspired to dilate on the beauties of humility: "you are aware that humility is the base and foundation of all virtues, and that without it there are none. It smooths away difficulties and is the means whereby we shall reach glorious ends; it makes friends of one's enemies, tempers the wrath of the choleric, abates the arrogance of the arrogant, and is the mother of modesty and the sister of moderation. In short, with it, vices cannot win a profitable triumph because its mildness and gentleness blunt the darts of sin."[40] Berganza's discourse on humility, which reveals his mastery of the rhetoric of contemporary sermons and devotional writings,[41] is framed by self-deflationary elements, his own criticism

[39] "Nos íbamos a la noria, donde, yo de bruces y él con un canjilón, satisfacíamos la sed como unos monarcas. . . . no hay mayor ni mejor bolsa que la de la caridad, cuyas liberales manos jamás están pobres, y así, no estoy bien con aquel refrán que dice: 'Más da el duro que el desnudo,' como si el duro y avaro diese algo, como lo da el liberal desnudo, que, en efeto, da el buen deseo cuando más no tiene" (p. 324-25).

[40] "La humildad es la basa y fundamento de todas las virtudes, y que sin ella no hay alguna que lo sea. Ella allana inconvenientes, vence dificultades, y es un medio que siempre a gloriosos fines nos conduce; de los enemigos hace amigos, templa la cólera de los airados y menoscaba la arrogancia de los soberbios; es madre de la modestia y hermana de la templanza; en fin, con ella no pueden atravesar triunfo que les sea de provecho los vicios, porque en su blandura y mansedumbre se embotan y despuntan las flechas de los pecados" (p. 234).

[41] For the accuracy with which the speech reflects commonplaces of current religious writings, compare Luis de León's discussion of the "humildad y mansedumbre de coraçón," exemplified by Christ, seated "indecorously" on an ass. "Dios . . . halló, como es verdad, que la primera piedra desta su obra era un ánimo manso y humilde, y vió que un semejante edificio tan soberano y tan alto no se podía sustentar sino sobre cimientos tan hondos" (*De los nombres de Cristo*, 2:89-90). See also Melchor Cano: "la cual [la humildad] es fundamento del edificio cristiano," and Francisco Ortiz: "en la misma Escritura Santa, que dice que el lugar de Dios es la paz, dice también que

of his comrade's predication in the introductory part of the exchange and his invocation of these lofty doctrines to account for his ingratiating techniques of acquiring masters at its conclusion. Such self-deprecation is hardly the style of the Stoic sage or censor, and it points to a most important aspect of the *Colloquy*, one which must be considered if we are to understand correctly its moral vision, its philosophical backgrounds, and its literary genre. In the following section I shall return to my point of departure, the question of the tale's genre, and attempt to deal with the type of complexity that the interlocutors' self-criticisms and self-implications bring to Cervantes' satirical personae and to the satirical discourse of the *Colloquy*.

THE UNASSERTIVE SATIRICAL VOICE: DIALOGUE AS A LIBERATING FORCE

An attempt to define the perspective of Cervantes' canine satirists must certainly take into account the forcefulness of their little homilies on humility and charity. However, perhaps more significant than the profession of such Christian sentiments is the way in which the dogs exemplify them in their discourse, that is, the way in which they allow them on occasion to soften the asperity of their criticism and, by so doing, consciously refuse to adopt the superior stance of the moral censor. For example, Cipión's harsh observations concerning

reposa donde hay humildad, y la misma humildad es verdadera paz y reposo y holganza, y por eso dijo la santa Verdad: Aprendid de mí, que soy manso y humilde de corazón" (cited by R. Ricard, *Estudio de literatura religiosa española* [Madrid, 1964], pp. 60, 65). In his colloquy on "la vanidad de la honra del mundo," the Spanish Erasmist, A. de Torquemada, defines authentic honor as the reward of virtue and condemns worldly honor, which his contemporaries have made a marketable commodity, as pride and, as such, opposed to Christian faith, which is "founded on humility" (*Coloquios satíricos*, p. 533). For the importance of the virtue of humility in Cervantes' writings and its significance as an indication of the impact of Erasmus on his development, see A. Castro, *El pensamiento de Cervantes*, pp. 299-300. Castro finds nothing in the text of the *Coloquio* that discredits Berganza's pronouncement of moral doctrine in this passage. In his study of the doctrines and methods of the Jesuit educators of the sixteenth century, F. de Dainville notes that, while Stoic philosophy furnished various doctrines which the Jesuits found congenial to their programs of moral instruction, their emphasis on humility as "le fondement et soutien de toutes les vertus chrétiennes" represented a rejection of the prideful self-reliance implicit in the classical ideal of autarchy (*La naissance de l'humanisme moderne* [Paris, 1940], p. 250). Here we see another of the numerous examples of the influence of Erasmus' thought on the Ignatian program of reform. See, on this subject, R. García-Villoslada, *Loyola y Erasmo* (Madrid, 1965).

the venality and ambitiousness of merchants and their determination
to ascend socially through the purchase of titles are followed by the
charitable qualification: "It is ambition, but it is a generous ambition,
the kind which seeks to improve one's position without doing harm
to others."[42] As Berganza alludes to the evils of constables and notaries, Cipión reminds him of the inhumanity of generalizing denunciations that exploit vulgar stereotypes of class or profession: "to speak
ill of one does not mean to denounce all."[43] If such retractions reveal
a generous, discriminating disposition in Cervantes' critics, the numerous self-incriminating statements that emerge in their survey of
foibles, as well as the mischievously self-deprecatory style of their
discourse, suggest a moderately indulgent attitude toward human failings and a conception of their critical role as far more complex than
those of the haughty Juvenalian censor, whom Cipión recalls in ad-
vising Berganza on the problems of satire, and the Stoic sage, whom
the more austere comments of Cipión might bring to mind.

Following Berganza's observation concerning the "generous ambition" of the merchants, we witness one of the most revealing of the
various exchanges that place the narrators in the foreground of the
tale, establish their identity as characters, and disclose their attitudes
as censors. The expression of tolerance concerning the foible leads both
narrators to consider the vice of slander, to condemn the "backbiting
defamers" who make a habit of "destroying family names," and to
confess their susceptibility to its appeal. Their discussion is marked
by the odd combination of levity and seriousness, of simplicity and
worldliness, and of innocence and cynicism which invests so many of
their pronouncements with an elusive, disingenuous quality and contributes so much to the fundamentally paradoxical spirit of the entire
work—a work that looks upon itself as a monster that edifies, presents
heroes whose unheroic nature is repeatedly stressed, offers criticism
that continually coils back on itself and joins it to the world it would
destroy, and develops as its central episode the confession of a witch,
who, although a worshipper of the devil, speaks eloquently of the
mysteries of divine justice.

As he analyzes the effects of slander, Berganza admits with a trace
of humor that he cannot control his impulses to "murmurar" ("I see
in myself that, in spite of being an animal, as I am, with every few
sentences that I utter, words come to my tongue like mosquitoes to

[42] "Ambición es, pero ambición generosa, la de aquel que pretende mejorar su
estado sin perjuicio de tercero" (p. 239).
[43] "Decir mal de uno no es decirlo de todos" (p. 269).

wine, and every one of them is malicious and derogatory"), attributes
the vice to the basic flaw with which all men have been born since
the fall of Adam and Eve ("doing and speaking evil we inherit from
our first parents and suck in with our mother's milk"), and supports
his argument by claiming that a child's first word is the imprecation
"whore," which he hurls at his mother while shaking his fist at her
in wrath. Cipión appears to be impressed by his companion's argument: "I confess my error and beg you to forgive me this time, as I
have forgiven you on so many occasions. Let us *blow our quarrels into
the sea, as little boys say*, and henceforth refrain from backbiting." The
shift in tonalities could hardly be greater or more swiftly managed.
Whatever we may think about the doctrine of original sin and its
implications, the posture and speech of the vengeful infant as its illustration conflict harshly with conventional notions regarding children's attitudes and behavior, which the following figure of speech,
based on the games of childhood, almost immediately reconfirms and
exploits. The startling reversal in the evocation of the child compels
us to look upon language from two diametrically opposed points of
view and simultaneously to take note of its power to heal and its
power to destroy. Accompanying the rapid movement from sophisticated, self-deprecating irony to the somber humor of the grotesque
and to the endearing banter of innocent children at play is a shift in
attitude and perspective from the weariness of worldly wisdom to the
nihilistic wrath of the darkest cynicism and finally to the ingenuous
hopefulness of humility and innocence. At this point Berganza appro-
priately commends himself to Jesus: "To Him I commend myself in
every event."[44] However, as if he can not bear to see the spiraling
discourse collapse on so conclusive and determinate a point, he immediately follows his profession of humility with a speech on the
difficulty of suppressing the urge to slander, which he illustrates with
an anecdote about a man who unsuccessfully sought to curb his impulse to swear by resolving to pinch himself and kiss the earth with
every oath. The story certainly qualifies the anecdote of the enraged
infant, which precedes it, as it presents a radically different, far more
indulgent perspective in which the vice is viewed. The exchange con-

---

[44] "Yo veo en mí, que con ser un animal, como soy, a cuatro razones que digo,
me acuden palabras a la lengua como mosquitos al vino, y todas maliciosas y mur-
murantes. . . . que el hacer y decir mal lo heredamos de nuestros primeros padres y
lo mamamos en la leche. . . . yo confieso mi yerro, y quiero que me le perdones,
pues te he perdonado tantos: *echemos pelillos a la mar, como dicen los muchachos*, y no
murmuremos de aquí adelante. . . . A Él me encomiendo en todo acontecimiento"
(pp. 240-41; italics added).

cludes in a tone of tolerance and good humor. Berganza resolves to imitate the man of his anecdote and to bite his tongue every time his utterances are touched with malice; Cipión encourages him with the humorous assurance that he will soon conquer his sin because he will quickly devour his tongue; and Berganza offers another profession of humility and piety: "At least I shall do my best, and may Heaven make up my deficiencies." The passage illustrates effectively how in the *Colloquy* such fundamentally serious and central issues as original sin, slander, satire, piety, humility, free will, merit, and Divine Grace are mingled with and, in fact, concealed beneath what appears to be trivial, how they are developed and fragmentarily disclosed in contexts of rapidly shifting perspectives and varied tones of humor and irony, and how the complex narrative voices of the work compel the reader to share the restlessness of the occupants of its fictional world, groping at the literary text, frequently redefining his awareness of what he is experiencing, and, in doing so, constantly discovering the instability of his perception of it. At the same time, the exchange reveals several of the principal stances which mark the protean commentary of the dogs: sophistication, simplicity, cynicism, self-mockery, and mischievous tolerance.

A similar effect accompanies Berganza's speech on humility, to which I have referred above. It follows closely on Cipión's eloquent discourse on the privileged position enjoyed by the poor and humble in God's service. Unexpectedly Berganza responds to the expression of such lofty sentiments with a mild rebuke: "All this, friend Cipión, is preaching."[45] Following Cipión's acknowledgement of the validity of the criticism and the promise to refrain from sermonizing, Berganza turns about to offer the elaborate speech on humility, which, in its personification allegory, its parallel phrases, repetitions, and amplifications, and its developed attention to rhythm, is a perfect example of contemporary pulpit oratory and devotional writing. While there is nothing in the conventionality of its ideas and style, despite what might be called an "overconcentration" of rhetorical conventions, that approaches parody, the mischievous way in which Berganza appears to disregard his injunction concerning sermonizing troubles our apprehension of the speech as a serious expression of moral doctrine. As if to complicate the perspective further, on coming to the *exemplum* of his sermon, the dog proudly describes how he "applied" his ethical wisdom by licking the boots of prospective employers and wagging his tail endearingly, and his flagrant confusion of the virtue with its

[45] "Todo esto es predicar, Cipión amigo" (p. 233).

appearance implicates his behavior and discourse in the processes of derangement that pervade the tale's survey of lawlessness. Thus the speech is introduced and concluded by elements that jarringly distract the reader from its doctrinal focus and compel him to apprehend it simultaneously as an impressive statement of Christian philosophy and as a constituent part of a satirical context dealing, on the one hand, with excessive sententiousness, on the other, with hypocritical piety. The plurality of meanings effected by the "fragile" coherence of the exchange is further compounded as the reader must ultimately cope with the possibility of subordinating its rifts to the ambiguities of the voice of the principal speaker and the character behind that voice and considering that the whole passage might be an elaborate pose of "sinfulness" by an ironic personality. However, the peculiar thing about the discourse on humility is the forcefulness that it maintains as a statement of doctrine despite the diluting effects brought about by Cervantes' interference with the reader's efforts to integrate its elements as a single system of meaning.[46] In this respect it is totally unlike the incongruous allusions to Biblical and liturgical texts in the much more monologic discourse of the cynical narrators of the pica- resque *Lazarillo de Tormes* and *El Buscón*, where the reader quickly grasps the principal aims of the unsettling energies released by the irony, namely the moral discrediting of the protagonist and the alien- ation of the reader from his world.[47]

[46] In his recent study "Cervantes' Sententious Dogs" (*Modern Language Notes* 94 [1979]:377-86), T. R. Hart notes that "the moral authority of a *sententia* does not derive from the person who cites it but from the whole tradition to which it belongs."

[47] A "self-negating moment" is essential to all authentic dialogue, which proceeds in the direction of truth through a sustained process of affirmation and negation, conditions any movement toward dogmatic assertion, always compels the reader or listener to exercise his own capacities of choice, and leads him to recognize ultimately the conditional nature of any truth. A tendency toward such self-negation is visible throughout the dialogue or the dogs. We witness it, for example, in Berganza's playing off antithetical proverbial utterances against one another: "puesto que dice el refrán: 'Quien necio es en su villa, necio es en Castilla,' el andar tierras y comunicar con diversas gentes hace a los hombres discretos" (p. 278). Similar effects can be observed in the undercutting of Cipión's truism on the necessity of trust in a society (see above) and in the discussion of the moral complexities surrounding the role of ambition in human behavior (p. 239). This "dialogizing" process can manifest itself in more subtle ways at the imaginative level of the discourse, as when Berganza exploits the metaphor of king to dignify the moment at which the dog and poet unite in genuine communication and friendship ("satisfacíamos la sed como unos monarcas") and almost immediately thereafter rearticulates it ironically to underscore the impoverishment and absurd pretentiousness of the latter's existence ("le seguí . . . imaginando que de las sobras de su castillo se podía mantener mi real" [pp. 324-25]). The analogy is simultaneously critical and celebrative; "king" as imagina-

One of the most significant aspects of the two passages under consideration is the manner in which Berganza implicates himself in the folly that he surveys. On occasions his self-denunciations are made more directly and forcefully, and it is only because Cervantes has elsewhere effectively characterized him as an ethical being with an ironic voice that we construe his avowals of sinfulness as ironic poses and render them intelligible in terms of the overall ethical and satirical purposes of the work.[48] For example, after resolving various times to curb his propensity to slander, he is caught flagrantly violating his resolution by Cipión, and he responds with a classical anecdote celebrating the heroic constancy of Corondas, who, on discovering that he had himself broken his own statute against the bearing of arms in the national assembly, immediately killed himself in proper execution of the law. Berganza concludes the exemplary anecdote with the traditional diatribe of satirical writing: "now things are not carried out with the consistency and rigor of days of yore. Today a law is made and tomorrow it is broken, and perhaps it is fitting that this should be so. Now one promises to correct his faults, and a moment later he

tive concept is at once a source of negative and positive energy. As G. Sobejano has correctly pointed out, the voluminous monologue of Guzmán de Alfarache is in reality much more "dialogical" than has been commonly supposed (see "De Alemán a Cervantes: Monólogo y Diálogo," *Homenaje al Profesor Muñoz Cortés* [Murcia, 1977], 2:713-29). However, aside from certain exceptional instances, such as the ironic declamation in celebration of begging, it does not consistently develop the kind of self-negating tendency that invests Cervantes' dialogue with such meaningful instability. One might compare the dogs' use of anecdotal and analogic qualification in their discussion of slander with Guzmán's account of his sleep before the Church of St. Lazarus (see above) or his description of his confession at the opening of Part II. In its verbal expansiveness and its rapid shifts of perspective through anecdotal spinoffs (i.e., the book appears in a bewildering proliferation of analogies—the viper which poisons, the blunderbuss which kills, the radish which nauseates, the banquet of Heliogabalus, a fine tapestry of corpses displayed by the executioner, a bear baited by a bloodthirsty mob) the picaro's discourse resembles that of Cipión and Berganza. However, we do not find that the shifts bring the changing perspectives into collision with one another. They ultimately collapse on a single point, and in their uniformity in tone they strive for effects which are far closer to those of conventional rhetorical amplification than to the enlivening provocation of the sustained dialogical destruction-construction of Cervantes' text. See *Guzmán de Alfarache*, 3:69-83).

[48] The characterization to which I refer has little to do with the psychologically or ethically consistent development of character which mark representational (e.g., novelistic) and exemplary fiction respectively. It is rather the creation of a satirical persona, whose unity lies in the style of its ironical discourse, an emphatically "free" discourse which adopts self-implications, reversals, and inconsistency as its norms. I am attempting to demonstrate that such a discourse accords perfectly with the ethical vision of the work, as well as with certain literary and cultural traditions behind the work.

falls into greater ones. It is one thing to praise discipline, and another to inflict it upon oneself; and indeed there is a great difference between saying and doing."[49] The speech is one of the most important of the various passages in the work that illuminate the utter depravity of the present with a beam of light emanating from a glorious past and that display both the protagonist and his world as distinctively unheroic. However, the self-denunciation continues, as Berganza immediately adds the vice of hypocrisy to his weaknesses: "May the devil bite himself, for I have no intention of biting myself—nor of exhibiting my heroic qualities behind this mat, where I am sure I am seen by no one who can praise my honorable resolution." The admission allows Cipión to proceed to a definition of the sin and a denunciation of hypocrites: "In that case, Berganza, if you were a man you would be a hypocrite, and all your acts would be fictitious and false though cloaked in virtue. All hypocrites behave this way so that they will be praised."[50] At no other point in the dialogue does Berganza, in his various poses, come so close to the unregenerate picaro, who preaches self-interest and a cynical acquiescence in the ways of a corrupt society. However, almost immediately the protean voice shifts tonalities, as the dog amuses himself by frustrating his companion's aroused expectations to hear the conclusion of the tale of the servants' nocturnal orgy. The mischievous nature of his assertion of "artistic freedom" is heightened by the means of his interruption: an anecdotal clarification of a Latin proverb which is, in fact, a glaring violation of his own recently expressed strictures on the flaunting of Latin by pretentious pedants. If we have found the advocacy of hypocrisy and slander disturbing, we are, nevertheless, quickly forced to qualify our impression as we witness the playful inconsistency with which he torments his audience within and outside of the work. We must then recognize that we are dealing with a Horatian satirical persona, in whom inconsistency, variation in tone and pose, and irony are fundamental attributes, that the calculated ironies in his advocacies of sin, unlike those in the statements of such cynical sinners and satirical personae as

[49] "Ahora no van las cosas por el tenor y rigor de las antiguas: hoy se hace una ley, y mañana se rompe, y quizá conviene que así sea. Ahora promete uno de enmendarse de sus vicios, y de allí a un momento cae en otros mayores. Una cosa es alabar la disciplina, y otra el darse con ella, y, en efeto, del dicho al hecho hay gran trecho" (p. 255).

[50] "Muérdase el diablo; que yo no quiero morderme, ni hacer finezas detrás de una estera, donde de nadie soy visto que pueda alabar mi honrosa determinación. . . . Según eso, Berganza, si tú fueras persona, fueras hipócrita, y todas las obras que hicieras fueran aparentes, fingidas y falsas, cubiertas con la capa de la virtud, sólo porque te alabaran, como todos los hipócritas hacen" (p. 255).

Lazarillo de Tormes, Guzmán de Alfarache (in his unregenerate poses), and Quevedo's Don Pablos, which they formally resemble, do not strike at the character of the voice uttering them, and that in the present case, the satirist's self-incrimination must be interpreted as part of a complex rhetorical strategy pointing up the general depravity of the present, with its slanderers and hypocrites, to which in reality he is ethically superior.

Probably the most shocking example of Berganza's self-deflations and the ambiguities of such ironic self-denunciation emerges in his account of his decision to "acogerse a sagrado." The election of the religious calling appears to be the climax of his spiritual development, as it follows on one of his most noteworthy ethical triumphs, his renunciation of revenge and his refusal to tolerate the moral compromises demanded by the career of an actor: "and as I was in the position of deploring these abuses without being able to remedy them, I decided to avoid the sight of them, and so I took sanctuary, *as do those who give up their vices when they are no longer able to practice them, though, to be sure, it is better late than never.* I say, then, seeing you one night carrying the lantern with that worthy Christian Mahudes, I noticed how contented you were and how righteous and holy was your occupation; and full of good envy I longed to follow in your footsteps, and with that laudable intention I presented myself before Mahudes."[51] The explanatory analogy which intrudes here strikes jarringly against the expectations which the preceding elements of the passage arouse and which the following clarifications tend to fulfill, and we must once again make an effort of recovery and release ourselves to a play of possibilities in order to integrate the inconsistent element and render it intelligible. If we read the statement merely for its self-evident condemnation of hypocrisy and hypocrites and emphasize its essential consistency with the numerous other judgments that the narrators make as moral satirists, we would not be wrong, but we would fail to respond to the challenge of the ambiguities of its context. If only for an instant Berganza paradoxically appears as both a frustrated "remedier of vice" and a frustrated "exerciser of vice." As an unexpected reversal in the speaker's self-portrayal, the statement acquires unmistakable traces of inauthenticity, irony, and irreverence, and,

---

[51] "Y como a mí estaba más el sentillo que el remediallo, acordé de no verlo, y así, me acogí a sagrado, *como hacen aquellos que dejan los vicios cuando no pueden ejercitallos, aunque más vale tarde que nunca.* Digo, pues, que viéndote una noche llevar la linterna con el buen cristiano Mahudes, te consideré contento y justa y santamente ocupado; y, lleno de buena envidia, quise seguir tus pasos, y con esta loable intención me puse delante de Mahudes" (pp. 328-29; italics added).

while they do not undermine its judgment of hypocrisy, they surround it with implications that are far more numerous and interesting than those of the moralizing observation in itself. On the one hand, the reach of the satire extends beyond hypocrisy to pious commonplaces and to those who mouth them. On the other hand, and this is the important point, Berganza refuses to allow his moment of moral triumph and conversion to be touched with the solemnity that traditionally attends the climactic moment of the confession, just as he has refused throughout his tale to let the retrospective judgments of his commentary take the form of the self-righteous, indignant pronouncements of the dogmatic censor. It is, of course, impossible to know whether or not Cervantes had in mind the conversion experience of the most popular meditative, critical narrator of the day, Guzmán de Alfarache, and designed Berganza's decision in response, whether as parody or allusion, to Mateo Alemán's text.[52] Nevertheless, it is interesting that Cervantes seizes the moment of conversion, traditionally the moment of intense insight into the self and precise definition of the self in terms of its purpose and destiny—at the same time, the concluding moment that "closes" the confessional text as an ultimately coherently integrated system of elements—and exploits its expressive power to heighten the aura of indeterminacy surrounding his own confessor, whose "act of renunciation" becomes in effect another of the numerous withdrawals from determinacy which endow the dogs' commentary with the instability and elusiveness characterizing the entire work. In perhaps its most striking moment of self-negation, the *Colloquy* abruptly retreats from its own climax and the repose that would attend its "proper" completion.

The four passages that I have analyzed are striking examples of the oblique, unassertive style of Cervantes' narration and of the way in which it forces the reader to confront "gaps" in the surface of the text, to venture out into the uncharted directions pointed to by ironic statement, and to resolve, tentatively and always on his own, the apparent

---

[52] The passage might recall for the contemporary reader Guzmán's meditation on the proper and improper motivation for the election of the religious calling and his candid analysis of the self-interest that led him to a false conversion and the decision to take up study for the priesthood in Alcalá. "Era piedra movediza, que nunca la cubre moho y, por no sosegarme yo a mí, lo vino a hacer el tiempo. . . . No hallé otro [remedio] que acogerme a sagrado . . . tendré cierta la comida" (*Guzmán de Alfarache*, 5:13-14). It is characteristic of Cervantes' dialogizing procedures to collapse the false and true conversion, which in Alemán's narrative are clearly separated experiences in the picaro's account of his life, into a single decisive, but extremely restless textual moment.

contradictions or to sanction their irreducibility.[53] It is a difficult style, "asserting" nothing but its own freedom and demanding no less from its addressee, but, in its cultivation of ambiguity for provocation and illumination rather than for obscurity, it can reward the responsive reader with an experience of what Friedrich Schlegel referred to as the most profound activity of the human consciousness as a reflective entity—its basic dialectic and dialogic movement as it passes through thought and counterthought, construction and deconstruction, in a restless drama, ever forward toward a fuller comprehension of truth and an awareness of its ultimate incompleteness.[54] All of these effects, which in their complexity go beyond those of any picaresque narration or Lucianic dialogue in Spanish literature, are, of course, distinctively Cervantine, and they powerfully manifest the preoccupations and ideas that shape the author's greatest writings: the difficulty of ascertaining truth, the multiplicity and relativity of experiential truth, the ways in which experience resists the reductive explanations afforded by dogma and authority, and the appropriateness of an ironic, "pluralistic," literary discourse, one that emphatically recognizes its own fallibility, as well as the fallibility of all traditional literary discourse, for a meaningful treatment of the complexities of experience and an adequate representation of the integrity of its "un-literary" particulars.[55] However, at the same time such effects have ethical

[53] For examples of this type of discourse in Cervantes' articulation of the theme of language, as well as its links to Erasmus' dialogic style, see below, Chapter VI.

[54] See E. Behler's discussion of Schlegel's observations on the dialogic character of thought as revealed in the Platonic dialogue, *Klassische Ironie, Romantische Ironie, Tragische Ironie: Zum Ursprung dieser Begriffe* (Darmstadt, 1972), pp. 83-84; also his chapter, "Ironie und Dialektik," pp. 85-103.

[55] The ironic discourse of the dogs is similar to that of Cervantes' various surrogates of the writer, e.g., Cide Hamete Benengeli and his editors, Periandro in his recitation (*Persiles*, Book II), Maese Pedro, and Chanfalla (see my *Cervantes, Aristotle, and the "Persiles"*), and it is usually audible when Cervantes appears in his works or refers to their quality. One can, for example, compare the dogs' performances in the passages under discussion with Cervantes' self-presentation in the prologue of *Don Quixote* I, where the author's pose of paralysis and ignorance is part of an ironic strategy aimed at the discreditation of the venerable conception of the perfect work of literature as an encyclopedic repository of knowledge and of the exalted classical figure of the *poeta doctus* as the conveyer of a primal truth, already revealed and sanctioned by authority and tradition. The implications of this strategy concerning artistic freedom and the value of a unique poetic voice, one who is quite happy to forget the name of his protagonist's village, are clear (see below, p. 191), but, lest they harden into assertion, Cervantes mischievously undercuts his spokesman by depicting him victimized by the vice he would condemn, redacting a prologue "given to him" and authorized by a friend and consulting the archives of the Mancha assiduously in an effort to ensure the historical accuracy of his narration. See also his pose as a demanding

implications concerning the voices that cultivate them. They, in fact, reflect an entire philosophy of criticism, and their presence supports the satirical vision that animates Cervantes' final exemplary tale.

As I have pointed out above, one of the most important consequences of such passages as the four I have analyzed is the characterization of the dogs and the establishment of their perspective as satirists. In all of them we note the irresistible urge to deflate the seriousness of their pronouncements, to implicate themselves in the vices they condemn, and, in so doing, both to soften the strength of their attacks and to lower their stature as moralists. Indeed, they could scarcely carry out more effectively the recommendations implicit in two of the most important passages of the work dealing with the nature, value, and practice of criticism. One approaches the issue in terms of literature, the other, in terms of moral philosophy. Cipión approves of his companion's satirical observations by recalling Juvenal's hackneyed formula: "Difficile est satiram non scribere," but he urges him to avoid vicious invective, to "expose (señalar) rather than to wound (herir)," and always to temper his criticism by the exercise of *discreción*:

Inasmuch as I have heard that a great poet of antiquity once said that it was a difficult thing not to write satire, I shall permit you to backbite a little, giving light but not drawing blood, that is to say, merely pointing out without wounding or ridiculing anyone in any particular thing. For slander is not a good thing if it kills one person, even though it makes many laugh. And if you can please without it, I shall consider you very discreet.

On another occasion Cipión scolds Berganza for yielding to the temptation to slander and invokes the traditional association of dog and Cynic philosopher:

Renaissance historian as he searches for and joyfully discovers the manuscript of a lying Moorish chronicler in Toledo. Berganza's invocation of the absurd poet Mauleón, "poeta tonto y académico" to excuse his abusive licenses is similar to the ironic self-deprecation contained in Don Quixote's comparison of his author, in his disorderly methods of composition, with Orbaneja, whose incoherent, improvisational paintings require explanatory tags (*Don Quijote*, 2:63-64). Later Don Quixote invokes both Mauleón and Orbaneja to describe Avellaneda's artistic methods (2:574), and one can see clearly how tentatively the comparisons hover between the pejorative and the laudatory, the positive and the negative. In their application to the *Coloquio* and *Don Quixote*, the rebuke which they imply clearly endorses artistic freedom and the value of imposing on the reader the task of engaging freely and critically with the text. Don Quixote's conclusion, that the result of the practices of Orbaneja is a work that will "require a commentary" if it is to be understood, followed by Sansón Carrasco's assurance that different types of readers understand it perfectly in their respective ways, is, in fact, an apt observation on the pluralistic nature of Cervantine discourse, which is particularly striking in such moments of ironic self-reflection.

Do you call slander philosophy? So it goes! Canonize, Berganza, canonize the accursed plague of backbiting, and give it whatever name you please; it will cause us to be called cynics, which is the same as calling us backbiting dogs; so for pity's sake I beg of you to be silent now and to go on with your story.[56]

As they attempt to set the limits for tolerable criticism in a work almost exclusively devoted to destructive criticism, the two exchanges recall Cervantes' examination of the satirist and the Cynic philosopher in the *Licenciado Vidriera* and point to the basic principles of the Erasmian program for criticism which nourished so much of the humanist satire of the sixteenth century.[57] Erasmus exhorted the critic to "correct with mildness," to find inspiration in the gentle firmness of Christ and St. Paul, and to reject the asperity, the pride, and the penchant for the reductive simplifications of stereotypes which characterize the Cynic philosopher and Juvenalian satire. Erasmus was well aware of the ways in which the literary genre founded by the avenging poet Archilochus and the critical philosophy preached by the railing Diogenes were difficult to reconcile with the tolerant spirit of his *Philosophia Christiana*. It is perhaps for this reason that he turned for inspiration to Lucian, whose satirical sweep was so broad as to include dogma of any sort, including the dogma of the self-righteous anti-dogmatist, and to Horace, whose denunciations are characteristically softened by his own self-implications in the corruptions of the world and his urbane discussions of the "value" of foibles.[58] Erasmus devel-

---

[56] "Por haber oído decir que dijo un gran poeta de los antiguos que era difícil cosa el no escribir sátiras, consentiré que murmures un poco de luz, y no de sangre: quiero decir que señales, y no hieras ni des mate a ninguno en cosa señalada; que no es buena la murmuración, aunque haga reír a muchos, si mata a uno; y si puedes agradar sin ella, te tendré por muy discreto" (p. 224). "¿Al murmurar llamas filosofar? ¡Así va ello! Canoniza, canoniza, Berganza, a la maldita plaga de la murmuración y dale el nombre que quisieres; que ella dará a nosotros el de cínicos, que quiere decir perros murmuradores; y por tu vida que calles ya y sigas tu historia" (p. 251).

[57] See my *Cervantes and the Humanist Vision*, chap. 3. Again the contrast with *Guzmán de Alfarache* is illuminating. The picaro's taste for what he calls the "salsa de murmuración" is curbed by no such ethical sensitivities. In a passage which Cervantes may have had in mind as he considered the problem of criticism in his story, Guzmán describes himself as a "perro de muestra, venteando flaquezas ajenas." With his characteristic lack of discrimination as a satirical railer, he relishes the image of himself as a madman throwing stones in all directions and assuming that, since everyone is born in sin, everyone deserves punishment. He describes his narrative as a "blunderbuss which kills." See *Guzmán de Alfarache*, 3:69-83, 89; also, above, "Introduction."

[58] Bulephorus, Erasmus' spokesman in the *Ciceronianus*, admits that he chose Horace as his principal model to be imitated because of an irresistible affinity of spirit which he felt while reading his words (p. 330). At another point in the dialogue

oped a satirical voice that, in its ironic self-deprecation, self-efface-
ment, and self-incriminations, in its cultivation of inconsistency, in
its self-conscious disavowal of the superior moral stance of the Juvenalian censor, and in its reluctance to allow a tirade to dominate a
satirical context, represented a type of satire that was consistent with
the program for humane criticism as set forth in the *Enchiridion*. Erasmus introduced his greatest satire, *The Praise of Folly*, with the assertion that he writes to produce pleasure rather than pain and that
unlike Juvenal he has chosen for his targets "the ridiculous rather than
the foul." Moreover, before allowing his spokesman to launch into
her merciless tirade against monks, logicians, grammarians, priests,
lawyers, astrologers, and other fools, he presents in her praise of her
followers an eloquent defense of the various foibles, such as self-love,
ambition, envy, and hypocrisy, which enable human beings to live
with one another in peace and harmony and to create civilization. If
the indulgent view of human failings and the bewilderingly oblique
manner of discourse that Folly employs in order to express it seem to
contradict the tone of uncompromising criticism and the relatively
straightforward presentation in much of what follows, Erasmus increases the readers' difficulties in resolving the ambiguities of the mock
declamation by including among the victims of Folly's invectives a
pedant named Erasmus, whose Biblical annotations contribute to the
obfuscation of the true meaning of the Gospels.[59]

In his relentless catalogue of the sins of the tongue, the *Lingua*,
Erasmus pauses twice to turn his satire back on itself by acknowledging that the very words that he is writing bristle with the evil that
he would correct. At one point he creates a critical listener or reader
and allows him to denounce his monologue: "At this point someone
will perhaps, and not entirely without reason, interrupt the course of
my words and say, 'All you are doing is reviling the evil tongue,
while we are waiting for a remedy.' " His critical commentary on his
text at another moment looks forward more directly to the inter-

---

Horace is acclaimed as the greatest writer of satires (p. 182). E. Dolet's unsympa-
thetic portrait of Erasmus is certainly accurate insofar as it analyzes the derivation of
his satirical persona: "He has forged for himself a verbal persona . . . out of Horatian
tags, filthy language from Apuleius, and the adages of Beroaldus. . . . And where
has he got his *sententia*-mask from . . . if not from Lucian, that most scurrilous and
immoral of all authors" (*De Imitatione Ciceroniana*, cited and translated by T. Cave,
The Cornucopian Text: Problems of Writing in the French Renaissance [Oxford, 1979], pp.
49-50). For the unobtrusive methods, the self-incriminating ironies, and the anti-
dogmatic posture of Horace's satirical persona, see R. M. Durling, *The Figure of the
Poet in Renaissance Epic* (Cambridge, Mass., 1965), pp. 13-26.
[59] See *The Essential Erasmus*, p. 164.

changes in the *Coloquio de los perros*; for he invokes as a self-reflection the Cynic philosopher, Diogenes, and recalls his rebuke by Plato:

There are many things which could be said about the evil tongue, but there is a risk lest, just as when Diogenes trampled all over Plato's cushions saying "I am trampling on Plato's pride," he got the answer "Yes, you are trampling on it, but with more pride of your own," so someone may say to me "Yes, you are ranting against the abusive tongue, but with more abuses of your own." For I admit that there should be a limit even in censuring evils, except that there is no limit to this evil, especially in these present times.[60]

The inclusion of himself amid his targets is a characteristic feature of Erasmus' satires,[61] and self-deprecation, by either the author or his

[60] "Hic orationis meae cursum fortassis aliquis non omnino sine causa interpellabit: *Tantum*, inquiens, *vituperas linguam noxiam, nos medicinam expectamus*. . . . Plura sunt quae de mala lingua dici poterant, sed periculum est, ne quemadmodum Diogenes calcans culcitram Platonis, quum addidisset, calco fastum Platonis, audiuit, *calcas tu quidem, sed alio fastu*, ita mihi dicat aliquis: *Debaccharis tu quidem in linguam maledicam, sed alia maledicentia*. Fateor enim et in malis insectandis modum esse debere, nisi quod huius mali nullus est modus, hisce praesertim temporibus" (ed. F. Schalk, *Opera Omnia*, Vol. IV, pt. 1 [Amsterdam, 1974], pp. 293, 332).

[61] See, for example, the colloquy *Cyclops*. At the conclusion of his portrayal of the stupidity, hypocrisy, and depravity of the monstrous Polyphemus, Erasmus surveys the corruption of the age, and he suddenly disrupts the dark tonality of the catalogue of woes with an unexpected reference to himself: "Kings make war, priests are zealous to increase their wealth, theologians invent syllogisms, monks roam through the world, the commons riot, Erasmus writes colloquies. In short, no calamity is lacking: hunger, thirst, robbery, war, plague" (*The Colloquies of Erasmus*, p. 422). As in the case of the fool who praises folly, the colloquy that denounces colloquies leaves the reader with a paradox and the various stimulating discomforts produced by its instability. In the playful dialogue introducing Battus' denunciation of the enemies of letters in the early satire, the *Antibarbari*, Erasmus appears in a form which resembles Folly's favorite poets and the scribbling dreamer of Cervantes' *Colloquy of the Dogs*: "Neque enim vereor, ne vestrum quispiam me prodat, modo possit Erasmi stilus conquiescere, qui quicquid noctu somniat, etiam interdiu chartis suis illinere solet" (p. 66). See also the unexpected shift in perspective at the climax of the *Sileni Alcibiadis*, when its lofty preachings are momentarily considered as the product of drunkenness (p. 296), and Erasmus' surprising appearance in his burlesque treatment of the Ciceronians' fanatical imitation of the style of their master: "Hinc tibi proferam Erasmum Roterodamum, si pateris. . . . Abicit ac praecipitat omnia nec parit, sed abortit, interdum iustum volumen scribit 'stans pede in uno' nec unquam potest imperare animo suo, ut vel semel relegat quod scripsit, nec aliud quam scribit, cum post diutinam lectionem demum ad calamum sit veniendum idque raro" (*Ciceronianus*, pp. 274-76). Characteristically Erasmus presents himself here as an *absurd* counterweight to the obsessed pedants of the Ciceronian school, who, inhibited by their reverence for their master, spend years preparing and rereading their writings, only to produce nothing. The absurdity of the extreme of carelessness and "spontaneity" compels the reader to locate on his own the norm at some point between the extremes.

satirical persona, can be observed in the Spanish satire that bears the impress of the Erasmian spirit. For example, in Antonio de Torquemada's *Colloquio satírico que trata de la vanidad de la honra del mundo*, the author's spokesman, Antonio, laments that his contemporaries have forgotten Christ's teachings on humility and blindly pursue the esteem of society, the "negra honra," with no concern whatsoever that it be an authentic reflection of virtuous conduct. However, as he deplores the absurdly complex rituals of salutation which society has developed for the conservation and celebration of its distinctions of honor and calls for "evangelical physicians" ("médicos evangelicos") to heal the illness, he cannot resist the temptation to laugh, and he goes on to implicate himself in the very madness he censures. Admitting that he too is "under the banner of this madness," ("debajo de la bandera de esta locura"), Antonio joins ranks with the followers of Erasmus' Stultitia and becomes one of the numerous sixteenth-century fools discoursing wisely on the nature of folly. If his benevolent attitude toward the victims of his ridicule and the admission of his own madness recall the tone of the most influential satire of the age, in his pose as a laughing Democritus ("in order not to weep, as did Heraclitus, I resolved to laugh with Democritus"),[62] he invokes the philosopher whose presiding spirit, as Johan Huizinga has noted, appears to have inspired the efforts of the greatest humorists of the humanist movement, from Erasmus, Rabelais, and Ariosto, to Cervantes and Ben Jonson.[63] In the Lucianesque dialogues of Bartolomé Leonardo de Argensola, an acquaintance of Cervantes whose literary achievements won him renown as the "Horacio de España," Democritus appears as a hero. In disillusionment with society, he has retired

Such self-deprecation is characteristic of the most influential voices among the numerous "praisers of folly" of the age. See, for example, "Thomas More's" patently nonsensical refutation of Raphael Hythloday's utopian "nonsense" at the conclusion of *Utopia*, or the meanderings of Ludovico Ariosto's narrator in *Orlando Furioso*. As the latter contemplates Orlando's frenzied reaction to the discovery of Angelica's faithlessness, he launches into a sententious tirade against the madness of love, only to conclude it with an admission that he himself is suffering from the very disease which he is condemning and that he himself is hopelessly involved in the "dance of folly" (XXIV, 1-3). See also *Cantos* XXIX and XXX, where he laments the inconsistency of men and defends gentle women against the foolish abuse of Rodomonte, only to turn about and pronounce his own sweeping denunciation of the frail sex and finally to admit that he is raving in madness. For the affinities linking Cervantes' artistic personae and Ariosto's narrative voice, see my *Cervantes, Aristotle, and the "Persiles."*

[62] N.B.A.E. 7:532, 539.

[63] *Erasmus and the Age of the Reformation*, trans. F. Hopman (New York, 1957), p. 155.

to a cave, where he spends his days laughing and writing a book about insanity, "the illness that is most widespread and least understood in the world." He justifies his withdrawal by denouncing the forms of madness that universally enslave man—self-deception, hope, fear, ambition, greed, the pursuit of fame, and "a certain specter that they call honor"—each of which may cause him to forsake his responsibilities to follow his natural reason, to "live with moderation," to be "firm of spirit," and to "conform to the simplicity of nature." The satirist is uncompromising in his criticism and in his profession of Stoic ethics. However, the austerity of his message is significantly softened by his interlocutor's eloquent defense of the creative value of man's follies. In a speech that recalls Erasmus' Stultitia's praise of folly and her invocation of a nature of vitality and abundance to support her argument against the Stoics' severe attitudes toward human weakness and the rationalistic conception of nature in which they are grounded, Hippocrates suggests that Democritus' demands on human beings are unnatural, and he points out that "vices" such as ambition and forgetfulness enable man to keep occupied and to cope with the vicissitudes of life and that his illusions make it possible for him to marry, to sail, and to build. Moreover, at the conclusion of an unsparing denunciation of the court, in which Argensola's persona employs such traditional satirical devices as the description of the "other world" (i.e., the court of Artaxerxes) and the grotesque visions of derangement that emerge in nightmares, Democritus must answer to the charge of inhumanity, and in words that recall Erasmus' fool's recommendations, he claims that his own laughter is a resource that has saved him from suicide, and he proceeds to defend laughter in general as a means of instruction and improvement.[64]

Whether or not the *Praise of Folly* was read in Cervantes' epoch, we observe in such works as Torquemada's and Argensola's satires a survival of Erasmus' complex satirical voice, a dialogic voice that enlivens its listener's perceptions by forcing him to cope with antinomies and

[64] *Obras sueltas*, 2:131-60. Leonardo de Argensola's work is based to a great extent on the spurious epistles of Hippocrates, sometimes referred to as the "Hippocratic novel." As M. Bakhtin has pointed out, it was a familiar text in the Renaissance, and humanist writers such as Rabelais no doubt found in its ambivalent treatment of the themes of wisdom, madness, and laughter a highly congenial spirit (*Rabelais and His World*, pp. 360-61). For Argensola's debt to his source, which was available at the time in numerous editions, both in Greek and in Latin, see O. H. Green, "Notes on the Lucianesque Dialogues of Bartolomé Leonardo de Argensola," *Hispanic Review* 3 (1935):275-94. For Cervantes' acquaintance with the brothers Argensola, see M. Fernández de Navarrete, *Vida de Miguel de Cervantes Saavedra* (Madrid, 1819), pp. 122-23.

paradoxes, that insists on laying bare the fundamental ethical problems underlying satire even as it pours forth its destructive energies, that emphatically refuses to adopt the monologic, morally uncompromising stance of the Juvenalian and medieval satirist, and that, through self-examination, self-criticism, and the continuing acknowledgement, through whatever means, of its own fallibility, attempts to reconcile criticism with the compassionate view of human nature and the fundamental ethical principles of the *Philosophia Christiana*.[65] In their appealing blend of wit, rigor, and humanity, Cervantes' irrepressible dogs are perhaps the most authentic European descendants of Erasmus' great fool.

[65] It is revealing to contrast Argensola's and Cervantes' satires, in their authentic conservation of the dialogism of Erasmus' mock declamation, with its contemporaneous, seemingly direct descendant, J.de Mondragón's *Censura de la locura humana y Excelencias della* (1598). Here the dominance of the unequivocal denunciation marks a return to a more traditional, monologic type of satire, the type which, in fact, was reasserted in the first Spanish adaptation of the *Praise of Folly*, López de Yanguas' *Triunfos de locura* (1521), with its introduction of Prudence as a debating opponent for Folly. The suppression of Folly's most subversive and humane message is in some ways analogous to Avellaneda's recreation of Cervantes' fools and the transformation of the fool which we note in Calderón's drama (see above). Nowhere in Europe is the "death of Erasmian folly" more striking than in seventeenth-century Spain and its literature of *desengaño*. For the problem of whether or not Erasmus' notorious satire was known in Cervantes' Spain, see M. Bataillon, "Un Problème d'influence d'Erasme en Espagne: *L'Eloge de la Folie*," *Actes du Congrès Erasme* (Rotterdam, 1969), 136-47. Bataillon revises his early conclusion that the *Praise of Folly* had little impact on Spain and suggests that the study of its influence should focus at this point, not on a search for concrete evidence of its transmission, but rather on the consideration of the presence of its spirit, as revealed, for example, in the affinities between the ironic praise of Lazarillo's autobiography and Stultitia's self-presentation and in the polymorphism of the theme of folly in the *Quixote*. Bataillon is certainly right in arguing that Mondragón's version of Erasmus' declamation is fundamentally medieval in spirit and should not be looked upon as either a bridge between Erasmus and Cervantes or as proof of the fact that the *Praise of Folly* was widely read in Spain at the time, as A. Vilanova suggests in *Erasmo y Cervantes* (Barcelona, 1949). For a clear account of the perspective and technique of the Juvenalian and medieval satirists, see A. Kernan, *The Cankered Muse*, pp. 37-80.

CHAPTER VI

Language: Divine or Diabolical Gift?

Keep talking, for the night
is slipping away.
—Cipión[1]

DON QUIXOTE AND THE COLLOQUY OF THE DOGS:
TWO PERSPECTIVES ON THE PLURALITY
OF LANGUAGES

Don Quixote: *Language and the Mysteries of the Self*

I am too spiritless and lazy by nature
to go about looking for authors to say for me
what I can say for myself without them.
—Cervantes[2]

LIKE MANY other great writers of the Renaissance, Cervantes was profoundly interested in the problematic relationship between words and things, in the arbitrariness of linguistic signs and systems, and in the possibilities for deception and confusion lurking in the most elaborate system of appearance created by civilization. Having spent so many years at those vital intersections of the Mediterranean world where the mingling of different civilizations, races, customs, and languages was dramatically visible in his daily experience, he was undoubtedly forced to confront such problems as existential facts in a way that enlivened whatever theoretical awareness of them he may have acquired in his youthful contact with humanist literature. A fascination with the subject of language is noticeable throughout his

---

[1] "Sigue; que se va la noche" (p. 282).
[2] "Naturalmente soy poltrón y perezoso de andarme buscando autores que digan lo que yo me sé decir sin ellos" (*Don Quixote*, 1:53).

writings, and the breadth and complexity of his engagement with this
subject are seldom matched by his contemporaries.

It was, of course, in the *Quixote* that Cervantes gave artistic form
to his most profound insights into the nature of language. In his
account of his adventurer's wanderings through a world both historically and linguistically alien, Cervantes found himself repeatedly exploring the shadows cast by Babel's ruins, registering his preoccupation with the cleavage between words and things, the instability of
language, the existence of differences between languages, and the relation of linguistic differences to distinctions of nationality, region,
religion, class, and existential milieus of a more microscopic and hence
less easily definable type—ranging from the family to the completely
individualized *circunstancia* of the self. Everywhere in the great novel
Cervantes reminds his reader that the totality of human language contains within itself an infinite number of speech systems, including
numerous literary languages, each with a problematic relationship to
"normal," or nonliterary discourse. And in exploiting the interaction
of such systems for fictional purposes, he constantly reveals his fascination with the way in which language is an authentic projection of
an individual, bearing all the nuances and peculiarities of an individual will and subject to change and growth concomitant with the
changing experience of the individual. In considering such manifestations of linguistic pluralism, Cervantes quickly, perhaps intuitively,
transcended any narrow literary, moral, or epistemological predisposition which might have guided his initial approach to such matters.
For the *Quixote* stands as a powerful affirmation of the value of linguistic fragmentation as the manifestation of the richness and the
vitality of the concrete human being and as a sign of the very copiousness that enables language to serve as an effective medium for the
expression of the inexhaustible variety and the nuanced particularity
of human experience. While the general awareness of the living nature
of language and the refusal to embrace the conventional negative view
of linguistic fragmentation and pluralism, traditionally embodied in
and supported by the myth of the Babylonian Confusion, were not
uncommon in humanist circles,[3] it remained for Cervantes to bring

[3] See, for example, G. Cardano's assertion that "utilitas vero quae ex varietate
linguarum habetur, est ut omnes animi affectus possint explicari" (*De Subtilitate*, cited
by C.-G. Dubois, *Mythe et langage au seizième siècle* [Bordeaux, 1970], p. 119). Vives
lamented that "peccati . . . poena est tot esse linguas," that words ceased to signify
the "rerum naturas" following Adam's fall, and that the confusion of languages "homines magis multo alienos facit à se se, quàm à bestiis suis, dumtaxat cicuratis" (*De
Tradendis Disciplinis, Opera Omnia*, ed. G. Mayáns y Siscar, 8 vols. [Valencia, 1782-

about in literature the complete liberation of speech from the traditional taints surrounding its acknowledged arbitrariness, its insubstantiality, and its plurality, and, by altering the customary emphasis from the relation between word and thing to the relation between word and self, to revalue its "inauthenticity" and to rediscover its existential truth and its inexhaustible riches precisely in its "cursed" indeterminateness, its promiscuity, and its adaptability. Cervantes was, of course, not a theorist of language, but he was well aware, in a way in which contemporary linguists were not, that each individual is a world, that each individual has a language appropriate to that world, and that both individual and his speech are in a state of flux in the continual interplay of self and circumstances that defines experience.[4]

1790], 6:299; *Clypei Christi Descriptio, Opera Omnia,* 7:34). At the same time he stressed that each language has its own natural laws, which must be respected, that each language is charged with the vitality of the people who speak it and grows and changes with its speakers ("quum linguae arbitrium sit penes populum, dominum sermonis sui, mutatur subinde sermo, usque adeo ut centesimo quoque anno prope jam sit omnino alius"), that languages must be cultivated to enable cultural, economic, and social interchange among peoples, and that grammarians must recognize the historicity of language and attempt to preserve "verborum omnium vires ac significationes" of the language of the treasured texts of the past (*De Tradendis Disciplinis, Opera Omnia,* 6:78, 299; *De Ratione Dicendi, Opera Omnia,* 2:105). A concentrated expression of the humanists' affirmative attitudes toward the "consequences of Babel" can be found in G. Pontano's celebration of the multiplicity of languages and variety and change within language as reflections of the plenitude of nature and the variety of peoples and customs, *De sermone libri sex,* ed. S. Lupi and A. Risicato (Lugano, 1954), pp. 5-6. For the history of man's thought concerning language, see Arno Borst's monumental work, *Der Turmbau von Babel: Geschichte der Meinungen über Ursprung und Vielfalt der Sprachen und Völker,* 4 vols. (Stuttgart, 1957-1963); for Cervantes' epoch, see 3:1048-1262. See also M. K. Read, "The Renaissance Concept of Linguistic Change," *Archivum Linguisticum* 8 (1977):60-69; "Renaissance Ideas on the Origin and Development of Language" [with J. Tretheway], *Semasia* 5 (1978):99-115; "Cause and Process in Linguistic Change: The Diachronic Study of Language in the Spanish Renaissance," *Archivum Linguisticum* 9 (1978):15-23.

[4] Perhaps the most striking presentation of the alteration of an individual's discourse brought about by his changing experience is Sancho Panza's conversation with his wife prior to the third sally. Both Teresa Panza and the translator of the chapter are befuddled by the peasant's new manner of speaking, and the translator, guided by theories of linguistics and literary decorum which cannot account for such a startling change in the character, recommends that the conversation be dismissed as apocryphal (*Don Quijote,* 2:73). As for the "promiscuity" of language, Don Quijote learns that "truchuela," or "little trout" can, in certain regions of Spain, mean "codfish," and that "canary," in certain social milieus, can mean "informer." In a little lesson in linguistics, Sancho is taught that "puta" can be a term of endearment in popular culture (see below). Such verbal flexibility would, of course, be impossible in the univocal, un-ironic discourse of Eden. Don Quixote frequently adopts a Cratylist position concerning the rigid alignment of word and thing, and Cervantes

As Leo Spitzer has pointed out, the discourse of Cervantes' great novel is marked by "linguistic perspectivism," and the numerous manifestations of this revealing feature of style can be properly understood only as reflections of the most essential and universal theme of the work—the perspectivism and relativism that characterize life on earth.[5]

Cervantes' implicit redefinition of language's potential for authenticity by displacing its warrant from externals (i.e., the things [res] of the well-founded nature [natura bene condita] with their inherent names), to the interiority of any human being who employs it to express his genuine identity is most forcefully presented as he introduces his own masterpiece as the unique product of his own voice. His progressive view of language underlies the entire prologue to Don Quixote I, with its notorious ridicule of the pedantry, ostentation, fraudulence, and inauthenticity in the imitative practices of Lope de Vega and its critical engagement with traditional theories of imitation. The ironies of the polemical dialogue of Cervantes and his "friend" reach well beyond their ostensible target and strike at the venerable conception of the poeta doctus as the creator of works that are sanctioned by tradition and authority and preserved and transmitted in a chain of revered texts extending backwards in time to some primal divinely revealed model.

---

occasionally draws attention to the naiveté of his view. When the author appears to endorse the knight's argument that Latin can illustrate and enrich the Spanish tongue, he is pointing to a linguistic plenitude which enables speech to provide an adequately nuanced instrument for the subtle dynamics of interpersonal and social relationships rather than to a linguistic hierarchy in which Latin enjoys a privileged ontological status as the language of Christendom or as a language that is "closer" than the vernacular to the true Adamic language (see Don Quijote, 2:361; compare Cervantes' modernist stance concerning the question of Latin and Spanish in the prologue to La Galatea [ed. J. B. Avalle-Arce, 2 vols. (Madrid, 1961), 1:6-7]; also, Don Quijote's words to Diego de Miranda [2:155-56]). The latter view of Latin appears in the Persiles, where linguistic fragmentation is viewed in a narrow moral perspective which is entirely traditional. The most familiar manifestation of Cervantes' skeptical attitude toward the Cratylist view of language is the instability in the proper names throughout the Quixote; for example, "Teresa Panza" and "Juana Gutiérrez" are equally arbitrary, equally valid, and equally insubstantial containers of the reality of Sancho's wife.

[5] "Cervantes saw them [dialects] as ways of speech which exist as individual realities and which have their justification in themselves. The basic Cervantine conception of perspectivism did not allow for the Platonic or Christian ideal of language." In the lexicological variants which he assembles from different dialects, Cervantes "must have seen not a striving toward the approximation of an ideal, but only the variegated phantasmagoria of human approaches to reality: each variant has its own justification, but all of them alike reflect no more than human 'dreams' " ("Linguistic Perspectivism in the Don Quijote," Linguistics and Literary History [Princeton, 1967], pp. 55-56.

Violently renouncing such a distinguished lineage for his "ugly step-son," Cervantes enunciates a principle of imitation ("la imitación per-fecta") which, while recognizing the importance of the proper adjust-ment of the literary utterance to the nature of its subject and the propriety of simplicity and clarity of style for the limited, satirical aims of the *Quixote*, at the same time places a good deal of emphasis on authenticity and self-expression. For him there is no need to turn to the "word of the fathers" to vivify his creation.[6] The friend who counsels Cervantes repeatedly refers to the work as its writer's own singular creation ("this book *of yours* has no need of . . . this writing *of yours* aims at no more than . . . you have only to see that *your* sentence shall come out plainly, with clear, proper, and well-ordered words . . . *expressing your intention to the best of your ability* and *setting forth your ideas* intelligibly without intricacies and obscurities"),[7] and Cervantes stresses the "sincerity" of his "history." Immediately there-after, by affirming his wish to forget the name of the protagonist's village, he flaunts his lack of interest in authentication, and in a muse of memory that might hand him a validating tradition, and he re-minds us that the single, authentic source of his history lies in his own consciousness.

Cervantes' insight into the living nature of language and his em-phatic rejection of his contemporaries' conventional view of imitation had been anticipated in the writings of his most influential humanist ancestor. In his polemical *Ciceronianus*, Erasmus championed a con-ception of proper imitation based on the priority of the self over any preexistent, authoritative literary tradition. His spokesman, Bulepho-rus, mocks the sterile, mechanical imitative habits of the Ciceronians, with their well-stocked memories and filing cabinets, and implicitly rejects their adherence to the belief in a single model language reflect-

---

[6] See M. Bakhtin's discussion of the power and lifelessness of authoritative dis-course. "The authoritative word is located in a distanced zone, organically connected with a past that is felt to be hierarchically higher. It is, so to speak, the word of the fathers. Its authority was already *acknowledged* in the past. It is a *prior* discourse. . . . It is considerably more difficult to incorporate semantic changes into such a discourse, even with the help of a framing context: its semantic structure is static and dead, for it is fully complete, it has but a single meaning, the letter is fully sufficient to the sense and calcifies it" ("Discourse in the Novel," *The Dialogic Imagination*, trans. C. Emerson and M. Holquist [Austin, 1981], pp. 342-43).

[7] "Este *vuestro* libro no tiene necesidad . . ."; "esta *vuestra* escritura no mira a más que . . ."; "procurar que a la llana, con palabras significantes, honestas y bien colo-cadas, *salga vuestra oración* y período . . . pintando, en todo lo que alcanzáredes y fuere posible, *vuestra intención, dando a entender vuestros conceptos* sin intricarlos y escu-recerlos" (*Don Quijote*, 1:57-58; italics added).

ing an essential, unchanging order in man and nature. He argues that language and literary style always reflect the personality of a specific individual producing a particular utterance ("nature created us to a certain extent for the sake of variety, endowing each one of us with a particular temperament, so that scarcely two human beings can be found who have the same capacities or interests . . . nature itself . . . demanded that speech be the mirror of the individual soul") and that, since nature has made each individual unique, any linguistic utterance must be judged in terms of the authenticity with which it reflects the particular "heart" beneath it ("speech becomes authentically living only if it is born in the heart and not if it is mere movement of the lips . . . the soul also has a kind of face, which is reflected in its speech as in a mirror, and, if one were to change it from its natural form into something else he would be doing nothing else but appearing before the public with a mask).[8]

[8] "Ad hanc [varietatem] nos natura quodammodo finxit suum cuique tribuens ingenium, ut vix duos reperias, qui eadem vel possint vel ament . . . natura . . . voluit orationem esse speculum animi"; "Ita demum vivida fuerit oratio, si in corde nascatur, non in labiis natet. . . . Habet animus faciem quandam suam in oratione velut in speculo relucentem, quam a nativa specie in diversum refingere quid aliud est, quam in publicum venire personatum?" (*Ciceronianus, Ausgewählte Schriften*, ed. W. Welzig, 8 vols. [1967-1980], 7:328, 196, 332). Needless to say, Erasmus' advocacy of such a radical theory of self-expression does not lead him to the intense interest in linguistic pluralism, individualized discourse, and the elevation of the vernacular and its dialects which we find in Cervantes' novel. While sensitive to the great variety in human nature and experience and sincere in his enthusiasm for the copiousness in language which enables it to manifest such variety, he does believe in the existence of an essential human nature (see my *Cervantes and the Humanist Vision*, chap. 2), and he is primarily interested in guiding man to the rediscovery of his true self, the Edenic self, and its true language, inspired by the Holy Spirit and manifesting purity of heart. Hence, he can maintain that there is one genuine linguistic form of self-expression, writing in the *Enchiridion*: "quando del coraçón del ombre salen palabras malas y de muerte, necessario se sigue que dentro ay escondida alguna cosa muerta. Y pues, como el Evangelio dize, lo que abunda en el coraçón aquello sale por la boca, de creer es que palabras limpias, bivas y de Dios saldrían por la boca, si la misma vida, que es Dios, estuviesse en el coraçón." Christ restores the Christian by offering him "palabras de vida," the single true language, (*El Enquiridion*, ed. D. Alonso [Madrid, 1932], p. 123); in the *Ratio Verae Theologiae*, Erasmus urges the theologian to avoid "fleeing to dictionaries, compendia, and indexes" for citations and arguments and rather to make his own heart a "library of Christ" and offer his fellows living water from his own inner spring (*Ausgewählte Schriften*, ed. W. Welzig, 8 vols. [1967-1980], 3:462). Erasmus neatly accommodates his theory of self-expression within his *Philosophia Christiana*, for man's authentic self embodies the spark of divine reason, and Christ, as *logos*, is both reason and word. Moreover, Erasmus could devote the labor of an entire lifetime to explicating the mysteries of the most ancient of human texts, the *Adagia*, a text which Christ himself did not hestitate to cite, as the expression of a relatively unalienated self, one which is close to the essential pure self of

The *Quixote*, then, offers itself from its very outset as "merely" the distinctive utterance of a private individual, and it abjures the kind of monumentality possessed by the canonized works of the literary tradition it playfully evokes. It acknowledges, even insists upon its own insubstantiality, and, as Cervantes' immense personal statement unfolds, it constantly draws attention to the insubstantiality of all human discourse. Yet Cervantes makes it clear that, far from being a limitation, such "emptiness" is what enables language to be "full" in the true sense of capturing and expressing the complex, changing reality of individual human beings and mediating between their lives. In his numerous fictionalizations of linguistic problems, we witness a fundamental drama which we could describe as the "decentering" of language, the conscious turning away from any absolute authority that might be invested in a single and unitary language. This drama reflects a radical alteration in man's linguistic consciousness, and in its background we can detect the affirmative attitudes toward the plurality of languages marking the most innovative of the humanist writings on the subject.[9] Cervantes' critical engagement with the belief

---

prelapsarian man. For the innovative character of Erasmus' theory of imitation in its stress on individuality, see H.-J. Lange, *Aemulatio Veterum sive de optimo genere dicendi: Die Entstehung des Barockstils im 16. Jahrhundert durch eine Geschmacksverschiebung in Richtung der Stile des manieristischen Typs* (Frankfurt am Main, 1974), pp. 116ff. For the ambivalences marking his attitudes toward language, see J.-C. Margolin, "Erasme et le verbe: de la rhétorique à l'herméneutique," *Erasme, L'Alsace, et son temps* (proceedings of a colloquium) (Strasbourg, 1971), pp. 87-110, esp. pp. 88, 94, and T. Cave, *The Cornucopian Text: Problems of Writing in the French Renaissance* (Oxford, 1979), pp. 35-51.

[9] Cervantes's modernity, in fact, stands out even when he is viewed beside the most progressive of contemporary theorists of language. In his *Diálogo de las lenguas* Damasio de Frías argues that there is nothing troubling about the fact that there are no intrinsic qualities in language, that the expression of the same concept can vary according to the individual will of the particular speaker, and that variety in usage is so great that one finds "diferencias de hablar" not only within the single nation, but also within any province and even within any city. In words that suggest the interpenetration of contemporary faculty psychology, skeptic philosophy, and progressive language theories, Frías points out that from the "intrínseca y natural diferencia de ánimos, inclinaciones y costumbres salió tanta diversidad de lenguas, y tan diversos términos y maneras de explicar sus conceptos con una perpetua inconstancia forzosa, y como, atrás os dije, necesaria en nuestra inquieta y mudable condición, yendo siempre a la manera de los ríos que guardando solamente perpetuos nombre y sitio, traen con todo cada día, cada hora y momento nuevas aguas." Language resembles the illusory representations and metamorphoses of a theater, and its laws are purely the result of usage ("el uso, maestro y señor que es del hablar"). However, Frías is capable of going only so far in his relativism, and at this point asserts the necessity of rational control of linguistic change, arguing that standards should be determined on the basis of the *good usage* of "discretos y autorizados hombres," and

in a hierarchy of languages parallels his subversive dialogue with traditional conceptions regarding the primacy of specific literary genres and styles. Both are integral parts of the more general liberating process through which the modern novel came into existence, a literary form responsive to man's demands to speak with his own voice and be heard despite the indifference and all the silences of a disenchanted universe. [10]

The Colloquy of the Dogs: Desengaño and the Language of the Earth

The man who is of the earth is earthly
and speaks from the earth.

—Erasmus

The first articulate word the child utters
is to call his nurse or his mother a whore.

—Berganza

---

invoking the social milieu of the aristocracy ("la gente noble y discreta") as the locus of this *discreción*. See *Diálogos de diferentes materias* (Madrid, 1929), pp. 242, 252, 271, 236, 244. Frías's position is very similar to that of Cervantes' licentiate, who appears to support Don Quijote when, angered by Sancho's effusion of proverbs and mispronunciation of the word *fiscal*, the knight denounces his squire as a "prevaricador del buen lenguaje." The scholar acknowledges that "sayagueses" and "toledanos" should not be expected to speak the same language and that Toledo's language itself breaks down into various dialects, but he insists: "el lenguage puro, el propio, el elegante y claro, está en los discretos cortesanos, aunque hayan nacido en Majalahonda . . . y la discreción es la gramática del buen lenguaje, que se acompaña con el uso" (2:181-82). However, what stands out in Cervantes' passage is the oppositional force of Sancho Panza's defense of his own individual mode of expression against the standards of the "friscales" ("no importa, yo me entiendo") and the vitality of his proverbial culture and the spheres of popular speech (the marketplace, the peasant world) in which his language is rooted. (One should compare his assertion with the powerful response to the discourse of the *poeta doctus* of the prologue.) Frías characteristically confines his interest in linguistic change to the enrichment of language from culturally elevated sources ("palabras nuevas y peregrinas"); as for the "plaza y el común trato del vulgo" (p. 272), it is the last place to which one should turn for authorization in adopting a change in usage, for its is always eager to confer value on the spurious (see pp. 272, 237). See my analysis of Cervantes' examination of the popular sphere of language in "la plática de los escuderos" below. For the modernity in Frías' theories of language, see Mary Lee Cozad, "A Platonic-Aristotelian Linguistic Controversy of the Spanish Golden Age: Damasio de Frías' *Diálogo de las lenguas* (1579)," in *Florilegium Hispanicum: Medieval and Golden Age Studies Presented to Dorothy Clotelle Clarke*, ed. J. S. Geary (Madison, Wis., 1983), pp. 203-27. For Angel Rosenblat's argument that the licentiate speaks for Cervantes' fundamental linguistic ideal in his response to Sancho, see *La lengua del "Quijote"* (Madrid, 1971), pp. 56-57.

[10] See M. M. Bakhtin, "Discourse in the Novel," *The Dialogic Imagination,* pp. 366-67.

In *El coloquio de los perros* Cervantes' approach to the theme of language is determined by his exemplary purposes, and, while his treatment of the theme's various facets is anything but simple, it is nonetheless far more conventional than in the *Quixote*, and its peculiar ambiguities and tensions can be accounted for much more easily in terms of the conservative linguistic theories advanced by the majority of his contemporaries. From the early moments of the tale, when the soldier and the scholar discuss the questionable veracity of the narration and the dogs discover their wondrous capacity to speak, to the final page, when Cipión refers to the "great benefit of speech" and Campuzano affirms the value of the written words that the convalescent has scribbled in his notebook in order to make his "dreams or absurdities" meaningful to the "eyes of the mind," Cervantes addresses himself to the problem of language, and there is no single theme or formal element of the work that more emphatically reveals how it was nourished by the major traditions of humanist thought. Unlike the picaresque heroes whom they resemble, the protagonists display an academic curiosity concerning the origins of words, the relation between words and things, and complex questions of decorum in speech. The dogs are capable of tracing the etymology of the word *philosophy* to its Greek roots and of invoking the professional exegete's distinction between letter and allegorical sense in order to render a bewildering prophecy intelligible. In the climactic central event, they find themselves involved in an analytical confrontation with a mysterious text, in which a tantalizing web of allusions would appear to ensnare anyone who might wish to grasp in it more meaning than the simple truth that language is multivalent, promiscuous, and infinitely adaptable and might in fact be as empty as a meaningless dream. Indeed, as we observe the dogs, in their role as readers, grappling with the ambiguities of their text and helplessly considering the possibility that they might be dreaming it, we must momentarily recall our own text, the "dreams or absurdities" ("sueños o disparates") which the Ensign has tentatively committed to paper, as well as his bewildered deliberations concerning its reality and value, and once again ponder the insubstantiality of the very words we are reading. At the same time the climactic moment of the *Colloquy* offers us a glimpse of Satan, the hideous goat-god, and significantly Cervantes' devil appears as a speaker who masters and delights in the multivalence of language. Declaring her intention to inquire of her paramour concerning the meaning of La Camacha's prophecy, Cañizares remarks: "Many times I have longed to ask my goat what end your adventures will have, but I never dared to do so because *he never answers our questions directly, but with distorted phrases and with several meanings*; so there is no use in asking our lord and master, since *with one truth he mixes a thousand lies.*"[11]

As I have pointed out above, Cervantes concentrates all the major themes of the *Colloquy* in the revelations of Cañizares' confession at its center, and it is no surprise that here we discover the key to its engagement with the problem of language. For if Cañizares and her partner are the archsinners, the ugly embodiments of all the evil practices of the society populating Cervantes' final novella, they are also the masters of its language. Traces of their dark idiom are audible in the speech of nearly all its characters and, of course, in the monstrous discourse of the work itself, a genuine colloquy of animals.

The dominant view of language of the *Coloquio* is expressed clearly when, early in the dialogue, Cipión cautions his comrade to restrain his tongue, for "on it lie the greatest miseries in human life" ("en ella consisten los mayores daños de la humana vida" [p. 219]). In his final tale Cervantes is not primarily interested in the tongue and its innumerable creations as the instruments through which the energy of an individual flows into forms that pulsate with his distinctive life. The tongue and its protean signs are rather viewed as dreadful weapons by which man deceives, enslaves, and scourges his fellow human beings. If Cervantes allows us to glimpse in the background of the wreckage on display everywhere in his tale the disastrous fall of the first man, his protagonists in their obsessive discussions of the dark potentialities of language remind us repeatedly of the ruins of the Tower of Babel. For they echo an ancient tradition which maintained that the troublesome gap between words and things and the pluralism of languages are consequences of primal sins and have created in speech a diabolical power which, as Vives put it, can "alienate human beings from one another more thoroughly than from the beasts which serve them."

The dark view of the consequences of Babel was extremely popular in the epoch of the Counter-Reformation, and the traditional attacks on human discourse, voiced frequently by theologians, mystics, and moralists, were reinforced by a rising current of criticism from skeptic philosophers concerning the inadequacies of language as a vehicle of knowledge and truth. Thus, ascetic writers such as Fray Dionisio Vázquez and Alejo Venegas de Busto reminded their followers that the

[11] "Muchas veces he querido preguntar a mi cabrón qué fin tendrá vuestro suceso; pero no me he atrevido, *porque nunca a lo que le preguntamos responde a derechas, sino con razones torcidas y de muchos sentidos*; así, que a este nuestro amo y señor no hay que preguntarle nada, porque *con una verdad mezcla mil mentiras*" (p. 295; italics added).

devil delights in the mastery of languages and thrives amid the Babylonian Confusion and its aftermath; the moralist Francisco de Miranda y Paz lamented that men, fearing "a bad name more than bad conduct," find words convenient instruments for the concealment of vices; and the great mystic St. John of the Cross yearned for a true language, which, like the word that descended to the apostles at Pentecost, would whisper soundlessly to the understanding of the "listener" and enable him to communicate directly with God.[12] At the same time the skeptic philosopher Francisco Sánchez derided contemporary attempts by etymologists to discover in names an identity with the essences of the things to which they refer, insisted that "words have no power to explain the nature of things apart from that given them arbitrarily by the one who bestows a name on a thing," and described languages as subject to perpetual corruption and change through usage in time.[13]

[12] See Vázquez, *Sermón de Pentecostés*, in *Sermones*, ed. P. Félix G. Olmedo (Madrid, 1943), pp. 98-102; Venegas de Busto, *Agonía del tránsito de la muerte* (Santiago, 1948), p. 100; Borst, *Der Turmbau von Babel*, 3:1147; Miranda y Paz, *El Desengañado. Philosophia Moral*, cited by Schulte, *El Desengaño: Wort und Thema in der Spanischen Literatur des Goldenen Zeitalters,* p. 209; San Juan de la Cruz, *Cántico espiritual* 13-14, *Obras completas*, ed. P. Simeon de la Sagrada Familia (Burgos, 1959), pp. 252ff.; see Borst, *Der Turmbau von Babel*, 3:1155.

[13] *Que nada se sabe* (Buenos Aires, 1944), pp. 109-113. I have been unable to consult Sánchez's original text, *Quod Nihil Scitur*, written in Toulouse in 1576. For the importance of skeptic philosophy in the contemporary writings informed by the spirit of *desengaño*, see H. Schulte, *El Desengaño*, pp. 139-48. For Quevedo's assimilation of Sánchez's skepticism and his exploitation of the philosopher's epistemological conclusions for his own moralizing aims, see A. Rothe, *Quevedo und Seneca*, pp. 58-63. As for the sixteenth-century obsession with etymological investigations and the search for the true language, marked by the perfect adequation of word to thing, C.-G. Dubois points out that a "nostalgie du mot pur qui n'est point signe arbitraire mais référence exacte aux choses, alimente presque toutes les recherches sur le langage . . . le mot est la clé magique qui ouvre tous les cabinets secrets de l'univers" (*Mythe et langage au seizième siècle*, pp. 28-29). For the importance of etymology as the quintessential science of those who sought to rediscover the code of Adam's perfect knowledge and the cabalistic and neo-Platonic traditions behind their interpretive practices, see pp. 77-81. Curiously, their elaborate efforts led not to the restoration of a simple language in which words and things were unequivocally identical, but rather to a hypertrophy of meanings and alleged correspondences surrounding individual words, which could only delight those thinkers of a skeptical bent who, like Sánchez, were fascinated with the multivalence and arbitrariness of language and welcomed any evidence in support of their rejection of the fundamental premises of the etymologists' theories. Cervantes' treatment of etymological thinking is consistently playful and satirical. See, for example, Don Quixote's erroneous analysis of *truchuela* as meaning "small trout," as well as his interpretation of the adequation of word and thing in the cases of "Rocinante," "Dulcinea," and "Beltenebros"; Sancho Panza's amusing conjectures concerning the correspondences between Benengeli, Berenjena, and Mor-

It is certainly difficult to determine to what extent writers of the age could not avoid confronting the pressures that issued from these various quarters, but there can be no doubt that a fascination with the instability of language and its inherent powers of confusion and deception were characteristic features of their greatest literature. While Cervantes could indirectly celebrate the experiential reality of language precisely in its essential unreality and Góngora could express his delight in linguistic multiplicity by composing a sonnet in verses of four different languages and justify the radical experiments in poetic diction and syntax of the nearly incomprehensible *Soledades* with the portentous claim that he had achieved in Spanish a pre-Babelic level of linguistic transparency,[14] the more typical responses to the heightened awareness of the insubstantiality of language failed to emerge from the lengthy shadows cast by Babel's ruins. Indeed, the old tradition of the dire consequences of the divine punishment asserted itself with renewed vitality under the impact of the resurgent ascetic Christianity and the powerful spirit of *desengaño* visible in nearly all areas of Spanish cultural and social life. If the entire earthly realm is illusory, a stage on which man is continually beset by the temptations of a diabolical antagonist and victimized by the weaknesses in his own nature, then the unreality of language is simply one more manifestation of the unreality of the temporal order, and its particularly protean nature makes it one of the most dangerous instruments of deception in the hands of the devil and his followers.[15] The prevailing somber

---

iscos, the great eaters of eggplants; or the discussions of the backgrounds of the Condesa Trifaldi and the beleaguered Princess Antonomasia. On the other hand, such humorous treatment of the problem occasionally can point to a serious conclusion, as when Sancho Panza's invention of the word *baciyelmo* suggests that, while the search for etymological roots in which things and words are identical is idle, words spring into being from real human experience, and a science of linguistics should seek their roots and geneses in experience. For the traditional critical engagement with language by the skeptical mind, see Hugo Friedrich's analysis of Montaigne's views of language (*Montaigne* [Bern, 1967], pp. 149ff.).

[14] *Obras completas*, ed. J. and I. Millé y Giménez (Madrid, 1961), pp. 466, 897.

[15] Just as writers of the age were fascinated with exploring the most attractive and colorful facets of the world of appearances and heightening their contrast with their "worthless" reality, they were similarly interested in exploring the most dazzling creations which are potential in the world of words, even while implying their fundamental emptiness. See Schulte, *El Desengaño*, pp. 210-11: "Der Illusionscharakter der Welt ist eine Grunderkenntnis der desengaño-Philosophie. . . . Auf diesem philosophischen Hintergrund ist das Barocktheater zu verstehen, aber auch die Barocksprache, die mit ihren manieristischen Stilfiguren zugleich Illusion schafft und durch das Bewusstsein ihrer künstlich-künstlerischen Existenz diese Illusion auch wieder zunichte macht oder zumindest die Desillusion als notwendige Kontrast-und Komplementärerscheinung zu der mit solcher Intensität und mit solch grellen Farben

attitude toward linguistic pluralism is most forcefully expressed in two of the masterpieces of the literature of *desengaño*—Quevedo's *Buscón* and Lope de Vega's *La Dorotea*. The reader of these works is repeatedly forced to confront the artificiality of language by witnessing a discourse abandon its roots in reality and develop according to the purely verbal logic of wordplays and self-generating conceits, discovering that the intelligibility of words persists despite their shocking dislocation from their normal contexts and referents, watching reality waver and disappear in the language that would encompass it, and listening to recurrent reminders that literary discourse is deceptive illusion.[16] In *La Dorotea* the pessimistic view of language is clearly implied by the repeated criticisms of literature as one of the vanities which men cling to in their refusal to come to terms with their mortality and by the protagonists' decision at the climax to renounce the literary circles of the court and their incessant futile babble in favor of the contemplative silences of the cloister and the active discipline of war.[17] The *Buscón* deals with the problematic character of language ironically, but its implications are no less clear. For here we observe perhaps the most satanic figure in Spanish literature displaying the prodigious powers over language that traditionally have been attributed to the devil, delighting in the logic of analogy and association governing autonomous verbal systems, and exploiting all the powers

---

dargestellten Weltpracht heraufbeschwört. Hier liegt der Zusammenhang mit der desengaño-Thematik, die in vielen Punkten eine theoretische Bergründung der barocken Sprachästhetik liefert. Eine weitere, spezielle Analogie besteht in der Übertragung des erschütterten Wirklichkeitsbewusstseins auf das Sprachbewusstsein. Genauso wie man an der Wirklichkeit irre geworden ist, weil sie so oft mit Schein täuscht, genauso ist man an der Sprache irre geworden, weil das Wort die Sache nicht mehr deckt. Die Wiederaufnahme nominalistischer Thesen durch die zeitgenössischen spanischen Philosophen ist eine interessante Parallelerscheinung." See also Leo Spitzer's comparison of the Baroque writer with a lover who adorns his beloved with the most dazzling jewels and yet at the same time is aware of the illusory character of all earthly beauty and of love itself (*Die Literarisierung des Lebens in Lope's Dorotea* [Bonn, 1932], p. 11).

[16] The best study of these features of Quevedo's style and their implications concerning the spirit of *desengaño* is L. Spitzer's "Zur Kunst Quevedos in seinem *Buscón*," *Archivum Romanicum* 11 (1927):511-80. He observes that this epoch "am Wort irre geworden ist" and "dem naiven und normalen Wortgebrauch entfremdet." The word becomes the "Spiegel seiner Zweifel." The *Buscón* clearly reveals Quevedo's thorough understanding of "das Illusionshafte, Ding-Vortäuschende der Sprache" and his pessimistic view of "Sprache als Ausdrucksmittel." Its striking "Wortspiel und Sprachbeobachtung fliessen beide aus einem indirekten und reflektierten Verhältnis zur Sprache und zur Wirklichkeit" (pp. 526-32).

[17] See A. K. Forcione, "Lope's Broken Clock: Baroque Time in the *Dorotea*," esp. pp. 470, 486-90.

for deception, disguise, and violence that are latent in words. Quevedo, of course, did not care to make a condemnation of his protagonist very explicit, but it is worth noting that his ironic depiction of Pablos' "successes" stirred up shock and protestations in his audience and that one of his detractors condemned the work as a perverse sermon, dictated by Satan to one of his most faithful ministers for the purpose of winning souls for hell.[18]

As I shall point out below, there is an ambivalence marking the treatment of the inherent promiscuity of language in the *Coloquio de los perros* which makes the work fundamentally different from Quevedo's and Lope's masterpieces. Yet it cannot be denied that its approach to the problem fully assimilates the traditions and attitudes that nourished the literature of *desengaño*. The tongue is the source of "the worst miseries in life." The devil is the master of the obliquities of language and reaps innumerable benefits by exploiting them. Everywhere Cervantes draws our attention to the consequences of the destructive powers in language. As he recalls his fall into misfortune, the enfeebled Ensign observes that it was not primarily the appearance of Estefanía that enslaved him but rather the seductive quality of her speech, to which he was exposed in "long and amorous colloquies": "her beauty was nothing to rave about, but she was such that she could excite love if one could communicate with her, because she had such a gentle speaking voice that it won its way through the ears into the soul."[19] Like the devil, the Ensign has the capacity to twist the connection between language and intention in such a way that "the most courteous of words" become an effective mask concealing treachery and "intentions so perverse and deceitful" that he shrinks from revealing them in his confession. In the central scene Cañizares boasts of her success at "simulated saintliness": "I pray little, but in public; I slander much, but in secret; it suits me better to be a hypocrite than to

---

[18] See *Tribunal de la justa venganza, Obras Completas* (verso) (Madrid, 1943), p. 1108. As I have pointed out in *Cervantes, Aristotle, and the "Persiles,"* a satanic aura hovers about Cervantes' most powerful figures of the artist (e.g., *Pedro de Urdemalas*). Like Quevedo's protagonist, they delight in the plurality of languages and styles and in the potential for deception and irony lurking in their illusory instrument. However, the "satanism" of Cervantes' playful figures should be seen as an aspect of their subversive role in liberating man from the tyranny of illusion and fear, and in conferring a kind of transcendental dignity on the nontranscendental order. It has nothing to do with the confirmation of a conventional ascetic attitude concerning the spectacular decay afflicting that order (see pp. 305-48).

[19] "No era hermosa en extremo; pero éralo de suerte, que podía enamorar comunicada, porque tenía un tono de habla tan suave, que se entraba por los oídos en el alma. Pasé con ella luengos y amorosos coloquios" (p. 181).

be a declared sinner, for the appearances of my present good works are obliterating my bad ones of the past from the memory of those who know me."[20] Berganza discovers that fools master a limited number of Latin phrases in order to present themselves before society as men of culture, and his description of their successes contains an association of language and deceptive clothing which emerges several times in the tale: "they go about deceiving the world with the tinsel of their tattered Grecian breeches and their false scraps of Latin." He observes that gossipers dignify their vicious slander by the designation of "Cynic philosophy" and that anxiety-prone *castellanos viejos* flaunt the Latin phrases of the certificate of *hidalguía* to assure society and themselves of their purity of blood. Berganza wonders with amazement how Cañizares "understands and speaks so much of God when her acts are so much those of the devil," and in a pathetically humorous scene he discovers the hard way the derangement of language that prevails in society. When the police chief of Seville commands him to attack the thief, he innocently decides to act according to the literal meaning of the words, "without disagreeing on a single point," bites his master, the constable, and learns in the ensuing melee how tenuous the relationship between words and reality can be.[21]

If Cervantes repeatedly displays the potential for deception and concealment in words, he similarly emphasizes how readily they become instruments of violence. As in the *Licenciado Vidriera*, Cervantes here reveals his fascination with the powers of language to destroy, the very powers that satirists such as himself have exploited from the most primitive ages of society. The dogs frequently expose slanderers and blasphemers, occasionally launch into their own invectives, and in descriptions that exploit the work's central imagery of mutilation, acknowledge the powers of speech to wound and kill ("slander is not a good thing if it kills one person, even though it makes many laugh"; "a backbiting slanderer has just blasted ten families and defamed twenty respectable men"). Berganza experiences Cañizares' words concerning his mother's infamy as "knife thrusts which pierced his heart." It is not surprising, in view of the nature and the prominence of the theme of language in the *Coloquio*, that its two most elaborate episodes climax in scenes of total chaos in which society is transformed into a

---

[20] "Rezo poco, y en público; murmuro mucho, y en secreto: vame mejor con ser hipócrita que con ser pecadora declarada: las apariencias de mis buenas obras presentes van borrando en la memoria de los que me conocen las malas obras pasadas" (p. 297).

[21] Berganza learns the same lesson when, after vainly searching for the wolf several nights, he discovers, much to his amazement, that "los pastores eran los lobos" (p. 232).

screaming, cursing mob. The description of the pandemonium in the inn, in which the Flemish sailor roars and grunts in his "mixed and bastard tongue,"[22] the enraged innkeeper's wife raves about her purity in bad Spanish and in worse Latin, and the others join in a confused chorus of "shouts and oaths" (p. 267), is just as characteristic of the *Coloquio de los perros* as are Preciosa's songs in the *Gitanilla*, and equally functional in developing a central theme and establishing a dominant tone.

It is similarly consistent with the obsessive reiteration of the theme of the destructive power of language that the gigantic figure of depravity who rises in the middle of the work is introduced in an act of vituperation which scatters the society about her ("Rascal, humbug, swindler and whoreson knave, there's no witch here!")[23] and that her request for a kiss is rejected by Berganza with repugnance. As in the description of Cañizares' belly during the dog's vigil, Cervantes is drawing on powerful imagery in the Christian tradition of writings on sinfulness, and his description of the hag's foul-smelling mouth echoes the imagery of the Psalmist: "Their throat is an open sepulchre, they have proceeded treacherously with their tongues, the poison of vipers lies under their lips. Their mouth is filled with bitterness and curses," words that Erasmus turned to repeatedly in the most influential denunciation of the sins of the tongue which the Renaissance produced, the *Lingua*.[24] Cañizares has the peculiar double func-

---

[22] The attitude toward the "foreignness" of a language here should be contrasted with that adopted by Cervantes in the *Quixote* (see below).

[23] "¡Bellaco, charlatán, embaidor y hijo de puta, aquí no hay hechicera alguna!" (p. 286).

[24] "Sepulchrum patens est guttur eorum, linguis suis dolose agebant, venenum aspidum sub labiis eorum. Quorum os maledictione et amaritudine plenum est" (Rom. 3:13; Ps. 5:11; see Erasmus' citation of the passage, *Lingua*, pp. 318, 326, 334). The prominence of Cañizares' mouth and belly in Cervantes' symbolic presentation of evil recalls Erasmus' emphasis on these two most troublesome members: "Anacharsis quum coenasset apud Solonem, hoc gestu repertus est dormiens, vt dextram admotam haberet ori, sinistram pudendis, videlicet ipsa re docens, duo membra maxime esse rebellia linguam ac pudenda, sed maiore cura cohercendam esse linguam, quam pudenda" (ed. F. Schalk, *Opera Omnia*, Vol. iv, pt. 1 [Amsterdam, 1974], p. 332). In the *Persiles* two of the most overtly symbolic characters, the lustful courtesan, Rosamunda, and the slanderous poet, Clodio, and their grotesque punishments—they are chained together and driven into exile from the kingdom which they have disrupted, and the poet is killed by an arrow piercing his mouth—can be seen as another symbolic elaboration of these sins and their catastrophic effects. The coupling of the two figures recalls, moreover, Erasmus' discussion of the violence of calumny and adulation. "Si calumniae copulem adulationem, fortasse videbor tale iugum inducere, quale sit, si quis draconem iungat simiae. Et tamen res tam diversae inter se cohaerent" (see pp. 318-19). On the possible influence of the *Lingua* on Cervantes, see below.

tion of explaining and embodying evil, and it is interesting that she is careful to point out that, in bringing God's inscrutable designs to fruition through suffering and evil, man sins in "intention, *word*, and act." While through symbol and theological disquisition she connects the problem of language with the deepest theological and philosophical themes of the work, she strikingly exemplifies the evils of language in her own actions. She is, as she herself boasts, an accomplished hypocrite, in her use of carefully chosen public prayers and discreet private "murmurings"; she consorts with the demonic master of the obliquities of speech; she pronounces the mysterious prophecy that sends the whole *Colloquy* spinning into indeterminacy; she utters a blasphemous conjuration of her master; and she vanishes from the narrative just as she enters, in a storm of violent imprecations and curses.

The connection between the destructive powers and uses of language and primal sins is made most forcefully by Berganza in the anecdote which I have analyzed above in relation to satire, the peculiar satirical perspective of the dogs, and the central theme of the mystery of lawlessness. As a concentration of Cervantes' principal themes in a single, powerful symbol, the passage is so rich in implications that I must turn to it once again. Describing his own weaknesses in the feral imagery that characterizes many of his most somber utterances, Berganza observes: "words come to my tongue like mosquitoes to wine, and every one of them is malicious and derogatory; wherefore I repeat what I have already said, that doing and speaking evil we inherit from our first parents and suck in with our mother's milk." He proceeds to support the assertion with a shocking anecdote describing an infant shaking his fist vengefully and calling his mother "whore!"—"the first articulate word which he utters" (p. 240). A nursing child joins the chorus of blasphemers that fills the world of the novella. Man's first word is a curse directed at his nurturer, a pathetic attempt to avenge himself on those who have burdened him with the affliction of inherited guilt. To appreciate the powerful implications of the symbolic anecdote, we should bear in mind that sixteenth-century humanist circles were fascinated with the possibility of rediscovering the lost Adamic speech and enthusiastically recalled the ancient tale of how the Egyptian king Psammetich discovered man's original, natural language by recording the first utterances of two infants raised in a forest by mute nurses.[25] Observing that their thinking seemed to rest on a

---

[25] See C.-G. Dubois, *Mythe et langage au seizième siècle*, p. 21. According to the tale, the first word was *Bec*, which means *Bread* in Phrygian; hence Phyrigian is the first and natural language.

popular notion, theologically fallacious, that "tout homme naît Adam" and that there is "une pureté initiale de l'âme enfantine," a "Paradis de l'enfance qui retrouverait, au-delà des siècles, communication avec le Paradis terrestre," C.-G. Dubois points out that they devoted considerable attention to the communication of infants and nurses. "Ainsi le 'baragouyn' des enfants et la langue des nourrices font l'objet d'une attention particulière, non par souci scientifique désintéressé, mais toujours par nostalgie d'un 'état' supposé naturel, identique chez tous les hommes, et qui n'est autre que l'état du premier homme encore en rapport avec la divinité."[26] The extent to which Cervantes was aware of such utopian aspirations as he traced his horrible infant is a matter of conjecture. Nevertheless, its moralizing and pessimistic message concerning the philosophy of language and its general relation to the contemporary ascetic and skeptical currents of thought which were colliding with the humanists' dream are impossible to overlook.[27]

The "Colloquy of the Squires": an Unfallen Language of the Earth

I confess that I realize that it's no dishonor
to call anyone "son of a whore."
—Sancho Panza

The prominence of conventional ascetic attitudes in Cervantes' engagement with the problem of language in *El coloquio de los perros* becomes all the more striking if we compare the discussion of the child's imprecation with the argument between Sancho Panza and Tomá Cecial about the questionable propriety of the latter's use of the same epithet in his enthusiastic description of Sancho's daughter. The exchange occurs in the carefully constructed dialogue—the "gracioso," "discreto," "nuevo," and "suave" *coloquio* of the squires, which Cervantes juxtaposes to the "grave" *coloquio* of the knights on the eve of Don Quixote's victory over the Knight of the Mirrors. The implications of the contrasts which Cervantes develops in these two scenes are too numerous to deal with in their entirety at this point. Suffice it to say that we observe a confrontation of two radically opposed

[26] Ibid., p. 57.

[27] Testimony of the familiarity of the tale of King Psammetich in Cervantes' Spain can be found in the *Tesoro de la lengua castellana o española* of 1611. S. de Covarrubias sadly rejects the possibility of discovering a natural language and notes that Psammetich's experiment was ridiculous, since *Bec* could just as well be French as Phrygian. Each language owes its origin to the will of the people speaking it. See ed. M. de Riquer (Barcelona, 1943), p. 758.

worlds and systems of values and attitudes. While their masters spend a sleepless night in dignified conversation about heroic adventures and the beauty of the ideals that inspire them in their lonely quests— glory, honor, sacrifice, and romantic love—the squires feel an irresistible urging to speak too. They leave the knights in order to search for a place where they can "talk squirelike" and enjoy a banquet which the "charitable" Tomá Cecial has provided, as if by "the art of enchantment." The banquet forms a festive counterpart to the discourse of the knights, and in its positive emphasis on the elemental needs of the body—food, sexuality, and sleep—it has the traditional carnivalesque function of "uncrowning," or rendering ridiculous, the lofty aspirations of the knights and the official attitudes and hierarchies of value that they reflect. For example, Tomá speaks scornfully of the stoical habits of the masters: "By my faith, brother, my stomach is not made for your thistles or your wild pears or your forest roots. Let our masters have them, with their ideas and their laws of chivalry, and let them eat what they order others to."[28] While discussing the absurdity of their masters' "search for adventures," Cecial notes the needs which Sancho's body is bringing to their attention and welcomes the opportunity for feasting: "All this while Sancho was spitting frequently a kind of dryish gluey saliva; and when the charitable woodly squire noticed it, he observed: 'All this talk seems to be making our tongues stick to our palates. I carry a pretty good loosener, though, here hanging at my saddlebow.'"[29] At the same time, the

---

[28] "Por mi fe, hermano . . . que yo no tengo hecho el estómago a tagarninas, ni a piruétanos, ni a raíces de los montes, Allá se lo hayan con sus opiniones y leyes caballerescas nuestros amos, y coman lo que ellos mandaren" (*Don Quijote*, 2:132).

[29] "Escupía Sancho a menudo, al parecer, un cierto género de saliva pegajosa y algo seca; lo cual visto y notado por el caritativo bosqueril escudero dijo:—Paréceme que de lo que hemos hablado se nos pegan al paladar las lenguas; pero yo traigo un despegador pendiente del arzón de mi caballo, que es tal como bueno" (Ibid., 2:131). For a provocative study of the carnival spirit of freedom informing much of the recreational literature of the Middle Ages and nourishing some of the greatest literary creations of the Renaissance, see M. Bakhtin's *Rabelais and His World*. Bakhtin's central thesis is that, through the various forms of "uncrowning" parody developed in the tradition of carnival, man experiences a release from the fears and restraints engendered by the tyranny of official values and enjoys a festive regeneration and participation in the bodily life and its temporal rhythms, a life of vitality, fertility, and growth, in which all human beings are equals and the distinctions based on official hierarchies are viewed as unessential. The carnival spirit resounds in Sancho's refusal to fight Cecial: "peleen nuestros amos, y allá se lo hayan, y bebamos y vivamos nosotros; que el tiempo tiene cuidado de quitarnos las vidas, sin que andemos buscando apetites para que se acaben antes de llegar su sazón y término y que se cayan de maduras" (2:138-39). This is not the occasion for a complete study of the numerous carnivalesque elements in the contrasting dialogues. However, I would point out

affirmative view of the fulfillment of such bodily needs, which we observe throughout the incident, and the scene of communion that unfolds as the two peasants share the meat pie, pass the wineskin back and forth, discover that sleep alone can "tie their tongues," and fall asleep together, "grasping the almost empty wineskin between them," powerfully support a celebration of charity, brotherhood, family loyalty, simplicity, and contentment with man's common, unheroic destiny. This celebration emerges in the dialogue of the two friends, a dialogue from which the crusading knights are, of course, excluded.[30]

---

that the pillow fight proposed by the squires is a festive, debasing counterpart to their masters' joust, just as the fool's horsemanship in the previous episode is a festive burlesque of Don Quixote's knightly figure, and that the enormous purple nose of Cecial, which Cervantes compares to an eggplant, is a common feature of the grotesque body of carnival tradition, a body in which a shocking emphasis on protuberances and orifices is exploited both to debase official values and restraints through sexual and scatological humor and to exalt the procreative energy and abundance of bodily life (see Bakhtin, chap. 5, "The Grotesque Image of the Body and Its Sources"). Moreover, in this scene we suddenly discover the important connections which Sancho and his ancestors have with the carnival fluid of truth, vitality, regeneration, and secular communion—wine. One of Cervantes' principal methods of comic reduction of the lofty world of chivalry is through its comic juxtaposition to food and alimentary concerns (e.g., the translation of the heroic manuscript is paid for with raisins, and the heroic chronicler's name turns out to be "eggplant"), and Sancho Panza, with his prominent stomach and shanks (i.e., Sancho Zancas), and his imperious appetite and digestive processes, provides, in his companionship with the knight, a constant source of a carnivalesque type of uncrowning imaginative energy. For his connections with traditional carnivalesque figures, e.g., Saint Pançart, who appears in Rabelais' *Pantagruel*, see Bakhtin, *Rabelais and His World*, pp. 21-23; F. Márquez Villanueva, *Fuentes literarias cervantinas* (Madrid, 1973), pp. 30-31; and W. S. Hendrix, "Sancho Panza and the Comic Types of the Sixteenth Century," *Homenaje ofrecido a Menéndez Pidal* (Madrid, 1925), 2:485-94. In recent studies, A. Redondo has shown that the episode of Sancho's rule in Barataria is thoroughly permeated by carnivalesque motifs ("Tradición carnavalesca y creación literaria del personaje de Sancho Panza al episodio de la ínsula Barataria en el 'Quijote,' " *Bulletin Hispanique*, 80 [1978]:39-70; and L. A. Murillo has analyzed the rich "festival mythology" of the *Quixote*, particularly those elements deriving from carnivalesque rituals, and argued that their effects are of crucial importance in investing the realistic action of the text with the "fictional semblance of a higher transcendency" we expect of epic narrative" ("*Don Quixote* as Renaissance Epic," in *Cervantes and the Renaissance*, ed. M. D. McGaha [Easton, Pa., 1980], pp. 51-70).

[30] The dialogue looks forward to Sancho's education of the duchess concerning the common destiny uniting men beneath all superficial distinctions of social hierarchies ("no hay estómago que sea un palmo mayor que otro" [2:299]) and to several episodes, toward the end of the novel, in which he joins with a natural society to enjoy a banquet and affirm the importance of charity, conviviality, good will, and simplicity: his adjudication of the dispute between the racers (chap. 66), his picnic with Tosilos (chap. 66), and his encounter with Ricote (chap. 54). The latter is by far the most important, as it follows Sancho's withdrawal from the deceitful, intrigue-ridden

The effectiveness of the colloquy of the squires derives in part from the vitality of popular language—the concreteness of its diction in its references to the everyday experiential worlds of work, body, and family, the earthy and organic energy of the metaphors underlying much of its slang, the gnomic resonances and immediacy of reference in its proverbial allusions, its "literary citations," as it were, the enlivening ambivalences of its obscenities, and the rapid movement of living dialogue, in which the speakers strive for authentic communication and self-expression rather than the elevation of the self and its sentiments through the mediating refinements of a preexistent elegant style. The power of all of this is heightened by the pronounced artificiality, the remoteness from experience, of the knights' colloquy with its lengthy, rhetorically composed sentences and speeches, its ornamental epithets, its mythological and geographical allusions, its epic literary citations, and its embodiment of sentiment in a conventional, highly abstract love sonnet. While the careful elaboration of stylistic contrasts draws our attention to the existence of different levels of discourse and to the conventionality of all linguistic utterances, Cervantes, in a way that is characteristic of his highly self-conscious stance as a writer, allows the scene constructed out of popular language to engender within itself a critical examination of the conventions of popular discourse, and, in doing so, he presents dramatically one of his most profound insights into the workings of language.

Cervantes' interest in the theme of language as he composed the scene is evident immediately at its introduction. On hearing Sancho's description of Dulcinea in concrete rustic similes ("my lady is as gentle as a yearling ewe, she is softer than butter"), the Knight of the Wood notes that he has never encountered a squire who "dares to *talk* where

---

official society of Barataria, his rejection of the powers, glories, and responsibilities of kingship, and his determination to return to his simple life as a farmer. Several details of this scene recall the colloquy of the squires: the festive banquet in which drinkers raise their wineskins in an ecstatic gesture ("clavados los ojos en el cielo, no parecía sino que ponían en él la puntería [2:449]) and which ends with most of the participants "sepultados en dulce sueño," the mockery of the cares of the official world as the celebrants return to the gay time of the feast and its regenerative laughter ("Y disparaba con una risa que le duraba un hora, sin acordarse entonces de nada de lo que le había sucedido en su gobierno; porque sobre el rato y tiempo cuando se come y bebe, poca jurisdición suelen tener los cuidados" [see Bakhtin, *Rabelais and His World*, chap. 4, "Banquet Imagery in Rabelais"]), the emphasis on communion and brotherhood during the drinking scene ("De cuando en cuando juntaba alguno su mano derecha con la de Sancho y decía: 'Español y tudesqui, tuto uno: bon compaño' "), and the connection of this intense communication at a fundamental level of experience with extra-official language—Sancho's sign language and the *lingua franca* in which universal brotherhood and good will are proclaimed.

his master is *talking*" and remarks of his own companion: "it will not be proved that he has ever opened his lips where I was *talking*." Sancho reacts with anger: "By my faith, I for certain have *talked*, and I can *talk* before another as . . . But let it be; it'll be the worse for stirring." Tomá Cecial immediately invites him to "*talk* in a squire-like way," and Sancho responds energetically: "you'll see whether I can compete with your most *talkative* squires." The narrator at this point concludes the introduction by calling attention to the contrasting styles of speech in what follows: "the two squires drew aside, and a *colloquy* took place between them which was as *comical* as their masters' was *serious*. . . . Knights and squires were separated, squires *relating their lives* to one another, knights, *their loves*."[31] The preoccupation with language continues throughout the scene and is visible even in such small details as Sancho's concern to explain the origin of the name of his beast: "Your worship may think I'm joking when I put such a price on my Dapple—for dapple is my ass's color."[32]

The tone of defiance in the squires' demands to speak is impossible to overlook. It is as if a voice that had been suppressed by an alien social and linguistic order were rising to make itself heard, and, as we quickly discover, its most assertive and eloquent claims to its rights are sounded by the squire who had never dared to open his mouth in his master's presence. Moreover, the peasants demand a freedom to go beyond any preordained limitations on their utterances, as they deride the cramped "love stories" which will consume their master's conversation and declare that they are going to talk about

---

[31] "Es mi señora como una borrega mansa: es más blanda que una manteca"; "—Nunca he visto yo escudero—replicó el del Bosque—que se atreva a *hablar* donde *habla* su señor . . . no se probará que [el mío] haya desplegado el labio donde yo *hablo*. . . .—Pues a fe—dijo Sancho—, que *he hablado* yo, y puedo *hablar* delante de otro tan . . . y aun quédese aquí, que es peor meneallo. . . . vea si puedo entrar en docena con los más *hablantes* escuderos . . . se apartaron los dos escuderos, entre los cuales pasó un tan *gracioso coloquio* como fue *grave* el que pasó entre sus señores. . . . Divididos estaban caballeros y escuderos, *éstos contándose sus vidas y aquéllos sus amores*" (*Don Quijote*, 2:127-28; italics added).

[32] "A burla tendrá vuesa merced el valor de mi rucio; que rucio es el color de mi jumento" (Ibid., 2:129). One might argue that Sancho's explanation of the name "rucio," which can be taken as a euphemism, reveals a concern for linguistic decorum. Such a concern is perfectly consistent with his position in the following discussion, when he appears to have forgotten his "authentic" language. The entire scene can be read as the rescue of Sancho Panza from an alien linguistic order, in which he has been acculturated through the influence of Don Quixote. One should recall the breakdown of communication in Sancho's dialogue with his wife at the beginning of the third sally and the translator's perplexity as he reads Cide Hamete Benengeli's account of the squire's "modo de hablar" (2:73-79).

"anything they might choose." Their entire dialogue pulsates with an expansive, transgressive energy, an urge to violate linguistic norms, to bring together things and levels of experience not customarily conjoined in official language.[33] The squires' rejection of conventional distinctions is evident in their fantastic materialization of the knight's lady as cooked food and the chivalric impulse as a digestive occurrence, in bizarre personifications of material objects (e.g., "a bit of cheese, whom four dozen carob beans accompany"), in the coinage of words and phrases releasing the defiant energies of paradox (e.g., "hablar escuderilmente"), and in figures of speech which, in their play with sacred cultural values, activate the disquieting powers of violations of taboos (e.g., the metaphorical transformation of the wineskin into an object of worship and the description of its adoration as an ecstatic religious act). So great is the impulse toward verbal liberation that Cervantes' narrator, characteristically a multivoiced reporter, cannot resist engaging in the inventive practices of his characters, as he describes the activities of the "bosqueril escudero." The release of the centrifugal energies in language culminates in a critical discussion of the most startling of the various grotesque combinations of disparate elements appearing throughout the scene.

[33] The tone of defiance in Sancho's voice, which asserts its rights to represent authentically the being to whom it belongs despite the conceptions of poetic truth, propriety in characterization, and decorum in style which dominate official literature, is one of the most important of the various features distinguishing the squire in Part II, who shows no patience with "reprochadores de voquibles" and "friscales de sus dichos." It is particularly audible in the opening literary colloquy (chap. 3), where he claims to be one of the "principales presonajes" of the history, and in the adventures in the palace world, where he speaks about his ass and mortifies Don Quixote, who would have him "sew up his mouth" and "hide his identity," where he continues to refer to his "regüeldos" despite Don Quixote's urgings that he contribute to the "enriquecimiento de la lengua" by using the euphemism "erutaciones," where he accedes to his master's command that he suppress his proverbs by mischievously stating: "no los diré, porque al buen callar llaman Sancho," and where his "folk tale," unlike the exasperating tale of la Torralba of Part I which it appears formally to resemble, most effectively conveys a satirical message concerning the patronizing strategies of the Duke (see II, chap. 31). To appreciate the transgressive aura surrounding Sancho's assertions of the value of his own language, one might recall the counsels of the influential neo-classicist, Torquato Tasso, concerning the necessity of concealing the authentic identity of the peasant in the "palace world" of the serious work of literature: "Sdegni ancora il nostro poeta tutte le cose basse, tutte le populari, tutte le disoneste . . . e se pur alcuna volta riceve i pastori, i caprari, i porcari e l'altre sì fatte persone, deve aver riguardo non solo al decoro della persona, ma a quello del poema, e mostrarli come si mostrano ne'palazzi reali e nelle solennità e nelle pompe" (*Discorsi dell'arte poetica e del poema eroico*, ed. L. Poma [Bari, 1964], pp. 112-13).

Following Sancho's loving description of his daughter ("tall as a lance, as fresh as an April morning, and as strong as a porter"), Tomá Cecial responds with enthusiasm: "Those are qualities . . . that fit her not only to be a countess, but to be a nymph of the green wood. Oh, son of a bitch, the little whore, and what muscles the rogue must have!"[34] While the contrast *condesa/ninfa–puta/bellaca* forms part of the carnivalesque uncrowning developed throughout the scene and brings into the dialogue of the squires a collision of high and low styles which replicates in a concentrated form the much more extensively developed interaction of the whole dialogue with that of the knights,[35] the most important linguistic implications of the statement for Cervantes' purposes lie in the obscenities themselves. Sancho finds the words insulting and indecorous and reacts angrily: "She's no whore, nor was her mother, and neither of them ever will be, God willing, whilst I'm alive. And speak more politely, for seeing that your worship was brought up amongst knights-errant, who are politeness itself, these words of yours don't seem very well chosen." Tomá Cecial protests that Sancho's remark is based on his ignorance of the "play of praises and vituperations," and assures him that parents should disown any children who do not merit such epithets. The good-natured Sancho, whose flexible and conciliatory attitudes toward linguistic precision and decorum are frequently contrasted with those of

[34] "Grande como una lanza, y tan fresca como una mañana de abril. . . . Partes son ésas . . . no sólo para ser condesa, sino para ser ninfa del verde bosque. ¡Oh, hideputa, puta, y qué rejo debe de tener la bellaca!" (Ibid., 2:129).

[35] Such grotesque blending of the lofty and the obscene is characteristic of the carnivalesque symposium, with which this scene of banqueting and gay conversation has such clear affinities. "The themes of table talk are always 'sublime,' filled with 'profound wisdom,' but these themes are uncrowned and renewed on the material bodily level. The grotesque symposium does not have to respect hierarchical distinctions; it freely blends the profane and the sacred, the lower and the higher, the spiritual and the material. There are no *mésalliances* in its case" (Bakhtin, *Rabelais and His World*, pp. 285-86). As for the startling presence of lofty and obscene (i.e., *ninfa-puta*) in the discourse of the peasant, it should be pointed out that a seemingly random mingling of voices and styles is characteristic of the entire *Quixote*, and one occasionally senses that the author is more interested in the life and interplay of languages than in the demands of coherent character presentation. The narrator himself is capable of such bewildering "double-voicedness," as frequently his apparently objective reporting suddenly incorporates Don Quixote's chivalric language as if it were his own. Oddly enough, such striking combinations of elevated and normal (or vulgar) discourse have the effect of recharging the high style with linguistic life even as they "deflate" it by pointing up its remoteness from the world of ordinary experience. They do this precisely by disclosing all that it consciously rejects or hides and hence by restoring an oppositional force within it. Cervantes reveals that what is absent in it has always given it life.

the rigid Cratylist, Don Quixote, accepts the explanation, remarking that if his friend really intends praise, he is welcome to "dump a whole whorehouse on top of him," his children, and his wife, "for everything they do and say is highly deserving of such praise."[36] However, not until after their feast do we discover that Sancho instinctively already understood the "play of praises" that his friend tried to clarify. For after enjoying an interminable, "mystical" draught of wine, "gazing at the stars for a quarter of an hour," he sighs and cries out ecstatically: "Oh the son of a whore, the rogue! And what grand ["católico"] stuff it is!" When Tomá draws his attention to how he has "praised this wine by calling it a son of a whore," Sancho concludes: "I confess that I realize that it's no dishonor to call anyone 'son of a whore,' when you mean it for praise."[37]

In this scene Cervantes depicts a natural society achieving a type of authentic verbal communication which accompanies its intense encounter at the elemental level of healthy bodily life and which is markedly absent in the exchange of monologues constituting the conversation of the self-absorbed knights. And one of its most striking and effective methods, as Sancho discovers in the little lesson in linguistics that Cervantes offers amid the farcical humor,[38] is to invert

---

[36] "Ni ella es puta, ni lo fue su madre, ni lo será ninguna de las dos, Dios quiriendo, mientras yo viviere. Y háblese más comedidamente; que para haberse criado vuesa merced entre caballeros andantes, que son la mesma cortesía, no me parecen muy concertadas esas palabras. . . . por esa misma razón podía echar vuestra merced a mí y hijos y a mi mujer toda una putería encima, porque todo cuanto hacen y dicen son estremos dignos de semejantes alabanzas" (*Don Quijote* 2:129-33).

[37] ¡Oh hideputa, bellaco, y cómo es católico! . . . alabado este vino llamándole hideputa . . . confieso que conozco que no es deshonra llamar hijo de puta a nadie, cuando cae debajo del entendimiento de alabarle" (Ibid., 2:132-33). F. Márquez Villanueva notes a similar rustic eulogy in Diego de Ávila's *Égloga ynterlocutoria*: "¡O hi de puta, y qué rabadilla / Debe tener la hi de vellaca! / Una espaldaza mayor que una vaca, / Y tetas tan grandes, qu'es maravilla!" and he points to the roots of Cervantes' comic treatment of his peasant figures in the comic techniques of Torres Naharro and his followers (*Fuentes literarias cervantinas*, p. 66). Both Cervantes and Torres Naharro owe a great deal to popular humor and particularly its carnivalesque forms, but what distinguishes Cervantes' scene from innumerable farcical exchanges between peasants in the drama of the period is its linguistic "self-consciousness," that is, the way in which it incorporates a critical analysis of the workings of the abusive praise of popular speech which it exploits for comic effects. For the importance of popular discourse in the *Quixote*, see A. Rosenblat, *La lengua del "Quijote,"* pp. 43-56; for its rich repertory of "expresiones exclamativas" of this type, see pp. 48-51.

[38] For Cervantes' mastery of the art of mingling the ridiculous and the profound, see L. Pfandl's "Die Zwischenspiele des Cervantes," *Neue Jahrbücher für Wissenschaft und Jugendbildung* 3 (1927):301-23.

in a shocking manner the customary meaning of words of praise and vituperation. The lesson has its parallel in the colloquy of the masters, as the Knight of the Wood tells Don Quixote: "my destiny or, to be more exact, my choice led me to fall in love with the peerless Casildea of Vandalia. I call her peerless because she has no equal, either in the greatness of her stature or in the perfection of her rank and beauty."[39] Cervantes intentionally chooses one of the most refined, conventional, and lifeless of literary epithets of praise, and the effect of its examination is both to point up, through a sharp differentiation of linguistic levels, the tremendous distance separating the worlds of literature and reality, writing and experience, knights and common people, "amores" and "vida,"[40] and official culture and popular culture, and to emphasize the superior vitality of popular discourse and the experience that nourishes it. Mikhail Bakhtin has pointed out that such manipulation of abusive language as we observe in Cecial's praise of Sanchica is a characteristic feature of some of the traditional forms of popular verbal culture (for example, the language of the marketplace) and that it is in fact quite common in the enormous spheres of un-

[39] "Mi destino, o, por mejor decir, mi elección, me trujo a enamorar la sin par Casildea de Vandalia. Llámola sin par porque no le tiene, así en la grandeza del cuerpo como en el estremo del estado y de la hermosura" (*Don Quijote* 2:134).

[40] In a stark antithesis which introduces the colloquies, the narrator emphasizes the unreality of the knights' amatory experiences, and an association of linguistic petrification and erotic stagnation runs through the entire episode. The burlesque of courtly love and the traditional female principle informing the knight's erotic mission is perhaps most striking at the point when the squires translate their master's experience of love into alimentary and digestive imagery. In one of the most carnivalesque moments in the episode, Cervantes turns to the sphere of concrete and elementary bodily life to uncrown the "sin par" maidens of romance and to materialize grotesquely the spiritual world of the questing knight. When Sancho asks him whether his master is "enamorado," Tomá responds: "Sí: de una tal Casildea de Vandalia, la más cruda y la más asada señora que en todo el orbe puede hallarse; pero no cojea del pie de la crudeza; que otros mayores embustes le gruñen en las entrañas, y ello dirá antes de muchas horas." Sancho replies in the same idiom: "No hay camino tan llano que no tenga algún tropezón o barranco; en otras casas cuecen habas, y en la mía, a calderadas; más acompañados y paniaguados debe de tener la locura que la discreción" (2:130-31). The contrast between the women of Sancho's world, who are described in terms of physical energy, organic growth, domestic excellence, family relations, and natural rhythms, and the knights' spiritual lady, who demands that her courtier continually prove his love through suffering and who expresses her regard for him by disdainfully crushing any hopes of union which he might entertain, recalls Cervantes' treatment of the sinister female type in *La Gitanilla* (see my *Cervantes and the Humanist Vision*, chap. 2). Compare *Don Quijote* I, chap. 25, where the female as a figment of the knight's imagination and an object of Platonic love is juxtaposed to the very real female, Aldonza Lorenzo, whose physical strength provokes Sancho Panza's outburst of enthusiasm in the same idiom: "¡Oh hideputa, qué rejo que tiene, y qué voz!" (1:312)

publicized or nonwritten speech of any language. In justifying his use of the obscenity, Cecial invokes the language of the public square, where "el vulgo" rewards the skillful thrusts of the bullfighter with verbal acclaim of this sort. Such ambivalent terms of abuse break down the customary associations and logical categories and divisions informing official language and enable human beings to reach deeper, more intimate levels of communication. The word is wrested from its familiar context, charged with the energy of an individual voice, and metamorphosed from the withering *flatus vocis* of conventional discourse into a revitalized mediator between two human lives. Bakhtin observes that "wherever conditions of absolute extra-official and full human relations are established, words tend to this ambivalent fullness. It is as if the ancient marketplace comes to life in closed chamber conversation. Intimacy begins to sound like the familiarity of bygone days, which breaks down all barriers between men."[41] As he conceived his scene of brotherhood and described Sancho Panza and Tomá Cecial moving toward the full human relationship that is denied their masters, Cervantes undoubtedly glimpsed the fundamental inadequacy of language as a channel for genuine contact between human beings, and, fascinated as he always was by the mysteries of his medium, he could not resist turning into fiction his insight into the power of linguistic paradox and illogic as means to which men have traditionally turned in their attempts to overcome that inadequacy and give expression to the ambivalences that mark any authentic emotional involvement.[42]

SERMO CARNIS—SERMO SPIRITUS: THE COLLOQUY AND ERASMUS' LINGUA

The comparison of the two scenes in which Cervantes exploits and comments on the power of obscene speech reveals clearly the fundamental differences between the *Quixote* and the *Colloquy of the Dogs* in

[41] *Rabelais and His World*, p. 421.

[42] In the extended and symmetrical presentation of a confrontation of official and popular levels of discourse and their respective experiential backgrounds, Cervantes' antithetical colloquies recall certain striking scenes in Rabelais' narratives, for example, the celebration preceding Pantagruel's grotesque creation of the pygmies, with its contrasting trophies, its carefully balanced stylistic oppositions, and its shocking juxtapositions of the heroic and the corporeal (see *Pantagruel*, chap. 27). However, Cervantes' text moves in very different directions, generating from the ambivalent powers of carnivalesque degradation a theoretical discussion of the complexities in the significative and communicative processes of language and incorporating that discussion in a novelistically developed encounter of individual consciousnesses.

their respective approaches to language. While the novel with its characteristic "existentialist" view of experience looks affirmatively at the ambivalences and "promiscuity" of language, the exemplary tale considers the same phenomena from a traditional moral and theological perspective.[43] However, for all its conservatism in this regard, its engagement with the problem of language is by no means as simple as the conventional lamentations on the dire consequences of Babel's destruction which proliferated in the ascetic and skeptical writings of the age. There are in fact some significant elements counterbalancing the overwhelmingly pessimistic statements which the *Colloquy of the Dogs* offers concerning language, and they suggest that, as in so many other major spheres of his thought, here, too, Cervantes' real affinities lie not with the narrow critical philosophy of the contemporary literature of *desengaño*, but rather with the tolerant, pluralistic vision of human possibilities and limitations that was characteristic of Erasmist Christian humanism.

In discussing the work as a satirical survey of the forms of evil and as a meditation on its sources, I have pointed out how Cervantes, in tones which are nearly imperceptible amid the destructive criticism, occasionally reminds his reader that man has the potential for goodness as well as for evil. In his treatment of the problem of language

---

[43] A comparison of *Rinconete y Cortadillo* and the episode of the galley slaves in the *Quixote* reveals the same differences: we view, on the one hand, a *corrupt* language, in which the deviation from a norm, sanctioned by nature, is constantly stressed and becomes the sign of moral inferiority; on the other, a living subspecies of Spanish, an authentic linguistic medium, perfectly adjusted to the particular expressive and communicative needs of its speakers. Similarly we find the moral-theological perspective on linguistic fragmentation dominating the exemplary *Persiles*, where the Babelic confusion of the northern world is an aspect of its theologically unregenerate state, its moral disorder, its ignorance, and its barbarity and is contrasted with the Latin of the Catholic world. This view appears in the *Quixote* only in one of its most romantic episodes—*The Tale of the Captive*. See my *Cervantes' Christian Romance*, pp. 90-91. For the *Quixote*'s respect for the integrity of each dialect and language, see Spitzer: "according to the creator of Don Quijote, dialects are simply the different reflections of reality (they are 'styles,' as the equally tolerant linguist of today would say), among which no one can take precedence over the other" ("Linguistic Perspectivism in the *Don Quijote*," p. 55). When I refer to the "characteristic 'existentialist' vision of the *Quixote*," I would draw attention to its implicit rejection of essences in its depiction of human beings, nature, language, and experience and its implicit endorsement of a philosophical point of view of the type which Cervantes' contemporary, the skeptic philosopher Francisco Sánchez, described in his treatise *Quod nihil scitur*: "Ni es de extrañar si fué sentencia de algunos, que de un mismo hombre, después de una hora, no puede afirmarse que sea el mismo que antes de ella . . . los accidentes son de esencia del individuo, los cuales, variando perpetuamente, le imprimen variación" (*Que nada se sabe*, p. 122).

we note similarly an occasional reminder that there exist more sublime registers of discourse than those generally audible in the strident world of the novella. If we examine these passages closely, we discover that the general tensions pervading the dialogue as it destroys and simultaneously reconstructs are reflected perfectly in its paradoxical approach to the nature of language. As strange as it might seem in view of its relentless depiction and exploitation of verbal violence, the colloquy begins and ends with discussions of the wondrous benefits of language, and no reader can fail to appreciate the forcefulness conferred upon them by their prominent position in the tale. Even more surprisingly, the dogs' words on both occasions contain a profession of faith in the power of language that recalls the great classical celebrations of speech as a humanizing and civilizing gift, bestowed upon mortals by the gods. Berganza and Cipión explain their mysterious acquisition of speech as a miracle, refer to language as a divine gift ("I find myself enriched by this divine gift of speech"), and declare that rational discourse is what distinguishes man from the beast: "what makes it all the more miraculous is not only that we speak but also that we speak intelligently, as if we had minds capable of reason; yet we are so devoid of it that the difference between brute beast and man consists in this, that man is a rational animal and the beast is irrational."[44] The favorable view of humanity as hierarchically placed above the beast and endowed with speech and reason as distinguishing characteristics is reasserted on several occasions in the dogs' dialogue.[45] Both dogs fear the imminent return to the "darkness of silence" ("I am fearful that when the sun rises we will be left in the darkness, our powers of speech gone"; "keep talking: the night is slipping away, and I would not like to find ourselves with the rising of the sun left groping in the shadows of silence"). They are deeply appreciative of the divine favor that has been granted them ("let us not fail to enjoy this blessing of speech and the incalculable boon of holding human

[44] "Me veo enriquecido deste divino don de la habla" (p. 213); "y viene a ser mayor este milagro en que no solamente hablamos, sino en que hablamos con discurso, como si fuéramos capaces de razón, estando tan sin ella, que la diferencia que hay del animal bruto al hombre es ser el hombre animal racional, y el bruto, irracional" (p. 210).

[45] One can compare the dog's veneration of language as the power by which man rises above the mute, isolated condition of bestial life with Sancho Panza's complaint that it is an excessive punishment to be forced to "coser la boca, sin osar decir lo que el hombre tiene en su corazón, como si fuera mudo." To be unable to speak is in effect to be "buried in life" (Don Quijote, 1:300). The same attitude toward the "divine gift of speech" lies behind the terrible penance which the lecherous Rutilio must suffer in the Persiles. He must wear the skins of animals and live for several years as a mute on the dark island of the barbarians.

discourse"), and in Cipión's final utterance he looks forward to the return of "this great benefit of speech."[46] Behind the dogs' enthusiastic pronouncements lies a traditional view of language reaching back to classical antiquity and perhaps most forcefully and concisely expressed in Quintilian's *Institutio Oratoria*: "And in truth that god, who was in the beginning, the father of all things and the architect of the universe, distinguished man from all other living creatures that are subject to death, by nothing more than this, that he gave him the gift of speech. . . . Reason, then, was the greatest gift of the almighty, who willed that we should share its possession with the immortal gods. But reason by itself would help us but little and would be far less evident in us, had we not the power to express our thoughts in speech. . . . Wherefore let us seek with all our hearts that true majesty of oratory, the fairest gift of god to man, without which all things are stricken dumb and robbed alike of present glory [luce praesenti] and the immortal record of posterity."[47] The view was frequently championed by the Christian humanists, who, in their characteristic syncretic approach to tradition, invoked it while emphasizing at the same time the dignity which Holy Scripture confers on the word as God's creative instrument and as the force incarnate in the divine mediator between man and God, Jesus Christ—the Word made flesh. At the beginning of his *Ecclesiastes sive concionator euangelicus*, Erasmus enumerates the powers and mysteries of Christ, "that Word which cannot be grasped, which expresses most surely the divine mind and which never deviates from the source of highest truth," and adds that man possesses nothing that is "more marvelous and powerful" than speech, the image of the mind. Moreover, there is nothing that separates man more thoroughly from the beasts ("a natura pecudum")

---

[46] "Estando temeroso que al salir del sol nos hemos de quedar a escuras, faltándonos la habla" (p. 256); "sigue; que se va la noche, y no querría que al salir del sol quedásemos a la sombra del silencio" (p. 282); "no por esto dejemos de gozar deste bien de la habla que tenemos y de la excelencia tan grande de tener discurso humano" (p. 312); "este grande beneficio de la habla" (p. 339).

[47] II, 12-15; XII, 30. See *The Institutio Oratoria of Quintilian*, ed. and trans. H. E. Butler (London, 1921-1922), 1:323, 4:513. For the classical origins of the view of language as a civilizing institution, its importance in the Renaissance as the "geheime Philosophie des rhetorischen Humanismus," and its opposition to the fundamentally different conceptions descending from late medieval nominalist philosophy (language as sign) and mystical Christianity (language as the divine *logos* manifesting itself through the soul of the individual), see K.-O. Apel, *Die Idee der Sprache* (Bonn, 1975). For numerous classical statements resembling those of Cervantes' dogs, see chap. 5. This fine study does not stress the manner in which humanists such as Erasmus could assimilate the latter two conceptions, which are considered to be "nichthumanistisches Sprachdenken."

and nothing that reveals his divine likeness more clearly than reason and language ("hominem non alia re propius accedere ad naturam aeterni Numinis, quam mente & oratione").⁴⁸ As F. de Dainville has demonstrated, the humanists' optimistic view of the civilizing powers of language was maintained by the Jesuit educators, and it became one of the fundamental principles underlying their highly successful program of rhetorical and literary study. We need only look at the influential *De Arte Rhetorica* (1577) of Cervantes' contemporary, the Jesuit Cyprian Soarez, to find a concise expression of the theories of Cervantes' dogs, themselves auditors in the Jesuit college of Seville, concerning the primacy of reason in man, the lofty alliance of reason and language, and the illumination which the light of reason through speech, its "admirable image," brings to the world.

There is such a likeness between reason [*ratio*] and speech [*oratio*] that the Greeks, who were preeminent not only in understanding but also in speaking, have named both with a single word, while the Romans, rivals of the Greeks in wisdom, gave both almost the same name. For speech is a kind of image of reason. God put reason in the mind, to which He granted rule of the whole spirit: the same highest maker placed the throne of speech in the loftiest and most noble part of the body: reason is a kind of light and illumination of life: speech is the perceptible glory and embellishment of reason: reason rules and checks a man's own spirit: speech also moves those of others: it is the admirable image of reason: the beauty of speech nevertheless proclaims that reason is hidden within.⁴⁹

---

⁴⁸ "Ille incomprehensibilis Sermo, divinae mentis certissimus enarrator & ab archetypo summae veritatis nusquam discrepans" (*Opera Omnia*, ed. J. Le Clerc, 5:772). See also P. Mosellanus: "Ac primum omnium quis nescit orationis usum unicum esse, quo nos naturae princeps et mundi fabricator deus prae caeteris donavit, et supra reliquorum animalium vilem conditionem evexit, quoque proxime ad suae imaginis divinitatem accedimus? . . . Sola est oratio quae nos homines facit sola cujus beneficio brutis praeferimur" (*Oratio de Variarum Linguarum Cognitione Paranda*, cited by L. Massebieau, *Les Colloques scolaires du seizième siècle et leurs auteurs* [Paris, 1878], p. 32); and Vives: "bestiae omnes sicut mente ita et sermone carent . . . ac quemadmodum mentem munere habemus Dei, sic etiam loqui naturale est nobis" (*De Tradendis Disciplinis, Opera Omnia*, 6:298). For the neo-Platonist Ficino, the gift of speech, which elevates us above the condition of the beast, proves that dwelling within us is "divina quaedam mens" (see Borst, *Der Turmbau von Babel*, 3:979). For the popularity of the classical celebration of language in the writings of Spanish humanists, see F. Rico, " 'Laudes litterarum'; Humanismo y dignidad del hombre en la España del Renacimiento," *Homenaje a Julio Caro Baroja* (Madrid, 1978), pp. 895-914.

⁴⁹ "Rationis, & orationis tanta est similitudo, vt Graeci, qui nonintelligendi solum, sed loquendi etiam principatum tenuerunt, vno vtranque vocabulo, Latini, Graecorum prudentiae aemuli, eodem pene nominarint. Est enim oratio quasi rationis imago quaedam. Rationem in mente, cui regnum totius animi tributum est, Deus Opt. Max. posuit: orationis sedem idem summus opifex in celsissima ac nobilissima cor-

It is perhaps symptomatic of Erasmus' interest in all the potentialities of speech that he cannot resist following his praise with a denunciation of the great perversion which results from man's abuse of the
divine gift. However, in the *Ecclesiastes* the humanist is concerned
primarily with the beauties of divine language and the modes of communication that the ideal preacher must employ to make its sancti-
fying powers accessible to human beings. In another work, the *Lingua*, Erasmus gives free rein to his interest in the sinful uses of the
tongue, and in its manner of conjoining a relentless exploration of the
darkest registers of language with a somewhat muted affirmation of
the powers in human discourse to uplift the desolate and cure the
spiritually ill, his satirical declamation resembles Cervantes' masterpiece more closely than any other important examination of language
in the age. In words that look forward to Cipión's attribution of life's
greatest evils to the tongue (see above), Erasmus exhorts his readers:
"Look around at all the grim tragedies in the world, and you will find
in almost every case that the source of all evils was an evil tongue."[50]
Man is born with the inclination to commit its sins. The tongue is a
weapon that can kill (p. 307). It is worse than war and death in the
catastrophes which it brings, for wars themselves would not exist were
it not for its abuses, and, while it tears apart all human bonds as
effectively as death, it does not reward its victims with the peace of
the afterlife (pp. 318-19). All the evils of the tongue observed by
Cervantes' protagonists, ranging from minor foibles such as the ostentatious display of Latin by pretentious intellectuals to the dreadful
perversion of Holy Scripture which emerges in Cañizares' confession,
appear in Erasmus' endless catalogue of woe: blasphemy, calumny,

---

poris parte collocauit: ratio est sicuti lux quaedam luménque vitae: oratio est rationis
decus & ornamentum: ratio regit ac moderatur proprium animum: oratio flectit etiam
alienos: rationis est species admirabilis: eam tamen intus latentem orationis pulchri-
tudo declarat" (cited by H.-J. Lange, *Aemulatio Veterum sive de optimo genere dicendi*
[Frankfurt am Main, 1974], pp. 38-39). For the Jesuits' preservation of the "héritage
de l'humanisme," in their belief in the value of language, see F. de Dainville, *La
Naissance de l'humanisme moderne* (Paris, 1940), pp. 65-68. Even while adopting the
ascetic, *desengañado*, attitude toward the immense distance between the omnipotent
creator and the infirm human being, the Jesuit L. Richeome noted the significance
of God's choosing to engender his divine Son and create the world by "opening his
mouth" and speaking: "Et ores qu'il n'aye point de bouche corporelle, il a voulu ce
nonobstant declarer sa vertu convenablement à notre infirmité, par tels mots prins de
la partie de l'homme, où il a peint au vif une image de la puissance de la volonté,
par le moyen de la parole" (*De l'adieu de l'âme* [1602]; see Dainville, p. 67).
   [50] "Circumspice quicquid est in orbe funestarum tragoediarum, comperies fere fon-
tem malorum omnium fuisse malam linguam" (*Lingva*, p. 286). The following page
references in my text are to this edition.

slander, betrayal, deceit, mendacity, perjury, swearing, flattery, ostentation, and garrulity. Like Cervantes' dogs, Erasmus asserts that it
is most difficult to avoid a sin of the tongue whenever one engages in
a lengthy conversation (p. 301); he denounces calumny as a particularly satanic sin (pp. 298, 316); and he laughs at intellectuals who
are so ostentatious that they insist on speaking Greek to everyone,
even to those who do not understand them (p. 352). In words that
look forward to Cervantes' creation of Cañizares, he expresses the view
that the belly and the tongue are the most rebellious parts of the body
(p. 332), and he voices his amazement at the fact that the same tongue
can offer hymns to God and pay homage to the devil in its maledic-
tions ("You boast of the psalms and hymns which you sing to God,
but with the same tongue you sing the song which the devil likes
best by blackening your neighbor's name; with the same tongue that
you use to bless God in words, you curse the parts of God's body").[51]
Erasmus describes in precise terms what Cervantes' Ensign discovers
in his misfortunes, that the poisons of the tongue insinuate themselves
gently and pleasantly into the mind of the listener, persuade him to
forget himself in the delights of the moment, and infect him with a
venom that is worse than that of the most baneful serpents. Like
Cervantes, Erasmus looks critically at the literary evils that flow from
the tongue—on the one hand, the foolish illusions of amatory poetry
and pastoral fiction ("in the plots of pastoral, shepherds are depicted
as being in love, and their herds, the mountains, the woods and the
rivers are upset by their afflictions"), on the other, the destructive
falsehoods of satire.[52] Like Cervantes' dogs, Erasmus on occasion pauses
to recognize how his tongue is infected by the illness which he would
cure, and he too invokes the figure of the Cynic philosopher as an
example of his own immoderate vituperation (pp. 332; 270, 293).

If the *Lingua* looks forward to the *Coloquio de los perros* in its obsessive reiteration of these themes, its dominant imagery, largely drawn
from the same sources in the central Christian writings on sinfulness,
is strikingly similar to that of the Spanish dialogue. Images of sickness
and physical decay pour forth on nearly every page. Language is a
venom that ravages its victims slowly and resists cures more effectively
than all the poisons of serpents. Evil speech is a disease more deadly

[51] "Iactas psalmos et hymnos, quos deo canis, sed eadem lingua canis cantionem
diabolo gratissimam obtrectans proximo, sed eadem lingua qua deo verbotenus be-
nedicis, dei membris maledicis" (Ibid., p. 325).

[52] "Et in Bucolicis argumentis pastores imaginantur [amantes], et pecori, et mon-
tibus, et syluis, et fluminibus suos affectus esse curae" (pp. 351-52; for the evils of
satire, see pp. 270, 316-17).

than cancer and rabies (p. 291). Erasmus begins his work with a description of the hideous effects of syphilis and goes on to emphasize that the illnesses of the tongue wreak havoc more widely and more contagiously: "This disease is neither simple nor new, it embraces all the sicknesses of the spirit, and there has never been a time so wholesome in its customs that no one complained about this evil."[53] The mouth of the slanderer is a foul-smelling pit whose noxious vapors are lethal to all they contaminate. Objecting to the defamatory conversation that perverts the banquet and its traditional function of bringing a community together, Erasmus asks: "But who vomits at table more shamefully than someone who pours out his choler, his hatred, and the infected pus of his spirit at a feast?"[54] Like Cervantes, Erasmus turns to the world of the predatory beast to add imaginative power to his diatribe: "What would you say, Paul, if you could now see Christians . . . being barked at, bitten, and torn apart by other Christians with the fury of dogs?"[55] The caluminator and his virulent tongue are likened to the scorpion, the dragon, and the serpent, and on several occasions Erasmus compares speech to the poisonous monster to which Cipión compares his companion's story—the squid.[56] Erasmus continually associates man's verbal communication with the acts of mutilation characteristic of the animal world ("For what kind of beast is there in the world which bites, tears at, and rips apart its own kind with such madness?"), and he proceeds to exploit the powerful imaginative effects of cannibalism to arouse his reader's repugnance at human beings' misuse of speech: "You will not eat the guts of an animal and yet you eat your brother's guts? For whoever denigrates his brother bites, yes, actually bites, wounds, and devours his brother."[57]

[53] "Pestis haec neque simplex est neque recens, vniversos animi morbos complectitur, nec vlla fuit aetas tam sanis moribus, vt de hoc malo non fuerit questa" (p. 235).

[54] "At quis indecentius mensam conuomit, quam qui bilem, qui odium, qui pestilens animi pus effundit in conuiuio?" (p. 320).

[55] "At quid diceres o Paule, si videres nunc Christianos a Christianis . . . rabie canina, allatrari, morderi, dilacerari?" (p. 330).

[56] See, for example, pp. 324, 332. Erasmus' introduction of the squid in order to emphasize the promiscuity or the potential for multitudinous deceptiveness lurking in language is striking: "Et nos nobis videmur pulchre religiosi pharisaicis quibusdam fucis, quum ignem gehennae circumferamus in lingua, quum aliud stantes aliud sedentes loquamur, quum linguam subinde vertamus in plures species, quam vllus se vertat polypus?"

[57] "Quod nam in orbe ferarum genus reperias, quod simili vesania sese mutuo mordet, lacerat, discerpit?" (p. 316); "Non comedis viscera pecudis, et comedis viscera fratris? Mordet enim omnino mordet, vulnerat, et comedit fratrem quisquis obtrectat fratri" (pp. 324-25).

In the *Colloquy of the Dogs* and the *Lingua* Cervantes and Erasmus are deeply concerned with the mystery of what the latter calls the "sermo carnis," the "vetus lingua" of unredeemed humanity. While Erasmus is content to invoke repeatedly the "sepulchral throat" denounced by the Psalmist to symbolize most effectively this speech, Cervantes compels us to confront it more directly. For as we move into Cañizares' dark cubicle at the climactic moment of his work, behold the witch's repulsive nakedness, and listen to the ghastly monologue issuing from her foul-smelling mouth, we sense that we are as close as it is possible to be to the ultimate source of this lawless language. However, both writers draw back from the abyss which they have explored so relentlessly; and with their characteristic breadth of vision they remind their readers, even amid such depths, that there are great civilizing and regenerative powers in language.

As I have pointed out above, the *Colloquy* begins and ends with a celebration of language and rationality as divine gifts which distinguish man from the beast and lift him out of the "dark silence" of animality. In perhaps a more cautious mood, the protagonist at another point refers to language as a "good on loan," given, as all the other neutral things of this world, by God and susceptible of proper use or abuse by its recipients. On several occasions Erasmus emphasizes the "double-edged" nature of the tongue, at once the most useful and the most destructive of instruments, a power which, when controlled by reason, draws men together in harmony, peace, and good will: "Double-edged part, from which so much harm abounds in the life of mortals, from which again so much usefulness derives, if a man controls it as it ought to be controlled. . . . The tongue is a Fury if it lacks someone who controls it. It is a horn of plenty if you use it rightly. It is Eris, who stirs up quarrels, but that same tongue is Grace, who binds with good will . . . it is all-healing if a healthy mind controls it . . . and it is the mother of peace and harmony."[58] While it is unequaled as a destructive agent when freed from all restraint, it is also a force that lifts men out of the order of savagery, erects cities, and founds laws (p. 331). Toward the end of the *Lingua* Erasmus' celebration of language evolves toward more mystical spheres. The emphasis turns from "recta ratio" (p. 247) and the "unsullied spirit, which rules and controls" ("animus integer rector, ac modera-

---

[58] "O membrum anceps, vnde tanta scatet pestis vitae mortalium, vnde rursus tanta manat vtilitas, si quis vt oportet moderetur. . . . Ate est lingua, si careat gubernatore. Copiae cornu est si recte vtaris. Eris est iurgiorum excitatrix, sed eadem est Gratia beneuolentiae conciliatrix . . . panacea est, si bona mens illam moderetur . . . eadem pacis et concordiae parens est" (p. 330).

tor" [p. 293], as keys to releasing the creative forces in language, to the cultivation of the "language of the spirit," the "new language," which Erasmus distinguishes sharply from the language of the flesh and its disruptive effects so spectacularly detailed in his work: "The flesh has its tongue, but the spirit has a very different tongue. The flesh speaks with the old tongue while the spirit has a new tongue, but one that is very different from that of the flesh."[59] The new language is the language of Christ, which mediates between the ineffable language of God and the angels and the flawed idiom of fallen man.[60] Erasmus exhorts his reader to imitate the language of Christ, which in contrast to the "vetus lingua"—"worthless, babbling, headstrong, untruthful, full of bitterness, quarrelsome, squabbling, tale-bearing, slanderous, immodest, a breaker of oaths, a giver of bad advice, undutiful, and blasphemous"—he describes as "a controlled tongue, a healing, gentle tongue, which binds together all things in heaven and on earth."[61] It is the language of simplicity, innocence, and charity, the "lingua medica" that heals and regenerates the body of Christians, torn apart as it is by the wounds inflicted by the language of the flesh. It is the language of the Good Shepherd, which "is able to bind together what is broken and to make firm what is weak,"[62] and, in a passage which may well have captivated Cervantes' imagination in his youthful encounter with the evangelical humanist's texts under the tutelage of López de Hoyos, Erasmus mentions as an example of those who speak the language of the spirit certain children who are innocent of malice and the good dogs who keep watch before God's house and minister to the wounds of the beggar Lazarus with their healing tongues.

The man who is of the earth is earthly and speaks from the earth. . . . The Psalmist makes mention of the tongue of a dog. Dogs were they who shouted "Away with Him, away with Him, crucify Him, crucify Him." Those who barked at Him as He hung on the cross "Thou that destroyest the temple of God" were dogs. . . . Paul tells us that these dogs should be avoided. However, there are also good dogs, who keep watch before the house of God, who have healing tongues and lick the sores of the beggar Lazarus. And there

---

[59] "Habet caro linguam suam, habet spiritus linguam longe diuersam. Caro veteri lingua loquitur, spiritus nouam habet linguam, sed ab illa longe diuersam (p. 335).

[60] See *Enquiridion*, p. 123 and my discussion above of Erasmus' views of linguistic authenticity and man's essential Edenic self.

[61] "Futilis, garrula, praeceps, mendax, amarulenta, rixatrix, conuiciatrix, delatrix, obtrectatrix, impudica, peieratrix, malesuada, impia, ac blasphema" (p. 364); "linguam modestam, linguam medicam, mansuetam, conciliatricem omnium quae in coelis et quae in terris" (p. 365).

[62] "Nouit quod confractum est alligare, quod infirmum est solidare" (p. 369).

are dogs who guard the flocks, who are silent in the face of the wolves, but who have barks and teeth for the sheep. The most harmful dogs of all are those who will not allow the voice of the Gospel to be heard.[63]

[63] "Qui de terra est, terrenus est et ex terra loquitur. . . . De lingua canis meminit psalmographus. Canes erant qui clamabant: *Tolle tolle, crucifige, crucifige.* Canes erant, qui oblatrabant pendenti in cruce: *Vah qui destruit templum* dei. . . . Hos canes vitari iubet Paulus. Quanquam sunt et boni canes, qui excubias agunt pro domo dei, qui linguam habent medicam, et lingunt vlcera pauperis Lazari. Et sunt canes custodes gregis, qui aduersus lupos muti sunt, aduersus oues vocem habent et dentes. Nocentissimi canes sunt, qui non patiuntur audiri vocem euangelicam" (p. 364). While Cervantes' dogs owe their existence far more to the power of their creator's imagination than to any specific thing he might have read or seen, the possibility that their genesis was affected by a recollection of Erasmus' *Lingua* is at least as plausible as the "authentic experience" which Amezúa, on the basis of the proven existence of a man named Mahudes, postulates as their source and offers as a supreme example of "el verismo cervantino" (see above, Chapter IV). In my consideration of the *Colloquy* and Erasmus' *Lingua* I am concerned primarily with the general similarities which link the texts in their treatment of language and with the spiritual affinities of their authors. As I have pointed out above, nearly all Cervantists who have dealt with the Spaniard's "Erasmism" have discovered that the question of direct influence or of proof of the fact that Cervantes read or did not read Erasmus' texts is difficult to answer. In his adaptation of sources, even those which did not meet official disapproval or censorship, Cervantes generally refashions the material he appropriates freely to meet his own imaginative needs and conceals evidence of direct borrowing. The *Lingua* was one of Erasmus' works that was translated into Spanish, and it enjoyed a success in Spain far greater than in any other country. As Bataillon points out, no fewer than nine editions appeared in Spain between 1531 and 1551 (*Erasmo y España*, trans. A. Alatorre [Mexico, 1966], pp. lvii, 313; a sixteenth-century Spanish translation of the *Lingua* can now be consulted in D. S. Severin's edition, which reached me following the completion of this chapter [*La lengua de Erasmo nuevamente romançada por muy elegante estilo* (Madrid, 1975)]), and the least that can be said about its transmission to Cervantes is what Bataillon conjectures about the availability to Cervantes of Erasmus' criticism of monks in the *Ecclesiastes* (a work not translated into Spanish), which may be echoed in the *Licenciado Vidriera*: "La transmisión oral es más verosímil; el Maestro López de Hoyos había leído el *Ecclesiastes*, como había leído la *Exomologesis*, y algo de estos libros condenados pasaba seguramente a través de sus lecciones" (p. 800). Moreover, citing as evidence the existence of the complete works of Erasmus in the library of the Count of Gondomar, Bataillon has more recently expressed the opinion that it is probable that the Index was not as successful in destroying the forbidden texts by Erasmus as has been commonly assumed and that it is quite plausible that men such as Cervantes and Lope de Vega read the *Praise of Folly* ("Un problème d'influence d'Erasme en Espagne: L'Eloge de la Folie" *Actes du Congrès Erasme* [Rotterdam, 1969], pp. 136-47). I suspect that a thorough comparative study of Cervantes' works and the *Lingua* will reveal more similarities than those I have pointed out in the area of general themes, general configuration of ideas, symbolism, and imagery. I would here add to my observations above the possibility that Don Quixote's anecdote (2:95) concerning Erostratus, the man who set the temple of Ephesus afire in order to win renown, an event recorded by Valerius Maximus, may have reached Cervantes via the *Lingua* (see p. 314), that Don Quixote's discussion of peoples'

In the *Colloquy of the Dogs* there is nothing that attenuates its overwhelming vision of evil comparable to Erasmus' discourse on the regenerative language of Christ, a peroration that lifts his reader far above the preceding survey of the devastation wrought by satanic speech. Quite the contrary, its efforts to affirm the divine potential in language, despite their striking appearances at the beginning and the end, seem muted, insubstantial, and marked by a tone of desperation. For one fleeting moment, however, we observe Cervantes moving toward a more extensive celebration of a language of innocence and charity. When the society of children forms around Berganza, they sell several "*Antonios*" in order to finance their picnics of butter cakes with the animal, whom they treat as a human being and as their king. As I have pointed out above, the little carnivalesque scene, even as it gently uncrowns the official world of the Jesuit college, presents a genuine society, characterized by innocence, charity, joy, true communication, and festive banqueting, and it functions as an ideal counterweight to the numerous fallen societies appearing throughout the novella. However, the significance of the scene in the present context lies primarily in the exchange of Antonio de Nebrija's famous *Arte de gramática* for the cakes of the "illicit" banquets. In its depiction of spontaneous acts of friendship and charity and its sharp dissociation of the pure communication of children and beasts from official discourse, it recalls the carnivalesque treatment of language in the "Colloquy of the Squires" in the *Quixote*. As if to reverse the implications of his description of the cursing infant and its disclosure of the satanic impulses informing man's first words, Cervantes here gives expression to the humanists' utopian belief that there existed a pure, transparent language prior to the fall, that vestiges of it are perceptible in the language of children and animals, and that in the restoration of his good nature through spiritual renovation man can restore his contact with this speech. The belief was perfectly consistent with the classical celebrations of language which they were fond of

---

willingness to gain fame and notoriety for their foibles may derive something from the same passage, that Cervantes' conception of Clodio and Rosamunda in the *Persiles* owes a good deal to the *Lingua*, not only in its personification of the catastrophic combination of lust and slander, the belly and the mouth, and adulation and calumny, but also in such details as the chain binding the two characters (see *Lingua*, p. 319), the arrow that punishes the slanderer (see *Lingua*, pp. 317-18), and Mauricio's admonitions to Clodio that criticism of a prince should be made in private (see *Lingua*, p. 304), that reproof should be corrective and fraternal (see *Lingua*, p. 298: "quae [errata proximorum] mansueta fraternaque monitione sanare debueramus"), and that "la lengua es el espejo del alma," a *topos* that appears at least twice in the *Lingua* (see, pp. 296, 326).

invoking and which stand at the beginning and end of Cervantes' *Colloquy*. For the original perfect order was thoroughly informed by the divine *logos*—reason and word, the latter written, as it were, throughout nature and in the heart of man.[64] Erasmus himself emphasized in the *Praise of Folly* that the people of the golden age had no need of grammars since speech was a faculty originally employed only for authentic communication, and, recalling Plato's arguments in the *Phaedrus*, he lamented that the evil genius Theuth had invented written letters and given the devil such a powerful weapon to use against man's happiness.[65] The most striking indication of the appeal of such beliefs to Cervantes is their echo in the *Quixote*, which, despite its fundamentally relativized, decentered language consciousness, can occasionally assert, free from any ironic discreditation, a contradictory hierarchical view of language's plurality, in which the imagined idiom of a primal age of natural perfection sets the standards of value.[66] In his nostalgic recollection of the fabled golden age, for example, Don Quixote notes that "the soul's amorous fancies were clothed simply

---

[64] The belief asserts itself in a similar way in the exemplary conclusion of *Rinconete y Cortadillo*, which emphasizes that Rinconete's "intelligence and good nature" enabled him to interpret the strange language of Monipodio's world as one of the various facets of an order which is "pernicious and opposed to nature itself" (*Novelas ejemplares*, ed. F. Rodríguez Marín, 1:216-18). In its genuine fascination with the details of the "fallen" discourse and its exploitation of verbal misunderstandings for comic effects, as well as for the depiction of evil acts, the tale stands closer to the completely emancipated linguistic world of the *Quixote* than it does to the *Colloquy of the Dogs*.

[65] See *Laus Stultitiae, Ausgewählte Schriften*, ed. W. Welzig, 8 vols. (Darmstadt, 1967-1980), 2:72-74. For the humanists' interest in the transparent language, natural or divine, see Dubois, *Mythe et langage au seizième siècle*, pp. 48ff., 57ff.

[66] In my analysis of the "Colloquy of the Squires" above, I have chosen to emphasize its implications concerning Cervantes' awareness of the living character of language. In its celebrative view of the superior vitality of popular discourse and proverbial literature vis-à-vis literary language and "official" literary forms, it can, of course, be seen as reflecting the author's seemingly contradictory belief in the perfect unitary language of an original order of nature. We glimpse the proximity of Sancho's language to this order when Don Quixote expresses admiration for the "verdadera tología" which springs from his squire's "buen natural" and manifests itself in "rústicos términos" (2:195), when the Duke's majordomo cannot control his amazement on discovering that "un hombre tan sin letras . . . que no tiene ninguna, diga tales y tantas cosas llenas de sentencias y de avisos" (2:406), and when, reborn from the "grave of silence" into which his master has thrust him, he pours forth the "contents of his heart" in an impressive string of proverbs (1:300-302). Sancho's entire being is intimately bound up with his proverbs: "ninguna otra [hacienda] tengo, ni otro caudal alguno, sino refranes y más refranes" (2:364). For the Erasmists' belief that a relatively unalienated self of mankind—i.e., a self in close touch with the divine *logos* and its original product, the *bene condita natura*—embodied its superior insights in proverbial wisdom, see my *Cervantes and the Humanist Vision*, chap. 2.

and plainly, exactly as they were conceived, without any search for artificial elaborations of words to enhance them,"[67] and, although the ignorant peasants, "gaping in bewilderment," fail entirely to understand the letter of his discourse, their actions indicate that its spirit is communicated perfectly. Probably the most eloquent expression of the dream of a pure form of communication and the possibility of a natural, nonofficial language of innocence is contained in the series of scenes in which Sancho, who occasionally boasts of his ignorance of grammar, achieves authentic communication with his donkey, his truest friend, with Ricote, and with the foreign pilgrims following his withdrawal from the official world of his government.[68]

CRITICISM, LITERATURE, AND THE LANGUAGE OF THE EARTH

No pleasure is comparable to the standing upon the
vantage-ground of Truth (a Hill not to be commanded, and where
the air is always clear and serene) and to see the errors and
wanderings, and mists, and tempests, in the vale below.
—Bacon, *Of Truth*[69]

[67] "Se decoraban los concetos amorosos del alma simple y sencillamente del mesmo modo y manera que ella los concebía, sin buscar artificioso rodeo de palabras para encarecerlos" (*Don Quijote*, 1:156).

[68] See, for example, his response to Sansón Carrasco, who warns him that "los que gobiernan ínsulas, por lo menos han de saber gramática": "Con la *grama* bien me avendría yo; pero con la *tica*, ni me tiro ni me pago, porque no la entiendo" (2:63). The shocking reversal of the *Colloquy*'s dominant perspective on animality in the college scene similarly recalls the carnivalesque celebration of innocent societies of animals and of men with animals in the *Quixote*. At the conclusion of their "plática," the squires, who have been divided from their masters, "sin hablar palabra, se fueron . . . a buscar su ganado; que ya todos tres caballos y el rucio se habían olido y estaban todos juntos" (2:137). The children's gesture of placing their hands in Berganza's mouth is comparable to the embrace and kiss which Sancho bestows on his "Rucio" following his flight from the corrupt world of illusion of Barataria. Cervantes' interest in the society of perfect friendship of Sancho's ass and Rocinante and their own language (e.g., "Solos quedaron don Quijote y Sancho, y apenas se hubo apartado Sansón, cuando comenzó a relinchar Rocinante y a sospirar el rucio" [2:92]) is another carnivalesque element of the *Quixote* which draws attention to the possibility of a nonofficial, more authentic means of communication than normal language. As D. McGrady and some editors of the *Quixote* have noted "suspirar" was a euphemism for flatulent pronouncement (see "The *sospiros* of Sancho's Donkey," *Modern Language Notes* 88 [1973]:335-37; for the importance of "images of the material bodily lower stratum" in the carnivalesque utopia, see Bakhtin, *Rabelais and His World*, chap. 6).

[69] *The Complete Essays of Francis Bacon* (New York, 1963), p. 7.

The glimpse of the festive society of children and animals at the Jesuit college fades quickly into the shadows that envelop the world of the *Colloquy of the Dogs*. Its utopian view of the possibilities of perfect communication is never reasserted, and it is elsewhere in language that Cervantes looks in order to discover its powers for redemptive purposes. While he repeatedly stresses the way in which the cleavage between words and things enables man to exploit language as an effective means of deception and betrayal, on one important occasion he reverses the direction of his argument to suggest that there is in fact a great civilizing power in the illusory nature of language. The startling turnabout lies in the very passage in which he acknowledges most candidly the destructive effects of the discourse of his final tale. As a clear assertion of authorial intent, the passage provided the point of departure for the first section of this study. However, like many other of the dogs' exchanges, the provocative discussion of names and things proceeds to problematize its assertions through the type of self-negation which I have analyzed above in connection with the elusive satirical voices of the dialogue. It is fitting to conclude by returning to it and recognizing the other face of its paradox—the moderating message it implies. Following Berganza's harsh words concerning the misuse of language by "learned fools, tiresome grammarians, and babblers in the vernacular striped gaudily in their lists of Latin phrases,"[70] Cipión castigates his companion for engaging in a deceitful use of words which is similar to the very abuses he is criticizing. He has in fact dignified the "accursed plague of backbiting" by referring to it as "philosophy": "And you call slandering philosophizing? That's a nice state of affairs! Canonize, Berganza, canonize the accursed plague of backbiting, and give it whatever name you please." Immediately after the rebuke, Cipión urges Berganza to avoid digressions as he continues, but unawares he violates his own principle of linguistic decorum. The mischievous Berganza will not allow an evasion which he discovers in his stern companion's speech to pass unnoticed. The dialogue then coils back on the problem of the relation of names to things and emphatically offers a view that would appear to contradict the position initially taken.

CIPIÓN: I mean that you should follow it consecutively without making it look like an octopus by the way you go on adding tails.
BERGANZA: Speak correctly; *the arms of an octopus are not called tails*.
CIPIÓN: This is the mistake he made who said it was not stupid or vicious

70 "Letrados tontos, y gramáticos pesados, y romancistas vareteados con sus listas de latín" (p. 250).

to call things by their proper names, as if it were not better, if it be necessary to name them, to speak of them by *circumlocutions and paraphrases that diminish the repulsion caused when we hear them called by their proper names.* Decent words give an indication of the decency of the one who utters them or writes them.[71]

Here Cervantes juxtaposes two contradictory extremes, each with a justifiable claim to validity, and allows them to reflect on one another and illuminate their respective strengths and weaknesses. As the paradox unfolds, there can be no doubt that a good deal of truth lies in the dogs' arguments both for candor and for concealment, both for the close alignment of name and thing and for the seemingly contradictory decorous use of linguistic evasion, but perhaps the greater truth to which the interchange points lies in its implications concerning the complexity of experience and the nonlinear character of authentic thought. For in coping with the ambiguities raised by the validity of opposites, we find ourselves compelled to confront the limitations of categorical thinking in general, and to experience the process of perspectivistic qualification and nuancing that is so fundamental to Cervantes' ironic discourse. In other words, "words should correspond to truth (i.e., things [*res*]), but not always."[72]

[71] Pp. 251-52; italics added. For the vulgar meaning of "rabo," see above, p. 6. Amezúa (*El casamiento engañoso y el coloquio de los perros*, pp. 506-507) finds in the passage simply a statement of Cervantes' adherence to the "excelente doctrina literaria" of linguistic propriety. The interesting aspect of the passage is, of course, its critical engagement with that doctrine, the striking presence of the "improper" within it, and its ultimate irreducibility to an unequivocal statement of doctrine. For the Spanish text, see my introduction, where I too emphasize but one of the various implications of its dialogical engagement with linguistic and literary problems.

[72] See Rosalie Colie on the effects of paradox: "Operating at the limits of discourse, redirecting thoughtful attention to the faulty or limited structures of thought, paradoxes play back and forth across terminal and categorical boundaries—that is, they play with human understanding, that most serious of all human activities" (*Paradoxia Epidemica: The Renaissance Tradition of Paradox* [Princeton, 1966], p. 7). Ernst Behler writes of Friedrich Schlegel's view of irony: "Diese 'Gymnastik des Geistes' stützt sich auf einen Bildungsbegriff, der den Gegensatz, den Widerspruch, die Antithese als das innere Prinzip der wahrhaft geistigen Erziehung auffasst, die Bildung als wesentlich 'antinomische' Funktion anerkennt. 'Alles was sich nicht selbst annihiliert, ist nicht frei und nichts wert,' sagt Schlegel, oder umgekehrt: 'Alles was etwas wert ist, muss zugleich dies sein und das Entgegengesetzte.' 'Das Zugleichsein zwei entgegengesetzter Zustände' findet er 'überall in der ganzen Natur,' woraus sich das Resultat ergibt: 'Jede nicht paradoxe Philosophie ist sophistisch' " (*Klassische Ironie, Romantische Ironie, Tragische Ironie: Zum Ursprung dieser Begriffe* [Darmstadt, 1972], p. 95). One observes this type of argumentation by mutually illuminating and qualifying antinomies throughout Cervantes' writing and in all spheres of his thought, from brief discussions of language such as the one that I have analyzed here to the impor-

In both its profound insight into the oblique, mediating nature of language and its paradoxical procedures the dialogue recalls Erasmus' writings on speech. In his colloquy *De rebus ac vocabulis* (*Things and Names*), his spokesman deplores the separation of words and substances and man's frequent recourse to the concealing label to avoid confrontation of the truth of his immoral actions. For example, the governor frequently takes comfort in the fact that his depredations are not designated as piracy; society is full of respected citizens, who are referred to by their professional titles rather than the more appropriate appellation of "thief," a truth that the naive Berganza discovers when he is beaten by the constables' associates. And just as Cipión finds consolation in the fact that the "Señor del Cielo" sees the truths behind the fraudulent titles and practices of the "señores de la tierra" and confers his authentic honors and titles only on those who serve him with "purity [*limpieza*] of heart," Erasmus' spokesman assures himself that, since a man's conscience is known only to God, it makes very little difference what he is named by other men if he is a thief in God's sight.[73] In this dialogue Erasmus is concerned primarily with the universal tyranny of appearances and the way language supports it. However, in his more elusive colloquy on the power of lies, *Pseudocheus and Philetymus: The Dedicated Liar and the Man of Honor*, he allows the suggestive paradox which enlivens Cervantes' passage to emerge amid his denunciation of an inveterate liar, who rejects outright the proposition that "man was endowed with speech in order to proclaim truth." While the shameless Pseudocheus defends lying as the fulfillment of man's nature and cynically boasts of his various ways of defrauding his clients and sowing dissension between men, Erasmus complicates our engagement with his reasoning by permitting him to remind us that the code of courtesy of a civilized society is based to some extent on lies and dissimulation and that lies are everywhere built into the common metaphors of the language.[74] As in the case of Cervantes' passage there is no question here of our misunderstanding the direction of Erasmus' ethical judgment. However, the startling

---

tant examinations of existential, philosophical, ethical, and literary concerns in such confrontations as Don Quixote and Sancho, Don Quixote and the Caballero del Verde Gabán, Don Quixote and the Canon of Toledo, Zoraida as Virgin and Zoraida as La Cava, the Gypsy as vital and the Gypsy as lustful, Marcela as lofty Stoic and Marcela as destructive egotist, etc. Everywhere conceptual binding springs apart, meaning is dispersed, and the reader is compelled to gather it and truly possess it.

[73] See *Colloqvia*, eds. L.-E. Halkin, F. Bierlaire, R. Hoven, *Opera Omnia*, Vol. 1, pt. 3. (Amsterdam, 1972), pp. 569-70.

[74] *Ibid.*, pp. 320-24; I take my translations from *The Colloquies of Erasmus*, ed. and trans. C. R. Thompson (Chicago, 1965), pp. 133-37.

paradox and the momentary mutual negation of the contradictory extremes force us to work through the ambiguities to a fuller and sharper awareness of the issues under examination and of the limitations of simplistic, categorical modes of thought. There is a good deal of subtle playfulness in Pseudocheus' observation that his way of addressing his friend as the "best of men" is based on an "egregious lie."[75] However, it is in the *Praise of Folly* that Erasmus presents this insight into the civilizing power of the "deceitful" instrumentality of language with the profound mischief that informs Cervantes' manipulation of paradox in the dogs' exposure of the complexities that mark the indirect relation between names and things, letter and spirit. After denouncing the absurdities of pride, chauvinism, and flattery, Erasmus' fool reverses her argument and begins one of her characteristic ironic revaluations of a vice.[76] She proceeds to rebuke those who are so inflexible in their refusal to take into account the obliquities and distinctions which trouble the relations between discourse, its source, and its referent, that they are incapable of making the fundamental distinction between the false vocabulary of the pernicious flatterers and the false vocabulary of the flatterers whose speech springs from genuine affection and contributes to the strengthening of the bonds of love joining men ("But nowadays this adulation has a bad odor, but only among those who are more concerned about the names of things rather than the things themselves").[77] Not only is flattery, when conceived thus, far preferable to the antithetical vice of asperity, but, moreover, the "empty" discourse which it employs turns out to be substantial in the most profound sense imaginable:

But this flattery of mine stems from a certain kindness and candor of mind, and it approaches virtue more readily than does asperity, or what Horace calls "inelegant and burdensome sullenness." My flattery raises the dejected spirit, it soothes those who are in mourning, mollifies the angry, and permanently unites the bond of love. It attracts children to the study of literature, the elderly are cheered by it, and under guise of praise, it cautions and

[75] See J.-C. Margolin's observations on Pseudocheus' discourse: "Erasme . . . veut surtout prouver qu'il y a mensonge et mensonge, que tout le monde ment plus ou moins . . . c'est en réalité vers une casuistique du mensonge et un exposé simple et vivant des paradoxes du langage et métalangage que nous sommes entraînés" ("Erasme et la vérité," *Recherches Erasmiennes* [Geneva, 1969], pp. 45-69, esp. p. 49).

[76] For her method of "rehabilitating" vices, see W. Kaiser, *Praisers of Folly* (Cambridge, Mass., 1963), chaps. 4, 5.

[77] "At hodie res quaedam infamis est adulatio, sed apud eos, qui rerum vocabulis magis, quam rebus ipsis commoventur" (*Laus Stultitiae, Ausgewählte Schriften*, 2:102; translation from *The Essential Erasmus*, ed. and trans. J. P. Dolan [New York, 1964], p. 132).

instructs princes in such a way so as not to offend them. In brief, it serves to make every man more pleasing and important to himself; this is truly the principal concept of happiness. What is more gracious than the way two mules scratch each other? But I shall not go on to tell you what a great part this flattery plays in your praiseworthy and forceful manner of discourse, in your medicine, and in the greatest part of all of your poetry. In conclusion, it is the honey and spice of all human discourse.[78]

As the concepts intertwined in the system of antitheses emerging in the passage recoil on one another (pernicious flattery/humane flattery; humane flattery/asperity; names/things), Erasmus compels his reader to view them from shifting vantage points and, in doing so, to discover the trace of inhumanity inherent in the conventional attitude toward the vice, the civilizing and creative energies which often underlie its practice, the absurdity of the traditional negative view of the gap between words and things, the problematic relations between spirit and letter, and the general inadequacy of the simplifications of categorical thinking. As in Cervantes' passage, the opposites only momentarily cancel each other out; we emerge from their collision and the self-reflecting, self-qualifying process that occurs therein with a nuanced understanding of their mutual necessity. While disclosing the processes of their perspectivistic thinking and subjecting the reader to the intellectually invigorating experience of following them in their "circunloquios," and "rodeos," both ironists make the fundamental point that in the illusory quality of language there lies a great civilizing power.

As Erasmus' passage makes clear, an enormous body of valuable literature and rhetoric in reality consists of such "empty" discourse. Cipión's brief discussion of civilized "circumlocutions and obliquities" might point to a redemption of literature that reaches far beyond that implicit in any conventional assertion of the divine power in language. For all their optimism, the dogs' initial and concluding panegyrics

---

[78] "Verum haec mea [adulatio], ab ingenii benignitate, candoreque quodam proficiscitur, multoque virtuti vicinior est, quam ea qua huic opponitur, asperitas, ac morositas inconcinna, ut ait Horatius, gravisque. Haec deiectiores animos erigit, demulcet tristes, exstimulat languentes, expergefacit stupidos, aegrotos levat, feroces mollit, amores conciliat, conciliatos retinet. Pueritiam ad capessenda studia litterarum allicit, senes exhilarat, principes citra offensam sub imagine laudis, et admonet et docet. In summa, facit, ut quisque sibi ipse sit iucundior et carior, quae quidem felicitatis pars est vel praecipua. Quid autem officiosius, quam cum mutuum muli scabunt? Ut ne dicam interim hanc esse magnam illius laudatae eloquentiae partem, maiorem Medicinae, maximam Poeticae: denique hanc esse totius humanae consuetudinis mel et condimentum" (*Laus Stultitiae, Ausgewählte Schriften,* 2:104; translation, with minor modification, from *The Essential Erasmus,* p. 133).

would leave the products of man's imagination "unemancipated," bound, as it were, to the cramped idiom of *logos*, nature, or Divine Will. However, Cervantes does not care to move in that direction. Quite the contrary, he repeatedly directs our attention to the deceitful and destructive effects of literary fictions. In a comment which recalls the imagery of the disastrous mutual seduction, the Ensign insists that he will not employ "rhetorical colors to adorn" his *true* story and make it more "pleasant" ("gustoso"). Offering his companion a lesson on the composition of short stories, Cipión similarly speaks of how writers can make "something out of nothing" by including "ornaments of words" and "dressing the stories up with words" (p. 219), and, as he does so, we momentarily glimpse the very tale we are reading thrust into the imaginative field of clothing, disguises, and deceptive gestures which pervades the entire work. While he labors among the shepherds, Berganza discovers with amazement that his employers devote their energies more eagerly to such prosaic chores as delousing themselves than to melancholic reverie, that their hoarse, grunting songs are in no way like the beautiful lyrics of pastoral romances, and that there are none to be found among them who bear the names of Amarilis, Lisardo, or Jacinto (pp. 227-29). He concludes that "all those books are dreams well written to amuse the idle, and *not truth at all.*"[79] When the dialogue looks at the more lofty traditional genres, it is even more pessimistic. Its gallery of fools includes two classical poets, who have studied the "rules" thoroughly and are struggling to realize those two great aspirations of Renaissance literary endeavor—the perfect heroic poem and the perfect historical drama. In the playwright Cervantes pokes fun at the classical ideal of the *poeta doctus*, the exalted purveyor of authorized truth, as well as at the distinguished doctrines of divine inspiration and verisimilitude. The youth gazes at heaven, bites his nails, mutters incomprehensibly, writes in snatches, and emerges from his trance with an oath of exultation: "By the Lord, this is the best eight-line stanza I have written in all the days of my life."[80] He is obsessed with the verisimilitude of his play, has carefully studied historical sources and "the whole of the Roman Catholic ceremonial," and refuses to allow his masterpiece to be produced because the director can find no purple robes for his cardinals, a color absolutely necessary for the perfect reduplication of

---

[79] "Todos aquellos libros son cosas soñadas y bien escritas para entretenimiento de los ociosos, y *no verdad alguna*" (p. 229); italics added.

[80] "¡Vive el Señor que es la mejor octava que he hecho en todos los días de mi vida!" (p. 320).

the historical circumstances of his plot. This is not the occasion to explore the rich literary allusiveness of this caricature or Cervantes' expert manipulation of the traditional satirical techniques of magnification and deflation in his treatment.[81] I would merely point out that the scene underscores the vacuity of the officially sanctioned type of "truthful" literature which he produces and that it is no coincidence that Cervantes, in portraying his ludicrous obsession, turns once again to the imagery of clothing and disguise which has so central a place in the imaginative vision of the *Colloquy*. The other poet is driven by similar obsessions, and here too Cervantes associates clothing with the literary offspring of his diseased fantasy. A crazed Horatian, he has outdone his master, spending not ten but thirty-two years in polishing his epic masterpiece, which includes a supplement to the *Historia de la demanda del Santo Brial*. After so much effort the hapless poet finds himself dying of syphilis, and he recognizes that his heroic poem about the "holy silk skirt," despite its observation of the prestigious classical rules concerning history, fable, invention, disposition, and *admiratio*, and despite its magnificent rhymes in *esdrújulos*, will probably die with him, for there is no magnanimous prince to dedicate it to in his depraved age (p. 331).

The survey of literary genres is complete and devastating. We observe God silently "speaking to the heart" of the sinner and we hear Berganza mention cryptically an approaching time when he will speak "with better reasons and with a better discourse than now," but we are ultimately left only with the "language of the earth" and the possibility that its illusory qualities, its corrosive energies, and its powers of provocation can somehow be enlisted in the service of truth. But the truth which the *Colloquy of the Dogs* would have us see is one that is hard to bear, and its revelation demands the destruction of all illusions. In its treatment of language the *Colloquy* is certainly more wide-ranging and ambivalent than the ascetic literature with which it has such clear affinities, but there can be no doubt about its dominant position on the subject. As he nears the end of his story, Berganza recalls his life as an actor and pauses to remark that the depravity of the society of actors is so great that all that he has narrated thus far would amount to nothing in comparison to what he could reveal about them. "Yet all you have heard is nothing to what I could tell you of what I have noted, learned, and seen of these people, their customs, their life . . . with countless other matters, some to be whispered in

[81] See A. Forcione, "Cervantes and the Freedom of the Artist," *Romanic Review* 61 (1970):243-55.

your ear, others to be shouted aloud, and *all to be engraved on the memory so as to disillusion the many who idolize fictitious figures and beauties of artifice and illusion*."[82] As a comment on the work itself and by implication as a comment on language and literature, Berganza's words accord perfectly with the Stoic ethical doctrine which emerges shortly thereafter in the dogs' last pronouncements. For the Stoics the theater has always been a favorite metaphor for the world, and the highest wisdom is that which enables the individual to see through the illusions which constitute man's numerous roles, to disengage from their tyranny, and to understand and accept, freely and self-consciously, the necessity of the civilized codes of deception which are essential to any community. The mission of the artist is to master and use the illusions of language in order to undeceive, to bring such lucidity and freedom to his readers, and he enhances the power of his demasking criticism by reminding them of the insubstantial quality of the very medium in which he works, of the fraudulence of his very own mask.

La Gitanilla, with its heavenly music and its beautiful vision of Maiden Poetry, concludes fittingly with a glance at the numerous poems which are being composed to immortalize its happy events and which in a sense replicate the celestial harmonies sounding through its world. The *Colloquy of the Dogs* leaves us with a tattered manuscript, an ambiguous prophecy, an unfulfilled promise of a continuing narration, and a good deal of doubt about whether its words represent dreams or realities. By comparison its vision seems terribly confining. It offers nothing to lift us upward to the starry spheres which shine above Preciosa's song, and only occasionally does it remind us of the possibility of their existence. Constructed out of the harsh "language of the earth," Cervantes' *Colloquy*, with its survey of abominations veiled perhaps by its concluding appeal to the "eyes of the mind," might even recall, if only for a moment, the demonic "long colloquy" which Doña Estefanía poured into the Ensign's ears in order to enslave his soul. And yet, it too rewards its reader with an experience of release, an experience that is far more sober, but no less exhilarating. It is the release that comes through purgation and attends the fearless confrontation of illusion and the discovery of truth. The irrepressible Berganza appears to understand this as he repeatedly insists on his

---

[82] "Pues todo lo que has oído es nada, comparado a lo que te pudiera contar de lo que noté, averigüé y vi desta gente, su proceder, su vida . . . con otras infinitas cosas, unas para decirse al oído, y otras para aclamallas en público, *y todas para hacer memoria dellas, y para desengaño de muchos que idolatran en figuras fingidas y en bellezas de artificio y de transformación*" (pp. 327-28; italics added).

rights to take advantage of the demystifying powers in his "miraculous gift" despite the admonitions of his more restrained companion. As his words pour forth in an incessant flow through the night, we discover that the *Colloquy*, for all its pessimism, ultimately offers a compelling affirmation of the value of human discourse. Like all things of the fallen world, language reveals its miraculous potential only when used correctly by human beings acting in freedom. In its unsparing vision, the *Colloquy* will allow for no illusions about the perfections of the word as the reflection of universal reason or divine truth, and, unlike the *Quixote*, it shows little interest in language as the living embodiment of the mysteries of human singularity. If there is anything miraculous in speech, it is to be found elsewhere, and it has something to do with that mysterious, nonrational process of self-transformation which, for Erasmus, is the central miracle of the Christian life.

The dogs' dialogue makes it clear that the "divine benefit of language" in reality lies in the powers of language as a critical instrument.[83] The reward which it bestows on the human mind that manipulates it properly is the kind of integrity that presupposes the liberation from all illusion. One of the great Renaissance apostles of clear vision, Francis Bacon, wrote of a "pleasure incomparable for the mind of man," which one experiences when one reaches the "Hill of Truth" and from its clear and serene height gazes down on the mists of error in which other men wander about aimlessly. It is probably this inner form of liberation from the darkness of illusion which Cervantes, ever conscious of the effects of his fiction, had in mind in his final scene, when he dramatizes his reader's favorable reaction to the stimulation of his text, with all its artifices, provocations, and inauthenticities, and watches him confidently step out of the imprisoning vision of lawlessness and return to life refreshed from the experience of reading. Silence is broken once again, a transformation has occurred, and dialogue begins anew.

---

[83] The critical instrument is perfectly at ease with its "flawed nature." As G. Bauer points out, it is characteristic of dialectical dialogue, certainly the dominant type in Cervantes' *Colloquy*, to acknowledge its oblique relations to its subject matter, to make reference to its provisional character, and to use hypothetical constructs to point to a meaning which lies ever beyond the fixing reach of language. Its verbal effusiveness is a sign of its effort to nuance thought and grasp for truth rather than a projection of the personality of a speaker, and its vitality, which can be intense, springs from the movement of the mind reflected in it. See *Zur Poetik des Dialogs* (Darmstadt, 1969), pp. 114-23; 223-28.

"I admire the art and invention you have shown in the *Colloquy*, and that is enough. Let us now go to the Espolón to refresh our physical eyes, as I have already refreshed my mind's eye."

"Let us go," said the Ensign.

And with that, away they went.[84]

[84] "Yo alcanzo el artificio del *Coloquio* y la invención, y basta. Vámonos al Espolón a recrear los ojos del cuerpo, pues ya he recreado los del entendimiento.

—Vamos—dijo el Alférez.

Y con esto, se fueron" (p. 340).

INDEX

Adam, 79, 89, 147, 188, 197, 203;
  Adamic language, 203
acedia, 90, 91, 141
Aesop, 27, 120, 125
Alemán, Mateo, 139; *Guzmán de Alfarache*, 7, 8, 11, 15, 26, 63, 66, 67,
  81, 82, 84, 91, 92, 97-100, 104,
  142, 143, 144, 146, 160, 161, 175,
  177, 178, 181; *Vida de San Antonio
  de Padua*, 89, 98
Alewyn, Richard, 26
Alexander, 156
allegory, 42-46, 195
Alonso Cortés, Narciso, 140
Amadís de Gaula, 43
Amezúa y Mayo, A. González de, 17,
  45, 55, 68, 78, 113, 114, 117, 140,
  143, 223, 228
anatomy, 22; anatomies of sin, 67, 72
anecdote, 17, 26, 175
Anthony, St., 133
anticlimax, 23, 32, 33, 36ff., 47, 57,
  106, 179
Apel, Karl-Otto, 216
aphorism, 17, 174
apocalypse, 34, 59ff.
Apollonius, Book of, 41, 42, 43
Apuleius, Lucius, 37, 38, 182; *The
  Golden Ass*, 47, 125
Aquaviva, P., *Ratio Studiorum*, 150
Archilochus, 181
Ariosto, Ludovico, 38, 39; *Orlando fu-
  rioso*, 35, 51, 184
Aristotle, 6, 9, 12, 22, 23, 24, 38,
  100, 166, 167, 194
ascetic Christianity, 15, 16, 18, 167,
  168, 198, 214, 233
Asensio, Manuel J., 96
Astrana Marín, Luis, 140
Atkinson, William C., 22, 23
Auer, Albert Alfons, 168
Augustine, St., 93, 96, 159; *Confes-
  sions*, 63, 89, 90, 91; *De Genesi ad
  Litteram*, 89
Avalle-Arce, Juan Bautista, 35, 52

Avellaneda, Alonso Fernández de, 13,
  139, 180, 186
Ávila, Diego de, 211
Ávila, Juan de, 75, 80, 92

Babel, Tower of, 188, 189, 196, 197,
  198, 214
Bacon, Francis, 226, 235
Bakhtin, Mikhail M., 56, 79, 185,
  191, 194, 205, 206, 207, 210, 212,
  213, 226
banquet, 105, 117, 144, 145, 147,
  204, 206, 207, 210, 224
Baroque, the, 66, 199
Bataillon, Marcel, 14, 15, 28, 142,
  150, 186, 223
Bauer, Gerhard, 37, 235
Behler, Ernst, 179, 228
Belic, Oldrich, 14, 101
belly, significance in Christian tradition, 77, 78, 219; in carnivalesque
  tradition, 79
Bible, 45, 46, 65, 72, 85, 89, 95, 98,
  114, 116, 155, 166, 174, 182, 216,
  218, 223; Ecclesiasticus, 80; Ephe-
  sians, 89; Genesis, 79; Hebrews, 64;
  Jeremiah, 76, 77; Job, 63, 64, 65,
  75, 89, 131, 143, 163; Kings, 110,
  111; Luke, 45; Matthew, 95, 96;
  Psalms, 65, 83, 84, 202, 220, 222,
  223; Romans, 89, 136, 202; 1 Thes-
  salonians, 89. *See also* Jesus Christ;
  Lazarus; and St. Paul
Blanco Aguinaga, Carlos, 15, 17
Boccaccio, Giovanni, 23, 133
Bollnow, Otto Friedrich, 144, 145
Borst, Arno, 189, 197, 217
Bosch, Hieronymus, 133
Brüggemann, Werner, 54
Buret, F., 66, 143
Burke, Kenneth, 33

Calderón, Rodrigo, 152
Calderón de la Barca, Pedro, 91, 139,
  186; *La cena del rey Baltasar*, 105; *El*

Calderón de la Barca, Pedro (*cont.*)
  médico de su honra, 79; *El sacro Parnaso*, 89; *La vida es sueño*, 72
Cano, Melchor, 169
Cardano, Girolamo, 188
carnivalesque spirit, 6, 91, 148, 153, 154, 205, 206-212, 224, 226
Caro Baroja, Julio, 6
Carvallo, Luis Alfonso de, 8, 10
Casalduero, Joaquín, 17, 21, 60, 114, 115, 126, 133, 151
Castro, Américo, 13, 15, 25, 51, 62, 95, 96, 97, 119, 161, 170
Cato, 37
Cave, Terence, 182, 193
Cervantes Saavedra, Miguel de: *El amante liberal*, 61, 62; *El cautivo*, 33, 139, 214; *El celoso extremeño*, 60, 153, 161; *El curioso impertinente*, 161; *Don Quijote*, 3, 6-9, 17, 21, 31, 35, 38, 39, 46, 48ff., 79, 91, 93, 112, 135, 141, 150, 153, 154, 179, 180, 186-95, 204-215, 223-26, 229, 235; *Entremeses*, 3, 31; *La española inglesa*, 48; *La fuerza de la sangre*, 41, 48, 139, 146, 147; *La Galatea*, 3, 190; *La Gitanilla*, 3, 4, 10, 14, 41, 46, 47, 48, 60, 61, 62, 122, 131, 132, 133, 137, 145, 147, 153, 202, 212, 234; *La ilustre fregona*, 41, 47, 48, 60, 61; *El Licenciado Vidriera*, 6, 7, 11, 22, 153, 181, 201, 223; *Las novelas ejemplares*, 3, 4, 13, 16, 60, 162; *Pedro de Urdemalas*, 200; *Rinconete y Cortadillo*, 57, 61, 62, 94, 99, 153, 214, 225; *El retablo de las maravillas*, 179; *El rufián dichoso*, 57, 94; *La señora Cornelia*, 48; *Los trabajos de Persiles y Sigismunda*, 3, 7, 9, 10, 38, 39, 44, 46, 48, 60, 61, 63, 64, 103, 111, 112, 126, 127, 133, 134, 137, 139, 143, 153, 156, 161, 179, 190, 200, 202, 214, 215, 224; *Viaje del Parnaso*, 7, 12, 13, 18, 24; novelistic techniques, 17, 35, 48ff., 140, 141, 187ff.; and picaresque literature, 57, 61, 62; and contemporary religious culture, 72, 116; self-presentation in his works, 179, 180, 200; and skepticism, 71; the "two Cervanteses," 17

charity, 153, 166, 167, 168
Charondas, 29, 125, 175
chivalry, ideals and laws of, 51, 205, 206; chivalric heroism, 212. *See also* romance
Christian humanism, 12-18, 98, 100, 146-53, 155, 156, 167, 170, 184, 185, 195, 214, 215, 216, 217, 224. *See also* Erasmus
Cizevsky, Dmitry, 118
Close, Anthony, 55
Cohn, Norman, 68
Colie, Rosalie, 228
comedia de honor, 161
Comenius, John Amos, 118
confession, 24, 41, 95, 96, 143, 156, 160, 178
conversion, 66, 89, 92, 93, 142, 144, 178
Coplas de Mingo Revulgo, 115
Counter-Reformation, 150, 196
courtly love, 212
Covarrubias, Sebastián de, 204
Cozad, Mary Lee, 194
Cynic philosophy, 5, 6, 29, 56, 155, 166, 171, 172, 173, 180, 181, 201, 219

Dainville, F. de, 150, 170, 217, 218
decorum, 5, 26, 27
Democritus, 184, 185
Des Périers, Bonaventure, 109
desengaño, 15, 16, 18, 53, 65, 77, 79, 91, 111, 139, 146, 159, 167, 168, 186, 197-200, 214, 218, 234
Deyermond, Alan D., 84, 96
Diálogo entre Laín Calvo y Nuño Rasura, 154
dialogue, 15, 16, 17, 24, 25, 26, 36, 37, 170, 204-213, 235; humanist dialogue, 17, 25, 26; dialogism, 14, 26, 174, 175, 185, 186, 210
Dickens, A. G., 150
Diogenes, 6, 155, 181, 183
discreción, 5, 26, 160, 180, 193, 194
divine mercy, the mysteries of, 80, 91, 92, 131ff., 143, 171
Dolet, Étienne, 182
Dominic, St., 155
Dostoevski, Feodor, 56

Dubois, C.-G., 188, 197, 203, 204, 225
Dunn, Peter, 144
Durán, Manuel, 52
Durling, Robert M., 182

Eckhart, Meister, 89
education, 28, 146-53, 160
El Saffar, Ruth, 102, 151, 152
Eliade, Mircea, 126
Elliott, Robert C., 6, 33
Enríquez Basurto, Diego, 65
epic, 54, 139, 206, 232, 233
Epictetus, 163
Epicureans, 70
Erasmus, Desiderius, 8, 25, 137, 147, 170, 192, 193, 235; *Adagia*, 14, 115, 150, 156, 192; *Antibarbari*, 153, 183; *Ciceronianus*, 181, 182, 183, 191, 192; *Convivium Religiosum*, 168; *Cyclops, sive Evangeliophorus*, 77, 78, 183; *De Conscribendis Epistolis*, 150; *De Copia Verborum et Rerum*, 150; *De Immensa Misericordia Dei*, 75, 81, 86, 92; *De Libero Arbitrio*, 80, 81; *De Pueris Instituendis*, 149, 150, 152, 153; *De Ratione Studii*, 149, 150; *De Rebus ac Vocabulis*, 229; *Disputatio de Taedio et Pavore Christi*, 167; *Dulce Bellum Inexpertis (Adagia)*, 164; *Ecclesiastes sive Concionator Euangelicus*, 216, 217, 218, 223; *Enchiridion Militis Christiani*, 74, 75, 85, 86, 92, 136, 161, 166, 167, 168, 182, 192, 222; *Exomologesis*, 223; *In Quartum Psalmum Concio*, 65; *Institutio Principis Christiani*, 114, 164; *Laus Stultitiae*, 115, 167, 182, 184, 185, 186, 223, 225, 230, 231; *Lingua*, 8, 182, 202, 203, 213, 218-24; *Paraphrasis in Evangelium Matthaei*, 150; *Pseudochei et Philetymi*, 229, 230; *Querela Pacis*, 164; *Ratio seu Compendium Verae Theologiae*, 192; *Sileni Alcibiadis (Adagia)*, 8, 14, 115, 156, 169, 183; Christocentric ideal of heroism, 155, 156, 161, 169; and the dignity of man, 168; educational philosophy, 147-53, 184; ethical philosophy, 166, 167, 168; ironic

discourse, 178, 185, 186, 230, 231; and the Jesuits, 149-53; pacifism, 164; *Philosophia Christiana*, 166, 168, 181, 186, 192; on satire, 181-86; and Stoicism, 166, 167, 168; theories of language, 192, 213ff.
Estella, Diego de, 77
Ettinghausen, Henry, 163
etymology, 195, 197, 198
evil, 18, 58-71, 90, 91, 102, 108, 126, 127, 131, 138, 140, 214
exemplarity, 13, 214
exemplum, 24, 173, 174
eyes of the spirit, 14, 76-79, 136, 156, 168

fable, 17
feritas, 15, 16, 146, 152, 153
Fernández de Madrid, Alonso, 75
Fernández de Navarrete, Martín, 185
Ficino, Marsilio, 217
Flaubert, Gustave, 56
folk tale, 209
fool, in Renaissance and Baroque literature, 91, 98
Forcione, Alban, 6, 7, 9, 12, 38, 39, 55, 58, 126, 131, 137, 139, 147, 160, 179, 181, 184, 192, 199, 200, 212, 214, 225, 233
fortune, 28, 29, 31, 42, 96, 144, 164
free will, 78, 80, 173
Freud, Sigmund, 97
Frías, Damasio de, 193, 194
Friedrich, Hugo, 198
Frye, Northrop, 22, 26, 37, 49

gamblers' mass, 94
García-Villoslada, Ricardo, 150, 170
Garin, Eugenio, 149, 150
Gilman, Stephen, 77, 95, 96, 97
Goethe, Johann Wolfgang von, 23
Gogol, Nikolai, 56
golden age, 225, 226
Gondomar, Conde de, 225, 226
Góngora, Luis de, 198
Gracián, Baltasar, 115
Granada, Fray Luis de, 59, 65, 76, 77, 79, 86, 92, 93, 111, 141
Green, Otis H., 185

Grimmelshausen, Johann Jakob Christoffel von, 26
Guillén, Claudio, 15, 96
Guzmán, Pedro de, 162
Gypsies, 107, 124, 132, 160, 162, 229

Hart, Thomas, 174
Hatzfeld, Helmut, 32
Hegel, George Wilhelm Friedrich, 96
Heliodorus, 9, 41, 44
Hendrix, W. S., 206
Heraclitus, 184
Heyse, Paul, 23
Hippocrateus, 185; "Hippocratic novel," 185
Hollen, Gottschalk, 94, 95
Homer, 37, 114
homo novus, 96
Horace, 9, 176, 181, 182, 184, 233
Huizinga, Johan, 184
humanitas, 15
humility, 27, 148, 153, 163, 164, 166, 169, 170, 173, 174

Inquisition, 156, 162
irony, 30, 53, 54, 55, 174, 177, 179, 180, 228

Jauss, Hans-Robert, 95, 96
Jesuits, 28, 29, 125, 147-53, 160, 162, 170, 217, 218, 224, 227
Jesus Christ, 45, 46, 60, 64, 89, 90, 92, 114, 115, 149, 155, 156, 163, 167, 168, 172, 181, 184, 192, 216, 222, 223
Job, Mass of St., 66. *See also* Bible
John of God, St., 155, 161, 162
John of the Cross, St., 197
John the Baptist, 161
John the Divine, 61
Jonson, Ben, 26, 184
Juan of Austria, Don, 48
Juvenal, 7, 100, 171, 180, 181, 182, 186

Kaiser, Walter, 230
Karrer, Wolfgang, 6, 46, 57, 96, 97
Kernan, Alvin, 12, 23, 31, 32, 33, 133, 134, 186
Könneker, Barbara, 14

Krauss, Werner, 149, 150, 151

Laín Entralgo, Pedro, 162
Lange, H.-J., 193, 218
language, 5, 6, 16, 17, 62, 87, 163, 187ff.; of animals, 224, 225, 226; of children, 172, 224, 225, 226; and Christian mysticism, 216; classical celebrations of, 215, 216, 217, 224, 225, 231, 232; as a critical instrument, 226ff., 234, 235; and decorum, 208, 210, 228; and individuality, 188-94, 235; natural language, 224, 225, 226, 232; and nominalist philosophy, 216; popular sphere of, 194, 207-213, 225; and reason, 215, 216, 217, 221, 225, 232, 235; of the spirit, 222-26; and usage, 193, 194
Lazarillo de Tormes, 15, 24, 29, 35, 63, 84, 95-98, 104, 107, 116, 142, 160, 174, 177, 186
Lázaro Carreter, Fernando, 15, 96
Lazarus, 66, 67, 74, 75, 91, 92, 95, 96, 99, 123, 222, 223
Lehmann, Paul, 56, 94, 95, 97
León, Fray Luis de, 25, 64, 83, 84, 86, 114, 115, 155, 169
León, Pablo de, 64, 65
Leonardo de Argensola, Bartolomé, 25, 154, 184, 185, 186
Levi, A.H.T., 150
limpieza de sangre, 27, 31, 105, 118, 119, 151, 163, 164, 169, 201, 229
literary theory, Renaissance neo-Aristotelian, 6-16, 21-25, 42, 55, 190, 191, 194, 209, 232, 233
Logroño, *auto de fe* of, 68
López de Hoyos, Juan, 222, 223
López de Yanguas, Hernán, 186
López Pinciano, Alonso, 12, 21, 22, 23, 25
Lotman, Jüri, 56
Loyola, St. Ignatius of, 150, 170
Lucian, 8, 17, 24, 25, 27, 32, 56, 70, 108, 141, 154, 179, 181, 182, 184, 185
Lucilius, 33
Lücker, M. A., 89
Lugowski, Clemens, 51

Lukács, Georg, 53, 54, 55
Luna, Juan de, 92, 98
Luxán, Pedro de, 25, 137

McGrady, Donald, 226
Madariaga, Salvador de, 52
Magnificat, 45, 94
Mahudes, 140, 162, 166, 167, 177, 223
Malón de Chaide, Pedro, 63
Marasso, Arturo, 50
Margolin, Jean-Claude, 149, 150, 193, 230
Mariana, Juan de, 152
Márquez Villanueva, Francisco, 206, 211
Marx, Karl, 96
Massebieau, L., 217
May, T. E., 99, 139
meditation, 75-79, 81, 113, 158, 159, 160
Meneses, Felipe de, 81
Menippus, 6, 25; Menippean satire, 22, 26, 100
Mercurian, P., 150
Mexía, Pedro, 25
microcosm, 4, 10, 131, 132
Milton, John, 19, 45
miracle, 39, 99, 164
miracle narrative, 17, 24, 131-46, 162
Miranda y Paz, Francisco de, 167, 197
Molho, Maurice, 60, 93, 101, 102, 152
Molina, Tirso de, 72, 83
Mondragón, Jerónimo de, 186
Montaigne, Michel de, 198
More, Thomas, 184
Moriscos, 107, 119, 121, 156, 160, 164
Mosellanus, P., 217
Murillo, Luis Andrés, 25, 53, 206

nature, the order of, 62, 131, 132, 133, 185, 190, 214; natural language, 191, 192, 197, 224, 225, 226; natural society, 148, 211, 212
Nebrija, Antonio de, 147, 224
neo-Platonism, 197
Neuschäfer, Hans-Jörg, 51
nominalism, 216

novel, 33, 35, 53-58, 97, 110, 214
novella, theory of, 23, 24

Oliver, Antonio, 156
original sin, 11, 25, 111, 112, 131, 147, 149, 188, 203. *See also* evil
Ortega y Gasset, José, 51
Ortiz, Francisco, 169
Osuna, Francisco de, 159
Ovid, 70

Pabst, Walter, 133
Pançart, St., 79, 206
Paparelli, G., 15
paradox, in Christianity, 65-71, 143, 144, 169, 170. *See also* evil
paradoxical discourse, 14, 98, 169, 185, 186, 209, 215, 227-31; rhetorical paradox, 98
Parker, Alexander, 25, 99
parody, 17ff., 44ff., 56, 62, 91, 93, 95, 97, 205, 206. *See also* travesty
pastoral, 48, 104, 112-17, 132, 147, 159, 219, 232
Paul, St., 24, 64, 74, 78, 136, 156, 166, 181, 220, 222, 223. *See also* Bible
Paul IV, Pope, 150
Percas de Ponseti, Helena, 50
perspectivism, 190, 193, 228, 231
Petrarch, 159
Pfandl, Ludwig, 211
Philip III, 15
Phocylides, pseudo-, 163
Pícara Justina, La, 28
picaresque literature, 7, 15, 17, 24, 25, 26, 28, 29, 32, 36, 56, 57, 58, 67, 91, 93-98, 100, 108, 127, 139, 141, 143, 144, 156, 157, 160, 174, 176, 177, 179, 195; picaresque hero, 26, 72, 82, 99, 104, 142, 158, 162, 176
Piero, Raúl del, 65
Plato, 25, 114, 166, 167, 183, 190, 225
poetry, 4, 48, 132, 219, 232; Maiden Poetry, 9, 10, 234
Pontano, Giovanni, 188
Pope, Alexander, 23, 32, 37
Price, R. M., 98

Proust, Marcel, 56
proverb, 88, 174, 207, 225
Psammetich, 203, 204

Quevedo, Francisco de, 25, 26, 46, 63,
65, 66, 67, 94, 95, 98, 99, 105,
127, 134, 139, 142, 163, 168, 174,
177, 197, 199, 200
Quintilian, 216

Rabelais, François, 8, 14, 37, 46, 56,
108, 184, 185, 206, 207, 210, 213
Ramírez Pagan, Diego, 155
Read, M. K., 189
Redondo, Augustín, 206
Rémy, Nicholas, 67
Ricard, R., 170
Richeome, L., 218
Rico, Francisco, 91, 96, 217
Riley, E. C., 13, 35, 42, 52
Río, Martín del, 67, 69
Rivadeneira, Pedro de, 63, 65, 77, 156
Robortello, Francesco, 6, 211
Rodríguez-Luis, Julio, 157
Rodríguez Marín, F., 109, 110, 151,
159, 160
Rojas, Fernando de, 62, 63, 87, 90,
91, 94, 95, 97, 99, 105
romance, 11, 12, 39, 43, 44, 47,
48ff., 62, 94, 96; of chivalry, 45,
49, 50-55; Greek, 95; theme of met-
amorphosis, 44, 45, 49ff.; theme of
prophecy, 44-55; theme of under-
world descent, 48ff. See also chivalry
Rosenblat, Angel, 211
Rothe, Arnold, 163, 168, 197
Russell, P. E., 55

Sánchez, Francisco, 197, 214
Satan, 45, 68-71, 76, 79, 88, 98, 105,
106, 195, 196, 199, 200, 219
satire, 5-18, 21ff., 100ff., 131-34,
170ff., 181-86, 201, 202, 233
Schlegel, Friedrich, 179, 228
Schulte, Hansgerd, 65, 77, 167, 197,
198
Seneca, 163
Shlonsky, T., 56
Siciliano, E. A., 151
Sieber, Harry, 53

skepticism, 67, 70, 192, 196, 197,
198, 214
Sklovskij, Viktor, 14, 31, 56
slander, 5, 28, 29, 172, 173, 180,
202, 219, 220, 227
Soarez, Cyprian, 217, 218
Sobejano, Gonzalo, 15, 16, 157, 175
Socrates, 6, 160
Solger, K.W.F., 54
Spitzer, Leo, 190, 199, 214
Starkie, Walter, 132
Sterne, Laurence, 37
Stoicism, 65, 144, 163-68, 170, 171,
185, 229, 234
Swift, Jonathan, 37
syphilis, 65, 66, 85, 143, 220, 233

Tarr, F. Courtney, 24
Tasso, Torquato, 25, 45, 209
Teresa de Jesús, St., 167, 168
Thomas, Keith, 68, 69
Timoneda, Juan, 42
Tolstoy, Leo, 144
Torquemada, Antonio de, 25, 115,
116, 184, 185
Torres Naharro, Bartolomé, 211
travesty, 31, 39, 46, 62, 88ff., 94,
109, 112-17, 142. See also parody
Tretheway, J., 189
Trent, Council of, 98
Trevor-Roper, H. R., 67, 162
Troeltsch, Ernst, 168
Truman, R. W., 96
Tynjanov, J., 56

Valdés, Juan de, 96
Valencia, Pedro de, 69-71
Valerius Maximus, 154, 223
Vázquez, Fray Dionisio, 196, 197
Vega, Lope de, 58, 139, 199, 200
Venegas de Busto, Alejo, 196, 197
Vilanova, Antonio, 186
Villalba y Estaña, Bartholomé de, 97
Virgil, 45-50
Virgin, the, 45, 47, 48, 61, 80, 81,
138-42, 161
Virués, Cristóbal de, 139
Vives, Juan Luis, 188, 189, 196, 217
Voltaire, 108

Waley, Pamela, 60, 135
Wardropper, Bruce W., 96
Wicks, Ulrich, 24, 29
witchcraft, 40ff., 59ff., 67-72, 164,
171

Woodward, J. L., 45

Yunck, J. A., 56, 57, 97

Zayas y Sotomayor, María de, 139

Alban Forcione is Professor of Spanish and Comparative
Literature at Stanford University and the author of *Cervantes,
Aristotle, and the "Persiles," Cervantes' Christian Romance: A Study
of "Persiles y Sigismunda,"* and *Cervantes and the Humanist
Vision: A Study of Four Exemplary Novels.*

Library of Congress Cataloging in Publication Data

Forcione, Alban K., 1938-
Cervantes and the mystery of lawlessness.
Includes index.
1. Cervantes Saavedra, Miguel de, 1547-1616.
Casamiento engañoso. 2. Cervantes Saavedra, Miguel de,
1547-1616. Coloquio de los perros. I. Title.

PQ6324.Z5F68 1984   863'.3   83-16129
ISBN 0-691-06588-8